SOCIAL STATISTICS IN USE

Social Statistics In Use

Philip M. Hauser

Russell Sage Foundation
New York

PUBLICATIONS OF RUSSELL SAGE FOUNDATION

Russell Sage Foundation was established in 1907 by Mrs. Russell Sage for the improvement of social and living conditions in the United States. In carrying out its purpose the Foundation conducts research under the direction of members of the staff or in close collaboration with other institutions, and supports programs designed to develop and demonstrate productive working relations between social scientists and other professional groups. As an integral part of its operation, the Foundation from time to time publishes books or pamphlets resulting from these activities. Publication under the imprint of the Foundation does not necessarily imply agreement by the Foundation, its Trustees, or its staff with the interpretations or conclusions of the authors.

Russell Sage Foundation
230 Park Avenue, New York, N.Y. 10017

© 1975 by Russell Sage Foundation. All rights reserved.
Library of Congress Catalog Card Number: 74–24747
Standard Book Number: 87154–375–3
Printed in the United States of America

Contents

Foreword	*vii*
Preface	*ix*
1. Why Statistics?	*1*
2. On Population	*23*
3. On Births, Deaths, and Health	*43*
4. On Marriage, Divorce, and the Family	*59*
5. On Education	*77*
6. On the Labor Force	*107*
7. On Social Security and Welfare	*135*
8. On Delinquency and Crime	*159*
9. On Consumption and the Consumer	*191*
10. On Housing and Construction	*209*
11. On Metropolitan Transport and Land Use	*233*
12. On Outdoor Recreation	*251*
13. On Governments	*273*
14. On Elections	*299*
15. On Public Opinion Polls	*313*
16. On Social Indicators	*339*
Index	*357*

Foreword

Margaret Olivia Sage instructed the Trustees of Russell Sage Foundation to use the funds she gave for "the improvement of social and living conditions in the United States of America. . . ." In carrying out this mandate, the Foundation has tried especially to take advantage of the findings and methods of the social sciences. These activities lead inevitably to data gathering and data analysis. People naturally wonder why all these data must be gathered, what good they are, and who uses them. These are fair questions and they deserve careful, thoughtful, detailed responses such as those provided in this book.

The Foundation has had a substantial program designed to bring the ideas of social science to journalists as one way of communicating with the general public about the need for the contributions of research in the social area. A parallel and larger Foundation program has set up training in social science for lawyers at several universities. The results have been substantial partly because in the last twenty years lawyers generally have grown much more attentive to the uses of social science.

Because data gathering for social purposes is often intrusive, people ought to know what such statistics are used for—how they help us make better decisions about our society. The American Statistical Association jointly with the National Council for the Teachers of Mathematics developed a set of essays explaining detailed uses of statistics to solve some very specific problems—national, state, city, personal, scientific, medical, and business. These essays in *Statistics: A Guide to the Unknown* can give one a feeling for the variety of uses of social and other statistics in a case-by-case way. What they will not and cannot do is provide a masterly overview of what is available in the statistical system and explain why this material is important and how it is used. Yet such an overview is needed if the citizen is to have a more comprehensive story of social statistics and their uses. In planning the project, Eleanor Bernert Sheldon and I thought that so much effort should produce more than a statement of uses of government statistics, something by itself of direct use.

Philip Hauser not only knew this material and sympathized with our desire to present it to the public, but he also knew how to get support from a variety of experts in this field. Thus, through their efforts, at last, we have a book that gives an honest overview of social statistics in use and one that also provides someone just beginning with a running start on knowing the kinds of statistics that are available and where they are to be found. The Foundation is deeply indebted to Philip Hauser and his colleagues for their contribution to our appreciation of the value of social statistics and their role in improving the social and living conditions in the nation.

Frederick Mosteller

Miller Research Professor
University of California
Berkeley, May 1975

Preface

This volume was undertaken at the suggestion of Eleanor Bernert Sheldon, now president of the Social Science Research Council, when she served on the staff of Russell Sage Foundation. Its purpose was to provide the educated lay reader with information on how statistics, especially those collected or compiled by government, are used; and in doing so to show justification for the census, government surveys, and other statistical undertakings which require public cooperation. It was felt that such information would help to allay admittedly mounting adverse public reaction to census and survey canvasses of the population and increasing concern about government statistical collections and record systems as potential sources for invasion of privacy.

The focus of this volume is mainly on social, as distinguished from economic, statistics, although the boundary line is not always clear and the statistics examined often have both social and economic implications.

To expedite the preparation of this volume, a number of experts were asked to prepare memoranda on the nature and uses of data in their fields of specialization. The memoranda were then edited and rewritten to achieve a non-technical readable volume which, hopefully, possesses more uniform style and treatment than would a series of separately authored chapters. Russell Sage Foundation provided the necessary funds to compensate the experts who prepared the memoranda and the author who wove them into this book.

Although I have enjoyed a long contact with government statistics in a number of capacities, including service as Deputy Director and Acting Director of the United States Bureau of the Census and as member or chairman of many government statistical advisory committees, I was necessarily dependent on the expertise of the specialists who prepared the memoranda for comprehensive coverage of the respective bodies of statistics and their uses. The significant contributions to this work then are those of the writers of the memoranda whose names and relevant affiliations are given at the beginning of each chapter. However, as author, I must assume responsibility for the editorial and rewriting treatments which varied from little to much and which did not always fulfill the desired objectives as well as intended. Hopefully, not too much damage was done to accuracy and balance in the statistical fields covered.

Publications to which reference is made are shown at the end of each chapter. These references, however, do not constitute comprehensive bibliographies. More detailed and updated sources of data can be found in the Appendix of the annually published *Statistical Abstract of the United States* (U. S. Bureau of the Census, Washington, D. C.: Government Printing Office).

I am, of course, greatly indebted to each of the experts who prepared the memoranda. I also wish to express gratitude to Dr. Sheldon, who, in addition to commissioning this work, provided counsel and encouragement throughout the period of its preparation; to Dr. Sheldon's colleagues at Russell Sage Foundation; and especially to Hugh F. Cline, president of the Foundation, who patiently provided the necessary financial and moral support to bring the work to a conclusion.

Finally, acknowledgment must be made of the faithful and skillful services of my co-workers, Mrs. Adele Kaye, Secretary, Miss Hana Okamoto, Administrative Assistant, and Mrs. Wilhelmina Crawford, Office Manager, in the arduous task of producing a number of drafts of the manuscript in readying it for publication; and of the tedious inputs of some of my students, especially Gabriel Alvarez, for completing bibliographical references.

Philip M. Hauser

Lucy Flower Professor of Urban Sociology
University of Chicago
Chicago, January 1975

SOCIAL STATISTICS IN USE

CHAPTER 1
Why Statistics?

The widespread misunderstanding and distrust of statistics and statisticians constitutes a major reason for writing this volume. Because hard facts are increasingly needed as a basis for policy formation, action programs and the evaluation of the impact of programs in our interdependent society, it is important that the general public gain an understanding of statistics and the role of the statistician. Perhaps the following summary points will help to bring this about, as a preliminary to considering selected areas of social statistics and the way in which they are used to serve public needs.

1. Statistics are quantitative facts collected, aggregated, and analyzed to provide intelligence, to facilitate understanding and to serve as a foundation for formulation of policy, development and administration of programs, and evaluation of the impact of programs.
2. The statistician is the professional specialist whose function it is to design, produce, and analyze statistics and to present his findings in an objective manner with probity and integrity for use by policy makers, administrators, researchers, and consumers in general.
3. The consumers of statistics constitute the audience for whom statistical intelligence is produced and who, it is assumed, want to "know the facts."
4. Although the relationship between consumers and producers of statistics must be a close one so that the information produced is relevant to the problems which confront consumers, this relationship should not in any way have the effect of impairing the integrity of the statistical undertaking as a fact-finding enterprise or of requiring the equivalent of a "directed verdict."

This volume is organized around bodies of statistics with examples of their uses. It should serve to counteract the occasional outbursts of anger directed at censuses, sample surveys, and other statistical undertakings in which it is represented that respondents are subjected to "harassment," "snooping," "invasions of privacy," and "government interference." The volume's basic premise is that public understanding of the uses of statistics is bound to result in the dissipation of hostile attitudes toward statistical undertakings, more effective and widespread use of the data, and better cooperation with agencies conducting collections of data and analyzing and publishing their results.

Because interpretations of statistics may often differ, as do those between Republicans and Democrats in an election year, statistics and statisticians often are mistrusted and may, also, be the butt of popular humor. It is almost a matter of folk wisdom to observe that "there are three kinds of liars—liars, damn liars, and statisticians." Moreover, the statistician's use of decimals—such as in stating that the average number of children needed to produce zero population is 2.11—often elicits humorous responses. One of the more elaborate responses of this type appeared in an article in *Colliers* (Miksch, 1950) which said among other things:

> The average statistician is married to 1.75 wives who try their level best to drag him out of the house 2¼ nights a week with only 50 per cent success.
> He has a sloping forehead with a 2 per cent grade (denoting great mental strength), ⅝ of a bank account, and 3.06 children who drive him ½ crazy; 1.65 of the children are male.
> Only .07 per cent of all statisticians are ¼ awake at the breakfast table where they consume 1.68 cups of coffee—the remaining .32 dribbling down their shirt fronts. . . . On Saturday nights, he engages ⅓ of a baby sitter for his 3.06 kiddies, unless he happens to have ⅝ of a mother-in-law living with him who will sit for ½ price . . . [p. 10].

The entire article is entitled "The Average Statistician (641.07 Words About a Pain in the Neck)." Moreover, statisticians themselves are not without a sense of humor: witness the title of the book, *How to Lie with Statistics,* by Darrell Huff.

No doubt the misuse and abuse of statistics, as well as of other forms of knowledge, are factors in such public distrust of statistics as may exist. Such distrust is generated particularly when politicians, in an effort to make the best possible case for themselves, especially in election years, use data with somewhat less than complete objectivity, impartiality, and competence. Even in nonelection years politicians and others have used statistics to serve their own interests, rather than that of the public, often to make themselves or their agencies "look good" or to justify policies or actions based on considerations other than the facts.

More serious than these general manifestations of distrust of statistics and statisticians are the negative attitudes and hostile reactions to specific government statistical undertakings. Perhaps an example or two of such reactions will help further to explain why it is desirable and necessary to clarify the role of statistics and statisticians. In planning the 1940 Decennial Census of Population, after almost a full decade of depression, new inquiries were placed on the population census schedule to provide the nation with information that would help guide government and private-sector policy and programs. They included questions on years of school completed; on the labor force, including employment and unemployment; restricted questions on income; on internal migration; on usual occupation; and on Social Security number. The context in which these questions were added is elaborated further below.

The new census inquiry on income generated a storm of protest, the history of which is enlightening. To begin with, at the sessions of the congressional committee concerned with the census, a southern congressman objected to the inclusions of the questions on income and on years of school completed with the observation that "these are socialistic New Deal inquiries designed to get the niggers dissatisfied." These questions were added, in fact, because of growing government interest in the welfare of the population and of business interest in obtaining marketing information. The congressman had foresight, however, because these questions have ever since played a significant role in pointing up inequities in the education and income of minority groups, and the statistics based on them have been widely used by civil rights and other organizations in their efforts to improve the status of the disadvantaged in the nation. The data have, of course, also been used by government and the private sector for various activities ranging from the planning of welfare programs to market analysis.

The proposed income question led a New England senator to initiate a vigorous campaign in opposition to it. He received considerable attention in the mass media. He tried to persuade the public not to answer the income questions because they were an offensive violation of the right to privacy. The Bureau of the Census was placed on the defensive in congressional committee hearings and was subjected to considerable editorial abuse by that part of the press bitterly opposed to what was regarded as an invasion of privacy and increased government interventionism. In the controversy the Bureau of the Census, with the support of the Department of Commerce and the White House, stuck to its guns, and printed millions of separate forms on which individual citizens could enter their income returns and, by direct mailing to Washington, escape the possible inquisitive eyes of local enumerators. Although some 20 million forms were printed, only about 100,000 actually were used. The public was not as worried as the senator imagined. The forms and the taxpayers' money (which paid for them) were not entirely wasted, however, because for many years they were used as scratch pads in the Census Bureau. It is noteworthy that, with the expansion of the income questions in 1950 to include more of the population and require more detailed returns, there was virtually no opposition.

Similarly, a vigorous campaign of opposition to the 1970 census schedule was waged by a congressman from the Middle West. He also felt the government was invading the privacy of the public, especially with the question relating to plumbing facilities used by the household. The fact that the 1970 census inquiries were very much like those in 1960 is certainly contrary to the impression created by much of the 1970 precensus hostile publicity. Moreover, the complaints about invasion of privacy in the 1970 census were often completely distorted as indicated by the well-publicized, although completely erroneous, claim that the 1970 census would require the person to report with whom he takes his shower. In fact, the census question read as follows:

Do you have a bathtub or shower?
☐ Yes, for this household only
☐ Yes, but also used by another household
☐ No bathtub or shower

This question, as experience since 1940 has shown, provides basic information on the quality of housing. The Bureau of the Census included it because government programs of urban renewal and public housing and the need of construction and related industries for knowledge about the nation's housing supply require information about housing quality. But the public clamor motivated a number of congressmen to introduce over 100 bills which would curtail the powers of the Bureau of the Census to ask questions and subject the final census schedules to the review of a congressional committee. This would, of course, represent a reversal of policy dating back to 1902, when the Bureau of the Census was established, and authority given for the design of the census schedules to the director of the bureau under the supervision of a member of the cabinet, now the secretary of commerce. Until that time the Congress itself determined the questions to be asked in the decennial census.

The administration supported the Bureau of the Census in the dispute about the 1970 census schedule, but it also undertook to review the decennial census operation through a Decennial Census Review Committee appointed as an advisory body to the secretary of commerce. This action mollified many members of the Congress and enabled the bureau to conduct the 1970 census without further harassment. As in connection with the furor over the income question in the census of 1940, the public cooperated well with the 1970 census operation. The belief that the public would refuse to answer census inquiries which they felt invaded privacy turned out to be completely unjustified. Moreover, under laws governing the conduct of the census, the privacy of the person is assured by provision for confidentiality which forbids the disclosure of any information about any individual and necessitates only the aggregation of information into statistics. Further explanation of why the "plumbing questions" were asked is contained below in historical context.

If the senator in 1940, the congressman in 1970, and that part of the public which they aroused in opposition to the census inquiries had fully understood the purpose of the questions and their ultimate use, it is doubtful that they would have pursued the course that they followed.

HISTORICAL BACKGROUND

Some form of summary reports was a prerequisite for the inventorying, distribution, and exchange of goods and services from the earliest times. In fact, various systems of writing, numerical notation, and recording were by-products of permanent human settlement. They evolved with the emergence of towns and cities which have been traced back to Mesopotamia, to Crete, to the Indus Valley, to the Yellow River Basin, and to Central America where evidence of the earliest clumpings of people and economic activities have been found. The invention of paper and pen in Egypt in the fifth century B.C., the development of government records in ancient Rome, and the preparation of tax and expenditure statements, including perhaps the drafting of the first budget by Emperor Augustus in A.D. 5, represent important milestones in the development of statistics as well as of accounting procedures and practices. The church and government both contributed to advances in record keeping during the medieval period.

The need for records and summary reports was not confined to government. Private agencies and businesses also contributed to the development of accounting methods. Considerable momentum to accounting practices accompanied the rise of Italian commerce during the thirteenth century. Record keeping enabled the merchants and investors to be informed about their financial positions and provided information also for creditors. Accounting became a recognized profession. Public accountants were at first part-time workers who traveled a circuit combining their profession with the practice of law or teaching. By the second half of the seventeenth century in England, however, full-time public accountants were practicing their profession.

The continued development of systems of records, the preparation of summary reports, and the refinement of accounting and auditing procedures are associated, of course, with increased urbanization. New technological and social-organizational developments resulted in ever larger clumpings of population and economic activities. Mankind, however, did not achieve enough in the way of technological development, on the one hand, and social-organizational development, on the other, to permit cities of 100,000 or more until as recently as Greco-Roman times. Man did not achieve enough technological and social-organizational development to permit cities of 1 million or more until probably as recently as the beginning of the nineteenth century. The increased size and density of populations were accompanied by increased division of labor and specialization. This meant greater economic and social interdependence and, therefore, greater vulnerability of the economy and society which required the development of mechanisms of coordination, integration, and control. These, in turn, required and generated the further elaboration of record systems, accounting procedures, and summary reports.

Accounting and auditing systems were needed by government and private business primarily for financial reasons. Paralleling the development of economic records and accountants, however, was the emergence of statistics and statisticians concerned with matters other than financial ones. Various scattered instances of governments collecting information, such as data on military manpower, can be traced back to antiquity.

The Old Testament mentions two censuses taken to obtain military manpower information. One was after the exodus of Israeli fighters and the nonmilitary Levites (Num. 1:45–47). The other was by Joab at the command of David (1 Chron. 21:2–5). The Romans took censuses every five years, including information about property to serve as a basis for taxation. Mary's and Joseph's presence in Bethlehem and the birth of Jesus there were related to one of these censuses. William the Conqueror caused the Domesday inquiry in England in 1086 to learn of the population and property in his new holding. In China a census was taken in 2 A.D., which may have been one of the more complete early censuses. This was likely because the census takers were authorized to cut off the head of anybody who refused to answer the questions.

Systematic collection of statistics on matters other than purely financial ones, however, did not begin until toward the end of the eighteenth and beginning of the nineteenth centuries. In the United States provision was made in the Constitution (Article I, Section 2) for a decennial census intended, of course, for the allocation of representatives in the Congress among the several states. The French Constituent Assembly required the publication of a statistical account of the resources in France and provided for a census to be taken in 1791. A number of other nations undertook the systematic collection and publication of statistics during the nineteenth century. Statistics, more than accounting, was the function of governments rather than of private business. The term "statistics" referred to "matters of state" reflecting the relationship between record keeping and the performance of government functions. The term "statists" was, in fact, sometimes used for statisticians during the nineteenth century. The Statistical Society of London for its Jubilee Session in 1884 asked that the views of "foreign statists" be ascertained.

Development of Statistics in the United States

Many years ago at a meeting of the Census Committee of the House of Representatives in Washington, a congressman inquired of the writer, then an official in the United States Bureau of the Census: "If American business has been able to get along for 150 years without statistics, why does it need them now?" The congressman might well also have included —in addition to business—government, labor, education, the church, welfare agencies, civic agencies, recreational agencies, voluntary organizations, and the general public.

The question is an important one. The congressman was in earnest in raising it. He was undoubtedly motivated by the many complaints he had received from his own constituents and from organizations throughout the country about the harassment of answering questionnaires and schedules for increasing numbers of surveys conducted by government agencies and also by private agencies—that is, by polling organizations, market-research organizations, and the like in the private sector. Moreover, his complainants often referred to the intimate nature of the questions asked, expressing the view that they represented invasions of privacy. They particularly resented canvasses in which compulsory reporting was required under penalty of law, as in the decennial census when refusal to respond carried with it the prospect of imprisonment as well as fines.

Why, indeed, is the citizen being increasingly subjected to surveys both by government and the private sector? This question is a reasonable one. The answer to it is difficult and complex. It requires an understanding of the basic transformation which America has undergone since its founding as an agrarian society under the federal Constitution, and of the developments which led to the emergence of the industrial and metropolitanized society in which we now live.

In 1789 when this nation was launched under her new Constitution and before the first census was taken, the citizen was not subjected to the present number of questionnaires. But, also, he was not constrained by traffic signals at street intersections; he was not compelled to go to school;

he was not required to make a contribution for the Social Security system; he did not need a license to conduct his business; he did not have to keep his sidewalk free of snow and sleet; he did not have to procure licenses for his pets; he did not need a building permit to put up his home, nor did he have to conform to requirements of codes and zoning in building it; and he was not subjected to regulations and fines for air and water pollution.

The proliferation of census questions and surveys and the conversion of their findings into statistics is only one of the many changes which have accompanied the transition of America from the "the little community" to the "mass society." The collection of information and the collation, publication, and dissemination of the resulting statistics is as much an index of modernization as the automobile and airplane, the radio and television, and the electronic computer. In that part of the world where most of mankind lives, the developing nations in Asia, Latin America, and Africa, censuses and surveys are still relatively scarce and statistics are virtually nonexistent. In the developing nations the citizen is not harassed by numerous questionnaires as is his counterpart in the economically advanced nations.

The extent to which a nation has a modern statistical system is in itself an index of economic and social development. In the post-World War II period, it has become national and international policy to induce economic and social development in less developed areas; at the same time it has become increasingly clear that the absence of statistics constitutes a major barrier to the planning and implementation of development programs. Thus the first step usually taken in such a developmental program is the conduct of a census or survey and the transformation of the information collected into statistics. Hard facts in the form of statistics are prerequisites for planning, for administrative guidance, and for the evaluation of the impact of programs.

Even with the relatively sophisticated state of statistics in the United States, there was not enough information during World War II for the planning and carrying out of various programs associated with the home and military fronts in the conduct of the war. With the establishment of the War Production Board to control production and the utilization of scarce resources during the war, many top businessmen were brought into Washington to develop and administer wartime programs. It was a standing joke among the civil service employees in the statistical agencies that the very same businessmen who had previously complained about the harassment of government questionnaires began their own Washington activities with a survey designed to get the necessary information for setting policy, for planning, and for the administration and evaluation of their programs. It was said, during that exciting time, that one could tell whether the businessman came to Washington by train or by plane. If he came by train, his questionnaire was longer.

Why Statistics?

In this nation's colonial period there was relatively little in the way of statistical information, especially on social as distinguished from economic matters. By the time the federal government was established in 1789, however, statistics had become an important tool in the conduct of government. Even during colonial times, there were statistics on population which became available in some of the colonies from 1610; on the slave trade from 1619; on the daily wages of workmen from 1621; on weekly basic diets in 1622; on exports and imports in 1697; and on bills of credit and Treasury notes in 1703. Indexes of wholesale prices can be calculated beginning in 1720, and those of tax collections were available from 1765. Private insurance company records were available from 1759. Most of these early statistics were concerned primarily with economic matters, but they also had important social implications.

In like manner, federal government statistics were first collected on such matters as government finances, foreign trade, water transport, balance of international payments, postal services, and patents. Early statistics collected and published by the federal government included information on hay, cotton, cottonseed acreage and production, prices, gold and silver production, iron ore and pig-iron production, currency stock and currency in circulation, public land sales, and banking. Although the information was largely economic in character, it is significant that information of a social nature also was collected. From the very beginning, for example, some data were gathered on military personnel, on elections, on membership in religious bodies, on medical schools and dentists, and on immigration.

The proliferation of statistics in the United States, as in the world as a whole, is to be understood as a function of social change, the result of the increased complexity and interdependence of the social order generated by increasing urbanization. As unprecedented problems emerged, government functions expanded to deal with them. When functions increased, the need for hard information as a basis for policy formulation, planning, administration, and evaluation of programs became apparent. In consequence, censuses and surveys and administrative records were increasingly used to compile needed statistics. This development is well illustrated by the history of the decennial census of the United States.

Development of the United States Census

Although the very first census in the United States, in 1790, was taken primarily under the constitutional provision for determining the apportionment of representatives to the Congress, it is noteworthy that it was not confined to a mere head count. The 1790 census included items such as the names of the heads of families and the age, sex, color, and the free or slave status of members of the household. Reflecting the interest of the government in manpower for military purposes, the age classification was asked only of males and restricted to an indication of how many were under and over sixteen years of age.

Thomas Jefferson, with his characteristic foresight, petitioned the Congress to expand the information collected in the census. When he was president of the American Philosophical Society, he sent a memorandum to the Senate, which reached that body on January 10, 1800, requesting that more information be gathered. In respect to the need for occupational information, Jefferson wrote:

> [I]n order to ascertain more completely the causes which influence life and health, and to furnish a curious and useful document of society in these States, and of the conditions and vocations of our fellow citizens . . . "a table was to specify" the number of free male inhabitants, of all ages, engaged in business, under the following or such other descriptions as the greater wisdom of the legislature shall approve, to wit: (1) Men of the learned professions, including clergymen, lawyers, physicians, those employed in the fine arts, teachers, and scribes in general. (2) Merchants and trades, including bankers, insurers, brokers and dealers of every kind. (3) Marines. (4) Handicraftsmen. (5) Laborers in agriculture. (6) Laborers of other descriptions. (7) Domestic servants. (8) Paupers. (9) Persons of no particular calling, living on their income . . . [Wright, 1900, p. 19].

As an aside, it is to be observed that to read and write in the United States in 1800 was to have a "learned profession."

Although the recommendations of Jefferson and others were ignored, the number of census questions had doubled by 1800, but they were still limited to the same topics: age, sex, color, and free or slave status. Age, although not required for slaves, was requested for females as well as males and in greater detail than in 1790. Reflecting the low longevity of the time, the upper age limit was "45 and upwards."

By 1820 the census questions included a number of new topics, both economic and social, indicating the problems which were engaging the attention of the Congress with the economic and social development of the nation. Questions were asked relating to workers engaged in agriculture, commerce, and manufacturing and, also, for the first time, there was a question on naturalization. In the next decade, 1830, the schedule required reporting the number of deaf and dumb and the blind, indicating the growing interest of government in the handicapped. In 1840 the information requested relating to work activity was expanded, with seven categories of occupation specified. Information also was required on pensions "for revolution and military services" as veterans became a new and growing responsibility of government. The census of 1840 was another milestone

Why Statistics?

in the development of statistics: for the first time the newly formed American Statistical Association (1839) made recommendations to the Congress with regard to the undertaking of the census. Expert advice from this association and many others has since become commonplace.

Many new problems confronted the federal government as social and economic change accelerated. Accordingly, Congress required six schedules for the census of 1850. Schedule "No. 1" related to free inhabitants and included many more population questions, including detailed occupation returns for all males over fifteen years of age. This evidenced the growing interest in the nation's work force, stimulated by the increasingly minute division of labor and the problems which accompanied it. Included, also, was a question on the value of real estate owned, information of both economic and social significance. The social inquiries included place of birth, whether the person had been married within the year, school attendance, literacy, and physical disabilities.

Schedule "No. 2" was for slave inhabitants and required information on the name of slave owners and the number of slaves and their characteristics. Schedule "No. 3" required information on mortality, including data on the characteristics of all persons who had died during the previous year. Schedules "No. 4" and "No. 5" were primarily economic in character; the former related to agriculture and the latter, to manufacturing, mining, fisheries, and all kinds of "mercantile, commercial or trading business." Major evidence of the increasing interest in social matters was schedule "No. 6," which called for "social statistics." For each political subdivision items were requested on evaluation of estates; annual taxes; colleges, academies, and schools; seasons and crops; libraries; newspapers and periodicals; religion; pauperism; crime; and wages. Although some of these items were obviously also economic in character, it is significant that they were labeled as "social" and interpreted as indicators of social differences. The census of 1850 may appropriately be viewed as the first census of the United States attuned in a major way to the statistical needs of the emerging mass society and providing information for at least a crude form of "social accounting." It also introduced some changes in census procedures which greatly improved the quality of the data.

The censuses of 1860 and 1870, in general, followed the pattern of the census of 1850. But General Francis A. Walker, who served as superintendent of the census of 1870, introduced some additions to the schedules for that statistical undertaking. General Walker, by the way, was president of the American Statistical Association from 1883 to 1896. The questions added to the population schedule included two on place of birth of foreign parents, two on "constitutional relations," and one on the month of birth of persons born during the year. The questions on place of birth of parents was in response to the growing interest in the increasing diversity of the population and the problems of acculturation and assimilation. The questions relating to "constitutional relations" were pursuant to the Fourteenth Amendment to the Constitution relating to the right to vote and its abridgment. The questions on month of birth of infants represented an early and continuing interest in fertility.

Five schedules were used in the census of 1880, one for each of the major areas of interest: population, agriculture, manufacturing, mortality, and social statistics. Again there were new population questions, mainly social in character, including relationship to the head of the household, marital status, illness, as well as disability and unemployment (months unemployed during census year). The questions on unemployment obviously had economic significance but there can be little doubt that there was interest in their social implications as well.

The censuses which followed continued to add new questions and, also, to drop old ones as conditions changed and as new problems faced the nation. Some of the more important additional questions were those relating to ability to speak English, immigration, tenure of home, and veteran status, which were carried in the census of 1890. The inquiries relating to English and immigration reflected increasing concern with the problems of acculturation of large numbers of European immigrants. Questions relating to home tenure were in response to the growing concern with problems of tenancy. Inquiries relating to veteran status were due to the increasing claims of veterans for government's assistance. New questions in the census of 1900 included inquiries on farm residence, duration of marriage and fertility, migratory flows, including migrants from rural to urban areas, decreasing birth rates, and differences in fertility among various subgroupings of the population which were beginning to attract national attention.

In 1910 an inquiry was added on "mother tongue" to provide information on ethnic origin. In 1930 a question was added on rent or value of home owned in an effort to find out about the social and economic status of families, which was becoming recognized as an important item for understanding various types of social problems. Another new question—whether or not the household had a radio set—was, of course, an effort to measure the diffusion of this new mass medium with important implications for communication, national defense, and marketing.

Following the severe problems generated by almost a full decade of depression in the 1930s a battery of new social questions appeared in the census of 1940. Added were inquiries on internal migration, years of school completed, and on the labor force, including employment status, income, usual occupation, and Social Security number. The decline in immigration with the passage of the exclusion acts during the 1920s and the acceleration in internal migratory flows led to great interest in internal migration as contrasted with the earlier interest in immigration. To make room for the questions on internal migration, inquiries relating to immigration were decreased. With the growing importance of education in the urbanizing society, a question on years of school completed was substituted for the earlier question on literacy which had become virtually meaningless. The grave situation created by the high level of unemployment generated pressures for obtaining information on the number and characteristics of the unemployed. It led to a series of developments culminating in the adoption of an utterly new approach for the measurement of the work force—the "labor force" approach, as distinguished from the "gainful worker" approach. It led, also, to the development of a new series of current statistics on employment and unemployment based on a sample survey initiated in 1940. This monthly survey, "The Monthly Report on the Labor Force," has since become the major means of measuring unemployment in the United States. The additions to the schedule in the 1940 census obviously reflected the growing national concern with problems of employment, unemployment, and the welfare of the American people. The new census inquiries were not without opposition, as indicated earlier. These questions were, in fact, added because of growing government interest in the welfare of the population.

In the census of 1950 the inquiries on income were elaborated and extended to larger proportions of the population. In the census of 1960 new questions appeared relating to mobility in response to the growing problems of transportation, decentralization, suburbanization, and the increasing mobility of the population. Questions were introduced relating to place of work, means of transportation to work, and length of residence in the same dwelling unit. The census of 1970 was in most respects identical with that in 1960. A few additional questions were added, asked only of a sample of the population, on occupational change, population of Spanish origin or descent, vocational education, and disability.

Privacy, Public Interest, and Confidentiality

As has been indicated above, the questions relating to plumbing generated some adverse congressional and public reaction in connection with the 1970 census. A question relating to plumbing facilities has been included in the decennial census since 1940. It first appeared in the Census of Housing taken in that year for the first time. The question ever since has provided what is regarded by experts as perhaps the best single measure of substandard housing. A housing unit without private toilet and bath facilities is generally a dwelling that is substandard by other criteria as well. In fact, in the 1970 census major reliance is placed on this question to determine substandard housing.

Has the government harassed citizens by making such an inquiry? Why does the government ask such a question? The answer is that the government since the 1930s has increasingly expanded its functions in respect to urban renewal and public housing, and has developed programs involving expenditures of literally billions of dollars, not to mention the displacement and relocation of millions of citizens. These programs have necessarily required information on the quantity and quality of available housing. They reflect the growing national determination to eliminate slums and to help provide decent housing for every family. To plan, administer, and evaluate the impact of its urban renewal and housing programs, the government necessarily required information of the type being collected in the Census of Housing. But the questions asked are felt by some people to constitute an invasion of privacy. Nevertheless, the government has taken the position, and the courts have upheld it, that information required for the general good transcends the right of the person to privacy. It may legitimately be held that it was not the business of government to make inquiries about plumbing in the first census in 1790, when 95 percent of the American people lived in rural areas, on farms, or in places of fewer than 2500 persons. But this position can scarcely be defended when the nation is 74 percent urban and 69 percent metropolitan, as in 1970; and when government policy and programs include urban renewal and public housing activities.

This, incidentally, was the general position taken by the Decennial Census Review Committee, of which the author was a member, in its report to the secretary of commerce in 1970. It recommended that the specific inquiries relating to plumbing and similar inquiries were well within the province of government, provided that the information collected from any individual person or family was kept completely confidential and was made available only in aggregative form; that is, in statistical tables which revealed nothing about any individual person or family. The Decennial Census Review Committee stressed the legal provisions which forbid the government to disclose any information about the person or to use census information in a manner inimical to the person's interests. It also recommended strengthened administrative provisions to assure the implementation of the confidentiality laws which have, in fact, been strictly enforced and upheld by competent legal authority and the courts.

Other Statistical Developments

The need for information by both the government and private sector generated many statistical developments in addition to those represented by the history of the population census. Early inquiries in schedules relating to industry, agriculture, and commerce foreshadowed the separate Census of Manufacturers initiated in 1904, the Quinquennial Census of Agriculture in 1925, the Census of Distribution in 1930, and the Census of Religious Bodies provided for in 1906. The newer censuses include, in response to chronic problems of urban housing, the Census of Housing first taken in 1940, and, in response to the chronic problems of urban transport, the Census of Transportation, initiated in 1963. Over the years the various censuses were supplemented by statistical programs designed to maintain on a current basis the key information collected in the census benchmark enterprises.

Similarly, statistical activities were greatly elaborated throughout the federal government. Statistical agencies emerged in the Department of Agriculture, the Department of Labor, the Department of Health, Education and Welfare, and throughout the federal establishment. The proliferation and elaboration of statistics, in response to emergent problems in the transition of this nation from an agrarian to an urban society, created new problems—additional demands upon respondents, duplication and overlap in the statistical work of federal agencies, and considerations of cost and efficiency. In consequence, in order to control, coordinate, and integrate the federal statistical programs, the Committee on Government Statistics was created in 1933 to review the situation and to make recommendations. Eventually, the recommendations of this committee led to the Federal Reports Act in 1941 and the creation of the Office of Statistical Standards in the Bureau of the Budget in the Executive Office of the President of the United States. Although this agency has been reorganized in what is now the Office of Management and Budget, the authority for coordination of federal statistics still is lodged there.

Furthermore, the increase in statistics and in their utilization was not restricted to the federal government. Similar developments have taken place in state and local governments and in the private sector. The proliferation of statistics in the private sector—in business, labor, civic and welfare organizations—matched that in government and for essentially similar reasons. Important private statistical data-collecting and publishing efforts include those of the National Conference Board, the National Bureau of Economic Research, the Dodge Corporation, Standard & Poor, Dun & Bradstreet, and McGraw-Hill. They also include the activities of the polling organizations such as those run by the Gallup, Roper, and Harris survey organizations; and such survey units as Audits and Surveys, National Analysts, the University of Michigan Survey Research Center, and the University of Chicago National Opinion Research Center.

The evolution of social statistics in this nation in response to the emerging needs of the changing social order is, of course, paralleled among other nations. The drive for internationally systematic and comparable statistics was initiated in the nineteenth century in the activities of the International Statistical Institute and its predecessors. Comparable international statistics are now compiled in a large number of annual and periodic publications of the United Nations and its specialized agencies.

Some idea of the breadth of social statistics now available can be gleaned from an examination of the *Statistical Abstract of the United States,* published annually by the U. S. Bureau of the Census. This publication summarizes the major statistics available for the nation from many sources, both public and private. A version of this volume is also available as a paperback publication entitled *Pocket Data Book* issued every two years. The volume is supplemented by *Historical Statistics of the United States: Colonial Times to 1957.* Another supplementary volume entitled *Historical Statistics of the United States: Continuation to 1962 and Revisions* updates this historical summary.

Social versus Economic Statistics

The data collected by governments in sporadic and then in systematic census undertakings originally were concerned primarily with sources of revenue, taxes, and expenditures, and also with military matters. As populations became increasingly large, societies grew increasingly interdependent, complex, and vulnerable, new needs precipitated new governmental functions, and new types of data were required. Problems associated with "urbanism as a way of life" required governments to become increasingly concerned with the welfare of their populations and, therefore, with the collection of information that would define these problems and permit the effective planning, administration, and evaluation of various types of programs. Much of the information first obtained by government was economic in character. More and more, however, governments are also collecting "social statistics." Many statistics, of course, have both economic and social implications. For example, statistics relating to unemployment, health, education, and housing are used both for economic and social analysis.

The distinction between the "economic" and the "social" has become easier since the passage of the Employment Act of 1946, creating the Council of Economic Advisors and requiring annual reports on the state of the economy. The statistics compiled and analyzed by the Council of Economic Advisors may be designated clearly as economic in character, although many of them also have social implications. The Employment Act of 1946 can be viewed as a sequel to the depression of the 1930s and the national concern with the state of the economy in the post-World War II period. It represents a systematic effort to collect and analyze information about the economy for the purposes of formulating policy and designing programs to assure high levels of employment.

At the present time, the "urban crisis" refers to many social—as distinguished from economic—problems, including slums, ghettos, crime and delinquency, alcoholism and drug addiction, racial tensions and intergroup conflict, family disorganization, increasing welfare rolls, and political and governmental problems. The growing attention to the urban crisis is pointing up the need for further systematic efforts to collect and analyze more social statistics relating to these types of problems. This development has, in fact, generated a movement to create a Council of Social Advisors calling for an annual report on the social state of the nation to parallel that on the economic state of the nation. In fact, a bill to create such a Council of Social Advisors was introduced into the Senate by Senator Mondale in 1967 and hearings were held on it.

The nation's increasing awareness of its social problems has also led to the consideration of the development of "social indicators" as basic types of social statistics that will play the same role in depicting the social state of the nation as the economic indicators depict its economic health. The Department of Health, Education and Welfare has issued one such report, *Toward a Social Report*. The Office of Management and Budget in the Executive Office of the President in 1974 published the volume, *Social Indicators, 1973,* after some five years of preparation.

In the chapters which follow some of the chief types of social statistics and their various uses will be described. Further consideration of "social indicators" will be reserved for the concluding chapter.

PREPARATION OF THIS VOLUME

In approaching the preparation of this volume, basic questions that had to be faced were "What is a 'use' of statistics?" and "Who is a 'user'?"

Statistics, as has been indicated, play a vital role in decisions which profoundly affect the lives of most citizens. For example, the cost and quality of housing, the need for schools and for other public facilities and services, and the growth or decay of entire communities are illuminated, while policies to deal with relevant problems are based upon the underlying body of statistical information. However, identification of the precise means by which these statistics exert their influence is difficult, and any evaluation of the actual use of an individual statistical series (or group of series) is necessarily largely impressionistic.

Several factors help account for this difficulty. Users and uses are broadly distributed in many parts of the economic system, in all levels of government, and throughout society as a whole. Users of statistics do not always make their needs known to the compilers of the data. In many cases, the users do not make direct use of primary statistical publications but instead draw their data from secondary sources. An example can be found in the remarks of a congressman who opposed the appropriations for a census because population figures were available in the press (*sic!*). In many instances it is difficult to know who the users are, exactly how the statistics are used, or the urgency of the needs which they satisfy. In addition, for many kinds of problems, a given body of statistics may be used in combination with other kinds of statistics. In such a case, it is difficult to assign a particular value to one set of the statistics alone. What is required to meet the need is an entire body of statistics, including data relating to a diversity of fields. It is then difficult to assess the role of any one of the statistical series by itself in its contribution to the solution of the problem as a whole.

Finally, the uses of statistics are handicapped by defects in the existing statistical system. Needed data sometimes do not exist. Data from different sources are not always comparable. The quality of some series needs improvement. Many uses which might otherwise be made of the statistics consequently are limited or discouraged altogether, thus compounding the difficulty of an accurate description of the extent to which the statistics actually are used.

In an effort to catalog uses of statistics one has to deal with three methodological or conceptual problems. First, what is a use? For example, how does one deal with the fact that a reader sees and makes note of a particular statistical finding, stores it mentally for further reference along with other information, and then uses it almost unconsciously in forming a judgment on some future occasion? Is this a use? It may be by far the most frequent manner of use of statistical data, but it is difficult to ascertain.

Second, it is not a simple task to identify a user, or at least to identify the proper person to answer questions about a use.

Third, how should one weight various uses to make the conclusions of greatest value? Should one give equal weight to the use made by a school child who crams a fact into a composition to get a better mark, and the use made by a congressional committee trying to arrive at a decision for framing a piece of legislation? Probably not. Both, however, certainly represent uses of the data.

The uses made of statistical data of a particular type could be analyzed in various ways. First, one could set down the general purposes that the user has in mind. These would tend to fall into identical broad categories regardless of the type of data being considered—economic, demographic, educational, health, or whatever—though the frequency of each type of use might differ from one category of data to another.

Second, one could study the manner in which the statistical data were used to achieve the specific purpose. This is a neglected field of study but

Why Statistics?

one that could have a considerable payoff in better data collection, improved system design, and more useful forms of presentation.

Third, one could study the users and classify them by the nature of their business. This has been done fairly frequently, but knowing who the users are does not in itself throw much light on the purposes of use or the manner of use.

In the materials which follow each of these approaches has been employed as necessary and feasible in an effort to illustrate the utility of the data.

A serious consideration of the uses of statistics in the service of society providing specific uses largely in the form of detailed case studies has been published under the appropriate title, *Statistics: A Guide to the Unknown* (Tanur, Mosteller, et al., 1972). That volume is organized around specific uses rather than around bodies of statistics, as is this one. The broad spectrum of interests covered is indicated by groupings of chapters under the following topics: "Staying Well or Getting Better," "Getting Sick and Dying," "Men and Animals," "Government Influences Man," "Man Influences Government," "Communicating with Others," "Man at Work," "Man at School and Play," "Counting Man and His Goods," "Forecasting Population and the Economy," "Measuring Segregation and Inequality," "The States of Nature," and "Modern Machines." These section titles alone strongly point to the fact that statistics are produced for use and not as an end in themselves.

The general plan followed in undertaking the present volume was to invite a knowledgeable person in a given field of statistics to prepare a memorandum in accordance with a general outline provided by the writer. These specialized memoranda served as a basis, then, for editorial treatment with varying degrees of rewriting to give the book better cohesion in subject matter and style. In each chapter based on such a memorandum, its author is given on the first page.

ORGANIZATION OF VOLUME

The following chapters consider specific bodies of statistics, broadly representative of social statistics but by no means covering the entire spectrum of social data. Selections of the fields discussed have been made on the basis of a number of criteria including the availability of well-defined bodies of statistics and information about their uses. Many other areas might have been incorporated including data such as those relating to communication, insurance of various types, social mobility, etc.

Chapters 2, 3, and 4 deal largely with demographic and health statistics. Chapter 2, "On Population," is concerned with the statistics based on the decennial censuses of population and their uses. Chapter 3, "On Births, Deaths, and Health," describes vital and health statistics and illustrates the manner in which they are utilized. Chapter 4, "On Marriage, Divorce, and the Family," considers these specialized aspects of population data and their multifarious uses.

The next four chapters focus on significant aspects of personal and social development and experience. Chapter 5, "On Education," treats the information available about this significant element in the socialization of the person and its various uses. Chapter 6, "On the Labor Force," is concerned with data about the nation's working population and the use of labor-force information. Chapter 7, "On Social Security and Welfare," focuses on data about those who earn benefits under the Social Security system or who become eligible for welfare programs. Chapter 8, "On Delinquency and Crime," considers the information available about persons who fail "to make it" in conventional legal channels and get caught in the toils of the administration of criminal justice.

The three chapters which follow relate to consumer expenditures and selected major areas of consumption. Chapter 9, "On Consumption and the Consumer," considers general aspects of consumption patterns and their social as well as some economic implications. Chapter 10, "On Housing and Construction," deals with a major consumer expenditure area, housing, which has significant economic as well as social impact. Chapter 11, "On Metropolitan Transport and Land Use," focuses on major elements which influence metropolitan structure and the circulation of goods and services. Chapter 12, "On Outdoor Recreation," treats an increasingly important element in the life space, greater time for leisure and recreation, especially outdoor recreation.

The next three chapters probe into the information available about factors related to public policy and the governance of this nation. Chapter 13, "On Governments," treats the statistics relating to revenues and expenditures of governments and describes the increasing usefulness of the data relating to this expanding element in the nation's economic and social activities. Chapter 14, "On Elections," describes the information available about elections on all three levels of government and points to its various uses. Chapter 15, "On Public Opinion Polls," although it does not embrace all aspects of public opinion measurement, is concerned with an area of growing interest and importance—that relating to significant national and international issues.

In the concluding Chapter 16, "On Social Indicators," consideration is given to the mounting interest in the use of social statistics to guide social policy and action in a manner paralleling that for economic policy and action following the passage of the Employment Act of 1946 and the creation of the Council of Economic Advisors.

Finally, it is to be noted that all references to publications within a chapter are listed at the end of each chapter. These references, however, do not constitute a comprehensive bibliography of sources of the data. For such a comprehensive and updated bibliography of the sources of statistics the reader is referred to the Appendix of the annually published *Statistical Abstract of the United States.*

REFERENCES

Miksch, W. F. "The Average Statistician (641.07 Words About a Pain in the Neck)." *Colliers,* June 17, 1950, p. 10.

Office of Management and Budget, Executive Office of the President. *Social Indicators, 1973*. Washington, D. C.: Government Printing Office, 1974.

Tanur, Judith M., Frederick Mosteller, et al. *Statistics: A Guide to the Unknown*. The Joint Committee on the Curriculum in Statistics and Probability of the American Statistical Association and the National Council of Teachers of Mathematics. San Francisco: Holden-Day, 1972.

U. S. Bureau of the Census. *Historical Statistics of the United States: Colonial Times to 1957*. Washington, D. C.: Government Printing Office, 1960.

———. *Historical Statistics of the United States: Continuation to 1962 and Revisions*. Washington, D. C.: Government Printing Office, 1965.

———. *Pocket Data Book*. Washington, D. C.: Government Printing Office, biennial.

———. *Statistical Abstract of the United States*. Washington, D. C.: Government Printing Office, annual.

U. S. Department of Health, Education and Welfare. *Toward a Social Report*. Washington, D. C.: Government Printing Office, 1969.

Wright, Carroll D. *The History and Growth of the United States Census*. Washington, D. C.: Government Printing Office, 1900.

CHAPTER 2

On Population*

The purpose of the Decennial Census of Population and its major official use is basic to the very structure of government in the United States.

When the founding fathers debated the organization of the Congress, they came to the conclusion that for the one house of Congress

> Representatives and direct taxes shall be apportioned among the several States which may be included within this Union, according to their respective numbers . . . .

They also established a means of finding out what these respective numbers would be by ordering that a census should be taken within each period of ten years. At the end of November 1970, when the results of the 1970 census were turned over to the president, there was another set of figures which showed how many representatives would come from each state after the elections of 1972. The method of making this computation is established by law. As a result of the 1970 census, nine states gave up a total of eleven seats to the five states which gained them.

Under the law the number of congressional districts in a state must be equal to the number of representatives to which the state is entitled. Moreover, in accordance with court decisions, the number of people in each district must be about equal. In 1971, nearly every state which had

---

* Based on a memorandum prepared by Conrad C. Taeuber, formerly associate director for population, U. S. Bureau of the Census.

more than one member in the House of Representatives found it necessary to set up new districts to take into account the fact that different areas in the state had not grown at equal rates since the old districts were established.

To enable the legislative committees charged with drawing up the new districts to do their job, it was necessary to provide them with population totals for every county, every place, every township or other subdivision of a county. In many instances statistics were needed for smaller areas, even down to city blocks in the larger cities. The same information was needed to draw up the new districts for state legislatures and for other elective offices. Population counts which were collected objectively and on a uniform basis throughout the area under consideration were required in order to draw up districts which would meet the tests provided by the courts.

Even the very first census of the United States, as has been indicated, involved more than a mere count of heads. Age data for males (under and over sixteen years of age) had definite uses for potential military manpower; the information on sex gave some picture of the population composition of the nation, not utterly unrelated to the political purpose of the census, since women were not as yet enfranchised; information on color and on free and slave status also provided a picture of the composition of the American people. Moreover, these data also had political implications because of the provision, under one of the great compromises at the Constitutional Convention, that only three-fifths of the slaves would count for the purposes of congressional apportionment.

In the second and subsequent censuses the inquiries asked of the American population were expanded, as has been noted in Chapter 1, to provide the Congress and the American people with the information necessary to handle the problems with which the nation was confronted. It may be stated, in fact, that a mere reading of the census questions, even without reference to the results obtained, provides considerable insight into the changing structure of the American economy and society and the changing nature of the nation's problems.

Through time the statistics derived from the decennial population censuses served many purposes—so many that it would be impractical, if not impossible, to try to list them all. Thus, only some of the more important and documented uses of the data will be set forth.

USES BY THE FEDERAL GOVERNMENT

There is a rapidly growing body of federal legislation which specifies or requires the use of population data for the allocation of funds or administration of programs. This legislation is of three types: (1) statutory provisions which use population and related data for allocating funds or for related types of action, such as grants-in-aid; (2) statutes which refer to one or more types of population and related data to be used in program administration; and (3) laws which clearly require, but do not specify, population and related information for their administration. The most important of these legislative enactments include the following:

1. Allocation of funds
   Elementary and Secondary Education Act of 1965
   Adult Basic Education Act of 1966
   Office of Economic Opportunity—Community Action Programs
   Research Facilities Act (Cooperative State Research Service—Department of Agriculture)
   Smith Lever Act (Cooperative Agricultural Extension Service—Department of Agriculture)
   Hatch Act and Amendments (Agricultural Experimental Stations—Department of Agriculture)
   Grants-in-Aid (State Technical Services—Department of Commerce)
   Grants-in-Aid (Office of Health, Education and Welfare—Guidance, Counseling, and Testing: Identification of Able Students)
   Grants-in-Aid (Office of Education, HEW—Land Grant Colleges and Universities)
   Grants-in-Aid (Public Health Service, Chronic Illness, and Aged)
   Grants-in-Aid (Outdoor Recreation Facilities—Department of the Interior)
   Grants-in-Aid (Water Resources and Planning—Department of the Interior)
   Appalachian Redevelopment Act of 1965
   Vocational Education Act of 1963
   Higher Education Facilities Act of 1963
   Social Security Act
2. Census data specified in statutes
   Public Works and Economic Development Act of 1965
   Fair Labor Standards Act of 1938 (as amended)
   Voting Rights Act of 1965
   Civil Rights Act of 1964
   The U. S. Housing Act of 1937 (as amended)
   Housing Act of 1948 (as amended)
   Housing Act of 1956 (as amended)
   Demonstration Cities and Metropolitan Development Act of 1966
3. Laws dependent upon census data
   Manpower Development and Training Act of 1962 (as amended)
   Elementary and Secondary Education Act of 1965 (Title VII, Bilingual Education Act)
   Immigration Act of 1965
   Urban Mass Transportation Act of 1964

Economic Opportunity Amendments of 1967 (Special Impact Program)
Jury Selection and Service Act of 1968
Federal Aid Highways
Housing Act of 1949
The Housing and Urban Development Act of 1970

Of the legislative acts listed above, ten were originally passed prior to 1960 and twenty-two subsequent to that date. With the advent of the "New Federalism" and a heightened national awareness of the social and domestic problems which confront the nation, it can be expected that population and related data will be involved even more heavily in the legislation from now on.

It is estimated that approximately $10 billion annually are now distributed by the federal government to the states or their subdivisions according to formulas which use population or housing data as a major element. In addition, large amounts of money are allocated annually by the states to counties and municipalities with population as a major factor in determining how much money each local government gets.

A matter which has received a great deal of attention in the administration, the Congress, and state administrations is the development of sharing the federal government revenue with the states. Population counts are a central element in practically all of the congressional bills introduced in favor of revenue sharing with the states. The revenue-sharing bill already passed and others being considered provide for initial distribution of funds to the states on the basis of a tax-effort formula involving state and national population figures. Since revenue sharing would be done on an annual basis, it would be necessary to have up-to-date population counts.

It is also possible that population counts would determine whether a local government would receive any shared revenue at all, since at least one major bill provides that sharing with cities and counties be limited to those with 50,000 or more persons. Another bill limits local sharing to metropolitan areas of 1.5 million or more inhabitants.

In addition, some bills have been introduced for distributing extra revenue-sharing money to low-income states, the amounts being determined by population size and personal income within the states. Other bills use income per person as a general basis for distribution to states. Population data enter into any program where, as it has been suggested, states might be credited with tax effort as measured by taxes per person.

Examples of other types of uses of the population figures by the federal government indicate further the many activities helped by census statistics for the benefit of the American people. Our lawmakers have the continuing job of anticipating changes which are likely to take place and trying to make ready for them when they occur. For example, in considering the lowering of the voting age, congressmen wanted to know how many young people, eighteen to twenty-one years old, there were and how this number was likely to change in the coming years. They wanted to know whether these young people were evenly distributed throughout the entire United States, or whether they were especially numerous in rural areas, big cities, or the suburbs. They also wanted to know how many of them were married, how many had jobs, how many were in college or in the armed forces, and how much education those who were no longer in school had completed.

There has been a continuing need to know the number of poor families and persons, as well as how many of them are white and how many black; how many are children and how many older persons; how many of the poor families have no man of working age; how many live in big cities, in suburbs, in smaller cities, or in rural areas; and how many of them are farming. There has also been a need for information on how many of these poor families in the cities have come there from rural areas, how many are long-time city residents, and how many have children who are attending school. There has been some indication that people who can leave the poverty areas to find better living conditions do so. How rapidly is this happening and what are the consequences for the families who are left behind?

Finally, it may be noted that the census population figures play a vital role in the nation's national defense. For example, with the adoption of Selective Service in connection with World War II, population statistics were used in helping to set state and local quotas for the draft; in estimating potential manpower for the military and on the home front; in making many decisions about consumer goods; in setting regulations affecting the job changes and movement of the population in the light of critical manpower needs; and in planning communication systems via first radio and later television for emergency use. Furthermore, the Office of Emergency Planning has used information on the number of persons and their location to develop plans and programs for air-raid shelters in case of attack, for adequate food and other supplies for use following an attack, and for many other parts of the programs necessary in an emergency.

USES BY STATE AND LOCAL GOVERNMENT

State and local government programs make up one of the most important and rapidly changing sectors of the national economy (see Chapter 13). Their annual expenditures in fiscal year 1971 totaled $171 billion, and have more than doubled since 1960. Their tax yields totaled $95 billion during 1971, up $8 billion or 8.4 percent from the previous year.

Local governments altogether spent more than $105 billion in fiscal

1971 for the various municipal, county, and other local services and facilities. Program planning and evaluation of each of the local governments is becoming increasingly affected and more complicated by the great population changes. Local governments face a continuing challenge to keep up with these changes in population size and composition which have resulted in increased need for public services as minority and lower-income groups have moved in and the tax base has diminished with the exodus of white and more affluent residents.

Population and related data provide an acceptable base of information needed in carrying out major programs involving cooperation between federal and local government agencies. These include such programs as housing for the elderly and handicapped persons and low-rent public housing, rent supplements, and home-owner interest subsidies. Urban renewal, model cities, and urban planning assistance programs require up-to-date information about the situation in the affected locality. The Department of Housing and Urban Development requires from local governments market analyses which include information on the housing stock, as well as on family income by tenure, migration trends, household size, housing quality, rents and values, and type and age of residential structures. Similarly, programs for the relief of poverty call for up-to-date information on the number and characteristics of persons below the poverty-income level, employment and unemployment, and the occupational skills of those in the community. There is need also for other information about the population affected: age, sex, race, family composition, level of education, and their recent migrations, as well as population shifts within the city and between the city and its suburban areas.

The Advisory Commission on Intergovernmental Relations believed that it would be desirable to count our population once every five years instead of once every ten years as we do now.

> The Commission views the census operation of the Federal Government as an important intergovernmental activity, essential to effective cooperation and coordination among Federal, state and local governments. Census data provide the factual basis for a multitude of policy decisions by the Congress, governors, mayors and other Federal, state and local officials and are required for the development of long-range plans for public facilities and services at Federal, state and local levels; the allocation of grants-in-aid by Federal and state governments; and the measurement of changing demands upon all governments as a result of shifting population patterns. The question of the need for a mid-decade census of population, unemployment, and housing is, therefore, relevant to the responsibilities of this Commission. It might be noted that there is a close parallel between many of the requirements of individual governments and the research needs of the Commission itself, since frequently

we examine the same questions of policy within the larger context of intergovernmental relations.

Because basic governmental problems at all levels are now, and will continue to be, shaped by the dynamics of population change, more current statistical measures of the social, economic and demographic characteristics of our citizenry are indispensable for designing and implementing governmental programs and policies to meet these challenges. We emphasize the importance of more current data since the tempo of population movements is altering significantly the characteristics of urban as well as rural areas over short periods of time; yet only the census of population and housing—of all the U. S. censuses—is taken as infrequently as once in 10 years.

The total of federal payments to state and local governments has risen sharply since World War II, from $900 million in 1946 to $6.3 billion in 1959 and to more than $21 billion in 1970.

One-third of the money spent by local governments—cities, counties, school districts, townships, and special districts—is supplied by federal and state intergovernmental payments. Most of the outside support comes in the form of state aid. In fiscal 1969, state aid totaled $23.8 billion, including more than $5 billion of federal funds channeled through the state governments. In addition, more than $2.2 billion in federal aid went directly to the various local governments.

Population statistics are used as a basis for distributing all funds under a number of important aid programs and are a major element also in the distribution of a sizable fraction of all federal and state grants-in-aid. Many of the grants to local governments are made only after the preparation of plans or programs in conformance with guidelines established by the Congress and administering agencies. Examples of statistical data required for these grants include total population classified by age, race, and sex; family income; population density; number of unemployed; housing supply and quality; and years of schooling for various elements of the population.

Administrative and legal actions under state laws use population data for achieving uniformity and fairness in programs for counties, municipalities, and other governmental subdivisions of states. The powers and duties of municipalities in many cases depend on the size and characteristics of their population.

In many states there are laws which specify the amount of capitalization needed before a bank can incorporate, basing the requirement on the population of the city in which the bank is to be located. Licenses of various types and taxes on those licenses frequently are determined by the size of the community in question. The number of officials and their salaries in many instances are determined by the number of people in the area they serve. A number of states have established classes of communities based on the size of their population. In every state, cities of the first, second, or third class have different powers and duties and it requires a count of the population to determine in which class a city falls.

The use of population statistics for administrative purposes may be illustrated by some of the provisions applying to the state of Kentucky.

1. Cities in Kentucky are divided into six classes depending on the number of their inhabitants, as follows:

First class	100,000 inhabitants or more
Second class	20,000 to 100,000
Third class	8,000 to 20,000
Fourth class	3,000 to 8,000
Fifth class	1,000 to 3,000
Sixth class	1,000 inhabitants or less

2. The size or class of a city determines its power to:
    a. Select its form of government—cities of second to sixth class may adopt the commission form of government. Cities of second, third, and fourth class may adopt the city manager form of government. There is a choice for some.
    b. Borrow money—maximum indebtedness depends upon the city class and named maximum percentages on the value of the taxable property therein which are as follows: cities of the first and second classes, and of the third class exceeding 15,000—10 percent; cities of the third class having a population of less than 15,000, and cities and towns of the fourth class—5 percent; cities and towns of the fifth and sixth classes—3 percent.
    c. Issue bonds—cities of first or second class, incurring indebtedness beyond income for the year, may issue bonds. The cities of the third class may do the same providing there is no limitation imposed by law. Cities of fourth, fifth, and sixth class need the consent of two-thirds of the votes cast to incur indebtedness.

Salaries of city officials in Kentucky depend on the classification of the city in which they serve. In cities of the second class the mayor may receive an annual salary of $4,000 and each commissioner may have an annual salary of $3,600. In cities of the third class the mayor and each commissioner may receive an annual salary of not less than $500 nor more than $3,000, to be fixed in the question submitted to the voters. In cities of the fourth class the mayor, police judge, and commissioners may each receive an annual salary for their first term under the commission form of government in the amount fixed in the question submitted to the voters. The salaries set for each office may not be less than the salaries then being paid for that office, the salary of the mayor may not exceed $1,200 per year and the salary of the police judge and each commissioner may not be more than $1,000 per year.

In the *Municipal Year Book 1970,* Table VI, "Salaries of Municipal Officials in Cities over 10,000," shows that salaries of officials, on the average, go down with the size of the city.

Most states have similar provisions and in many instances the use of the population counts affects many other government functions. Moreover, the number of officers of certain types a city or a county can have depends on the size of its population. In many states the salaries paid to judges and other governmental officials depend on the size of the population which they serve.

The sharing of tax money between the states and the counties and cities is often on the basis of the number of persons in the area being served. For many cities, this is an important source of their tax money; a resident may be worth $25 or more per year to his community in the form of money received from the state. Similarly, money is distributed by the federal government to the states; and in many instances the number of persons living in the state is an important element in the amount to be turned over. In some of the highway funds, the number of rural residents is a major factor in determining the amount of money to go to the state. For some programs, including Vocational Agriculture, the number of farm residents is taken into account in deciding how much money is to go to each state. As has been indicated, the proposals for revenue sharing between the federal and the state governments, which have been discussed by the Congress, include population and the state's efforts to raise its own revenue as a basis for determining how much is to go to each state.

Other cases illustrate the range of legal provisions using population statistics. In one state, a county with 400,000 or more persons may establish a tunnel authority. Population size is an element in determining the power to regulate the practice of cosmetology, the office hours of county officials, the licensing of barbers, the regulation of black powder in blasting in mines, the establishment of a tax on beer, and so on. In another state, the size of the population affects the method by which school districts make their purchases, the registration of architects, the administration of pensions and relief funds, the use of the university hospital, the number of banks which may be chartered, and whether or not a main-line railroad is allowed to run through the business district of a city. The list of such applications of census figures to local administration is a very long one. These few examples illustrate how much dependence is placed on the population data. Clearly, if all areas are to be treated fairly, it is necessary to have up-to-date, comprehensive, and reliable information about the population.

Cities and counties often have to borrow money in order to provide essential facilities or services. When they try to sell their bonds they frequently need to show how the population of the area is growing. They also need statistics to show how many persons would benefit from the improvement which is to be financed with the money to be raised by the bonds, and to provide an indication of future growth as a measure of the ability to make the payments which will be required. Population statistics are often essential in such negotiations.

Other specific examples of the use of population figures are given below.

> A police department related trends in crime to the characteristics of the people in the areas in which arrests were made and decided on that basis how to allocate its manpower within the city. For example, juvenile delinquency was related to the number of young people in the area.
>
> Plans to develop swimming pools in a suburban county were developed within three limitations: it must be an outdoor pool; it must be situated on public property and it could not be self-supporting. An optimum-size pool would serve approximately 700 families. Selecting priority locations for such a public pool called for the use of information on the number and location of families, especially those with children and youths who might be expected to use the pool.
>
> Information showing the number of persons within an area in the city was used as a basis for developing a voter registration campaign and for studying its effectiveness.
>
> Information about the people and their places of residence was used to study residential segregation and the changes which were occurring. They were frequently used to delineate areas that required attention and to persuade the local authorities to take effective action.
>
> Census data were a factor in planning for the extension of sewer lines in rural areas, taking into account the density of the population.
>
> A director of planning reported that an attorney for a disgruntled applicant for a zoning action threatened to move a black family into a house he owned. The census figures showed that there were already a number of such families in that area, and thus the threat turned out to be no threat at all and the action was not contested.
>
> A county planning board needed data on the number of people and how that had changed in order to answer the question, "How many people shall we plan for?" They wanted to know who was moving away and where the migrants from the city were going. The planning of a transportation program for the county was at stake.
>
> A planning board writes, "Not only are we able to continually update the projection of health facility needs, but we can study and evaluate the change in hospital service areas within a metropolitan area as to age, sex, economic levels, etc., and relate these changes to the services offered by the hospitals."

In planning for a city program for the housing of the elderly, data were sought on the number of the elderly and their location within the city, as well as the circumstances under which they were living. Knowing these facts enabled the planning board to choose a site close to the former homes of the elderly. Public housing for the elderly was constructed in the light of these findings.

A health department related births, deaths, infant mortality, and illegitimacy to the characteristics of the population of the area in which these events occurred and planned its programs on that basis. The programs included provision for the immunization of children and adults and other health services.

A local school board came to the census to get information on the number of children of elementary school age living in families with low incomes to help them in determining how to distribute funds among the schools in their area.

A school board faced with a rapidly changing population asked for information on the number of white and black families in the area which they served and for each of the neighborhoods in that area, and used this, along with their own information on behavior problems in the school and the academic records of the several schools, to plan a program for improved racial relations in the community.

The school board of a large city asked for information about the changing distribution of the population within the city in order to draw up new boundaries for their school system.

Information on the race and size of the population was used in connection with information on school transfers to develop a plan for future construction of schools in a large city.

USES BY THE PRIVATE SECTOR

Who needs population information? It would be easier to answer the question, "Who doesn't need such information?" for practically no one would be included in that list. When a census has been taken, the results are published and the statistics then are printed and distributed. They give figures for every state; for every county; for every city, town, or village; for every township; and for neighborhoods in each of the large cities. This information is reprinted in newspapers, almanacs, encyclopedias, school books, and in many magazines. Printed reports are available in many libraries, and are used widely.

In addition, if people need more information than they can find in the printed reports, they can ask the Census Bureau to make special tabulations, for which they pay. Many people and organizations do that. In the year 1968 nearly 900 organizations and individuals paid the Census Bureau for preparing some special summaries which they needed. This was information from the 1960 census, which was already eight years old at that time but was still needed. The buyers of these special tabulations included a root beer company, a university, a professional association, a drug manufacturer, a large manufacturer of electrical appliances, a firm which sells drugs and other products from door to door, a bank, a large oil company, a county government, a firm which prints many books for use by businessmen, a large department store, a hospital, a research firm, a firm specializing in convenience foods, a paint manufacturer, a chain of ice cream stores, a private welfare organization, a small community newspaper, a church, a restaurant chain, and many others.

The needs of the above persons and organizations were very clear. They needed to know something about the numbers of the people they were serving or hoped to serve—where they were; and whether they were old, young, or middle-aged; lived in families or institutions; were rich or poor; well or poorly educated; white, black, or of other ethnic backgrounds; and also how rapidly the situation in any area was changing. There was interest in how many teen-agers were living in homes with above-average incomes; how many children of elementary school age were living in homes with very low incomes; how many homeless men there were in a community. In every case they were interested in people. Sometimes they wanted to know about all of the people, sometimes only about certain classes of the people. In all cases they found that the best source of such information was the population statistics based on the census or some of the sample surveys which the government carries out.

By taking advantage of the fact that the government had collected such information to meet its own needs, the private organizations could get necessary information at far less cost than if they had had to go out independently and get their own. One additional benefit of this arrangement is that it cuts down the frequency with which the citizens of the country are called upon to supply the same information.

Business Use

Perhaps the most readily documented use of population statistics in the private sector is that by the business community. Every businessman constantly is faced with a variety of questions concerning his operations. Will there be more or fewer people who will want his product? Should he expand one line of production while cutting back on another? Should he move to the suburbs and continue in his downtown location, or should he give up his downtown location and concentrate entirely on the suburbs? Is business likely to pick up in the smaller cities of the state as more people move into them? Is the number of teen-agers likely to go up or down, and what does this mean for the type of clothing, records, school equipment, movies, entertainment, sports, and other activities he should be featuring? Are more housewives going to be working and, therefore, providing a better market for laundry and cleaning services, restaurants, prepared foods, and similar services? Is the number of young couples increasing and thereby creating more demand for rental housing? Is the number of older couples without children increasing and does this mean that there is need for more medical care, travel service, recreation, and so on? Is the number of senior citizens likely to increase and does this mean a need for more special services and facilities geared especially to older citizens? Young people and older people have different tastes with respect to clothing, automobiles, home furnishings, entertainment, reading matter, beauty care, medical care, and virtually all other goods and services. They have different values in regard to the use of money and credit, with younger people more ready to buy on credit than were their parents.

Companies which specialize in selling root beer, hamburgers, advertising, automobiles, beauty products, paint, home repairs, gasoline, and oil, along with the owners and developers of shopping centers all study such statistics carefully before deciding where to locate another store or franchise and what it should emphasize in its sales efforts. Bankers study these figures in deciding where to locate branches, what kinds of services are most likely to appeal to the people in the neighborhood, what kinds of new industries should be helped to get started in an area, and how much expansion there is likely to be.

The owners of supermarkets study the proposed location for each store very carefully to make sure that the new store will be situated so that it has a good chance of success. Firms which franchise drive-in eating places, miniature golf courses, and similar establishments make careful studies of each proposed location to make sure that it has a chance of success.

Electric power companies, gas companies, and the telephone companies need to be ready with their services when the population grows, and they make their plans for years in advance, projecting as best they can where the population is likely to grow and by how much, and where it is likely to decline.

A relatively detailed illustration of the use of census data by business is afforded by an investigation which the author made some years ago, at the request of a manufacturer who was considering the relocation of his plant. This head of an industrial establishment wanted to know whether, by reason of difficulties in recruiting labor, especially female and white-collar workers, and the increasing deterioration of the area in which his main plant was located, he would be well advised to abandon his plant in the inner city and move to suburbia. The problems facing the plant were exacerbated by the changing composition of the area which was losing white inhabitants and gaining Negro residents.

Census data were analyzed for both the area in which the industrial plant was located and for alternative sites. The data utilized in the analysis included trends in population size and composition; labor-force size and composition; general location of industry; location of plants of the specific industry, accessibility through mass transit and by use of the automobile; and the number and composition of workers.

The conclusions of the study indicate the usefulness of census data to business and industry in general. On the positive side it was indicated there were certain advantages if the plant remained where it was:

1. The loosening of the labor market could eliminate recruiting difficulties.
2. The plant was already located in a central position with respect to potential labor.
3. The increased use of Negro labor could resolve recruitment problems even if the labor market remained tight.
4. The concentration of workers in the same industry in the area in which the plant was located and the ability of the industrialist to compete favorably for such workers would enable him to outbid competitors for labor at costs below those which relocation would necessitate.
5. The deterioration of the general neighborhood had reached a level which would give it a high priority for government programs designed to renew the area, both for residential and industrial purposes.

If the plant remained where it was, negative factors also were reported. These included the following disadvantages:

1. Continued location in an area which would experience further deterioration for several years.
2. The disruption which would be caused by renewal activities.
3. The difficulty of acquiring additional land in the intensively used inner city.
4. The prospect of a change in racial composition of the area and transition to a larger proportion of Negro workers.

A similar analysis of the situation which would be encountered if the plant were moved to a specified alternative location resulted in the following considerations:

1. Additional land for plant improvement and attractive landscaping would be available at relatively low cost.
2. The move would increase by relatively little the distance to work for the plant's longer-service employees, many of whom had already moved.

On Population 37

    3. The move would enable the plant to continue a high proportion of white but aging employees and possibly reduce the proportion of Negro employees.

However, the move would also require recognition of the following facts:

    1. Any possible gain in the proportion of white employees could be short-lived because they were aging and the proposed new location was in the path of continued Negro advance.
    2. It was doubtful that the move would improve the prospect of recruiting white-collar workers because it would not be as centrally located.
    3. The move, which at the outset would place the plant in a less deteriorated area, could in a relatively short time, as the trend indicated, subject the plant to the problems of another deteriorating area. In the interim the area in which the plant already was located might be rehabilitated.
    4. The proposed new site would put the plant in an area in which other industries already present would, by reason of higher wage rates, place the plant in a disadvantaged competitive situation for labor.
    5. The suburban location would require a separation of display and sales operations and manufacturing functions, and involve split management.

Similar analyses were made for other potential sites with similar types of conclusions.

The study did not make a specific recommendation on site location. But, in presenting the factors to be considered, based mainly on the analysis of census data, the management was able to reach its own conclusion. It decided, to complete the story, to remain where it was—a decision which turned out to be a wise one.

Other specific examples of the use of census figures for business are shown below.

    An existing shopping center used data to help decide whether or not there was enough business in the area to support another major food-chain outlet.

    A department store used the data to help get proper zoning and favorable financing for a new store.

    A savings and loan association used population data to determine the feasibility of applying for a new branch facility and of obtaining approval for it.

    A metropolitan newspaper used population figures to help evaluate the performance of dealers in handling circulation in specific territories.

    An automotive supply chain used them to help in reorganizing a direct mailing system to obtain greater sales at less cost.

    A large manufacturing concern reported that in selecting a site for a plant they considered the following: at maximum employment the plant should not require more than 2 percent of the people in the labor area or 10 percent of the eligible workers. This was expected to level off at 500 employees; therefore, there had to be at least 5000 workers available within a twenty-mile distance.

A bank official stated that he used the census reports on population to help in planning branch bank locations and, also, in developing an advertising campaign. He had also run for public office and reported that he made use of the population figures by neighborhoods in his district to plan his campaign.

A business firm used the information about the numbers of people, families' age, income, ethnic classification, and education to identify neighborhoods which had certain characteristics in order to plan its major advertising for various products.

A number of national magazines have issued special editions in which they modified the advertising and sometimes the editorial matter to make the magazine of greatest interest to the people to whom it was sent.

A supermarket chain wanted to know in what localities they could find the most promising sites for new stores. What were the characteristics of their potential markets? For this they needed to know the store's possible "trading area" and the changes in that area over the last several decades.

The manager of location analysis for another supermarket organization made the following observations:

> The two foremost market criteria of retail trade area are the number of persons and the quality of competition. We desire to have a minimum of 10,000 persons living within the first mile from the supermarket site and a minimum of 15,000–20,000 in the primary trade area. But we need to know more than the number of potential customers. For example, the race and country of origin may suggest special merchandising or type of store. Recent migrants from the South often represent lower purchasing power. They demand more chicken, pork, cheaper cuts of beef and greens relative to other food store items. In Slavic neighborhoods heavy competition may be encountered from ethnic meat markets and bakeries. In Jewish neighborhoods the small delicatessen becomes a significant competitor. This may encourage a supermarket chain to install a delicatessen department and to give more personal service.

The specific examples cited are only a sample of the uses of population data by business. Are such uses of benefit to the general public? The answer is decidedly in the affirmative because anything that increases the efficiency of business operations results, sooner or later, in increased productivity or better distribution of goods and services and, therefore, contributes both to better returns on investment and higher levels of living for the American people. The U. S. Department of Commerce has field offices in many major cities where businessmen and others can come for help in finding the information they need.

Social and Civic Uses

There are, of course, many social and civic uses of the data. For example:

A council of churches studied the statistics for a city and its neighborhoods to plan for the location of churches and to plan special church programs to meet the needs of the people in the neighborhoods of the churches. One problem which came to their attention was that of serving single working women. The reports which they had from some local people had suggested a large concentration of single working women in one area of the city—the census statistics showed how many there were and, in this instance, made it unnecessary to set up a special program because there were not enough there to justify it. They were also particularly interested in the figures on the length of time which people lived in the same house and neighborhood as a help in developing the programs for the churches in neighborhoods with high population turnover.

In another city statistics were used by the Community Chest to decrease overlapping programs and to develop programs according to needs. They depended particularly on figures showing:

    Population and population change by census tracts
    Distribution of age and sex groups and the trends in their distribution
    Population density and land use
    Welfare rates
    Juvenile delinquency rates
    Participation in recreational programs

The census data made possible a determination of the areas of greatest need and the kind of need, and helped establish program priorities.

Another example is given by a home for the elderly, seeking to extend its services to the entire community and to make its facilities available to persons who were not living in the home, which asked for figures on the number and location of elderly persons within the possible service area.

WHAT ABOUT THE FUTURE?

Everyone who is concerned about the future of his job, his business, his city, his state or his country needs information on how the population is changing. This is true whether the individual is part of the government or is making his own work, business, residential, educational, recreational, or other plans. The outlook is different for an area which is growing than for one which is declining slowly or rapidly. The continuing movement of young people from an area may leave behind an elderly population which is no longer able to provide all of the community services. The movement of young people, with their small children, into a suburban area may create a critical need for more schoolrooms, more medical facilities, and a rapid increase in other services.

City planners, real estate developers, the gas and electric companies, as well as the telephone company, the post office, and the local businessmen, continually need information on how the population of an area is changing. They try to find out what is likely to happen in the future. We take it for granted that we will have streets and roads, water and sewer lines, electric power, gas, stores, doctors, teachers, hospitals, and schools when and where we need them. But providing these and other services often takes a long time and, therefore, it is necessary to plan ahead. One of the important elements in such planning is having some information on how many people there are, where they are, and whether their number is likely to grow or decline.

Forecasting population growth for the nation as a whole is difficult. Since the end of World War II we have had what many people called a baby boom—some even talked of a population explosion. But since 1957 the birth rate has dropped, and in 1968 we had the lowest birth rate—i.e., number of babies per thousand of the population—up to that point in our history. The birth rate and the number of babies went up again in 1969 and 1970 and down again from 1971 to 1973. However, since the number of babies born in the 1950s and much of the 1960s was unusually large, we will have an unusually large number of young men and women starting their own families and having children all through the 1970s and well into the 1980s; as a result the birth rate will almost certainly rise again.

What is important here is not only the number of young men and women, but also the age at which they marry, how many of them marry, and how many children they are likely to have. Demographers and population experts also need to know whether the average time between the marriage and the first child is getting longer or shorter, and how much time there is between the arrival of the other children. All of this helps in looking ahead to the growth of the population. Will we have 250 million or even 300 million people in the future? Answers to these questions have much to do with what we expect the federal, state, and local governments and the private sector to do between now and then, and how we as individuals look on the prospects for the future.

When it comes to looking ahead to the likely population of a state, a city, or part of a metropolitan area, we need information not only on how many people there are now, but on how the number moving in or out is likely to change. Americans are a mobile people, and they are free to move anywhere within this large country that they consider desirable. But this movement changes communities and what they can provide, as well as what they need. Without such information, the government cannot do what is expected of it, and this is true also of schools, churches, hospitals, and the entire business world.

Every businessman and government official who is responsible for planning the actions to be taken in the future must take into account the changes in the population which may take place. Will we continue to grow as we have been doing, will our future rate of growth be higher than it was in the past, or are we likely to grow less rapidly than before? Will we need more schools for young children, or more homes for the aged, or both? Can we look forward to a larger number of young people ready for jobs or for college than in the recent past? Are we likely to see a rapid increase in the number of young people getting married, starting their own homes, and needing to buy all of the things that go to make up a modern home? And what about the birth rate? Is that going up or down, and what does that mean for our future growth? Answers to such questions as these affect the production of all kinds of goods, the production of homes and of schools, plans for expanding water and sewer lines, telephone and electric power lines, and, of course, the location of shopping centers and individual stores.

While no one can foretell the future with certainty, it is still necessary to make the best judgment possible about probable developments. For this purpose we need good statistics about the changes in the population which have taken place and of those which are likely to take place. Here, one of the important statistics relates to the total number of children which women have had in the course of their lifetime. If that number is about 2110 per 1000 women, it means that the population is stationary so long as approximately the same proportion of women marry and have children. If, however, women are having about 3000 children per 1000 women—as they were doing not so long ago—then the population is in for some rather rapid growth. With numbers of this type and with some knowledge of the changes in the education of women and of the shift of population from rural to urban areas, it is possible to gain a better appreciation of likely future changes than can be done without such statistics.

Looking ahead it is almost certain that government functions will increase, not decrease, as our society continues to change and as new problems emerge which require collective action for their solution. At the moment increased concern with the nation's health and the relatively high death rate points to increased government interventionism in matters of health insurance and improved delivery of medical services. Should this happen, the need for new information about health and the use of medical services and facilities is certain to require new questions on sample survey and census questionnaires and more responses from the American people. Some of the new questions will undoubtedly be regarded by a few persons and agencies as further invasions of privacy; new protest campaigns, therefore, are likely.

In this connection it is well to quote from the *Report of the Decennial Census Review Committee to the Secretary of Commerce* (July 1971):

> Failure to collect and compile census data would severely handicap governments—state and local as well as Federal—in their administration of many programs affecting, among other things, health, housing, urban renewal, education, poverty, welfare, agriculture, employment and national defense; and severely handicap many activities to the administration of private, civic and welfare programs [p. 30].

It is also in order to quote from a court decision in the same report on the importance of census statistics:

> The authority to gather reliable statistical data reasonably related to governmental purposes and functions is a necessity if modern government is to legislate intelligently and effectively. (*United States of America* v. *William F. Rickenbacker,* 309 F 2nd 462 cert. denied, 83 S. Ct. 542, 1963).

The trial judge said in his decision requiring a citizen to answer the census questions that "Congress has the power to compel relevant testimony necessary for legislative purposes" (p. 22).

Coupled with the power to compel response to the census questions, however, is the requirement that the information provided be kept confidential by the government and be made public only in aggregate form—that is, as statistics which disclose no information about any individual person or organization. Such confidentiality has, indeed, been maintained by the Bureau of the Census, and additional safeguards for doing so are being developed as the questions increase in scope and privacy.

REFERENCES

Municipal Year Book 1970. Washington, D. C.: The International City Management Association, 1971.

Report of the Decennial Census Review Committee to the Secretary of Commerce. Department of Commerce, Washington, D. C., July 1971.

CHAPTER 3

On Births, Deaths, and Health*

Vital and health statistics provide information about births and deaths; marriages and divorces; illness; health care; and health resources and facilities. Data on illness, called "morbidity statistics," include "notifiable disease" data (information about contagious diseases), disability data from household interview surveys, diagnostic and other data from health examinations, and hospital discharge surveys. Health-care statistics include data on utilization of physician, dentist, hospital, and other health services from the household interview, hospital discharge, and other surveys. The statistics on health resources and facilities deal with health manpower data and information on hospitals, rest homes, and other health-care facilities.

Varied uses are made of these statistics. For example, marriage and divorce statistics, dealt with in the next chapter, provide information on family formation and dissolution; birth statistics measure the fertility of the population; and death statistics measure the attrition of the population. Mortality statistics also provide an actuarial base for life insurance and pension purposes, whereas the statistics on causes of death have long been used to identify problems of public health importance and in epidemiological studies, that is, causes of illness and death. With the growing emphasis on delivery of health care, there is increasing demand for data on medical

---

* Based on a memorandum by Theodore D. Woolsey and I. M. Moriyama, National Center for Health Statistics, Health Services and Mental Health Administration, U. S. Department of Health, Education and Welfare.

care utilization and on health manpower and facilities for planning and operational purposes.

The demand for vital and health statistics and the nature of these demands are constantly changing, and depend on health progress, current program interest, and emerging problems. With the increasing complexity of health and social problems, the nature of the demands becomes more sophisticated and increasingly difficult to meet. This gives rise to suggestions for new data systems to supply information deemed necessary for various specific purposes.

The users of vital and health statistics are about as varied as the uses of the data. They range from research workers concerned with scientific studies of disease or of population dynamics to business interests concerned with forecasts of the baby food market. However, of the various consumers, the health industry is probably the biggest single group of users of vital and health statistics.

HISTORICAL PERSPECTIVES

At the beginning of the century, public health was preoccupied with problems of sanitation and control of communicable diseases. Fumigation and quarantine still were accepted public health practices. The gastrointestinal infections, the diseases of childhood, and respiratory diseases, especially pneumonia and tuberculosis, were frequent causes of death.

Since that time significant inroads have been made into the infectious disease problem by sanitation—purification of milk, water, and the environment—and by the discovery of various antigens—toxins, enzymes, proteins—and their application in the immunization of the population, especially during childhood. Much progress was made despite the relatively slow public acceptance of chlorination of water, pasteurization of milk, and vaccination. Venereal disease control activities were conducted under the name of social hygiene until the disease was made a household word in the late 1930s.

The late 1930s also saw an acceleration in the downward trend in infectious diseases as a cause of death with the discoveries of a succession of therapeutic agents for treatment. Pneumonia sera, the sulfa drugs, penicillin, and the wide spectrum of antimicrobials contributed to the rapid decline in death rates. The vaccine against poliomyelitis has virtually eliminated the disease and all but wiped out the serious consequences of this infection. It is expected that the recent discovery of vaccine for rubella (German measles) will have a significant effect on the incidence of congenital defects.

Along with the fight against infective diseases, federal legislation early in the 1900s initiated programs of maternal and child health. Maternal mortality which was once a serious problem, especially in hospitals, has been practically eliminated over the years. Infant and childhood mortality rates are also now at the lowest levels in the history of the country, but have not yet reached the irreducible minimum, and are still above the levels achieved in a number of other countries. With the reduction in the infant mortality rate, there has been a shift in the problem of infective diseases in the postneonatal period (the last eleven months of the first year of life) to medical problems during the neonatal period of life (first month). Congenital anomalies and other birth defects are assuming greater relative importance. The question of premature live births is very much involved in unfavorable pregnancy outcome. Also of concern is the problem of pregnancy wastage, the magnitude of which is not precisely known but thought to be sizable.

The large decrease in death rates from infective disease and in infant and childhood mortality has played a significant role in increasing the life expectancy of the population. The demographic consequences of this and declining fertility have been the aging of the population. This, in turn, has resulted in an increase in the chronic noninfective diseases—the degenerative diseases—particularly heart disease, cancer, and stroke.

The decline in the infectious diseases and the increase in the degenerative diseases called for a change in emphasis of public health programs. By the end of World War II, the various public health programs to control specific diseases were firmly established. However, many of these control programs were handicapped by inadequate knowledge of the causes of the disease.

With the increase in degenerative chronic diseases, another major shift in emphasis took place after World War II. Public health authorities became more and more concerned with medical research and increasing millions of dollars were made available in the form of research grants. At the same time, the specific disease public health programs gave way to the Comprehensive Health Planning Program and to the Regional Medical Program. The effect of this was to shift emphasis from disease prevention programs to a health-care delivery system for the treatment of diseases. These new programs required increased planning and evaluation. In addition to this change in direction of public health programs, there has been a move in a number of cities and states to integrate activities in public welfare, medical care, mental health, and public health under one administration established to deal with human resources.

Other significant developments were the Social Security program of Medicare, a health insurance scheme for those 65 years and over, and the federal-state Medicaid program which provides health insurance coverage for the poor. The latter reflects the growing concern with the inequities in health and the health services of the poor—disproportionately minority groups.

The postwar period called attention to a new and serious health hazard in the form of ionizing radiation and fallouts from atomic bomb explosions, and the potential hazards of atomic energy employed for peaceful purposes. Atmospheric pollution from other sources, such as smoke and motor vehicle exhaust gases, caused discomfort and disease as well as economic waste in most of the urban centers. The widespread use of pesticides commercially and in the home created a new kind of health hazard not only to the user but to the general public eating food containing poisonous substances. Another problem of the environment resulted from the discharge of industrial and other wastes into public streams and rivers. The pollution of the waterways is affecting the ecological balance, and making unsuitable for recreational and other purposes many areas of the country. Thus, some of the problems have come full circle. Environmental sanitation is again a serious issue but the enormity and complexity of the problems in the highly industrialized country of today defy easy solution.

In addition to the difficulties brought about by the trend toward a more heavily urbanized population, a good part of the national social and economic problems of today stems from sheer growth in numbers in this country. This is of relatively recent origin. For many years, both the birth and death rates declined with considerable regularity until about 1936 when the birth rate began to turn upward. Until that time, the demographers were concerned about the possibility of a declining population. However, the birth rate continued to rise during the period of World War II and record numbers of births were reported annually through the postwar years. More than four million births were registered each year between 1954 and 1964. The peak in the crude birth rate was reached in 1957, after which the rate again began to decline.

The resurgence of the birth rate during the war and postwar years contributed enormously to the population growth of this country. The obstetricians and the hospitals were the first to experience this wave of births. The pediatricians were the next to accept responsibility for giving care to the babies. In time, elementary schools, high schools, and colleges were affected by the increasing student population. As consumers, they began to have an impact on various businesses catering to teen-agers and young people. As these youngsters reached the marriageable age, the marriage rate began to be affected. Subsequently, there will be another wave of births which will cause smaller ripples in another cycle in the future.

The war and the postwar boom in the birth rate has contributed significantly to what has been referred to as the population explosion. By 1968 the total population of the United States reached the 200 million mark. The 1970 census recorded 205 million Americans.

DATA DEVELOPMENT

Except for the decennial population censuses which were used to collect statistics on births and deaths, no regular system for collection of vital and health statistics was available at the beginning of this century. Because of the need for statistics on the health of the United States population, the American Medical Association and the American Public Health Association memorialized the Congress to authorize a permanent Census Office for the annual collection of birth and death statistics. Such an office was established in 1902. Although the statutory authority provided for both the birth and death registration areas, work on the birth registration was not started until 1915. Thus, national statistics on deaths became available starting in 1900, and on live births and stillbirths in 1915. Both areas included about ten states and the District of Columbia at the beginning, and more and more states were added as they became qualified for admission to the registration areas. Not until 1933 did both the birth and death registration areas include all the states of the Union.

While mortality statistics provided information for health programs, the annual publication of data failed to satisfy the need for current statistics on communicable diseases for surveillance and control purposes. The various states declared certain diseases to be "notifiable," and physicians were required to report to the local public health authorities each new case of a notifiable communicable disease. In the early days, certain of these notifications resulted in the quarantine of the household in which the disease occurred. Subsequently, the reports were used only for statistical purposes. The completeness of reporting of notifiable diseases deteriorated when the reports were no longer used as a basis of administrative action. However, the statistics continued to be useful in detecting and tracing the course of various epidemic diseases.

With the decline in mortality to a relatively low level and with the increasing emphasis of public health programs on the control of chronic diseases, there was growing dissatisfaction with mortality statistics and the notifiable disease statistics as the only bases for program use. In response to the growing demands for statistics on illness in the general population, the National Health Survey Act was passed in 1956. Basically, the National Health Survey consists of three major components: the Health Interview Survey, the Health Examination Survey, and various surveys of patients cared for in institutions.

The Health Interview Survey, started in 1957, is a continuous survey of the civilian noninstitutional population by interview of a sample of households. This is essentially a national survey, but limited data are available for broad regions and for a number of large metropolitan areas. In addition to statistics on disability from various causes by different demographic characteristics, data are available on the utilization of medical care, health insurance coverage, personal health expenses, dental visits, and so on.

Because the Health Interview Survey is conducted by lay interviewers, the quality of data on causes of disability is limited by the diagnostic information known to the respondents. Thus, the amount of diagnostic detail available is limited. The survey gives particular emphasis to morbidity as it affects the individual and society. The Health Examination Survey was instituted in 1959 to get at diseases defined in clinical terms and to measure the extent of diseases of which the affected person may not be aware. In this survey, the household interview survey schedule is supplemented by a thorough physical examination and certain selected tests in mobile examination facilities. The sample of the population examined is relatively small—usually approximately 6000 persons. This is basically an ad hoc survey taking a particular population segment—generally an age group—for each cycle of the survey. Because of the small sample, only national estimates of disease prevalence usually are obtained. This survey, too, is confined to the noninstitutional population.

Another source of diagnostic data is the Hospital Discharge Study. This is a national sample survey of discharges from hospitals which was instituted in 1965. From a sample of records of patients discharged from short-term hospitals, data on discharge diagnoses are compiled.

It was mentioned earlier that the Health Interview Survey and Health Examination Survey relate to the noninstitutional population. In 1963 the Institutional Population Survey was started to collect information and data on patients in various institutions offering long-term medical, nursing, or personal care. These data are for the United States as a whole, and the sample usually covers a two- to three-month period. Also included are reports on diagnostic data as well as statistics on utilization of medical-care facilities.

Finally, a series of statistics on health resources, namely, manpower and facilities, was established starting in the year 1966. This series was originated in response to demands for data needed for planning future health resources.

There are other important data sources such as the Medicare program of the Social Security Administration, the Medicaid program for the indigent, the annual census of patients in state mental institutions, the state crippled children's program, and the several cancer registries. Many local ad hoc surveys and studies have been and are being made, and these continue to be important sources of data for many purposes.

With the development of new knowledge in demography and health and in statistical methods, old techniques of measurement are being found to be inadequate and more sophisticated approaches are being devised. For example, until recent years the simple measures of fertility such as the crude birth rate (births per 1000 persons per year) and the birth rate by age of mother were being widely used as indices of fertility. However, when the birth rate began to change drastically as during the depression baby bust and the postwar baby boom, and as interest in the national population prospect increased, more refined measures were needed for assessment purposes. This led to the development of the "cohort fertility analysis"—the analysis of births to a set of women throughout their reproductive life, which in combination with data on birth expectations derived from surveys provided better understanding of fertility changes and prospects. The surveys also provided information on differences in childbearing and family-planning practices which aided materially in the interpretation of the important factors underlying the trend in fertility.

In the future, it is expected that even better methods will be developed to cope with old problems, and new techniques will be devised to meet emerging problems in health and demography.

USES OF VITAL AND HEALTH STATISTICS

Vital and health statistics have been used for a wide variety of purposes. These purposes may be considered under four broad headings: (1) the planning and management of public and private programs relating to health; (2) research in areas involving health and health services and demography, that is, general population growth and composition; (3) teaching and clinical practice; and (4) legal purposes. Let us consider more specifically each of these types of uses.

Planning and Management

Planning, administration, and evaluation of public and private health programs, a major use of the statistics, often has involved the identification of new problems. Examples of this use of the statistics include the identification of the rising problem of chronic respiratory disease, including lung cancer and emphysema; the slow trend downward in infant mortality; indications of epidemics; nutritional deficiencies among the poor (based on a ten-state survey). The information about nutritional deficiencies attracted the attention of Congress and resulted in a number of specific provisions to deal with the problems.

Another type of use is represented by the effort to prepare for the future based on analyses of the statistics to discern trends and to use the trends to project future problems and needs. Examples of this type of statistics use include the projections of anticipated needs for medical and related services by various subgroupings of the population; projections of the population subgroups themselves in order to estimate future medical needs; and the use of statistics on uncorrected vision defects among children in relation to the birth rate trends, to estimate the needs for vision conservation services in the schools.

Another type of planning and management use is represented by the choice of strategies and procedures for dealing with specific problems. One example of this is the use of statistics on disability and deaths, among other types of data, for making "cost-benefit analyses" of disease-control programs. Studies were made to measure the costs of various disabilities and causes of death against the cost of programs to deal with them. The cost-benefit analyses studies were made for a number of disease-control programs, for example, for arthritis and for motor vehicle injury prevention. Another example of such a use is that of putting the diseases and causes of disability or death in rank order to determine what are their economic costs and, thus, to provide administrators with a basis for deciding which problems they should first tackle.

Still another administrative use of vital and health statistics is that of measuring the "market" for proposed new health services. This involves estimating the cost of such programs, preparing budgets for them, and, in general, creating a plan for administrating and evaluating their impact. For example, estimates have been made of the cost of a continuing program of nurses' education based on an analysis of the number and types of nurses available and needed for the future. Estimates have also been made of the cost of a program for controlling diabetes involving early detection from survey data on untreated cases in the population. In the private sector, pharmaceutical companies use statistics on illness, including those showing new occurrences ("incidence") and those indicating what proportion of the population has the illness at any one moment in time ("prevalence"), to estimate the market in new drugs. Moreover, it should not be surprising that casket manufacturers and manufacturers of baby products are interested in the statistics about deaths and births for their own specific marketing purposes. It may be of interest that some years ago the writer had occasion on the same day, at a luncheon and a dinner meeting, to address a national organization of casket manufacturers utilizing death statistics and a baby diaper service utilizing birth statistics to help these industries determine their future markets.

Still another general management use of vital and health statistics is that involved in educating the public about health matters. Such information is provided in congressional hearings as a background for new legislation; it is given to the White House and to presidential commissions for planning future administration proposals. Some examples of this type of use are represented by the report of the National Commission on Heart Disease, Cancer and Stroke, which included many statistics on death and illnesses to document the size of the health problem represented by these diseases. Another use was in the congressional hearings that resulted in the Medicare legislation. The statistics given at that hearing included data on the trend of insurance coverage for hospital and surgical care for people 65 years of age and over. Another example is that given by the reference above to the use of statistics about nutritional deficiencies which led to enactments to provide more food for the poor.

Statistics indicating the frequency of accidental injuries of various types are used widely in education campaigns to warn the public of various types of risks including accidents in the home, in motor vehicles, and at work. The National Commission on Product Safety used health statistics to make estimates of injuries resulting from unsafe products that had important implications for legislative and administrative control on behalf of the consumer.

Health statistics also are used for measuring the input into programs in terms of money costs, personnel, facilities, and other resources; and also for monitoring the process, that is, maintaining continuous watch over the programs and their results. For example, statistics on the operations of Medicare are used continuously to determine what problems need attention and also as a basis for adjustments in the operations of the system. Another example of such a monitoring use is given by the statistical system being developed to keep track of family-planning services provided by programs subsidized by the government.

Finally, an important management use of health statistics is that which permits administrators to measure progress toward their objectives or goals. This involves measurement of program output that provides a basis for the evaluation of the program. Many examples of this type can be cited. One is the use of statistics on cigarette smoking to measure progress in programs designed to reduce the amount of smoking and thereby to reduce lung cancer deaths. A statistical program has been developed to monitor the effects of the improved food-stamp and commodity-distribution programs so as to tell whether they are successful in helping the poor to obtain more and better food. Data also are analyzed for the white population and for the various minority groups to determine whether or not racial and ethnic differences in medical care are diminishing or increasing. Needless to say, such information is of special importance under conditions of ongoing interests in civil rights and the elimination of discriminatory practices against minority groups.

Research

Health statistics serve many research purposes across a wide variety of public and private agencies and personnel. One use of the data is that involving the discovery of new facts about population changes, about the development of disease and injuries, and about the workings of the health-care systems. For example, all the statistics about illness, deaths, or health care, when collected for the first time, have provided new knowledge about not only the situation at the time the data were obtained but also the prospects for the future. Information about illness and the use of medical care by age, sex, marital status, and color or race of the population provides a sound basis for estimating future needs as different elements of the population grow at different rates.

Data on nonfatal injuries provided the first reliable information on this subject that was useful to all parties concerned with health care. Another example of such a use is afforded by the study of a sample of birth certificates in relation to date of marriage which provided new knowledge about the frequency of premarital pregnancies.

Vital and health statistics are used also in research to determine causes of illness and death and to test hypotheses about the causes. For example, it has been observed that there seems to be an association between multiple sclerosis and latitude (position on the earth from north to south) which has led to various attempts to explain the cause of that disease, including the notion that it is probably produced by a virus. Comparisons have been made of heart disease and stomach cancer as causes of death among Japanese in Japan, in Hawaii, and in the western United States in order to test hypotheses about the development and risks of these diseases.

Vital and health statistics are used also to coordinate research findings from various cause-of-disease and cause-of-death studies. For example, the results of in-depth community studies of heart disease undertaken in Framingham, Massachusetts, and Tecumseh, Michigan, became more meaningful when the disorder rates in those areas were compared with those for the country as a whole, to examine the differences so that it could be determined whether the communities studied were or were not like the rest of the United States. Finally, the statistics are used to feed computers which are instructed to show how health problems and the need for health care would change under different conditions such as changes in the birth rate, or the death rate, or the marriage rate, or the divorce rate, or causes of death, and the like. The availability of computers has, of course, greatly improved the power of analyzing vital and health, as well as other, statistics and of using them to provide better knowledge about present and future health matters.

Teaching and Clinical Practice

The available vital and health statistics often are used in medical and other schools to provide students with knowledge about the history of a disease or the workings of the health-care system. The National Center for Health Statistics often receives requests from medical colleges for various reports. The data also are used in order to get a picture of the distribution of anthropometric and medical characteristics of the population as a whole so as to be in a better position to tell when a person is different enough from the general population as to indicate an abnormality. For example, the information about differences in blood pressure by age, sex, height, and weight makes it possible for an examining physician to tell better whether a person's blood pressure is normal or abnormal. Similarly, information about differences in blood glucose tolerance levels provides a better basis for diagnosis of diabetes for an individual case.

Legal Uses

Health and vital statistics often are used in connection with lawsuits in the nation's courts of law. As an illustration, the Post Office brought suit against a company which was offering health insurance through the mails and used statistics on illnesses to show that a very large proportion of all illness would not be covered by the insurance policies offered. "Life tables" showing the average number of years of life remaining to persons at different ages based on the death statistics often are used to make an estimate of the value of a man in cases where compensation is sought for injury or death. Such information is used to estimate the money value of a person. Vital and health statistics are used in various types of lawsuits in malpractice cases, in which the doctor is accused of inadequate or faulty practice, to support arguments involving the death rates following specific operations or treatments.

Vital and health statistics are used on documents for nonstatistical purposes in the interests of individual persons. The basic vital records on births, deaths, marriages, and divorces are used by millions of persons every year to provide proof of age, citizenship, marriage, death, and the like. The copies of these records are issued to the persons named on them or their parents or others legitimately concerned for legal proof of such facts about the person.

The basic records are also used to monitor individual patient care. Although there is no standard record of medical treatment, either for hospital inpatients or outpatients, nor is there a standard record of medical examinations, hundreds of millions of such records are created each year for the purpose of helping health maintenance or the treatment of individual patients. Hospital patient records maintain a continuous record of the person's medical history and serve as a basis for statistics as in the case of the Hospital Discharge Survey statistics which are based on forms copied from basic hospital patient records. Efforts are underway to develop and to get acceptance of standard hospital discharge records. Such records would not only be of great help in the next treatment of the patient but could serve, also, as an important document in a legal suit and as a better basis for improved statistics. Efforts also are being made to get standardization of physicians' records to improve basic information not only for the treatment of the person but also to provide better statistics. Almost every element in the health industry requires some type of record for administrative purposes that may also serve other purposes, including those relating to the medical treatment of the person, and as a source for better statistics.

Further, vital and health records are used to identify specific types of cases for further and generally more intensive study. A scientific sample of such records can be used for intensive follow-up to get information in greater depth than that which can be obtained from the record itself. It may be observed that various records, including those of marriages and deaths, have been consulted to trace persons for longitudinal studies, that is, studies designed to see what happens to the person or family in relation to health matters over a long period of time. In Hagerstown, Maryland, for example, a sample of people have been studied for the outcome of chronic disease over a period of twenty years. Marriage records were used to give information about name changes for women and death records showed those lost to the study because they had died.

USERS OF VITAL AND HEALTH STATISTICS

The National Center for Health Statistics (NCHS) has made an effort to identify the users of vital and health statistics. This effort was necessarily restricted to obtaining information from those relatively easy to identify as users. Since vital and health statistics are published and distributed widely and are available for use by anyone with access to the data, it is obviously impractical, if not impossible, to identify all users. The NCHS sent out a questionnaire to a mailing list based on its own publication mailing list combined with a number of other lists believed likely to include users after removing duplications. Questionnaires were sent to 5192 respondents, of whom 4057 replied.

Column (a) in Table 3.1 shows the percentage distribution of users as obtained from this survey. Observe that the largest single group of users as classified was a combination of "universities, faculties, students, and hospitals other than university hospitals, clinics, and nursing homes." Twenty-eight percent of all the respondents fell into this category. The next largest single group of users were state and local health departments and other state and local governments with 17 percent, and the federal government, except the legislative branch, with 13 percent. The legislative branches, federal, state, and local government accounted for another 2 percent of the users. The basket category "other" including scientific or professional societies, attorneys, private physicians, individual researchers, consultants, laborers, and others not classified elsewhere accounted for another 17 percent of the users. It is possible that the governmental offices at the federal, state, or local levels are underrepresented in this distribution compared with university and hospital users. This is because the former tended to be in the list of names of offices while the latter were more frequently included as the names of individuals. Many uses in a single governmental office would show up as a single use whereas several different individuals on a faculty would show up as separate uses.

Of the 4057 replies received, 81 percent indicated they had used health statistics and 77 percent used statistics of the National Center for

Table 3.1. Users of Vital and Health Statistics by Category of User

Category	(a) Percent $N = 5192$	(b) Percent $N = 2426$
1. Legislative branch of federal, state, or local governments including administrative staff	2	1
2. Planning councils for health facilities and services	4	2
3. Federal government, except legislative branch	13	15
4. Universities, faculties, and students	28*	40*
5. Hospitals, other than university hospitals, clinics, nursing homes		
6. State and local health departments and other state and local government	17	17
7. Insurance companies: health, life, disability, and casualty	6	4
8. Other business and industry	7	8
9. Voluntary nonprofit health, welfare, and social service agencies	3	5
10. Publishers, editors, journalists, and reporters	3	2
11. Other, including scientific or professional societies, attorneys, private physicians, individual researchers, consultants, labor unions, and other n.e.c.	17	6
	100	100

* Categories combined because of inability of respondents to make the distinction.

Health Statistics. Sixty percent of the respondents had used the statistics of the NCHS within the preceding six months. The distribution of those respondents is indicated in column (b) of the table. As for *all* respondents, the larger proportion, the most frequent single users were represented by categories 4 and 5, "universities, faculties, students, hospitals other than university hospitals, clinics, and nursing homes." State and local health departments and other state and local government agencies constitute the second most frequent users of the data and federal government, except legislative branches, the third. It is noteworthy that the combination of items 7 and 8, insurance companies—health, life, disability, and casualty— and other business and industry represent 13 percent of all users and 12 percent of the users within the preceding six months of the NCHS statistics. Business users other than insurance companies included pharmaceutical manufacturers, manufacturers of health products, food manufacturers, advertising and marketing agencies, suppliers of goods and services for infants and children, automobile manufacturers, banks and investment firms, research and consulting firms, public utilities, and others.

The variety of users of vital and health statistics is, of course, to be understood in light of the identification of such data not only with the field of science and large professional groups, but also the very large health-related industry that has private profit, private nonprofit, and government components and involves an annual dollar flow of over $60 billion that may well become $100 billion within a short time.

LOOKING AHEAD

Trends can be observed in the health field which will greatly influence the demand for vital and health statistics. Such trends are the increases in activities such as (1) planning, (2) evaluation, (3) model construction, and (4) outcomes. The discernible trends are almost certain to increase the demand for vital and health statistics and require greater detail and elaboration of the data.

Many activities have been greatly extended at state and metropolitan levels in recent years. Under sections 3.14a and 3.14b of the Public Health Service Act there has been a great increase in planning activities on state and community levels which has led to increases in demand for statistics in geographic detail. Since many of the present health statistics are prepared for national estimate purposes only, the demand for state and local information is not yet being met.

Interest in the results obtained from various health programs has stimulated greater efforts at evaluation and these programs also call for geographic detail. For example, the Office of Economic Opportunity and the Health Services and Mental Health Administration are providing funds for neighborhood health centers in an effort to study ways of improving health-care activities to reach the poor. Likewise, the National Institute of Mental Health is setting up a network of community mental health centers. The National Center for Health Services Research and Development is increasing demonstrations of new types of health-care delivery systems in metropolitan areas and in entire states. Such activities require statistics so as to determine what impact these experimental programs actually are having and thus serve as the basis for possible extension of the programs to broader areas. The types of new demands may well require the creation of entirely new data systems to supplement the present national sample surveys.

The use of the computer, as has been indicated, has made possible the construction of different models of systems which can be manipulated in order to determine what would happen if various elements involved were changed. Increasing interest in constructing such mathematical and statistical models of health systems also requires greater detail and scope in health statistics. The use of such data in computer-run models can produce results very much the same as actual experiments conducted in the field.

Perhaps the greatest deficiency in the available vital and health statistics are those relating to the "outcomes" of various programs. Information about such outcomes would permit better decisions about programs to accomplish desired objectives. For example, injuries and deaths from automobile accidents now are covered in available statistics, but suppose several different strategies were developed for reducing such injuries and deaths. Four such programs might include (1) educating and influencing the behavior of drivers, including persuading the drivers and passengers to use seat belts; (2) improving the automobile's safety characteristics and equipment; (3) improving the safety characteristics of streets and highways; and (4) enforcing laws more rigorously and/or increasing penalties. In order to determine which of these proposals or which combination of them might be most effective in reducing injuries and deaths it is obvious that statistics would be needed to measure the outcomes of experiments with such programs. At this time there is no provision for supplying the kind of information that would enable planners and administrators to determine which would be the best approach to use.

It is almost certain that vital and health statistics are likely to be expanded and elaborated in scope and in geographic detail in the years which lie ahead. It will undoubtedly mean increased approaches to the general public as well as to health agencies, institutions, and personnel for additional data. Widespread dissemination of information about the ways in which the statistics outlined above are used to enhance the health benefits that the public receives should serve to increase the public's understanding of reasons for vital and health statistics and, therefore, increase public cooperation with the agencies whose task it is to produce and analyze the data.

CHAPTER 4

On Marriage, Divorce, and the Family*

THE DEVELOPMENT OF THE STATISTICS

Family

The major source of statistics on families is the United States Census. However, early decennial censuses did not include a count of families but only data concerning households, and the definition of household varied over the years so that the figures are not entirely comparable. The first census in 1790 defined a household as a dwelling unit and all persons residing in it; later censuses modified the definition of household.

Beginning with the census of 1890 the marital status of the population has been published. Since that date, for persons fourteen years of age or older the count is available for the single, married, widowed, and divorced. In general, successive decennial censuses gave more comprehensive statistics on families.

In the 1930 census family coverage was considerably expanded. Information was collected on size of family; number of children by age; number of employed persons; number of live-in lodgers; the race, age, and sex of family head; and, regarding the house, its rental or value. Detailed information was published for each state and large city and for selected counties. The 1940 census compiled similar data but published only summary tables.

---

*Based on a memorandum by Hugh Carter, formerly in the National Center for Health Statistics.

In 1940 limited family income data were collected and published for the first time and data were obtained, also, on the characteristics of the house occupied by family in the nation's first Census of Housing. In 1940, also for the first time, each person in the family was classified by his relation to the household head. In 1950, although there was some cutback in coverage, there was another innovation in that duration of current marital status and family living arrangements data were obtained. The 1960 census included separate reports on women by number of children ever born, child spacing, families, persons by family characteristics, age at first marriage, marital status, as well as other family data. The 1970 census provided statistics on family composition, persons by family characteristics, marital status, age at first marriage; also reports on fertility (women by number of children ever born, child spacing and current fertility, marital selection, and fertility).

Up to 1944 information about families in the nation was collected only in the decennial census. However, beginning in 1944, annual reports based upon the Current Population Survey (CPS), a sample survey conducted by the Census Bureau, have provided national data on family characteristics and marital status. The CPS provides much more information on families for the nation as a whole than that made available by the decennial censuses. In addition to the regular yearly information on marital status, the CPS frequently is used by other agencies to compile data on various aspects of family life.

Family statistics for limited areas also are compiled by private agencies as well as state and local area governments. For example, for an intensive analysis of the Eastern Health District of Baltimore, Maryland, a house-to-house survey provided full details of the families living in the area and periodic resurveys provided changes for all families. With such statistics, meaningful family rates can be computed.

Many private agencies conduct national sample surveys of families to use as a panel for obtaining desired information. Numerous marketing agencies find out consumer preferences; university and other research organizations determine attitudes toward the ideal size of the family and many other questions; polling groups frequently use a sample of families to learn of voter preferences.

Marriage and Divorce Statistics

Statistics on marriages and divorces were late in developing in the United States. During the colonial period the various colonies tended to follow the customs of the countries from which the settlers came and there was a lack of uniformity in the officials who could perform marriages and those who had custody of marriage records. Divorces, if granted under any circumstances, were treated as very special events. At various times divorces became possible as the result of a legislative act. In the early history of the United States an attempt was made to obtain data on marriages during the preceding time period through the regular decennial censuses. However, the results were unsatisfactory because of incomplete reporting of events and, therefore, this approach was dropped.

The maintenance of records of marriages that occurred was the responsibility of local civil officials, such as county clerks; the records were referred to for various legal purposes, such as settlement of estates. However, with many local clerks and with a highly migratory population, it was frequently difficult to locate the marriage record of a deceased person. Some states established a statewide index or file of marriage records and this proved so useful that gradually nearly all states established such files. In 1970 only three states (Arizona, New Mexico, and Oklahoma) did not maintain such files. As a by-product of state files of marriage records it became possible to obtain simple statistical reports of marriages in the various states. A few states issued detailed analytical reports on marriages each year; most states limited themselves to a few summary tables, however, giving the number of marriages by county and by month. Some states did not issue any reports on marriages.

The recording of divorces followed an even more tortuous path than did that of marriages. After divorce proceedings were lodged in state courts, divorce records became the responsibility of the courts granting the divorces. Very gradually state indexes or files of divorce records were established. In 1970 only five states did not maintain files of divorce records. These were Arizona, New Mexico, Oklahoma, Indiana, and Minnesota. Some of the states issued annual reports of divorces granted with a few analytical tables.

The first comprehensive statistics on marriages and divorces for the United States as a whole were issued in 1889 and were the result of a national survey covering the years 1867–1886. It was conducted under the direction of Carroll D. Wright, then commissioner of labor. The coverage of divorces, with many details, was more complete than that for marriages. This was due to the greater interest of the lobby group that for some years had urged such a survey before the Congress. The New England Divorce Reform League, later known as the National Divorce Reform League, contained numerous clergymen in its membership who expressed concern over the rising number of divorces and the lack of uniformity in the state marriage and divorce laws. Since the first years of the twenty-year period covered in the survey fell immediately after the Civil War when many local governmental units were not functioning normally, the incompleteness of the reporting of marriages and divorces was probably greatest for the earlier years. With respect to marriages, it was clear that the survey obtained an incomplete count; with respect to divorces, which were more completely reported, it obtained the date of marriage, cause of divorce, number of children, and whether the petitioner was husband or wife.

After the passage of twenty years a second survey was conducted on marriages and divorces. President Theodore Roosevelt stated that the statistics to be obtained would hasten uniform marriage and divorce laws and so safeguard the family. This second national survey covered the years 1887–1906. There was a count of both marriages and of marriage licenses for the states that required the issuance of marriage licenses. The divorce schedule contained eighteen items. These included occupation of the parties, whether the case was contested, and whether intemperance was a contributing cause.

Ten years passed before another national survey of marriages and divorces was conducted. For the single year 1916 national data were obtained. After this survey there was another lapse of some years before anything further was done about national statistics. Beginning in 1922 and continuing through 1932, the U. S. Bureau of the Census issued annual reports on marriages and divorces based upon mail surveys sent to responsible state and county officials. The report for 1926 contains estimates of events for the years 1907–1915 and 1917–1921, the missing years in the earlier surveys. Following 1932 the principal source of marriage and divorce data was the Metropolitan Life Insurance Company through its *Statistical Bulletin, The Jeweler's Circular-Bulletin,* compilations by the Federal Home Loan Bank Board, and estimates prepared by Professors S. A. Stouffer and L. M. Spencer of the Department of Sociology of the University of Chicago for the years 1933–1936. During this period when official national data were not available, the need for such information became increasingly apparent.

There was a clamor for marriage and divorce statistics by family welfare agencies, clergymen, sociologists, and other social scientists, and the need for such data also was experienced by business groups and government agencies. For example, jewelers wanted the information to help them in planning the sale of engagement rings and other wedding items; life insurance companies wanted the information because of its obvious marketing value. The Home Loan Bank needed the information to aid in planning for the housing market.

In response to such needs the 1940 census included an attempt to obtain data by purchasing copies of the marriage and divorce transcripts from the states that could provide the information. However, the coverage was incomplete and this attempt was not resumed for a number of years. Beginning in 1948 tables of marriage and divorce statistics were prepared by the states for use in issuing national statistics. A number of states could only give a count of the number of events; for some states it was necessary to prepare estimates from scanty available sources.

Beginning with 1957 a "marriage registration area" (MRA) consisting of twenty-nine states was established; this was followed in 1958 by a "divorce registration area" (DRA) of fourteen states. States were admitted to these areas as they met specified minimum standards of excellence in reporting. In 1971 the MRA consisted of forty-two states and the DRA of twenty-six states. So the goal of national coverage is still a distant one.

For the year 1960 a special effort, reasonably successful, was made, with the cooperation of many demographers and sociologists, to obtain full national coverage. Statistics were compiled based upon a sample of transcripts obtained from the states. This procedure, similar to that long employed in preparing birth and death statistics, is now the generally used method.

Another development to provide improved information about marriages and divorces occurred in 1968. In that year uniform report forms were adopted for the states and it was recommended that all states use these forms, but it will probably take some years yet before all comply. Thus, it is clear that the statistics derived from the marriage and divorce forms based upon reports to state vital statistics offices are still far from complete despite the substantial demand for these data.

THE USERS OF MARRIAGE AND DIVORCE STATISTICS

A comprehensive survey of users of divorce statistics was conducted at the end of the 1950s. These results were published in a report by the National Committee on Vital and Health Statistics (1962). In 1958 and 1959, a survey of researchers was made with responses from sociologists, lawyers, members of the Population Association of America, and a variety of research people in other fields. A survey also was made of users of divorce data other than researchers. In addition to the special surveys designed to obtain information about who uses the data and how they are used, an indication of uses is given by the requests received for information by the Marriage and Divorce Statistics Branch of the National Center for Health Statistics.

The requests that could be identified represent only small fractions of all the users of the data. In the years 1967–1970, for example, 21,951 analytical reports on marriage statistics were distributed as well as 27,829 reports on divorce statistics. In addition, the official volumes of the *Vital Statistics of the U. S.* include "marriage and divorce volumes," various excerpts from these volumes, advance reports, provisional data published in the *Monthly Vital Statistics Report,* reprints of papers published outside the National Center for Health Statistics, copies of the statistical bibliography of marriages and divorces and registration materials. An analysis of these requests by Dr. Alex Plateris of the Marriage and Divorce Statistics Branch in December 1970 is summarized in Table 4.1.

Table 4.1. Users of Marriage and Divorce Data by Types of Users

Type of Users	Marriage Data	Divorce Data
TOTAL	100.0%	100.0%
General public	22.8	28.2
Government	16.4	14.4
Business	17.7	12.6
Consumer groups	0.7	0.3
Students	4.4	7.7
Educators	12.2	11.3
Minority groups	3.0	2.1
Women	0.2	0.3
Youth	0.5	0.5
Clergy	1.4	1.8
Aged	0.2	—
Communication media, including authors of books	19.4	20.3
Research groups	1.2	0.8

Persons who did not state their affiliations are classified as "general public" and thus this particular category may be inflated somewhat because they may properly belong to a different group. It is difficult to say how representative the types of users indicated in the table actually may be. Simple requests which require merely the enclosure of a publication are definitely underrepresented. This may disproportionately involve student users.

As in the case of most government-collected statistics, government agencies themselves are among the major consumers. Among the federal agencies which requested information about marriages and divorces were the Departments of Labor, Defense, Agriculture, and Justice, the U. S. Information Agency, the Library of Congress, the House of Representatives, the Senate, the Veterans Administration, and the Selective Service System.

THE DATA REQUESTED

Although the information on marriage and divorce is relatively limited in scope and detail, the requests for information covered virtually all that was available and frequently pointed to gaps in the statistics. With respect to marriage the statistics requested included such items as median age at marriage; duration of marriage; historical trends in marriage; age of women at remarriage and remarriage rates; teen-age marriages; interracial and interfaith marriages; births to teen-age marriages; monthly marriage totals and seasonal adjustment of marriage rates; marriage rates of college students; projections of marriages and marriage rates; age at remarriage of widowed women; age at marriage of couples who were divorced; number and proportion of marriages in which the bride is under 18 and the groom is under 20; duration of marriage to a divorce decree; number and rate of marriage of persons over 65; age of marriage by number of marriages, first, second, etc.; common-law marriages; comparative marriage rates for the United States and other countries; states with laws authorizing common-law marriages.

With respect to divorces the information requested included the following: numbers and rates of divorces; number of children involved and year of birth of children involved in divorce; the age and education of divorced persons; other characteristics of divorced persons; divorce by duration of marriage; divorce rates of interracial and interfaith marriages; variations in divorce by various characteristics including place of residence, occupation, income, and so on; divorce in teen-age marriages; likelihood of divorce in interracial and interfaith marriages; projections of divorces and divorce rates; income of divorced persons; comparison of divorce rates for couples with or without children; real cause for divorce and legal cause for divorce; economic status in divorce; religion of the divorcing persons; the impact of marriage and divorce on fertility; demographic and social aspects of childlessness; premarital pregnancy; legislation affecting divorce and the family; marriage and divorce data as social indicators; comparative divorce rates for the United States in relation to other countries.

Both marriage and divorce requests included information not only for the nation as a whole, but for regions, states, and localities.

THE USES OF MARRIAGE AND DIVORCE STATISTICS

General

Despite the limited nature of the data on marriage and divorce and the late development of social statistics in this area, the available information is in wide demand and is used extensively. A survey in the late 1950s indicated the prevailing situation. The results of the survey are contained in a report by the National Committee on Vital and Health Statistics (1957). A large group of responsible persons in business, colleges and universities, government, and private research organizations were asked whether they made use of marriage statistics and, if so, to indicate the nature of the use. Over 80 percent of them reported that they used the data. The specific uses to which they put marriage statistics were estimating the number of households (70 percent), analysis of social trends (54 percent), and estimating future market for products (41 percent). Smaller proportions used marriage statistics for estimating future school needs, determining future needs of utilities, university teaching, lecturing, and sociological research. The uses of marriage statistics listed included housing estimates, market analysis, demographic research, articles and textbooks, credit and insurance, and special studies.

Other uses of the marriage and divorce statistics which were catalogued by the National Center for Health Statistics included studies of marital adjustment, studies of jurisprudence, development of legislative proposals, evaluation and planning of counseling programs, planning of child-welfare programs, long-term trend in family disruption, divorce laws, and history of the effort to establish uniform laws.

Federal Government Uses

The major use of marriage, divorce, and family statistics by government is that relating to the preparation of legislative proposals and the administration of programs affecting the family. This is evident by considering some of the proposed legislation before the Congress of the United States in 1970–71, which requested analysis of marriage and family data undertaken by members of the Congress and their staffs. The data also were used by the executive departments sponsoring proposals affecting the family. For example, President Nixon's proposal to provide a minimum income to all families with children if they were unable to provide for themselves made it necessary to know the number of families by composition and by income. For families falling below the poverty level it was essential to have figures on income, on size and composition, and on place of residence. It was necessary also to have statistics on families headed by women, whose situation was quite different than those headed by men. Considerable detail about the characteristics of poor families was needed to prepare estimates of the cost of the president's proposal. For example, information was needed on the age of parents and children; on the physically handicapped—the blind, the deaf, the disabled; on urban or rural residence. Moreover, to estimate future costs it was necessary to prepare estimates of the number of families that would fall into various categories in future years. Effective consideration of this proposal or, indeed, of any form of welfare reform is necessarily dependent on possession of the actual facts.

Apart from this specific proposal by President Nixon, considerable attention has been paid in recent years to the problem of poverty in the United States. To estimate with reasonable accuracy the magnitude of a social problem is an important first step toward solving it. This essential step has been taken with poverty (U. S. Bureau of the Census, 1970). A number of series of social statistics were involved in preparing this estimate. First, estimates had to be made of total population for 1969 by marital status, race, number in family, household composition, and place of residence by region and by urban-rural area. Second, estimates were made of the cost of maintaining a family of each size indicated at a minimum decency level in each area. Third, it was necessary to design a comprehensive and representative sample of the population of the entire country and to conduct a survey to determine the income of each family. From these data it was possible to estimate the number of families below the poverty level. Further, it was necessary to repeat this process from time to time (annually) to indicate what progress, if any, had been made in solving the problem. Thus, it is now known that during the past decade the number of poor persons has been reduced by 15 million only to rise again in 1971. Also, with such data it is possible to note the intractable elements of the problem. For example, in ten years the poor families headed by a man have declined sharply while families headed by women still show a disproportionate number in the poverty group.

The statistics on poverty serve as a factual basis for determining government policy and programs that vitally affect not only the poor, but also all taxpayers in the United States and the economic and social fabric of the nation. A variety of national health-care proposals are being advanced. Doubtless these will be debated at length. Medicare, applying only to persons over 65, has raised questions about possible appropriate action for other age groups. Statistics on families, by composition, income, residence, and other characteristics, will be an important component in consideration of possible new programs. Health care is a family problem and social statistics of families will play an important part in the discussion.

Determination of the cost of changes in Social Security rates and coverage is tied closely to family statistics. Estimates of costs in future years is dependent upon estimates regarding future family composition. Data on joint survival for spouses of various ages make possible close estimates of the onset of widowhood and widowerhood. Such actuarial tables relating to families are essential to insurance computations.

Much legislation has been proposed to control pollution of the environment—air, water, noise, and so on. In each instance the family becomes a prime object of concern in efforts to improve the environment. Air pollution not only affects the health and well-being of individuals but has major impact upon families. Thus, in the debates that will ensue in Congress over pollution controls social statistics of families frequently will be used. One of the most important and involved requests for marriage data originated in the Selective Service and dealt with marriage figures for draft-age men. Such statistics were necessary to assess the impact of the Executive Order of September 10, 1963, exempting married men from the draft, and was to be used as background material for the evaluation and changes in those rules.

State and Local Uses

Innumerable questions come before state legislatures that to be accurately answered require data on families. For example, the impact of state sales taxes is primarily upon family units. In consequence, the users of family statistics for tax purposes are the administrative agencies proposing the taxes and the legislative committees passing upon the proposals.

Many other state legislative proposals have primary impact upon families. Changes in marriage and divorce laws are considered in terms of their presumed effects upon families. To know the marital status of the population and eligible families is essential in planning for public housing construction and urban renewal. Many state programs allocate funds to counties and cities based upon population and families. State educational funds paid to local school boards must be planned years ahead. This requires detailed figures on families: size, composition, and age of children.

Real property and other local taxes must be planned to meet the needs of present and future families residing in the locality. Failure to obtain adequate family data has caused thousands of planning failures—school buildings too small or too large, street networks too ambitious or inadequate, water and sewer plans not suited to community needs.

Education and Research Uses

Increasingly the family is recognized as the basic unit for analyzing social change in American society. The social sciences stress the importance of family data for this purpose. In consequence, it should not be surprising that textbooks and analytical reports on marriage and the family are filled with statistical data. A few representative textbooks illustrating such use in the schools are listed in the References; see Burgess and Locke (1945), Kephart (1966), Udry (1966), Kenkel (1960), Kirkpatrick (1963), Winch (1971), Glick (1957), Goode (1956; 1963), Jacobson (1959), Carter and Glick (1970). Many other sociological studies and reprints deal with families or imply the strong interaction of individual and family. A great deal of such sociological research has been published. Much of this appears in the *American Sociological Review, American Journal of Sociology, Journal of Marriage and the Family,* and numerous other technical journals. Some examples of the studies of marriage, divorce, and the family which have had important implications for public and private policy and programs and have provided a better understanding of the family in its cultural context in our society follow.

> Paul C. Glick of the Bureau of the Census analyzes the changes in the composition of the family from marriage until the death of one spouse. Vital statistics, census data, and income information are used to give a picture of the family in its changing phases from formation to dissolution. Changes in the family cycle that have taken place during the past 80 years are also shown.
>
> Professor Jean Clare Ridley of Columbia University showed that family size varied inversely with activities outside the home. Such data were of great interest in illuminating the relationship of the wife's nonfamily activities to fertility and had special importance to public and private agencies concerned with population projections.
>
> Wilson H. Grabhill and Paul C. Glick, both of the Bureau of the Census, showed that rates of childlessness among married women in the midst of childbearing ages were as low as 8 percent a century ago, but rose in the depression years of the 1930s to a peak of 20 percent, thereafter falling again to about 10 percent in the 1950s. This information was of great interest for assessing population growth and family structure.
>
> Through original use of social statistics of marriages, divorces, and births, Professor Harold T. Christensen of Purdue University has shown the extent of premarital pregnancy and its impact upon divorce. He showed the variation between Denmark, Utah, and Indiana in both the extent of premarital pregnancy and in subsequent divorce. This analysis was of great interest to church leaders, legislators, students of the family, and others interested in public policy and possible legislation.
>
> Professor John Hajnal of the London School of Economics analyzed change in marriage patterns. Using data from the United States and several European countries he showed that the then current baby boom was more prevalent in urban than in rural areas, among the well educated more than among the less educated, among employees more than among employers. These data clarified various aspects of changing fertility and family patterns.
>
> Professor John H. Burma of Grinnell College, using marriage license data from Los Angeles for the period 1948–1959, anticipated the increase of interracial marriages that have been witnessed during the past decade. Lacking data on the result of interracial marriages in Los Angeles, he checked on the previous marital status of each couple. From these limited data he indicated

that marriages of a Negro man and a white woman had a greater than expected probability of being entered into by persons previously divorced. Other interracial marriages, however, had less than the expected number of previously divorced persons.

Professor Lee G. Burchinal of the National Science Foundation and others, using data from the state of Iowa, indicated that marriages of persons who were members of different churches showed smaller differences in survival rates than had been commonly assumed. These facts were of great interest to church leaders and students of contemporary culture.

Using census and vital statistics data it was shown by Hugh Carter that remarriages of women of childbearing age increased substantially between 1890 and 1960, especially among the previously divorced.

Since the family is a basic social institution there is widespread interest in the dissolution of marriages—the number and nature of the dissolutions and the social consequences of such dissolutions. Unfortunately, social statistics in this area are incomplete. We do not know precisely the yearly number of dissolutions, much less the demographic characteristics of the persons involved. The ramifying social consequences of such dissolutions can be inferred only from special studies and not from comprehensive social statistics.

Since all marriages must ultimately end by the death of one of the marital partners, the general question comes down to premature dissolutions of marriage by death, divorce, or separation. Looking at long-term trends it is evident that such dissolutions by death have been greatly reduced because of better health conditions. Thus, widowhood early in life has been substantially reduced and the number of orphans has decreased. On the other hand, dissolutions by divorce have substantially increased. It is impossible to say with any assurance whether separations have changed in volume in a significant manner. Something can be said about the persons most likely to dissolve their marriages. They are more likely to marry very young, to be urban dwellers, to be Negroes rather than some other race. This much can be inferred from census and vital statistics data.

In considerations of the health of the American people the family is often regarded as a health unit. This is illustrated by a number of studies which have helped to provide a factual basis for public and private policy determinations and programs. Examples of such studies follow.

E. H. Hare and G. G. Shaw, writing in an English journal, showed that as family size increased various indices of mental and physical health problems for the father, and especially for the mother, increased, possibly due to the increased strain in caring for the greater number of children.

The same authors showed that poor health of one parent was associated with poor health of the other parent and of the children. Neuroticism in one parent was associated with neuroticism in the other.

The high rate of deafness in Finland (130.7 per 100,000 population) prompted a study of over 500 cases of a deaf person marrying another deaf person by J. S. Lumio and others. The authors found that 52 percent of deaf children of such couples were deaf because of a genetic factor.

A compilation of statistical data on family hospital insurance coverage by P. I. Ahmed was designed for use by health planners. The statistics indicate a large segment of the population has inadequate hospital insurance.

A careful survey of prevalence of mental health impairment in part of New York City was based on a sample survey of families and a psychiatric interview. The resulting statistics were employed in planning needed mental health services not only in New York but also in other large cities.

By relating statistics of families to family income and health characteristics, information useful to health planners was provided by R. R. Fuchsberg. Thus, he found that as income increases the number of disability days decreases per person.

The above examples of research in which the family was the essential unit of study point to the kind of information that is becoming available to provide a better understanding of what is happening to the American family. Such knowledge, largely statistical, is obviously of great importance in providing a factual foundation for policy and for programs, public and private, that relate to the basic social institution in this and other nations—the family. By reason of the rapidity with which social change in general is affecting the family, the need for comprehensive and accurate facts about marriage, divorce, and the family is certain to increase and require more and better statistics than are now available.

Business Uses

For many marketing purposes the family, rather than the person, is the consumer unit. In consequence, market analysts often work with family as well as with person statistics. Some examples of family studies oriented to business use are presented next.

An example of the use of family statistics for marketing purposes is given by a cheese company test of the potential market in Denmark. In order to determine the possibility of entering the urban market in Denmark with a cheese product, a company made a survey and conducted a test campaign in two small cities. On the basis of the data obtained a careful analysis was made of the number of families classified by number of children and level of income. In this case the resulting potential sales of the product fell below the break-even profit point. This gave the executives of the company information necessary to determine policy. Similar market surveys are widely made for many product lines.

Twenty-two cooperating Florida producers of frozen orange juice analyzed families using and not using the product. Promotion was directed to first use or to greater use. The campaign based on the data resulted in a substantial increase in sales of the product.

Using census family statistics including income levels and occupation of family head, Harry L. Hansen shows (1) the number of families now owning stocks and their characteristics; (2) the number of potential family stock owners and their characteristics. The report further points out the most effective approach to such families. As a result of follow-up promotions stock sales by members of the New York Stock Exchange were increased greatly.

Other specific uses of family data by business enterprises indicate the multiplicity of ways in which such data contribute to business efficiency and, thus, to the national level of living. Some examples are given below.

A large department store in the southwest area was supplied with considerable data on population characteristics, family income, and other related information to be used in a promotional mailing program.

A utility company was furnished data on family income, educational attainment, and class of worker for selected cities in New England.

A paint manufacturing firm obtained information on housing units, population, and family income for census tracts to be used for advertising purposes.

A southern manufacturer of heating equipment asked for material that would be helpful in extending their market. Considerable time was devoted to supplying census data on families and on housing, reports on heating and cooking equipment, fans, blowers, and unit heaters. They also were furnished with general information concerning the making of marketing surveys.

A western telephone company requested information on household population data for a state; intrastate migration by counties and Standard Metropolitan Statistical Areas and immigration; and the historical trend of average age of marriage. Data were to be used in forecasting new household formations from 1964 to 1970 in order to predict the number of telephones to plan for. Sources used: Special Mobility Census Reports and Vital Statistics Data.

A realty firm in the South requested statistics and economic data to be used in a study to establish the feasibility of locating a large department store in the city. It was supplied with information on retail trade, wholesale trade, population, number of families, various age groups of the population, and family income.

OUTLOOK FOR STATISTICS ON FAMILIES, MARRIAGE, AND DIVORCE

There has been a great increase in the critical international comparisons of family and marriage statistics within recent years. The United Nations' *Demographic Yearbook* contains data from all countries that can supply the requested information. Regarding marriage the following information is requested by the United Nations: (1) characteristics of the event —date of occurrence, date of registration, place of occurrence; (2) characteristics of bride and groom—date of birth (or age), industry, literacy or level of formal education, marital status, number of previous marriages, occupation, place of usual residence, status (as employer, employee, etc.). While not all countries (including the United States) can supply all the requested information, some countries do so. The *Demographic Yearbook* does not publish all the information it receives. It has issued one of its annual volumes featuring marriage and divorce data. The United Nations has the original completed questionnaires sent in by member countries on file in New York. It also has summary cards with important information. The United Nations regularly publishes a few simple tables on marriage by countries and no doubt the quality of the data in most countries will improve under United Nations encouragement.

The publication of divorce data from the various countries will also probably expand under the stimulation of the United Nations. (A small and decreasing number of countries do not grant divorces.) The recommended items for inclusion in divorce data are (1) characteristics of the event—date of occurrence, date of registration, place of occurrence; (2) characteristics of the divorcees—date of birth (or age), date of marriage, industry, literacy or level of formal education, number of dependent children, number of previous marriages, occupation, place of occurrence of marriage, place of usual residence, status (as employer, employee, etc.). Most countries, including the United States, cannot supply all these items of information for every divorce granted, but the United Nations standards will doubtless stimulate better reporting of divorces and thus promote improved international comparisons. It seems probable that in the future family statistics will be improved in quality and will be more widely used. Since there are many different types of families, it is evident that the most useful statistics will classify the original data by types of families. There will be information by age of husband and wife and by differences in age of spouses. Other useful subclassifications already frequently used will include racial composition; income class and sources of income; and stages of the family-life cycle.

There will be more sophisticated use of statistics on families. Market surveys, rather than computing rates per 1000 population, will compute them per 1000 families and will not lump all families together but will compute rates per 1000 families with specified characteristics. Public opinion polls will not be limited to samples of the population by such characteristics as age, sex, and political affiliations, but will also sample families. Government planners will make detailed use of family statistics to project the effects of specified policies. City and regional planners, budgetary officials, and legislative aides will place more reliance on family statistics. Educational administrators will make detailed studies of families to project estimates of the future student population and to obtain useful information on types of families from which highly motivated students can be recruited. Students with personality and adjustment problems will be studied in terms of family background. Minority group leaders seeking insight that will make it possible to raise the status of the group will come to use family statistics. In certain groups the family structure is a source of strength; in others it is a source of weakness. Leaders will use information about families to plan remedial programs. In the fields of medicine and public health there will be increased recognition of the family, rather than the individual, as the effective health unit. Increasingly, longitudinal studies of families will be made to gain insight into health programs.

In all aspects of life it seems probable that increased reliance will be placed upon family statistics.

CONCLUDING OBSERVATIONS

Statistics relating to marriage, divorce, and the family have, as has been indicated, many uses. Not least among them is that of providing the general public with the important facts about the family as the basic social institution. These statistics tend to uplift the level of popular discussion relating to marriage, divorce, and the family by substituting facts for prejudices and folk tales. For example, the more extreme types of statements frequently voiced by some journalists about the imminent disappearance of marriage and the death of the family are not borne out by the data.

Moreover, the areas of disagreement among informed persons regarding wise public policy concerning the family will be narrowed. Witness the effect on family life of the program of Aid to Families with Dependent Children. It became clear from the available data that the program frequently tended to disrupt families and changes were introduced into the program. As improved marriage and divorce data become available, supplemented by long-term in-depth studies of families with special problems (divorce, poverty, illness, etc.) and comparisons with families lacking such problems, it will be possible to discredit many of the statements frequently made about family life based upon tradition or prejudice. Thus, it frequently is stated that divorce has a disastrous effect upon the children or that it has a beneficial effect upon the children. Or, it is stated that poverty in families is due to unwillingness of family members to work. Again, it is asserted that adequate medical care is available to all families either through payments for services or charity by physicians and hospitals. As more comprehensive statistics become available, however, such statements are supported or discredited as the data may indicate.

REFERENCES

Burgess, Ernest W., and Harvey W. Locke. *The Family: From Institution to Companionship.* New York: American Book Company, 1945.

Carter, Hugh, and Paul C. Glick. *Marriage and Divorce: A Social and Economic Study.* Cambridge, Mass.: Harvard University Press, 1970.

Glick, Paul C. *American Families.* New York: Wiley, 1957.

Goode, William J. *After Divorce.* New York: Free Press, 1956.

———. *World Revolution and Family Patterns.* New York: Free Press, 1963.

Jacobson, Paul H. *American Marriage and Divorce.* New York: Holt, Rinehart and Winston, 1959.

Kenkel, William F. *The Family in Perspective.* New York: Appleton-Century-Crofts, 1960.

Kephart, William M. *The Family, Society and the Individual,* 2d. ed. Boston: Houghton-Mifflin, 1966.

Kirkpatrick, Clifford. *The Family: As Process and Institution,* 2d. ed. New York: Ronald Press, 1963.

Metropolitan Life Insurance Company. *Statistical Bulletin.* New York: Metropolitan Life Insurance Co., monthly.

National Center for Health Statistics. *Monthly Vital Statistics Report.* Washington, D. C.: Government Printing Office.

———. *Vital Statistics of the U. S.* Washington, D. C.: Government Printing Office, annual.

National Committee on Vital and Health Statistics. *Improving National Divorce Statistics: A Report of the Subcommittee on the National Divorce Statistics of the U. S.* Washington, D. C.: Government Printing Office, 1962.

———. *National Vital Statistics Needs: A Report of the United States National Committee on Vital and Health Statistics.* Washington, D. C.: Government Printing Office, 1957.

Udry, J. Richard. *The Social Context of Marriage.* Philadelphia: Lippincott, 1966.

United Nations. *Demographic Yearbook.* Statistical Office of the United Nations, Department of Economic and Social Affairs. New York: United Nations, annual.

U. S. Bureau of the Census. *24 Million Americans: Poverty in the United States: 1969.* Current Population Reports Series P-60, No. 76, December 16, 1970. Washington, D. C.: Government Printing Office, 1970.

Winch, Robert F. *The Modern Family.* Rev. ed. New York: Holt, Rinehart and Winston, 1971.

CHAPTER 5

*On Education**

Education is a large and complex activity in the United States. Public and private expenditures for formal education at all levels were estimated at about $90 billion for the 1972–1973 school year. About 30 percent of the nation's population—over 60 million people—is enrolled in some kind of classes, and almost three million people are teaching these children and adults. More than eight million of these students are enrolled in colleges and universities for degree credit. The 1972 graduating classes, for example, were awarded over three million high school diplomas and almost 900,000 bachelor degrees. The federal share of support for education was $11.6 billion in 1972, and about $12.8 billion in the fiscal year ending in June 1973.

This great enterprise is administered mostly by the fifty states (plus the territories), and about 17,000 school districts which hire the teachers and other employees, admit the students, choose the curriculum, build the schoolhouses, receive financial support from a number of different sources, and expend these funds under budgets which they adopt and administer.

Even a summary statistical description of this vast activity must include several kinds of components: the demographic base for the school population, enrollments in the various types of schools, educational attainment of various components of the population, the principal kinds of

---

* Based on a memorandum by Ezra Glaser, formerly of the U. S. Office of Education.

77

educational institutions, financial data, the staffing of these institutions, their physical plants, the achievement of the students, educational technology, and some account of research, development, experimentation, and demonstration in the conduct of the enterprise. That there is need for all of these kinds of information is beyond dispute.

Not all of these aspects of education are described with equal completeness and detail. In particular, the organization of information for the end of the listing can be suggested in only a very partial and incomplete manner. There are no definitive time series of national statistics to measure the changes in educational methods and practices, the application of research findings, or the predisposing conditions under which particular modes of education can be counted on to succeed. Most vexing, perhaps, is the inability to relate changes in measures of "educational outputs" to changes in the "mix" of inputs—the direct expression of how to get the most for the dollar spent on education for any particular subpopulation of students.

The degree of the availability of data forms a pattern. Generally, the items that can readily be conceptualized and reported (a student enrolled in the third grade, a full-time high school teacher, a dollar spent in a particular school district) are available as consistent time series of national statistics, often with geographic structure and a good deal of subject-matter detail.

But convenience is only part of the explanation. Public demand for information about the educational establishment and its business necessarily began with elemental considerations: the number of children of particular age, the number of teachers, etc. The public business of education shared some traditional characteristics with other public business: the accounting for public monies, the various budget processes, the estimation of future need for programs, etc.

In recent years, the demands of the public for information about the performance of the national educational activity have greatly escalated. This questioning has ranged from the objectives of the educational enterprise itself, to its effectiveness in doing its chosen job, to its way of measuring its successes, to the explanations, if any, of its successes and its failures. Moreover, all of the questions are to be answered separately for different ethnic groups, for poor children, for the educable retarded, the physically handicapped, the children of migratory families, the children with particular definable learning difficulties.

The growing federal role is measured by both the increasing federal share of the national education budget and, also, by the growing number of arrangements to support specific activities. The demand for information therefore originates partly at the federal debates over money, where the education appropriations must compete with other national programs, and where one categorical program (aid for migrant children, assistance to school libraries, schoolroom construction, improvement of administration of state educational agencies, experimental schools) must compete with all of the others within the educational support mechanisms. "Rational" decision-making demands that predictable outcomes be matched against specific plans and budgets. The citizenry has taken up the cry with the demand for "accountability"—the demonstration that the basic machinery is "effective"—for a number of definitions of "effectiveness."

A convenient explanation of the absence of predictions about outcomes can point to public ignorance of the costs, staff, response burdens, and technical difficulties of constructing information systems with the necessary properties. This explanation is at least partly specious, since there is not even a demonstration of a model for experts which computes the differential outcomes for given combinations of input factors (staff, money, teaching methods). What may seem "practical" and "necessary" to a nontechnical public has proved to be too difficult, in the present state of technique for such projections.

AVAILABLE DATA

Elementary and Secondary Schools

The major sources of educational statistics are given in the References to this chapter. In general, the United States Office of Education (USOE) collects data from the state departments of education on pupils, teachers, instructional rooms, and estimated expenditures of public schools, and publishes them annually. Biennially, more comprehensive statistics on organization, staff, pupils, and finances are published based on information collected from the states. Similar data for nonpublic schools are published by USOE using its own surveys. Additional information is provided by the state education agencies, the United States Catholic Conference (formerly the National Catholic Welfare Conference), and by the U. S. Bureau of the Census.

The most useful general summary of educational statistics in the United States is the *Digest of Educational Statistics,* published annually by the National Center for Educational Statistics (NCES) of the U. S. Office of Education. It often publishes data several months before they appear in their more specialized reports, and it refers to all the major sources, public and private. The *Digest* is a large compendium which will often meet the needs of an administrator or researcher.

Many of the publications can be obtained from the federal, state, or local agencies that publish them. Both published and unpublished papers are often available through the USOE National Center for Educational Communication, 400 Maryland Avenue, S. W., Washington, D. C. 20202. Searches for papers can be made with specified descriptors in the computerized files of the Educational Resources Information Center (ERIC). ERIC papers can be purchased in microfilm or hard copy.

Demographic Base Statistics relating to education must be considered in relation to general population statistics, especially the age distribution of the population. That part of the population in each age group which is enrolled in school is given in national summaries (U. S. Office of Education, annual). The U. S. Bureau of the Census (see Chapter 2) provides the age-sex distribution of the population in elaborate geographic detail for the total population and for ethnic subpopulations. Moreover, in addition to the decennial censuses, the Census Bureau conducts a monthly survey—the Current Population Survey—which periodically collects data on enrollment in school by age group and, also, on educational attainment. The U. S. Office of Civil Rights (1968) publishes a *Directory* which gives the ethnic composition of individual schools.

The basic working statistic of a school system is its enrollment—the number of pupils or students being served. Enrollment statistics are available nationally from the beginning of the century from kindergarten through higher education, for public and private schools, and with increasing detail over the years. Enrollment in federal schools for Indians dates from 1929–1930, and other special categories are also available (residential schools for exceptional children, federal schools on federal installations). The standard sources are available from the NCES.

Enrollments Current enrollment data are available in great detail by individual grade by state. The *Directory of Public Schools* contains enrollments for each individual public school in the country, with summaries for the school districts and the states.

Enrollment in specific courses in high school science and mathematics and in foreign languages are reported from time to time. Reports on programs for seven classes of handicapped students and for gifted students occasionally are released.

Data for nonpublic schools are shown separately for nonchurch-related schools; and the church-related schools are divided into eleven religious groups, all classified by nine geographic regions.

As important as enrollment data may be, the apportionment of funds is sometimes computed on *average daily attendance* (ADA). This information is published by states, along with related statistics: average number of days attended per pupil enrolled, average length of term in days, and average daily attendance as a percent of enrollment.

Educational Attainment The source for basic information on the educational attainment of population—the amount of schooling completed—is the decennial census and the Current Population Survey conducted by the Bureau of the Census. Data are given for the population 25 years of age and older by sex and race. Also available in the census reports is the percent of the population that is attending school, by age, sex, and race. Retention rates from the fifth grade to college entrance are estimated by USOE.

Educational Institutions The local basic administrative unit for education is the school district or local educational agency (LEA). They vary, by states, from a single LEA in Hawaii to 1526 in Nebraska (1971). With the increasing complexity of educational programs and the growth of elaborate reporting systems, the smaller LEA's gradually are disappearing; the number of public elementary and secondary school districts shrank from 128,000 in 1931–1932 to 84,000 in 1949–1950, and to 17,000 in fall 1971. These LEA's administered some 66,000 public elementary and 25,000 public secondary schools in fall 1971.

Financial Statistics The approaching $100 billion annual cost for all formal education would be enough to generate demands for detailed information on the sources of funds and the way in which they are expended. The public business must also respond to the rising penchant for "accountability" (i.e., demonstration that the enterprise is well administered and does its job) and to the statutory requirements of the many categorical federal and state support programs.

Public education is supported by federal, state, and local (including county) funds and also from student fees, private gifts and grants, and other sources. These data are available for individual states.

Expenditures are separated first into capital and current operating accounts. The latter are separated further into several "purposes": administration, instruction, operation of plant, maintenance of plant, fixed charges, and other school services. These detailed classes of expenditure are available for the individual states.

A number of useful comparisons are published: capital and current expenditures per pupil in average daily attendance in public elementary and secondary schools, by state, with the total ranging from $501 in Mississippi to $1,327 in New York; per capita current expenditure for public elementary and secondary education as a ratio to per capita personal income, from 3.65 in the District of Columbia to 7.55 in Vermont (1971–1972). Estimates are also available for current expenditures per pupil in average daily attendance for 1971–1972, ranging from $543 in Alabama to $1,466 in New York.

A general indicator of the national importance of education is the expenditures of regular educational institutions as a percentage of the Gross National Product (GNP). Wide swings in the percentage since 1929 arise from fairly stable expenditures for education, compared with a fluctuating GNP. In prosperous 1929, 3.1 percent of GNP was spent for education, but in 1933 4.1 percent was spent, reflecting the depression-level GNP. During World War II expenditures for education fell below 2 percent as GNP rose while enrollment decreased by reason of military service. The postwar years witnessed a steady climb of educational expenditures as a proportion of GNP, to 7.5 percent in 1969 and 8 percent in 1971. Although GNP was increasing during this period, expenditures for education rose even faster.

Expenditures are published for elementary schools, secondary schools, and higher education separately. A good deal of detail is available for special kinds of schools or pupils (handicapped, retarded, etc.), by state. For example, expenditure for vocational education is published by source (federal, state, local) by state, and often by type of vocational program.

The construction of school buildings and other educational facilities usually is financed by local bond issues. Fifteen of the states require voter approval for school bond issues for some part of the financing of school systems, thirty-two of them require approval for any school bond issue, and three states require no approval. The percent of the par value of school bonds which have been approved has been falling for several years, from 79.4 percent in 1965 (about $2½ billion approved) to a low of 41.4 percent in 1971 (about $1⅓ billion). The report on the number of bond elections, the number of approvals, the value of approvals, and the interest rates are compiled by the Investment Bankers Association of America under a contract with USOE.

School Staffing The number of classroom teachers in elementary and secondary schools is reported by state. A more complete description of the staffing of the schools adds the numbers of principals, supervisors of instruction, librarians, guidance counselors, and others. Noninstructional personnel (such as maintenance) also are reported.

Some of the characteristics of teachers are described: age, sex, marital status, years of teaching experience, and highest degree held. Secondary school teachers are classified according to the subject in which the largest portion of their time was spent.

Salaries of teachers are reported by the NCES, the National Education Association (NEA), and the Office of Business Economics in various forms, for example, with adjustments for the purchasing power of the dollar.

School Plant The number of schools is an obvious measure of the size of the physical plant for educational activities. It is published for elementary schools and four types of secondary schools: traditional, junior, senior, and junior-senior.

A measure that better reflects size is the instructional classroom. Public classrooms are described by age, fireproof status, character of building, and state.

More generally, school facilities are classified as public or private; elementary, secondary, or combined; for a number of kinds of rooms—library, auditorium, cafeteria, gymnasium, etc., including rooms that serve more than one of these functions.

The number of pupils on curtailed sessions reflects schoolroom shortages and the estimated shortages also are expressed, by state, in terms of the number of additional rooms needed to reduce classes to specific sizes.

Educational *achievement* is measured by performance on a variety of tests, as distinct from *attainment,* which is expressed in terms of the last grade of schooling completed. While there are many tests available, several have enjoyed a fairly general use This facilitates meaningful comparisons between schools or school districts as well as year-to-year changes. Norms for the entire nation and for geographic areas are also available.

Publication of scores, norms, and other information about the tests is by the proprietors. Among the most generally used tests are the following:

California Achievement Test, which includes reading and vocabulary comprehension
Iowa Test of Basic Skills
Metropolitan Achievement Test of Reading
Stanford Reading Tests

Some of the available tests cover skills other than reading—mathematics, science, etc.—but reading tests are the most extensively used.

There is also an active current literature about tests of achievement and their interpretation: questions of cultural bias, responsiveness to changes in materials being taught, etc.

The National Assessment of Educational Progress (NAEP) differs from the usual practices of achievement testing. It is a test of a sample of the population to measure capability in several subjects: reading, mathematics, and science. The testing is not for class units, since there is no intention to associate the results with any particular teaching program. Reports are issued by USOE.

Educational Technology, Research Educational research covers a number of subjects ranging from individual tutoring to the administration of state school systems. The schools of education publish many papers on these subjects. Individual scholars also prepare research papers for conferences, journals, and for completing the requirements of graduate degrees. Many of the papers contain statistics on the kinds of instructional methods used in the various school systems, the use of audiovisual equipment, computer-assisted instruction, and analytical and interpretative comment on all of the subjects enumerated in this section.

The larger universities have substantial collections of these publications in their libraries. In addition, the USOE maintains an index of the research literature through the National Center for Educational Communication (NCEC). Among other services, NCEC maintains a large-scale computerized index—the Educational Resources Information Center—for use by the public.

Federal Programs There are many programs of financial assistance by the federal government. Most of them operate through grants to the states. The Elementary and Secondary Education Act of 1965 and its amendments provide for aid to schools in low-income areas, to handicapped children, to children whose home language is not English, to children of migrant families. Other categorical programs assist the operations of the state educational agencies, school libraries, and other institutions on the educational scene.

A quantitative description of these programs can be obtained from various sources. The identification and measurement of the target populations (of students and institutions) form an important part of the legislative hearings that lead to the passage of the statutes. The annual appropriation hearings provide current reviews for the federal share of about 8.8 percent of the total funds for public elementary and secondary education. The reports on educational finances include amounts for federal programs, and the annual reports of the USOE review their purposes and activities.

Higher Education

In the U. S. Office of Education's *Digest of Educational Statistics,* 1970, the following statement appears: "The United States has gone a long way toward providing universal elementary and secondary education for its citizens. While regulations differ somewhat from one jurisdiction to another, it may be said in general that free public education is available to all and that school attendance is compulsory between the ages of 7 and 16" (p. 23). No such statement can be made for higher education. There is great diversity in the control, programs, degrees or certificates offered, costs, student charges, sizes, and other characteristics of these institutions.

More than two-fifths of the approximately 2500 institutions of higher learning

> are under the control of State governments or of cities, counties, or other subdivisions of States. Seven institutions are controlled by the Federal Government. The remaining 58 percent of the institutions are controlled by religious denominations, professional organizations, or self-perpetuating groups of public-spirited persons. Publicly controlled colleges and universities tend to be much larger than their privately controlled counterparts. About three fourths of all college students attend public institutions [USOE, *Digest of Educational Statistics,* 1972].

Enrollment Degree-credit enrollment in higher education rose from about 2.3 million in 1950 to an estimated 8.2 million in 1972. During this interval the population 18 to 24 years of age rose by about 50 percent, from 16 million to an estimated 25.9 million, accounting for only a small part of the increase in enrollment. Enrollment per 100 persons 18 to 24 years of age rose from 14.2 to 31.7. Enrollment data and related statistics are obtained directly from the institutions by the USOE annual survey, *Opening Fall Enrollment in Higher Education.* Several kinds of data, therefore, are available for the individual colleges and universities. Most of the information in the following discussion is based on this survey.

Enrollment in higher education is published for individual states, for public and private institutions separately, by sex of student and full-time or part-time attendance. The same detail is presented for individual institutions. State figures also can be shown for detail of control: if public, for state or local control; if private, for nonchurch-related or for major denominations of church affiliation.

A substantial detail of programs (degree-credit, extension, nondegree, occupational-oriented) and subjects (aeronautical technology, forestry, journalism, education, police technology, etc.) is published.

Enrollment in special types of institutions also is provided. Those colleges predominantly attended by black students are reported in terms of the sex and academic level of the students, degrees conferred, faculty, and type of college. Enrollment and finances for land-grant institutions (for specific federal-support programs) also are reported.

Two-year junior or community colleges are included in the opening fall enrollment surveys, making a wealth of information available: their number, enrollment by sex of student, state location, control, etc.

Slightly more students attend colleges and universities in their own state than was earlier the case. In 1968, 83 percent attended in their state of residence. The change might be associated with increased fees in many public colleges for out-of-state residents, and also with the establishment of many new community colleges that can be reached by commuting. A systematic study of these relationships was made by the National Center for Educational Statistics of the USOE in the fall of 1968. Each state reported the number of residents attending an institution of higher education, the number and proportion of these attending in their home state, and the number in other states. For each state, there is also the number migrating into that state and out of it.

A statistical description of the student population can be obtained from the various reports of the USOE and other sources: enrollment for degrees, for advanced degrees, by sex of student, and by course of study or major subject. The U. S. Bureau of the Census reports age, sex, and ethnicity of students, their residence (urbanization), marital status, and years of college. Most of these factors are cross-classified with the type of institution, its control, and the citizenship of graduate students, as well as the number holding stipends.

Educational Attainment Educational attainment for higher education is measured by the award of degrees of several levels, associate degrees, and certificates. These data are available by sex of the student receiving the award, subject of specialization, type of institution, level of degree or certificate, state, and individual college or university.

Institutions Institutions are described by type, control, number of years in the curriculum, kinds of formal awards, size of student body and faculty, and the listing of the individual colleges and universities. In addition, the USOE *Education Directory* contains listings for the individual institutions.

The institutions themselves are described in many ways. The formats include such summaries as statistical distributions by size of enrollment, by type (two-year, universities, etc.), and control to listings of individual institutions.

Financial Statistics Financial statistics of colleges and universities are published by USOE in a variety of reports. Revenue, by source for institutions with different kinds of control, is available for the individual states. The contributions of students in the form of tuition and fees, and room and board rates are also given.

Current expenditures are classified into about a dozen major categories, and appear in the basic financial reports published by the USOE. Statistics on endowments and the value of physical plant per student are reported, as is additional detail for the land-grant institutions.

Staffing The staffing of higher education is the subject of reports by the USOE and the American Council on Education. The numbers of teachers and other professionals, by sex, academic rank, kinds of positions, and types of institutions are given. The statistical description of college faculty members includes such demographic factors as their age, sex, citizenship, race, father's educational attainment, religious background, current religion, marital status, and the number of their children. Their professional background is also described: highest degree held, faculty position during graduate work, year of last degree, major field, present rank, and type of appointment, for each sex separately, as well as type of institution. These data are from a sample survey of the Carnegie Commission on the Future of Higher Education.

Salaries of faculty members are reported separately for universities, other four-year institutions, and two-year institutions by academic rank for nine-to-ten-month and eleven-to-twelve-month contracts. Median salaries are published by academic rank, size of institution, and control. Median salaries for a number of administrative (nonteaching) positions are also available.

The value of the physical plant of institutions of higher education is reported in total and per student, classified by control and academic level of the institution.

Teaching Technology and Research Teaching technology and research into educational methods are the subject of an extensive literature, as in the case of elementary and secondary education. The data are available in libraries and access is facilitated by the USOE indexing services.

Federal Programs Federal programs to assist higher education are numerous. One group which might be considered a form of aid is more realistically a payment for research performed. These programs vary from "grants" of the National Science Foundation and the National Institutes of Health to purchased research services by the Atomic Energy Commission or the Department of Defense. The difference is indistinct so there is no clear summary of these separate forms of support. The reports of the various federal agencies provide details. A second group of assistance programs provides for payments to the institutions under a large number of laws, beginning with the Northwest Ordinance in 1787, which authorized land grants for the establishment of educational institutions, and the first Morrill Act in 1862, which authorized public land grants to the states for the establishment and maintenance of agricultural and mechanical colleges. A third group of assistance programs takes the form of aid to students: grants, low-interest loans, and guaranteed loans.

Various reports on federal programs that assist higher education have been prepared by the National Center for Educational Statistics of the U. S. Office of Education. They provide a substantial amount of detail on the types of programs and agencies administering them, as well as comparisons over several years. A number of the programs have quite specific objectives making a long list of "categorical" assistance programs, as distinct from general financial aid. A historical perspective of population of ages 18–24, going back to 1867, is given in *A Statistical Portrait of Higher Education* (Harris, 1972). This is an excellent general source book for higher education, with 700 tables of data.

Adult Education Enrollment in adult education schools (over 13 million in May 1969) is published by sex, race, and age for six sources of instruction: public or private school, college or university part-time, job training, correspondence courses, community organizations, and tutor or private instructor. Reports on adult education programs present, also, descriptions of courses and other services provided, and information on ethnic group and language spoken.

Adult education can better be understood in conjunction with labor-force participation of the students—data available from census labor-force statistics.

Limited space has dictated that some important aspects of education not be covered in this summary review: education of the handicapped, of the gifted, and of "special" students in several categories. There is no treatment at all of curriculum development; teaching methods; the training of teachers, counselors, and administrators; the organization and dissemination of the research literature. Each of these subjects has its own organization of information, some of which is appropriately in statistical form.

USES OF EDUCATION DATA

The educational establishment in the United States must be one of the most complicated legal organizational entities the world has evolved. The formal elementary and secondary education of almost 50 million children and youth is the responsibility of the fifty states and some 17,000 school districts that vary in size from almost 200 districts with 25,000 or more pupils to something less than 2000 districts which operate no schools of their own. The responsibilities of the state educational agencies (SEA) and of the local educational agencies vary from one state to another. In the making of important decisions and the adherence to administrative styles, the local educational administrations wander over a broad spectrum. Moreover, with the present emphasis on neighborhood control, even such large school districts as major cities of the nation are decentralizing the control of their elementary and secondary schools to administrative units representing the ethnic, economic, and social perceptions and ambitions of the locality.

The planning and management of the huge and complex education activity in the United States must take account of three factors. The first is its large scale. The second is the decentralization of operation—which differs from one locality to another—but with support originating at different levels of government. The third factor arises from the multiple goals of the educational process and the community's attempts to choose the goals and direct the schools toward them ("neighborhood control," "public accountability").

Each of these factors takes on real meaning only after it is expressed quantitatively. By necessity, then, almost all of the constructive discussion about the purposes, plans, financing, management, progress, and consequences of education must presently come to the questions: How much? How many? It is not too much to say that the statistical resources almost provide a second language without which purposeful discussion can hardly proceed.

It obviously is impossible within a reasonable space to describe all the uses of the vast outpouring of statistics from the enormous educational complex in the nation. There have been attempts to learn what information actually is used by school officials, and for what purpose.

An example of a "user survey" is "A Survey of the Decision Processes and Related Informational Requirements for Educational Planning and Innovation" for sixty-five school districts in the three San Francisco Bay area counties (Rittenhouse and Chorness, 1969). The National Center for Educational Statistics of USOE also supported a "user study" by the Stanford Research Institute which asked a number of educational administrators and others what information they used and how frequently. Some of the results were used to assist in the redesign of the NCES data systems.

To present at least some of the highlights on the use of educational data the discussion will be presented under the following headings:

1. Administrative reports and information systems
2. Special studies
3. Projections
4. Advisory committees
5. Legislation
6. Allocation of funds
7. Use in one large LEA

None of these reviews is exhaustive. Rather, examples are given with the intention of suggesting the way in which the statistical data form a foundation for some aspect of educational administration for the particular schools, SEA's, or LEA's covered by the exemplary study.

The picture that emerges is clear. The many differences from one situation to another notwithstanding, an enormous amount of data are currently in use to plan, budget, administer, review, and legislate for the operations of the many components of education in the United States.

There is strong evidence of the habitual utilization of statistical data from regular reporting systems and management information systems by those who administer and serve the schools. Since the evidence is from active practitioners, one must conclude that national, state, and local preparation of statistical information is the foundation upon which decision-making in the educational community stands.

Administrative Reports and Information Systems

Many federal support programs include statutory provisions requiring annual reports for the operation of the program. Accordingly, the states report each year on their operations under Title I of the Elementary and Secondary Education Act. Typical reports describe the services provided (assistance with reading, health services, educational counseling, kindergartens, more school hours, teaching of English as a second language, etc.) and the groups aided (children from low-income families, the handicapped, delinquent, and migrant). Also included are basic demographic data including the ethnic composition of the LEA's receiving Title I funds. Results of the programs usually are presented in the form of the subjective opinions of officials or as achievement test scores.

The annual reports for the vocational education programs describe the elements of the programs (aptitude testing, counseling, etc.). They also make use of the occupational outlook studies of the U. S. Department of Labor. Planning is in terms of estimated number of jobs of various sorts anticipated to become available in the local labor market over the ensuing six years and estimated labor-force participation rates for women (Nassau County, N. Y., 1969 report).

A number of the states have developed information systems intended to provide their education officials with reports necessary to the management of their large and complicated organizations. There seems to be no systematic analysis of the contents of these reporting systems. However, they have attempted to arrange for the automatic generation of the data which the SEA's report to the agencies of the federal government, and to some of the professional associations. The design process often centers on the systems analysis for computerizing the flows of data and the generation of routine reports.

An example of this development is the New York State Educational

Information System (NYSEIS). It is intended to provide a "complete range of information and data processing services to the school districts in New York State" (NYSEIS, 1969).

Many of the state information systems are in development; their current status and the availability of statistical information from them can be learned by addressing the individual SEA. One might safely anticipate that most states will eventually have such rationalized information systems, capable of comparing state data to national data, and presumably to those of other states.

The USOE is developing a rationalized reporting system to be used in program evaluation. Reports are already available which contain the necessary combinations of financial items, program variables, and information about the students, including socioeconomic status. The Joint Federal/State Task Force on Evaluation played a leading role in the design of the reporting system; it was composed of representatives of SEA and USOE. It worked with the National Center for Educational Statistics which was ultimately responsible for the design and operation of the program. It is now absorbed into the Committee on Evaluation and Information Systems (CEIS).

Special Studies

Rather more complete analyses than those in routine annual reports appear in special evaluation studies. Of particular interest here is the treatment of statistical data. Whereas the annual reports tend to display information that flows conveniently out of the programs, evaluators are typically unhappy about the absence of kinds of information they particularly want.

For example, an "Evaluation of the Guidance Program in the Los Angeles City Adult Schools" (Stewart, 1967) laments the absence of data on student's vocational interests, aptitudes, preferences, personality, out-of-school activities, and work experience, and the inadequacies of data on the student's personal, social, and mental status. Two forces seem to be at work here: the answers to difficult questions about such a complex matter as a large-scale educational program require a good deal of data, and they must be organized in particular ways. This practically never happens unless a special study is organized for the specific purpose of answering the particular array of questions. No amount of "background" information suffices; this is also an illustration of the paucity of data on educational "process," which was noted in the opening section of this chapter.

An example of such a special study is the *Evaluation of Family*

Service Program of Clinton County, N. Y. (Alexander, 1967). This special study concerned the training of women as aides in home economics education. Items included formal education, occupation of husband, family income, testing of knowledge before and after a course of instruction, and oganizational participation of the aides.

A more complete study was the *Quality Measurement Project* of the New York State Department of Education (Goodman, 1967). Achievement scores for various skills and three grade levels were related to expenditures for education and measured IQ. Critically, the relationships were controlled for socioeconomic status.

Educational attainment is often useful when related to other factors. For example, the U. S. Department of Labor prepares estimates of educational attainment for nine occupational classes by sex and race. The relation of attainment to income is expressed in at least two ways: annual money income (in fifteen-interval detail) for detailed attainment classes, by sex and age for the population 25 and older; estimated income of men by years of schooling from age 18 to death, and from age 25 to 64 (sometimes called "lifetime income"). These types of analyses serve a useful purpose in quantifying one aspect of the value of an education viewed as an investment in human resources.

A new element facilitating special studies is to be found in the creation of the National Institute of Education (Public Law 92-318, Education Amendments of 1972), which will likely develop a statistical reporting system as an integral part of each project which is designed to improve a group of schools through the application of research results. The very form of the program dictates the essentiality of the data. The search is for best practice under particular conditions, with an immediate need to observe and assess the consequences of changes. In an important sense, it is difficult to separate the operations of a particular project from the statistical analysis that brought it into being or from the evidence that the intended benefits were or were not achieved.

A number of uses of the information described are obvious. The floating of a school bond issue would not be considered without a review of the trends and recent experience in bond referenda, and the interest rates would be proposed with an eye to the money market. Teacher salaries would be repeatedly reviewed by planning and budgeting units in preparing for future years, and the same kinds of information would play a part in the fixing of salaries, no matter what procedure was followed (collective bargaining, etc.).

The preceding section of this chapter provided a general description of the kinds of data most basically used and their sources. In actual use, combinations of data usually are more revealing than each kind considered in isolation: demographic (ethnic, family income), with program (federal funds for state programs to aid the educationally disadvantaged), and with output data (changes in achievement scores or educational attainment). If one restricted himself to primary sources of data—rather than cited references—the greater importance of certain standard sources would stand out more clearly. Census data are rearranged and republished by many "sources" and in many forms. The standard time series of the National Center for Educational Statistics enjoy the same reuse. The same is true of such nongovernmental sources as the National Education Association and a number of other professional organizations which collect their own data. The federal government foregoes collecting data where private sources can supply them.

Projections

One of the typical uses of past and current statistics of all kinds is to form a basis for making projections. Educational statistics are not an exception. The planning of the whole educational operation presumes some perception of the future needs for schools and schoolrooms, for teachers and administrators. One approach is for the national statistical system merely to provide data as they come available and leave the projections to the individual user. The other approach is to have a single expert agency organize the data as completely as possible—demographic data and information about educational activities—and estimate for a convenient span of years into the future on the general assumption that trends (enrollment rates, retention rates, class sizes, per-pupil expenditures) will persist for limited periods.

The second approach is that used by the U. S. Office of Education. The National Center for Educational Statistics publishes an annual volume: *Projections of Educational Statistics*. This report presents estimates each year for a span of ten future years for a great deal of the nation's educational business. In general, all of the subjects on which there are current reports are represented in the ten years of projections: descriptions of the school-age population, enrollments, degrees, institutions, teachers' finances, etc.

The estimates are thus presented in a consistent and useful form in far greater detail than any consumer could afford, unless he were to organize a duplicate agency to NCES, with access to the same information. These reports allow the individual scholar, planner, or administrator to have a constructed quantitative picture of education for each future year at his fingertips, up to ten years ahead. While there is a good deal of structural detail (different kinds of colleges, etc.), the estimates are for the United States as a whole, without geographic detail. The planning organizations in the state educational agencies can be guided by the national estimates, but they must prepare their own. The methods of projection and the assumptions behind the specific estimates are set forth in the publication.

State projections of elementary and secondary enrollments and degree-credit enrollment in institutions of higher education, by sex, are made available upon request (through the National Center for Educational Statistics), but they are not published.

Short-term forecasting of kindergarten and first-grade enrollments for small areas can be accomplished by using preschool-age population data for single years of age. Longer-term forecasts require estimates of birth rates, and additional uncertainties arise from the need to predict migration patterns. These analyses, too, depend upon census data.

Advisory Committees

The U. S. Office of Education has an array of advisory committees to assist in deciding which kinds of data are most important to the educational community. The SEA's are represented through the general advisory committee to the National Center for Educational Statistics. The Committee on Evaluation and Information Systems (CEIS) recently absorbed several advisory groups of which the most general in function was the long-standing Committee on Educational Data Systems (CEDS) which was a subcommittee of the Council of Chief State School Officers. CEDS regularly reviewed the current data collection plans of NCES in detail. Moreover, special advisory groups have been created for many particular statistical collections such as the Library General Information System (LIBGIS), a longitudinal survey—Study of the High School Graduating Class of 1972—and, particularly important, the Joint Federal-State Task Force on Evaluation. All of these are now part of CEIS.

Similarly, the advisory committees of the U. S. Bureau of the Census convene regularly to advise on the contents of the data collection programs of that bureau. The attendance in schools and educational attainment are standard items in both the decennial censuses and the monthly Current Population Survey from time to time. The census provides an excellent example of the way in which the usefulness of educational information is greatly improved when related to other demographic data: age, sex, ethnicity, family status, labor-force classification, etc. The census data are therefore responsive to the opinions of advisory committee members who speak for the educational community and who base their judgments on the analysis of the data already available.

Legislation

All of the uses of educational statistics described above are, of course, relevant to use by administrative and legislative officials on all levels of government as a basis for legislation relating to education. Statistical data become a central element in the design and passage of federal laws, in their administration and evaluation, as well as in the operation of state and local educational agencies. Reference to any recent hearing relating to education in the U. S. Congress, a state legislature, or on a city council or county board is certain to document this assertion. Especially significant in this regard are the uses of statistical information in hearings resulting in the passage of the landmark federal enactment of the Elementary and Secondary Education Act of 1965. The identification and measurement of the target populations (of students and institutions) form an important part of such legislative hearings that lead to the passage of statutes. Moreover, the annual appropriation hearings provide current reviews for the federal share of about 7 percent of the total funds for public elementary and secondary education.

In addition to specific congressional studies and hearings, the most compelling reports that have led directly to action are those which dealt with ethnic desegregation of school systems. The periodic reports of the U. S. Civil Rights Commission are examples in point. There are also many reports on the desegregation of particular localities. In "The Status of Integration in the St. Louis Public Schools in the 1966–1967 School Year" the St. Louis Board of Education describes the racial composition of professional personnel and student populations in the individual schools, along with twelve specific integration activities. One of these is the determination of school district boundaries which would promote racial integration.

A statistical analysis of the factors associated with a greater or lesser degree of integration in Mississippi utilized data from the census, sources in the U. S. Department of Health, Education and Welfare, and the SEA in conjunction with a primary data collection from 147 LEA's. The information related to the schools, the community, and the characteristics of the desegregation program for each school district (Palmer, 1971).

Many localities have made special studies of desegregation problems, with recommendations for action. The assignment itself dictates the use of the results. Several examples are cited: *Improving Ethnic Balance and Intergroup Relations* (California State Department of Education, 1968) recommends changes for improving the education of minority-group children, some of which involve school reorganization and redistricting. A similar report covers the New Haven (Calif.) Unified School District (1967), the Corona Unified School District (1967), and the Vallejo Unified School District (1968).

Allocation of Funds

Perhaps the most direct use of statistical data for the administration of educational programs is the computation of the distribution of federal funds to the states under a number of statutes. The key role of census data stands out clearly (see also Chapter 2).

Population by income level has been used for the allotment (formally to individual counties in this case) of some $1.5 billion a year on the basis of the number of children aged 5 to 17 in families with income, at the last census, below $2,000 (and below $3,000 for a sub-program) per annum, under the Elementary and Secondary Educational Act of 1965 (ESEA, Public Law 89-10, Title I) for "financial assistance to meet the special educational needs of educationally deprived children."

Population by educational attainment has been used for persons 16 and over with less than a completed high school education, for allotment of funds under the Adult Education Act (P. L. 88-452, as amended by P. L. 89-750, Title III).

There are a variety of laws providing funds to the states on the basis of the most recent census data: age 18-22 for the Higher Education Act and the National Student Vocational Loan Insurance Act; total resident population for the Bankhead Jones Act (grants to the states for agricultural experiment stations); age groups 15-19, 20-24, 25-65, and 15-20 (annual survey data) for two provisions of the Vocational Education Act; total residential population for Library Services and the Construction Act Amendments of 1966; age group 3-21 for education of handicapped children; age group 5-17 and total resident population (annual survey) for ESEA, Title III (supplementary education centers) and the National Defense Education Act of 1958, Titles III (instructional assistance grants and loans) and V (guidance, counseling, and testing). Data from the census, along with data from the U. S. Welfare Administration and from the USOE (Division of Compensatory Education) are used to compute assistance to state agencies for Aid to Families of Dependent Children, and neglected, delinquent, corrective, and foster children.

A number of programs that are not based on census data use statistics from USOE itself to compute state distributions of federal funds.

Examples are elementary and secondary school enrollment data for strengthening state departments of education (ESEA, Title V); public and nonpublic enrollment for library resources (ESEA, Title II); public plus nonpublic enrollment grades nine to twelve for higher education facilities (P. L. 88-204, Title I, Section 104); high school graduates, public and nonpublic, for college work-study programs (P. L. 88–452, Title I, Part C) and for public community colleges (P. L. 88-204, Title I, Section 103); enrollment in institutions of higher education for loans to students in higher education (P. L. 88-452, Title I, Part C) and for education opportunity grants and work-study programs (P. L. 89-329, Title IV, Parts A and C); full-time and full-time equivalent enrollment for improvement of educational instruction (P. L. 88-204, Title I, Section 104 and P. L. 89-329, Title VI).

The USOE also provides data for computations, sometimes in conjunction with data from other agencies, for the distribution of funds to the state agencies for children with certain educational problems: current expenditure per pupil, and other data for the handicapped (USOE Bureau of the Handicapped), neglected children and delinquent children [USOE Bureau of Elementary and Secondary Education (BESE)], children in migratory families (U. S. Department of Labor), and adult corrective education (USOE BESE), all under ESEA, Title I, Part A.

One of the most obvious uses of statistical data, then, is in the design and enactment of legislation for a variety of classes of persons needing special educational services, and for the administration of these programs of financial assistance after the statutes become operational. The whole philosophy of state-operated education with financial assistance from the national government depends upon such objective criteria for the parceling out of funds as those listed in the above examples. Indeed, complaints arise from those jurisdictions which believe that more current data or more recent estimates would increase their share of some program fund—whatever their attitude toward statistical reporting on other occasions—and they sometimes become exponents for more frequent collections or more prompt availability of statistics.

Use in One Large LEA

The public school system of Fairfax County, Virginia, enrolls almost 136,000 students (September 1972), operates 164 schools, and employs over 7200 instructional personnel. Its 1972 budget was approximately $150 million.

The Fairfax County school system has a computerized statistical information system that provides data for the operation of the system and prepares reports to the State Department of Education in Richmond. State law requires a school census every three years. In addition there is a census twice a year to count children of federal employees, for the computation of federal payments to the county as a "federally impacted" school district (first authorized by a 1941 amendment to the Lanham Act of 1940).

The monthly Pupil Membership Report presents enrollment data for each individual school for the preceding five months, by each grade, compared to the "rated capacity" (classroom space) of the school, and to "program capacity." The last takes account of the provision of special space for the educable mentally retarded, the gifted, and for preschool programs. Summary tables highlight changes in these quantities for the attention of administrators. Most of the report is in the form of a computer printout, and a monthly report is approximately thirty to thirty-five pages; it is dated the middle of the month following the last month reported.

The periodic report, Program Capacity for Elementary Schools, presents a full detail of the components of program. The February 1972 report listed a rated capacity of 82,770 pupil spaces in the elementary schools but only 75,657 program capacity, a shortage of 7113 pupil spaces required for "special programs and special services."

The Annual Financial Report lists receipts of state school funds in eighteen distinct accounts, nine federal sources, three city-county sources, the appropriated district budget, and about twenty other noncapital sources; and seven from loans, bonds, and investments.

The many specific federal programs in support of education have been noted above, and their manner of using statistical data reviewed. There is a corresponding statistical control system at the LEA, where management must have a current and orderly review of the many special funds and their use. Much more is involved than mere financial audit; there is also a large and complex educational activity to be managed effectively.

The disbursement accounts not only function as cost accounts, but they relate appropriate expenditure items to teaching staff, administrative and service staff, and average daily attendance of pupils.

Six management objectives were adopted by the LEA (decrease in dropouts, increase in attendance, development of interpersonal relationships, etc.). Each principal plans his school year in terms of activities that aim at improvement in relation to the standard objectives. A report for the school year summarizes the results for each individual school.

OUTLOOK FOR THE FUTURE

The trend of preparation and publication of statistics on education in the United States has been toward better unification of the basic statistics and the addition of new kinds of materials. Continuation of this trend depends upon various factors: the organization of the statistical activities of the U. S. Office of Education and the U. S. Bureau of the Census; the resources committed to these activities; the participation of the states and the localities and of the broader educational community in the national statistical program; the establishment of standards of terminology and technical practices and adherence to them; and a continuation of work of such nongovernmental associations as the National Education Association, the American Council on Education, and the United States Catholic Conference.

The survey programs of USOE now are planned as a unit, under the technical supervision of the National Center for Educational Statistics, and with the advice of the Committee on Educational Data Systems, a subcommittee of the Council of Chief State School Officers. Historically, an abundance of new legislation and the accompanying reorganizations of the education components of the U. S. Department of Health, Education and Welfare have impeded the implementation of a unified program of national educational statistics. With adequate financial support and staff—especially in NCES—the trend of improved unification and adequate coverage of the nation's educational business should be expected to continue.

The variety and complexity of educational institutions and their many activities make it particularly important that they comply with two classes of standards: standards of classification and terminology, and standards of technical statistical practice.

The formidable task of providing a dictionary of consistent terms to describe the many aspects of education, and to obtain agreement on their meaning has been a cooperative program of the USOE and a number of professional associations. In 1953, USOE published the first of its handbooks on terminology, *The Common Core of State Educational Information,* initiating the State Educational Records and Reports Series. The handbooks now comprise seven volumes. The principal purpose of developing and adopting standards of terminology is to assure comparability of records kept at all administrative levels, and consequently the statistical reports that derive from them.

The scale of effort can be illustrated by the preparation of Handbook VI, *Standard Terminology for Curriculum and Instruction in Local and State School Systems* (USOE, 1970). (The Handbooks are widely available in educational agencies, university libraries, and professional associations, and they may be purchased at the U. S. Government Printing Office.) The definitions themselves are hierarchically arranged and occupy 200 pages of oversize format (the book is almost ten by twelve inches). There is a coded numbering system for the more than 3000 definitions, suitable for use in computerized records. Some seventy-six professional associations participated in the preparation of the definitions. Thirteen "cooperating associations" joined with the USOE in the planning, development, preparation, and revision of the definitions (especially the work of making them consistent and mutually exclusive at the several hierarchical levels). These thirteen associations formally endorsed the final handbook and called upon the educational community to adopt the standard practices as promptly and completely as possible. The actual preparation of the contents occupied more than five years.

It is no small effort to overhaul record systems and reporting systems for the state educational agencies, the local agencies, and the many other organizations that keep records and provide data for the national system of educational statistics. With time, the use of the standards should become virtually universal.

The variety and complexity of education in the United States also make for difficulties in the design and administration of data collection, analysis, and reporting. The federal government, under the impact of proliferating war agencies in 1942, was given a general mechanism for unifying statistical systems and maintaining technical quality with the passage of the Federal Reports Act. Many agencies have provided for technical review within their own walls or proposed statistical reporting systems before submitting their plans for the required approval of the Office of Management and Budget (formerly the Bureau of the Budget). The National Center for Educational Statistics and the Office of the Deputy Commissioner for Development provide this technical service for the USOE. Many innocent-appearing surveys have proved to require surprisingly advanced techniques of sampling, instrument design, and quality assurance in order to obtain the sought-for information. The gradual improvement of the consistency and quality of educational data should continue, with the pace largely dependent upon the staff resources committed to this demanding work.

New kinds of statistics—or improvements on underdeveloped kinds—are planned by USOE. Two will be noted: evaluation studies and longitudinal studies of students.

The evaluation of programs which are designed to improve educational services is a particularly difficult task. Typically, such programs offer improvement in very few of the factors that can influence the performance of pupils, teachers, and schools. It has proved most difficult to isolate the contribution of individual programs to any improvement observed. This circumstance has caused some serious problems, and has invited two technical errors: (1) the failure of reports to distinguish between "We did not succeed in measuring what we wanted" and "There was no measurable effect"; and (2) the presumption that failure to "prove" that a program had made a contribution was the same as actually "proving" that the program had in fact made no contribution and was therefore a waste. Both of these errors fail to separate the events in the real world of education from the difficult statistical problems of measurement. Presumably, it would be easier to perform statistical measurement in a laboratory, with the essential controls, randomization, replication, etc., but researchers and administrators have quite properly been wary of substituting such an artificial experimental environment for real children in real schoolrooms being taught by real teachers.

There have been a few controlled experiments with "performance contracting"—an arrangement under which a private contractor undertakes to teach pupils, and is paid in accordance with a formula that depends upon the gains in educational achievement of the pupils.

There have been several attempts to survey a group of students by following them over a period of years with the intention of relating their later histories, especially their successes and failures, to a number of factors from their earlier lives. A large-scale study was launched by the NCES in the spring of 1972: A Survey of the High School Graduating Class of 1972, with an initial nationally representative sample of 20,000 seniors. The study will attempt to relate the socioeconomic backgrounds, educational experiences, school characteristics, etc., to their future educational activities, their early work histories, and other aspects of their young adult lives. The expressed plans and intentions of the youth in the sample will be resurveyed at intervals and matched against the actual events of their lives.

A longitudinal study of several "follow-through" programs by the Office of Economic Opportunity and USOE will attempt to evaluate these early school grade programs.

The federal government cannot obtain much information about education without the participation of the state educational agencies. A great deal more than passive consent is involved. Representatives of the states serve on advisory committees, and assist in the design of individual surveys and in the planning of the national statistical system itself. A principal instrumentality for this participation is the Council of Chief State School Officers—largely through its subcommittee, the Committee on Educational Data Systems.

The evolving plans of the USOE include measures to strengthen the cooperation of the federal government and the states. There is already provision in the Elementary and Secondary Act of 1965 (and its amendments) for support of state educational agencies in their record-keeping and other administrative activities. A new program of the NCES—The Common Core of Data for the 1970s (it will probably become known by the label CCD-70)—would provide for matching federal funds for a class of reporting and record-keeping activities by the states. It also comes under the advisory purview of CEIS. The combination of improved technical practices, adherence to the standard handbook definitions, and federal-state support of statistical operations holds promise for continued improvement of the information necessary for the planning and administration of the nation's educational activities.

The educational activity of the nation is not static: new issues constantly arise and old ones change shape enough to create demands for new kinds of information. For example, the Serrano case in California (*Serrano v. Priest* in California State courts) dealt with the distribution of funds among the local school districts of the state. A requirement of equal cost per student was discussed against a background of property value and property tax rates throughout the state. Since that decision, almost every state has become involved in similar cases. In the District of Columbia a similar principle was adjudicated, but in this case the issue was the lack of equality in subareas within the school district.

The emergence of "performance contracting" as a solution to the problems of improving the effectiveness of education made new uses of data on pupil achievement (i.e., to determine the pay of a teaching contractor), bringing with it all of the problems and unsettled questions concerning the validity of present methods of achievement testing.

As new programs are proposed and new problems come to public attention, new kinds of statistical data will be required; the national system of educational statistics will be modified in order to try to meet the new demands.

Finally, the decennial censuses have provided the most complete data on the educational status of the population, especially in small area geographical detail. These census data provide the foundation for a substantial part of the national surveys of the USOE. Moreover, the Current Population Survey samples—with less geographic detail—are the best source of population data, including enrollment and educational attainment. Special studies by the U. S. Bureau of the Census, usually acting on behalf of USOE, and specially prepared estimates form an important part of the USOE publications. The dependence of the ten-year projections of educational statistics upon the data of the U. S. Bureau of the Census has been noted above.

Ten years is a long time to wait for new data, especially for rapidly changing parts of the country: the growing suburban edges of the metropolitan areas, the decaying or reaborning central cities, the areas of suddenly changing land use. Because of this, there have been repeated demands for a quinquennial census—perhaps less complete than the traditional decennial census, but filling an important gap in our knowledge about our country. Education is only one subject that would benefit importantly from the initiation of the often-proposed five-year census.

An innovation in the organization of census data promises to make the decennial censuses much more useful to the educational community. The National Center for Educational Statistics has recently completed a system for the allocation of census data to the individual school districts (excepting those with less than 300 persons). The project required the detailed mapping of the country for school district boundaries and for the census areas. Each census area that occupied more than one school district then had to be split into parts to be assigned to the individual school districts.

The publication of 1970 census data for the school districts is scheduled for the summer of 1975 under the title, "Social and Economic Characteristics of the School Districts." Tapes containing these data have been available for some time, and specific inquiries can be addressed to NCES. Color microfilms of maps for the entire country can also be purchased. Revisions in school district boundaries are constantly being made; their effect on the census data is also estimated, making "current" data available which express the 1970 census characteristics for the new geographic units.

There are two formats of census data on the computer tapes:

1. "First-count" census summary tape, showing fine geographic detail but relatively few items of information.
2. "Fourth-count" census summary tape, for a more gross geographic grid (and therefore with more estimation in the data for a school district), but with a wealth of socioeconomic detail: nativity, mother tongue, family income, number of children, number of children aged to five years and six to seventeen for families below the "poverty level," educational attainment for persons over 25 years of age and vocational educational attainment (nonhigh school graduates) for those 16 to 65, and labor-force status (employed, unemployed) with occupation (including elementary or secondary school teacher).

These data are for persons residing within the school district, rather than for enrollees. It is important to realize that the detail of the fourth-count tapes is fully usable only for the larger school districts. The low-density cells of the tabulations are subject to relatively large sampling variances, and are more likely than the larger numbers to shift over time in their relative sizes.

This new organization of census data will be a standard resource of the national statistical system for future years and will be directly applicable to the planning and management of the nation's school systems.

REFERENCES

Alexander, Frank D. *Evaluation of Family Service Program of Clinton County, N. Y.* Ithaca, N. Y.: College of Home Economics, Cornell University, September 1967.

California State Department of Education. *Improving Ethnic Balance and Intergroup Relations.* An Advisory Report to the Board of Education Santa Barbara City Schools, 1968.

Goodman, Samuel M. *The Quality Measurement Project.* A Research Activity Conducted by the New York State Department of Education, New York State Department of Education. Albany, 1960.

Harris, Seymour E. *A Statistical Portrait of Higher Education.* A Report for the Carnegie Commission on Higher Education. New York: McGraw-Hill, 1972.

Nassau County Vocational Center for Women. *Second Annual Report, 1969.* Mineola, N. Y.

National Center of Educational Statistics. *Projections of Educational Statistics.* Washington, D. C.: Government Printing Office, annual.

New York State Educational Information System. *NYSEIS Systems Design, Phase II, Final Report.* New York: Price, Waterhouse and Co., July 1969.

Palmer, James M. *Mississippi School Districts: Factors in the Disestablishment of Dual Systems, Final Report.* State College, Mississippi Social Science Research Center, Mississippi State University, 1971.

Rittenhouse, Carl H., and Maury H. Chorness. "A Survey of the Decision Processes and Related Informational Requirements for Educational Planning and Innovation." Paper presented at Western Psychological Association Convention (Vancouver, B. C.), June 18, 1969.

Stewart, Robert M. "Evaluation of the Guidance Program in the Los Angeles City Adult Schools." Ed.D. thesis submitted to University of California, Los Angeles, 1967.

U. S. Office of Civil Rights. *Directory of Public Elementary and Secondary Schools in Selected Districts, Enrollment and Staff by Racial and Ethnic Group.* Washington, D. C.: Government Printing Office, 1968.

———. *Earned Degrees Conferred: Associate Degrees and Other Formal Awards Below the Baccalaureate.* Washington, D. C.: Government Printing Office, annual.

On Education

―――. *Opening Fall Enrollment in Higher Education.* Washington, D. C.: Government Printing Office, annual.

―――. *Standard Terminology for Curriculum and Instruction in Local and State School Systems.* Handbook VI. Washington, D. C.: Government Printing Office, 1970.

―――. *Vocational and Technical Education.* Washington, D. C.: Government Printing Office, annual.

U. S. Office of Education. *Directory of Public Schools.* National Center of Educational Statistics, occasional.

CHAPTER 6
On the Labor Force*

TYPE OF DATA AVAILABLE

Definition and Scope

The term "labor-force statistics" refers to data on the working population—those who are employed and those who are trying to find jobs. In addition, the information provided relates to the kind of work people do; the kinds of places in which they work; their input in terms of hours worked per week or weeks worked per year; their earnings; the duration of their unemployment, if jobless; and various other facts about their attachment, full-time or part-time, to the labor force. The last is of great importance today when much of our working population consists of married women and young persons still in school who work on only a part-time basis.

For many years, the only source of information about the work force of the country as a whole was the decennial census of population, and this was generally limited to a description of the kind of work persons usually did—their gainful occupations. Early in the present century, information on the number of persons on payrolls in some manufacturing industries began to be collected by the U. S. Bureau of Labor Statistics. The system was expanded to cover more industries and by 1937, estimates of employment in all industries except agriculture were published. This type of data

---

* Based on a memorandum by Gertrude Bancroft McNally, formerly of the U. S. Bureau of the Census and the U. S. Bureau of Labor Statistics.

was furnished by employer records and came to be called "establishment data" or "payroll statistics," as contrasted with household data provided by enumerations of the population in censuses or sample surveys.

With the onset of the Great Depression of the 1930s, need for information about the *unemployed* became urgent. The 1930 Census of Population included a special question on persons who were out of work. During the decade many local surveys were conducted, such as a series in Philadelphia, to try to measure the number of people for whom jobs had to be provided. The work-relief programs of the New Deal were launched without any hard evidence of the numbers of unemployed and needy. Many estimates of the unemployed were made based on the changing payroll statistics and guesses about the size of the "working population." During the 1930s estimates of the number of unemployed differed by many millions. In 1937, Congress authorized a so-called Census of Unemployment, based on registrations at the post offices throughout the country. Fortunately, a sample survey designed to check the accuracy of the self-registration also was undertaken, in which the information was obtained by direct interview. The check sample survey clearly showed that the self-registration was defective. Thereafter, no one supported the idea that the nation's unemployment statistics could be obtained by voluntary declarations of the population uncontrolled by scientific statistical procedures.

The need for clear-cut definitions of employment and unemployment became increasingly apparent through the confusing and contradictory experiences in the 1930s. The measurement of unemployment proved to be a difficult task because of both human and political concerns. The present way of measuring the labor force was developed in time for use in the 1940 Census of Population, and has remained substantially unchanged with only some sharpening ever since. It took many experiments in surveys and censuses during the 1930s to discover a good way of measuring unemployment. It became clear that the questions must relate to a short and specific period of time in the recent past; and that a system of priorities of activity had to be established because within a short time a person could be employed, seeking a job, or outside the labor force. Consequently, the questions determining employment status were based on what the person was doing during the calendar week before the census data. Persons who worked at any time during that week were counted as employed; those who had no work during the week but looked for work were counted as unemployed. With a few exceptions other persons were outside the labor force.

The theory underlying these concepts, developed after experience had been gained, was that this measurement of unemployment represented the number of people for whom the economy had failed to provide jobs, and, equally important, who were currently putting pressure on the labor market for jobs.

While the planning for the 1940 decennial census was under way, experimentation was conducted in the Work Projects Administration to test the above and similar definitions in a small population sample survey, which could be conducted every month to guide the administration on the changing number and nature of unemployment. This survey was launched officially in 1940 and eventually was taken over by the Bureau of the Census as part of its Current Population Survey operated each month. By 1971, 50,000 households were being interviewed in 449 sample areas in 863 counties and independent cities. This survey is the source not only of the labor-force statistics analyzed and published by the Bureau of Labor Statistics, but of the demographic and income statistics published by the Bureau of the Census. It also serves as an instrument for special studies.

Monthly Household Data

The household survey, in 1970 in its thirtieth year of operation, each month provides estimates for the total civilian population of the United States not resident in institutions. These include estimates of employed and unemployed persons sixteen years of age and over (prior to 1967, fourteen years and over), by age, sex, color, marital status, and relationship to household head. Estimates of the employed and unemployed have been carried back to 1929 on an annual average basis by relating the new statistics to earlier census and payroll statistics.

The characteristics of employed persons which are published include major occupation and industry groups, hours worked during the survey week, reasons for part-time employment, reasons for absence from job and whether or not pay was received.

For unemployed persons the information given includes occupation and industry of last job, reason for unemployment, and duration of unemployment. Both absolute numbers and rates are published, that is, the unemployed persons of a specific sex, age, color, etc., are shown as a percent of the labor force of employed plus unemployed of that same sex, age, or color, etc.

Many of the monthly statistics are seasonally adjusted so that they are more useful in economic analysis.

Once a quarter, additional data on persons not in the labor force are published as averages of three months' reports. These statistics show how many persons not in the current labor force want a job and their reasons for not looking for work. Collection of such information on a regular basis was initiated in 1967 in response to pressure for some direct measure of the number of discouraged workers—i.e., those who had given up the search for work because they thought they could not find a job.

The concern with this "discouraged" group is traceable to two main sources. One was the manpower planning group which had set a goal of developing programs to help not only the unemployed but, also, the underemployed, those with not enough work or suitable work, and those who could be brought back into the productive labor force. The other concerned persons were the economists who, in their analysis of the level of economic growth needed for full employment and utilization of other resources, expected that prosperity would bring back into the labor force those who had dropped out due to discouragement or had not thought it worthwhile to look for work. Jobs would be needed for them as well as for the unemployed.

Much other information about the work force is compiled but published only in special reports or used in connection with in-depth studies. Examples are the employment status of Vietnam veterans; the age, sex, and color of the labor force in occupation and industry groups; and the employment status of persons living in poverty areas.

All of the information described above is available for the United States as a whole. From time to time, however, estimates of the major categories for the four census regions—Northeast, North Central, South, and West—also are published, but the demand for these broad groupings of states appears to be modest.

Need for individual state and local area labor-force data, however, has been urgent for a long time. Except for the decennial census, this need has not been met by household surveys on a regular basis because of prohibitive costs. When the Current Population Survey sample was expanded to 50,000 households in 1967, reasonably accurate estimates for the ten largest states and twenty largest Standard Metropolitan Statistical Areas (SMSA's), and central cities of fourteen of them, could be prepared by averaging the monthy statistics for a calendar year. Data for the nine census divisions were also made available. Only the major totals with a few classifications by age, color, and sex currently are provided.

Annual and Other Special Surveys

With the ongoing monthly survey, supplementary questions on problems that require only annual or occasional measurement are feasible at relatively small cost. Since 1948, questions on work experience during the preceding calendar year have been asked early in the year, and beginning in 1956, these data were combined with income data for families still in the sample in March; in 1971, the two surveys were consolidated in March. On a broader time scale than a single week, these statistics describe the composition of the annual work force—weeks worked either full-time or part-time, total weeks and number of periods of unemployment, occupation and industry of longest job, and similar data for all persons 16 (or 14) years old or more in the civilian population at the time of interview. They also show earnings by occupation or industry of full- or part-year workers, by sex, color, family status, and other characteristics.

Annually, since 1948, information on the family characteristics of the labor force have been collected in March or April. These surveys have traced the increasing tendency of mothers of children at various ages to work for pay and have also shown the effects of unemployment on families.

Another annual survey, conducted in October of each year since 1947, reports on school enrollment, and provides statistics on employment and unemployment of in-school and out-of-school youth and of high school graduates and dropouts.

A fourth type of recurring survey gives the years of schooling of the population and the labor force. This project has been conducted annually in March since 1964, and for selected years back to 1948.

Except for the years 1961, 1967, and 1968, surveys of persons holding more than one job during the survey week have been conducted every year since 1956. Occasional studies were made prior to that time, the first in 1950. A major purpose of these surveys is to permit the coordination of estimates of employed persons from household surveys with estimates of employment obtained from various types of establishments. They also measure the amount and nature of "moonlighting," that is, holding more than one job. Although this practice is often popularly condemned as a contributing factor in high unemployment, these studies have shown otherwise.

Each year since 1948, information on the hired farm work force has been collected for the Department of Agriculture, providing measurements of weeks worked during the year, earnings at farm and nonfarm work, extent of migration, and similar problems.

Finally, many special studies too numerous even to list here are concerned with continuing problems of manpower quality and utilization. Some examples are detailed studies of special samples of the unemployed and of out-of-school youth; studies of job tenure and job turnover; eligibility for pensions; formal training of workers; mobility of married women in and out of the labor force; child-care arrangements of working mothers; extent and nature of volunteer work. In connection with its program of research on poverty, the Office of Economic Opportunity provided funds for an expansion of the Current Population Survey in the spring of 1966 and 1967 for a Survey of Economic Opportunity. Detailed questions were asked on income and assets, work experience, and a variety of other topics such as union membership. This sample was designed to permit estimates for blacks as well as whites.

Studies of labor-force behavior of four population groups over time, covering expectations and attitudes as well as standard items, have been conducted for the Department of Labor. The data are being collected by the Bureau of the Census and analyzed by Herbert Parnes at Ohio State University. The groups studied are young men and women 14 to 24 years old, women 30 to 44 years, and men 45 to 59 at the time of the first interview. This research seeks to trace for a five-year period the employment and unemployment experience, education, training, economic status, health, job attitudes, and many other facts that may explain how and why persons enter or leave the labor force, change jobs, and make other types of adjustments in their working lives.

Labor-Force Statistics from Decennial Census of Population

The decennial censuses since 1940 have provided information on the size and composition of the labor force for the nation, states, metropolitan areas, cities, counties, and small urban places. Prior to 1940, the census data were essentially limited to occupational inventories and some personal characteristics for individuals who were reported as "gainful workers," that is, persons with an occupation.

The most detailed statistics in the census volumes are for the country as a whole, for states, and for the larger areas within states. More information is given for the 1970 census than for 1960, largely because of greater computer capacity, just as the statistics for 1960 exceeded the output of the two previous censuses. In addition, access to the 1970 census tapes for further tabulations by interested buyers was made much easier.

Insofar as possible, the concepts, definitions, and classifications used in the census are the same as those used in the Current Population Survey. But some simplification of questions is necessary and some marginal groups are not measured because of the greater problems and costs of the mass census operation, much of it relying on self-enumeration. On the other hand, much greater detail in such fields as occupation and industry statistics, and for various cross-classifications by age, race, ethnic origin, residence, etc., is feasible with the larger samples used in the census.

Census Employment Survey

Following the completion of the 1970 census field work, the Census Employment Survey was conducted in sixty cities, and in groups of rural counties in four states. Samples of addresses were drawn in the "poverty areas" of these cities—the poverty areas having been established by the Census Bureau in cooperation with local groups, roughly on the basis of the poorest census tracts. The rural counties were selected as examples of poor rural areas, and the samples of households drawn on an "area" basis from maps and field listings.

The survey provides the usual labor-force information for those household members, plus many facts about work-seeking activities, education, training, earnings, transportation, child-care problems, and health—too numerous to have been included in the decennial census itself. A special feature of the survey is the interview with the person himself, instead of with any responsible member of the household.

This survey is modeled on an Urban Employment Survey in the slum areas of six cities (New York, Detroit, Chicago, Los Angeles, Atlanta, and Houston) conducted by the Bureau of the Census for the Bureau of Labor Statistics during fiscal years 1969 and 1970.

Labor-Force Statistics Based on Employer Reports— Nonagricultural Employment

A system of employment and earnings data, based on reports from samples of employers, began as a national enterprise in 1915. By the 1920s, the coverage of manufacturing industries was fairly complete, under a program of cooperative effort between the states and the Bureau of Labor Statistics (BLS). Gradual expansion of this effort resulted by 1937 in estimates for all industries except agriculture. A major factor in the expansion was the need for estimates of unemployment. In the absence of a direct measurement at that time, unemployment was estimated by subtracting employment as shown by these statistics from an estimated total labor force. In those years, the labor force was believed to change in size only as the population and its basic characteristics changed. This belief was shattered as the monthly labor-force statistics became available.

Originally, the estimates from the sample employers were adjusted to the statistics based on the industrial censuses. The requirement of employer reports to the federal government in connection with the Social Security program for old age and survivors' insurance and to the various state governments under the unemployment insurance laws made it possible to shift to these much more timely anchoring points.

In the interest of economy and of reduction in demands upon employers, the establishment-based program became a cooperative effort of the BLS and state agencies (primarily state employment security agencies affiliated with the U. S. Training and Employment Service, formerly the Bureau of Employment Security, in the Labor Department's Manpower Administration). The employer reports used for the BLS estimates also are used by the state for state and local area estimates. The state agencies mail the forms to the appropriate employers, edit them, and send on to the BLS the data required for the national series.

Monthly publications of the BLS present a statistical series on employees on nonagricultural payrolls in major industry divisions for the United States back to 1919; estimates of current payroll employment in great industrial detail—upward of 400 separate industry groups and subgroups; and estimates of current payroll employment in the major industry divisions for states and selected labor market areas. A series on job vacancies in manufacturing by industry and summary data for selected areas were published for the first time in October 1970; more detailed statistics were scheduled for publication.

Other important characteristics of current establishment employment —weekly hours and earnings, and turnover rates in specific industries and in states and areas—are provided.

The state agencies themselves compile and publish more detailed statistics for the state and major areas within states on employment levels in specific industries, hours, earnings, and similar data. In 1971, out of 230 Standard Metropolitan Statistical Areas, 209 had local data on current employment, hours, and earnings for detailed industry lists.

Agricultural Employment

Estimates of farm employment based on reports from over 25,000 farmers are published monthly by the Economic Research Service of the Department of Agriculture. They show total farm employment, number of family workers and hired workers, by states, with quarterly data on wage rates. Since there is a substantial amount of double counting of individuals working on more than one farm, these "establishment" reports provide somewhat higher estimates than those from the household survey in which a person is counted only once and in the job at which he worked longest in the survey week.

Labor-Force Statistics Based on Administrative Records

Unemployment Statistics Through the records of state unemployment insurance systems, numbers of persons drawing benefits for unemployment in covered industries are available every week for the United States, states, and individual labor markets (usually SMSA's). Numbers of persons filing their first claims in a period of unemployment, as well as those exhausting their benefits are also available. Claimants under nonstate systems (railroad retirement, ex-servicemen, and federal employees) are reported as well. These data are combined to furnish a rate of "insured unemployment," which is lower than the total unemployment rate from the Current Population Survey but generally follows the same pattern, after allowance for the different seasonal movements.

Because the insured part of the labor force does not include all persons who may be looking for work (e.g., persons from "uncovered" industries such as agriculture and private household work, or state and local government, new workers, persons reentering the labor force, those who have exhausted their benefits or have not yet accumulated sufficient rights in a benefit period or are ineligible for other reasons), the estimates of total unemployment are prepared for states and local labor markets, using a number of estimating steps, to build up the count of insured unemployed. These are produced every month in 150 major labor areas, and are published locally as well as in the Department of Labor publication *Area Trends in Employment and Unemployment*. Unemployment thus estimated, combined with total employment estimated largely from establishment reports gives an estimated "work force" to which the unemployment figure is related, and from which an unemployment rate is computed.

This effort was initiated during Word War II and has been considerably expanded and refined since then. Thus, the insurance system provides two unemployment rates—one a rate of *insured* unemployment, the second, a rate of *total* unemployment that is as consistent as possible with the concepts of the household survey approach. The second is most useful in state and individual area programs.

Work History Records The Social Security Administration of the Department of Health, Education and Welfare maintains a 1 percent sample of all persons who have Social Security account numbers and have been employed in industries covered by the system. The person's age, sex, and race are recorded when he applies for a number. Into the file are placed his earnings and industry each calendar quarter that he remains in a covered job. The file also contains information on the geographic location of place of employment. In this manner, records for about 90 percent of the employed are maintained—a vast body of data on job mobility, for states and localities, as well as for the United States. This is in addition to the comprehensive statistics on employment and earnings from the operation of the system.

Data on Scientific and Technical Manpower Statistics on scientific and technical personnel are analyzed by the National Science Foundation. The data come from its own National Register, statistical surveys for its use conducted by the Bureau of Labor Statistics, other surveys, and other sources such as the decennial censuses.

Other Data Sources

The preceding sections attempt to cover the major systems of labor-force statistics. Important sources of data that have other major aims are the National Health Survey of the Public Health Service (see Chapter 3) which relates health and disability to employment status, occupation, and income; surveys of the aged by the Social Security Administration [the first in 1963, the second in 1968, based on interviews with samples of beneficiaries and other persons 65 years and over (see Chapter 7)] which examine the economic characteristics of this population group; and a longitudinal survey of persons aged 50 to 63 in 1969 to trace retirement processes—the Longitudinal Retirement History Survey, also conducted by the Social Security Administration, as is a Survey of New Beneficiaries (workers newly retired)—to find out about their reasons for leaving their last job, their earnings, coverage by other pensions, and similar data.

USES OF DATA

The General Public

The general public "uses" labor-force statistics, like many other statistics, to form political opinions, to judge the state of the economy, to learn about the magnitude of changes in society which have attracted attention through individual experience. To a large extent, the public is a secondary user, the various news media being primary users, selectors, conveyors, and interpreters.

The overall unemployment rate is considered by business-cycle watchers to be one of the most important economic indicators, and its changes in critical periods make headline news. Following on this, the unemployment figures and rates also have important political uses as indications of the success or failure of the administration in power to deal with a problem which, since the Great Depression of the 1930s, has had top priority in every country. Rising unemployment in 1960 and 1970 as measured by these figures undoubtedly affected election results in both years.

A good example of public use was the controversy at the end of 1970. The efforts of the government in 1969 and 1970 to reduce inflation without an intolerable rise in unemployment were judged by the news media and then by the public by the national unemployment figures. Estimates of unemployment in specific areas and states prepared by the State Employment Offices may have even greater impact on public opinion than do the national figures, since they give support to what is known locally through personal experience or through news stories about specific layoffs.

The growing sophistication of the press in reporting the monthly labor-force figures has helped to educate the public on the differences in unemployment, particularly the higher rates for blacks than for whites and the extreme rates for black youth. This awareness has helped to gain support for special training and employment programs for disadvantaged elements of the population.

In addition to the data on unemployment, other labor-force statistics used to educate or influence the public include those relevant to the general civil rights movement, to the problems of ethnic minority groups, and to the women's liberation crusade. For example, the occupations and earnings of blacks or Mexican-Americans or Puerto Ricans contrasted with those of whites or of men compared with women, provide measurements of social and sex discrimination in our society.

Whether or not labor-force statistics affect individual behavior is debatable. They have shown, for example, great increases in the number and proportion of married women working outside the home and a great expansion in part-time employment. When an individual woman starts to look for a part-time job, the news item that there are 6 million women working part-time may help convince her family that this is appropriate for her, too. Probably, however, the telling argument is not national numbers but the specific want ads together with the friends who are enjoying part-time work and the extra money it brings.

Government

Apart from their use as economic indicators, labor-force statistics now are used mainly by government in connection with manpower programs. These programs, which are numerous, are generally joint responsibilities of federal and state or local bodies.

National Goal One of the few American national goals contained in legislation is that stated in the Employment Act of 1946: that it is the federal government's responsibility to use all practicable means to create and maintain conditions under which "there will be afforded useful employment opportunities, including self-employment, for those able, willing and seeking to work, and to promote maximum employment, production and purchasing power."

That 1946 act also provided for a Council of Economic Advisors to the President. A major responsibility of the council is to prepare the annual

President's Economic Report which was required by the same legislation. This is transmitted to the Congress, where it is reviewed by the Joint Economic Committee of the Senate and House, partially in hearings where expert testimony of other persons is solicited. The Joint Economic Committee then prepares its own report on the recommendations and content of the president's report.

Essential to these policy deliberations and determinations are the labor-force statistics, which measure how close the nation has come to the employment goal. Because they provide not only national total measurements, but also statistics for numerous population subgroupings, they are very useful for diagnosis of the situation and projections to the future. In other words, they serve as measurements of the health of the economy, and also as tracers of changing problems within elements of the population —youth, blacks, older workers, slum residents, the poor, women, etc.

General Economic Indicators The unemployment rate, based on interviews with sample households in selected areas—ranging from 41 areas in 1940 to 449 in 1970—can be regarded as a statistical miracle. It is compiled and published rapidly each month and has an uncanny power to reflect the cyclical changes in the total economy. For this reason, the unemployment rate is featured in the Congress's Joint Economic Committee's publication *Economic Indicators;* and in the Department of Commerce's *Business Conditions Digest.* In the latter, it is included as an indicator along with the unemployment rate for married men, both from the Current Population Survey and the average weekly rate of insured unemployment. For analysis of the business cycle these are called roughly "coincident" indicators, a category which also includes total nonagricultural employment from the household survey and man-hours and employees in nonagricultural establishments.

"Leading indicators"—those which move down or up early in the contraction and expansion phases in the business cycle—include from establishment reports average overtime hours worked, the average work week of production workers in manufacturing, and the accession and layoff rate in manufacturing. Initial claims for state unemployment insurance benefits are also leading indicators as they show new spells of unemployment.

"Lagging indicators," those that move up and down late in the business cycle, include the percent of the labor force that has been looking for work for fifteen weeks or more.

Indicators for Specific Localities As has been noted above, unemployment estimates for specific areas are based on unemployment insurance figures and estimates of local total employment, largely based on establishment data. These estimates are used to classify by level of unemployment 150 major areas and, thus, to guide the allocation of certain types of federal contracts. Several hundred smaller areas also are classified by unemployment level when they have substantial unemployment. The classification scheme is as follows:

Areas of substantial unemployment
Unemployment in the area is—
1. Six percent or more of the work force, discounting seasonal or temporary factors, and
2. It is anticipated that the rate of unemployment during the next two months will remain at 6 percent or more, discounting temporary or seasonal factors.

Areas of persistent unemployment
Areas (labor market areas, usually SMSA's) or cities of 250,000 or more, or counties, where unemployment has averaged 6 percent or more during the most recent calendar year and the rate has—
1. Averaged 6 percent or more and has been at least 50 percent above the national average for three of the four preceding calendar years; or
2. Averaged 6 percent or more and has been at least 75 percent above the national average for two of the three preceding calendar years; or
3. Averaged 6 percent or more and has been at least 100 percent above the national average for one of the two preceding years.

In addition to these classifications based on unemployment rates, the Department of Labor has designated areas of concentrated unemployment or underemployment (in 141 cities, parts or all of 163 counties, 31 Indian reservations, and Puerto Rico, in October 1970). These include all places participating in the department's "Concentrated Employment Program," a "coordinating mechanism designed to combine individual manpower programs into a comprehensive system of services and to concentrate the impact of these programs on specific urban slum neighborhoods or impoverished areas" (*Manpower Report of the President*). The designated sections of cities also include all "target areas" under the "Model Cities" program of the Department of Housing and Urban Development, plus Indian reservations of 4000 or more population.

Federal Procurement Preferences Firms are eligible for preference in federal procurement programs under Defense Manpower Policy No. 4 (revised) if they agree to employ a stated percentage of their newly hired workers each month from among the disadvantaged residents of areas with one or another of the above designations. "Disadvantaged" persons are those who are poor and, also, one of the following: (1) a school dropout; (2) under 22 years of age; (3) 45 years or older; (4) handicapped; or (5) subject to special obstacles to employment resulting from any other factor such as being a member of a minority.

Firms in areas of substantial or persistent unemployment are also eligible for preference under the Buy American Act.

Public Works and Economic Development Act, 1965 Areas of *persistent unemployment* are recommended to the Department of Commerce for designation as "redevelopment areas." Areas of *substantial unemployment* are also eligible for public-works grants and development facilities if they were so classified during the preceding calendar year.

Trigger Figures for Extended Unemployment Benefits Under the Employment Security Amendments of 1970, P. L. 91–373, a program of extended benefits (beyond the state legal maximum number of weeks) shall be triggered when the seasonally adjusted rate of *insured* unemployment equals or exceeds 4.5 percent in each of the three most recent months. The trigger is "off" when the unemployment rate drops below 4.5 percent in each of three consecutive months. (The rate was 4.5 percent in November 1970 for the first time since 1963.)

In an individual state, the trigger is "on" when its insured unemployment rate averages 4 percent for any consecutive thirteen-week period, and is 20 percent higher than the average rate for the corresponding thirteen-week period in each of two preceding years.

The extended benefit period begins with the third week after a week for which there is a national "on" indicator or a state "on" indicator, whichever happens first.

The federal government reimburses each state for one-half the cost of the extended benefits.

Manpower Development and Training Act of 1962 Massive increased use of labor-force statistics by the government began with the Manpower Program of 1962. The body of data accumulated through the Current Population Survey and from other sources such as decennial censuses, state employment offices, and establishment statistics was the foundation for such use. What had seemed for the most part general purpose descriptive statistics to provide knowledge without any specific policy value all of a sudden became essential for program planning. Of course, many studies, governmental and private, and some extensive congressional committee investigations (e.g., the Special Senate Committee on Unemployment Problems, established in 1959 under the chairmanship of Senator Eugene J. McCarthy; the Subcommittee on Employment and Manpower of the Senate Committee on Labor and Public Welfare, chaired by Senator Joseph S. Clark in 1963; and the Joint Economic Committee almost annually) had examined the problem of persistent, high unemployment during the 1950s and early 1960s. Without repeating the arguments that were carried on in the committee hearings and documents, in learned journals, and among experts wherever gathered, one can summarize briefly: one school, chiefly monetary and fiscal economists in and out of government, contended that only an increase in total demand for goods and services could substantially reduce unemployment; the other school, chiefly labor economists, argued that the high level of unemployment was attributable to frictions in the labor market—that is, shifts from job to job, and the stranding of workers without needed current skills, education, and training. The tax cut of 1964 was a victory for the first group, and the Manpower Development and Training Act of 1962 was a victory for the second.

That act of 1962 authorized a national program of training for unemployed and underemployed workers, and specified the need for a large expansion in research to guide manpower policy and programs. Like the Employment Act of 1946, it required an annual report by the president to Congress and a report by the secretary of labor to the president on manpower requirements, resources, utilization, and training. The responsibility, on paper at least, was established for the whole network of problems of working life ranging from forecasts of total labor demand and supply to techniques for training the unskilled, uneducated welfare mother to get and hold a job. This was, perhaps, the first time, apart from war mobilization periods, that the United States set up anything that could be called a national manpower policy. This bill produced not only important programs but, also, stimulated public and legislative interest in labor problems and resulted in great expansion of statistical and research activity.

Each of the annual reports, and many of the policies they consider, are founded on labor-force statistics compiled by various levels of government or developed by research projects in the field of labor-force activity. Some examples of use of the labor-force statistics follow:

> The persistently high rate of unemployment among teen-agers pointed to a need for an enlarged program of youth training, which was achieved in the 1963 amendments to the act.
>
> The handicap of lack of basic education, repeatedly demonstrated by national data and by the experience of the training programs with individuals, led to the inclusion of basic education in the training plans.
>
> Sharp rises in unemployment statistics in the off-season for agricultural, construction, and certain other types of workers underlined the need for study

and action. Concentrating at first on the construction industry, the secretaries of labor and commerce undertook to find ways by which the federal, state, and local governments could reduce seasonal unemployment, chiefly through the contracting procedures. In 1968, heads of federal agencies were instructed by the President to follow certain procedures leading toward this objective.

Studies of persons not in the labor force, conducted chiefly by the Bureau of Labor Statistics, showed time and again that many people wanted regular jobs but were not looking for them because of ill health or disability—the chief reason for adult men—or because of family responsibilities—the chief reason for women. Ill health was much more frequent among black men and women. These findings have been useful in helping to direct executive and legislative attention to the need for child-care centers and better delivery of more adequate health services.

Studies of how out-of-school youth and laid-off workers look for jobs revealed sharply the great defects in the workings of the labor market. Accordingly, continuous efforts have been made to strengthen the federal-state employment service system, in particular its ability to help unemployed and disadvantaged workers with the new programs including store-front neighborhood offices in slum areas, and special services to rural residents. Also, the 1968 amendments to the act provided for a program using the most modern computer and communications methods to get job seekers and job opportunities together. By the end of 1970, job banks—essentially daily computer printouts of unfilled job orders—were in operation in seventy-six of the largest cities. In addition, different experimental and fully computerized systems are being tested in four states.

Continuing data on unemployment rates and the occupational distribution and earnings of black workers, dramatized by protest and other visible forms of unrest, have strengthened somewhat the governmental efforts to open up jobs to this minority group. Through the Civil Rights Act of 1964, executive orders dealing with federal government, its contractors, and subcontractors, and the Civil Service Commission, there has been some progress. Voluntary action by employers for reasons of public service, public relations, or need for workers in a tight labor market must also be credited.

Initially, emphasis was placed on vocational training in the traditional classes supported by federal grants to the state vocational system. The deficiencies of the vocational system in relation to existing job opportunities became clear to many who had previously been ignorant or uninterested. As a result, impetus was given in 1963 to a redesign of this system, and to some obvious improvements. For example, office occupations were made eligible for funds, and enrollment in classes in health-related occupations nearly doubled. New programs were started for young persons with special educational handicaps and given highest priority in the 1968 amendments to the Vocational Education Act.

Many other examples could be cited of policies that emerged from efforts to solve problems originally revealed by statistical data on some aspects of the labor force. Perhaps most noteworthy is the Family Assistance Plan, which specifically recognizes the magnitude of the problem of inadequate earnings as a cause of poverty. Until late in the decade of the 1960s, unemployment and unemployability were judged to have the highest priority. But the great number of year-round full-time workers whose earnings left their families below poverty levels pointed to the need for some form of income supplementation.

Altogether some twenty-four federally assisted manpower training and support programs are or have been in operation as of 1970 (e.g., Job Corps, Neighborhood Youth Corps, Work Incentive Program, Manpower Development and Training Administration). Very few, if any, were developed without some use of national or local labor-force statistics to define the scope and to measure their effectiveness in relation to need.

The Manpower Training Act of 1970 would have restructured and consolidated these programs, giving more authority to state and local governments. It contained a provision for increasing appropriations to the states when the national unemployment rate equals or exceeds 4.5 percent for three consecutive months, with further increases when the rate equals or exceeds 5 percent for three consecutive months. Although passed by the Congress the act was vetoed by the president. But it serves to indicate the direction in which the nation is heading.

Projections of Labor Demand and Supply   In addition to the use of labor-force statistics as tracers of problems and measures of progress, an increasingly important role is in the area of forecasts or projections. These range from national estimates of the size and age-sex composition of the labor force at some future date (color, educational attainment, and other variables also are provided) to forecasts of demand and supply for specific occupations such as elementary school teachers. The Bureau of Labor Statistics has a continuing program of such projections for the country as a whole, based on a variety of techniques (such as input-output analysis, matrices of industry and occupation statistics, and demographic techniques). Some states and labor market areas also prepare similar projections to guide their planning of vocational training, taxation, and employment service operations of all kinds. For use in specific job counseling and placement work, state employment offices prepare "area skill surveys" based chiefly on employer interviews which forecast demand for specific types of workers in local labor areas.

In several recent statutes, Congress has required that federally financed education and training programs be set up to meet specific local and regional manpower requirements which must be developed from projections: federal-state employment services are required to provide information on current and long-range needs by industry and occupation in order to (1) assess job opportunities under the "reasonable expectation of employment" clause of the Manpower Development and Training Act; (2) counsel and guide young people under the Economic Opportunity Act of 1964; (3) provide manpower information for community economic development under the Economic Development Act. State Boards of Vocational Education are required to take account of information about current and projected manpower needs in allocating funds under the Vocational Education Act of 1963.

The Council of Economic Advisors uses labor-force projections to estimate, both for the short and the long run, the number of jobs that will have to be provided by the economy to achieve full employment. The labor-force projections themselves may be based on the assumption of adequate growth in the economy. Again, the labor-force, occupation, and industry projections are used to develop other projections such as Gross National Product; income payments; income tax payments; demand for factors of production other than manpower, such as electric power, water, etc. Similar projections have been prepared for river basin areas (e.g., Delaware River basin) and other subregions (San Francisco Bay region, for example).

Another by-product of the projections, not strictly statistical, is a guide to employment prospects in a large variety of occupations. At the national level, this is contained in the Bureau of Labor Statistics publication, *Occupational Outlook Handbook,* which has wide distribution in the high schools of the country. Selected occupational guidance material also is prepared by the United States Employment and Training Service (formerly Bureau of Employment Security) of the Department of Labor.

The government is not the only source of projections. Many research groups such as the National Planning Association also are engaged in this activity, and also depend essentially on population and labor-force statistics for their ingredients.

Other Uses Space does not allow the enumeration of all the ways that labor-force statistics are used in the examination of many different governmental policy problems. One additional example might be cited, however. The extremely high unemployment rates of teen-agers in the United States, far higher than in any other industrialized country, have generated much concern in and out of the government. One possible cause that has been tentatively put forth is that federal and state minimum wage laws requiring rates of pay, which have been periodically increased, have priced young workers—inexperienced and untrained—out of the labor market. Employers, especially those in smaller communities, are unwilling or unable to pay such rates, and therefore do not hire young people. If this is so, then one solution might be to legislate lower minimum rates for new, young workers (as is done in the United Kingdom, for example).

A detailed study of the problem was completed in 1970 by the Bureau of Labor Statistics: *Youth Unemployment and Minimum Wages,* Bulletin 1657. This examined the changes in the labor-force status of young people —particularly their unemployment rates—in relation to demographic changes, school enrollment, military requirements, and shifts out of agriculture. A survey of hiring requirements in ten metropolitan areas was undertaken by mail and telephone follow-ups to get at other types of information. Its findings were that employers most frequently were reluctant to hire teen-agers because of legal restrictions on hiring youth for hazardous jobs, the military draft, their undependability, and their lack of training. Examination was made of the state experience with minimum wage differentials for youth and their effect on youth employment. A similar review showed the effect of youth wage rate schemes on youth employment in Western Europe, Canada, and Japan. The study concluded that increases in the level and coverage of the federal minimum wage, although hard to disentangle from other causes, probably had a small effect on the employment of youth. Legislation which permitted a *substantial* difference in rates for young workers—especially those 16 and 17 years old—would increase their employment prospects, but would be inconsistent with wage-setting institutions on the American scene. Clearly the mass of evidence assembled was not strong enough to justify the recommendation of a change in policy. Any further consideration of this question would have to take off from a new base of accumulated evidence.

Labor

Organized labor uses labor-force statistics in much the same way as the economists in the federal government do—to check on the performance of the economy; to evaluate (perhaps more critically) administration policy especially as it relates to the fluctuations in employment and unemployment; to estimate levels of employment that could be reached, and shortfall from such levels; and to document areas of need for special programs in relation to manpower. Representatives of labor testify before congressional committees on specific legislation, or before the Joint Economic Committee, and need as much or more than any group the facts about the working population. Labor union economists and spokesmen, being closer to the people who are subject to unemployment and underemployment, have been, in the past, consistently interested and engaged in the controversies over the measurement techniques. They have testified before technical review committees, congressional committees, and the like, and have been responsible for mobilizing opinion in favor of definitional changes that have slightly broadened the concepts. As an institution, labor has always provided support for expansions of statistical programs in this area.

Of more immediate day-to-day use are some of the establishment data on levels of employment in specific industries, and on earnings and hours worked. When an industry as defined by the Standard Industrial Classification is organized by a single union, the payroll data are especially pertinent to union planning and even to bargaining. Estimates of industry employment levels by state provide essential information on shifting locations of possible membership.

Of particular interest to labor union representatives are some of the special surveys conducted in connection with the Current Population Survey—those relating to annual income and earnings, to weeks worked, occupation, industry, and demographic factors; job mobility and length of time with current employer; overtime hours and premium pay; eligibility for pensions. One of the questions asked in the Survey of Economic Opportunity was union membership—repeated in the spring of 1971 as part of the Current Population Survey; this provides not only an estimate of the total who are members of labor unions, but information about their age, sex, race, average earnings over the year, employment status, residence, etc. Each union may know, or claim to know, these facts about their own membership, but until the 1966 survey, such data were not available anywhere for the movement as a whole. The further and great advantage is that many comparisons are possible with the unorganized segment of the labor force.

Business

The most common use of labor-force statistics by business is probably for economic indicators and for the purpose of evaluating governmental programs and performance. Judging from the prominence given the monthly unemployment figures in the financial pages of the regular press, and in business and financial journals (e.g., the *Wall Street Journal* regularly has a front-page chart and story), the reader must assume that this particular indicator is of prime importance to business. Many of the other series also are featured, particularly those listed earlier as leading cyclical indicators—overtime hours worked, initial claims for unemployment insurance, and layoff rates.

The more academic business journals, bank letters, and research groups prepare the same type of economic analyses and forecasts that are produced by the federal government, and use the labor-force data in much the same way. Labor-force and industry employment projections also are used quite intensively by some business economists as a framework for projecting the future course of their own segment of the economy and their market. (A favorite example is the manufacturer of work clothes who turned to the occupational and industry projections to determine the number of blue-collar workers who would need his product.)

Some use of data on the characteristics of the labor force and the size of the pool of unemployed is made in selecting new plant locations, although it is not clear how important this is in relation to other factors such as taxes, water supply, transportation costs, population size, level of education, and extent of union organization. There is some evidence, for example, that industries using a large proportion of women in their work force prefer to locate where there is a good supply of women *not* in the labor force whom they can easily recruit and train, rather than relying on already experienced workers who would need to be retrained and perhaps have higher wage expectations. On the other hand, there is no doubt that the expansion of certain types of industries requiring large proportions of highly skilled professional and technical personnel, such as the development of Route 128 establishments near Boston, Massachusetts, was due to the proximity of universities in the area, which could supply such persons.

As with labor, businesses in industries that are shown separately in the Standard Industrial Classification make use of the establishment statistics on employment, hours worked, earnings, extent of overtime, job vacancy and turnover rates, to compare their own records with those of the industry as a whole. In fact, statisticians for business enterprises constantly try to persuade the government to produce statistics that are relevant to their particular line, and therefore always are concerned with greater subclassifications and finer detail.

Businessmen want data for the communities in which their enterprises are located which would tell them the size and detailed characteristics of the available manpower pool in order to determine, among other things, how tight the labor market is and what their hiring policies and recruitment efforts need to be. They also want turnover statistics for specific industries in particular localities, for comparison with their own.

Students

Many of the labor-force statistics and publications analyzing them relate to the employment problems of students but it is doubtful that students, as such, are aware of this (unless, as thousands do, they are engaged in writing school papers or in research projects involving manpower problems, race and sex discrimination, unemployment, and the like).

Sources of information that are used, at least at the high school level, are the *Occupational Outlook Handbook* and the *Occupational Outlook Quarterly,* both published by the Bureau of Labor Statistics. The former is a compendium of information about the requirements, earnings, and probable demand for a host of individual occupations—professional, technical, clerical and sales, blue collar, and service. The *Quarterly* has current articles, usually based on recent surveys and research projects, which convey facts about salient manpower issues, job opportunities in broad terms, and related problems, written in a popular style for student education. For example, the 1970 fall issue carried an article on the projected demand and supply for women in professional occupations during the 1970s, emphasizing the sharp decline in opportunity for teaching, a field that has absorbed 40 percent of women professional workers. The Manpower Administration through the U. S. Training and Employment Service prepares guidance materials on particular occupations, such as *Job Guide for Young Workers, Career Guide for Demand Occupations,* and *Health Careers Guidance.*

At the community level, there are various programs of vocational guidance conducted by public employment services or vocational education personnel. Apparently they vary greatly in quality and effectiveness, but they all depend on some knowledge of local conditions and of growth trends in occupations. Much of the guidance is based on national projections of the size and composition of the labor force, developed at the federal level. For example, workshops for vocational educators sponsored and funded by the National Defense Education Act in the mid-1960s centered around the occupational information and projections current at the time.

At the graduate level, a burst of interest in manpower problems has occurred perhaps in some part as a result of the funds provided for research contracts and grants in the Manpower Development and Training Act (MDTA), the Economic Opportunity Act, and the Social Security Act. The original Manpower Act provided a directive to the secretary of labor to develop a comprehensive research program, as indicated earlier. About 1 percent of the cost of the MDTA training programs was reserved for funding research—amounting to many millions of dollars over the first eight years that the act was in effect. In February 1970, twelve universities were selected as centers for manpower research and the education of manpower specialists, and were given four-year grants amounting to $3,150,000 by the Department of Labor.

A catalog of these research projects and grants extends over more than 200 pages. It lists and describes active and completed research contracts under MDTA, the Economic Opportunity Act, and the Social Security Act; institutional grants, doctoral dissertation grants, and research grants under MDTA; and completed reports for 1963–1970. Faculty and students at more than 100 colleges and universities have received funds for research from these acts. With few exceptions, their work has involved the analysis and/or development of statistical or other types of data about the labor force and such problems as employment, occupational choice and training, work motivation, job discrimination, measurement techniques, labor market information, and related isues.

Educational Institutions and Educators

Perhaps more than any other type, educational institutions have "benefited" indirectly most from the public acceptance of the writings of labor-force statisticians—that the lack of a high school diploma and, indeed, a college degree is a major factor in low income, persistent joblessness, immobility in low-status jobs, and other handicaps in earning a living. This evidence, plus the social handicaps of little schooling, and the exemption provisions of the selective service system, probably have been primarily responsible for the extraordinary rise in the *rate* of college enrollment—over 60 percent of high school graduates now as compared with 50 percent at the start of the 1960s go on to college, according to the Office of Education.

During the 1960s, growing awareness of the issues of poverty, racial discrimination, women's rights, minority groups, and urban decay was naturally reflected in schools and colleges, and generated attention, if not formal courses, in these areas of concern. Discussion and examination of the information relevant to the problems focused interest on labor-force statistics not previously exceeded since the days of the Great Depression. Data on employment and unemployment, earnings, types of job opportunities, and progress or lack of it over time was the starting point. As indicated earlier, the stimulus to research provided by government action programs also had its effect through educational institutions.

One area of education that has reputedly ignored labor-force data until fairly recently has been the vocational education in the public schools, financed heavily through grants to states by the federal government to support training in specified occupational categories. For years, the emphasis was on agriculture, despite the long-run downward trend in employment in this industry, and on home economics, even though the proportion of women working outside the home was rising fast. With the Vocational Education Act of 1963 and the amendments of 1968, recognition was given to the need for updating. The first legislation allowed for training in all occupations except those requiring four or more years of education. As a consequence, both high school and postsecondary enrollments increased markedly, especially in the newly approved fields of office education, and in health occupations training. Increased cooperation with the Employment Service also was achieved as a result of the act.

The 1968 act, taking account of the changes recommended by the National Advisory Council on Vocational Education, required that higher priority be given to the needs of the disadvantaged and the mentally and physically handicapped. Greater emphasis is also to be placed on postsecondary education and to continuing education for persons of all ages to keep up with changes in occupational requirements. To what extent this has been an added impetus to the growth of community colleges and technical institutes cannot be determined.

Minority Groups

Testimony of the importance now given statistics by minority groups is the pressure they exert upon data collectors for information about themselves—blacks, Mexican-Americans, Puerto Ricans, American Indians, Asians, and others. Not too many years ago, in contrast, Negro organizations were opposing the racial designation in any public record or statistical operation, and, of course, they still are for job applications.

Economic data, particularly relating to income, earnings, types of jobs, and unemployment experience, are used by organizations representing these groups to measure progress and discrimination, for their activities directing public opinion and exerting political pressure. The Urban League, for example, fully exploits the census data and the Current Population Survey findings and, indeed, took many steps during the 1970 census field collection operations to try to improve the coverage of the black population. One of this organization's major contributions was overcoming some of the opposition to the census expressed by the more militant groups which professed to see the operation as part of a program leading up to genocide. The league also is engaged continually in trying to upgrade black employment, even through individual actions, and therefore needs the occupational and earnings data and projections.

Government-sponsored groups which make demands on the statistical establishment for all types of data are the Cabinet Committee on Opportunity for Spanish-Americans, the National Council on Indian Opportunity (which wants a data bank in addition to employment and income data for separate tribes), and the Indian Health Service at the Department of Health, Education and Welfare. The Bureau of Indian Affairs in the Department of the Interior is, of course, a prime consumer. The National

Conference on Indian Awareness, among private groups, also wants a data bank, and organizations of urban Indians are active as data seekers.

Japanese-Americans have the Japanese-American Citizens' League, Japanese Community Youth Council, and, along with other Asian groups, the Council of Oriental Organizations. In general, they seek to encourage social and economic planning for the communities or neighborhoods in which the disadvantaged members of their group live.

Women

Beginning during World War II, the steady and sometimes spectacular increases in the employment of women, despite marriage and baby booms, have fascinated public and private personnel including all types of social scientists. The system of labor-force statistics has reflected these trends and has been continuously extended to provide greater detail. In fact, a catalog of such statistics would now have "by sex" after almost every title. Consequently when women were urged to look at the labor-force problems of their sex, they found an abundance of data—becoming more abundant with every passing year.

Women's organizations of all kinds use the labor-force statistics. The Women's Bureau of the Department of Labor has for many years popularized the findings of various censuses and surveys originally in the interests of trade unions with women members, who were steady consumers. Business and professional women's organizations, the American Association of University Women, and more recently, the many groups that have arisen with the women's liberation movement are other examples. Major public bodies set up to look at discrimination against women in the labor market whose reports were founded on labor-force statistics include the President's Commission on the Status of Women, appointed by President Kennedy in 1961; the Task Force on Labor Standards of the Citizen's Advisory Council on the Status of Women; and the Equal Opportunity Commission.

The principal issues on which labor-force statistics provide light and ammunition are equal pay for equal work; equal opportunity and access to jobs and promotions; equal opportunity for training, for education in any field, for managerial, and supervisory positions. In both professional and nonprofessional occupations, women often are passed over for training and promotion because they are believed to be temporary workers in whom it is not worth making an investment. Employers, and perhaps many female employees too, have not yet come to realize that the majority of women, even married women, who work, are in the labor force the year round.

As in other areas of social tension, young scholars are choosing the problem of women's rights for study and making wider use of the data that have been compiled. This will give impetus, in the end, to demands for more and better data.

The Aged

Agencies and organizations working on the problems of the aged are generally concerned about adequacy of income, medical care, housing, and quality of life, rather than their place in the labor market. A major exception is discrimination in hiring because of age, but this relates to discrimination at age 40 or 45, not to the truly aged.

The problems of the "older worker" have received great attention during the last several decades, for although their unemployment rates have not been excessively high, they have suffered from long stretches of joblessness once they were out of work, and have faced barriers in seeking new jobs. Early retirement, which has many other causes, has often been a way out; the labor-force participation rates of men 55 or more—i.e., older men—which have been falling rather steadily, are evidence of this.

In 1964, the Civil Rights Act was passed, reflecting in part the work of the President's Council on Aging. This act directed that a study be made by the secretary of labor on problems faced by older workers. The study (U. S. Department of Labor, 1965) provided detailed information on the job handicaps of this group. By 1967, enough support was generated, and the Age Discrimination in Employment Act was passed. This makes it illegal for employers of twenty-five or more persons in industries affecting interstate commerce to deprive anyone aged 40 through 64 of his employment opportunities because of age. Employment agencies and labor unions also are forbidden to discriminate. The act calls for research and educational programs related to employment of older workers but funds have so far been insufficient for this effort.

The Manpower Administration has stepped up the activities of the state employment offices so that placements of older workers have shown some increase. It also allotted 20 percent of the training slots in MDTA programs to older workers in 1966; only about half of these have been used, probably because these workers tend to resist retraining and employers continue to resist taking them on. Other programs aimed at the older group have had proportionally greater success but have not had much impact in terms of numbers.

In summary, labor-force statistics have certainly been one of the intelligence items that have helped to delineate problems of senior citizens, to direct attention to them, and to influence policies and programs designed to deal with them.

The Social Security Administration has responsibility within the federal government for those who are aged chronologically. Studies conducted by this agency have shown the importance of some form of employment for income and morale maintenance among the able-bodied, and have doubtlessly helped to raise the maximum earnings provisions of beneficiaries under the law.

OUTLOOK FOR THE DATA

Although federal budgetary restrictions operate to hold back increase in volume and scope of federal programs of labor-force statistics, as will the scarcity of other public and private funds, there is every reason to think that the inevitable needs of programs for alleviation of unemployment and poverty, for manpower utilization, and for economic growth will, in the long run, lead to further statistical expansion. The proposed "New Federalism" pointed to greater responsibility for planning and administration of social and economic programs by the states and, through them, local governments. The current demand for data of this kind below the federal level is already very strong; in fact, much legislation now assumes that such data are available and that the only requirement is that the statistics should be used. Actually, often only crude approximations to adequate statistics exist, and they would not stand scrutiny under a bright light. Nothing is so much needed in this field as a comprehensive system of labor market information on a state and local basis. The establishment of this goal in the 1968 amendments to the Manpower Act may generate new support and effect some progress.

The wave of interest in manpower research cannot be expected to subside. The 1970 census has provided material for some years to come, as has the Current Population Survey. Unfortunately, neither of these sources is geared to providing the kind of insight on psychosociological factors that private or academic research is better suited to do. Understanding of causes and cures of the individual's inability to accommodate to labor market requirements, even when his need is great and demand is strong, is far from adequate.

Programs that are in the initial stages, such as the collection of detailed occupation statistics from employers, or those that have been temporarily shelved, such as the expansion of the CPS sample to obtain regular, badly needed data on the economic problems of minority groups, will, it is hoped, be expanded or revived.

Apart from program-oriented research, the last decade has seen the development of new interest among social scientists in analyzing labor supply and demand by means of more sophisticated techniques including econometric models. Need for input for their models has turned their attention to the need for more detailed labor-force statistics not previously of much concern to them. The economists' and other social scientists' establishments may, therefore, be expected to add its pressure to that of other consumers to the drive for more data.

In short, whatever the outlook for the supply of statistics may be, the demand for additional and better labor-force data is certainly unprecedented and can only continue to increase.

REFERENCES

Manpower Report of the President. Washington, D. C.: Government Printing Office, 1974, annual.

U. S. Bureau of Labor Statistics. *Occupational Outlook Handbook.* Washington, D. C.: Government Printing Office, annual.

———. *Occupational Outlook Quarterly.* Washington, D. C.: Government Printing Office, quarterly.

———. *Youth Unemployment and Minimum Wages.* Washington, D. C.: Government Printing Office, 1970.

U. S. Council of Economic Advisors. *Economic Indicators.* Washington, D. C.: Government Printing Office, monthly.

U. S. Department of Commerce. *Business Conditions Digest.* Washington, D. C.: Government Printing Office, monthly.

U. S. Department of Labor. *Area Trends in Employment and Unemployment.* Washington, D. C.: Government Printing Office, biennial.

———. *The Older American Worker—Age Discrimination in Employment.* Report of the Secretary of Labor to the Congress under Section 715 of the Civil Rights Act of 1964. Washington, D. C.: Government Printing Office, 1965.

CHAPTER 7

On Social Security and Welfare*

WHAT THE PROGRAMS DO

One of the important functions of any society is helping those who are unable to provide for themselves: the aged, the sick, the disabled, the widowed, and orphaned or deserted children. In primitive societies, these functions are carried out by the tribe or the extended family. For centuries in Western society, the church played an important role in assisting those in need. Increasingly, in the last few decades, this function has been taken over by governments. In the United States, two major sets of public programs have been created to fill this need: the Social Security system and public assistance (often called "welfare"). Both Social Security and welfare had their genesis as federal programs in the great depression, but both have been greatly expanded and altered in the intervening decades.

Social Security was originally an extension of the concept of insurance against risk of income loss. It was modeled on private insurance and pension schemes, although the public system differs in many respects from its private analogs. Under Social Security, everyone who is employed in "covered employment" (now almost all jobs) is required to have a Social Security account distinguished by a Social Security number. A percentage of his paycheck is deducted by his employer, and a like amount is added by the employer and forwarded to the federal government for crediting

---

* Based on a memorandum by Alice M. Rivlin and Robert D. Reischauer, formerly of the U. S. Department of Health, Education and Welfare.

to that employee's account. After the employee has been covered for a certain number of quarters, he is eligible for benefits if he becomes disabled or upon retirement, and his survivors are eligible for benefits if he dies. The amount that a beneficiary receives is related to the amount the employee has paid. Over the years, however, Congress has raised the benefits above the levels implied by amounts paid, and has changed the ratio of benefits to amounts paid, primarily to improve the lot of the aged poor. People employed in occupations newly covered have been awarded the benefits to which they would have been entitled if they had been covered during their working lives, and all individuals aged 72 and over have been "blanketed in" so that they may receive benefits even though they would not otherwise have been entitled to them. Hence, the Social Security system has drifted away from its original resemblance to an insurance or pension system, and has become one of the ways in which the current working generation ensures a better life for older people, especially those who would otherwise be living in acute poverty.

When the Social Security system was created, it was expected eventually to reduce poverty drastically by maintaining the income of the aged, the disabled, and survivors—as indeed it has. It was recognized, however, that poverty would persist among those who were not yet covered, and also that some people were poor for other reasons, such as desertion, unemployment, or low productivity often associated with minority-group status. To help states and localities meet part of this need, Congress created the public assistance system. The federal government was authorized to pay part of the cost of state assistance programs in specified amounts for certain categories of poor people. Current federally aided public assistance programs are Old Age Assistance (OAA), Aid to the Blind (AB), Aid to the Permanently and Totally Disabled (APTD), and Aid to Families with Dependent Children (AFDC). The last program is primarily for mothers with children and no male breadwinner, but some families with disabled or unemployed fathers are included. Not all the poor are covered by these federally aided public assistance programs, so the states have sometimes, at their own expense, extended aid to other poor persons (these programs are known as General Assistance).

Public assistance is only one of the programs that provide aid to the poor. Others include the Food Stamp Program, administered by the Department of Agriculture, Medicaid and other programs which pay for medical care of the poor, public housing, and the entire range of job training and similar programs. Only public assistance will be considered here.

REASONS FOR NEEDING STATISTICS

Public assistance and Social Security programs have grown rapidly over the years, especially in the last decade. Between 1960 and 1970, federal outlays for Social Security benefits (not including Medicare) rose from about $12 billion to $30 billion, and those for public assistance rose from $2 billion to over $4 billion. In 1971, approximately 20 percent of the population received benefits from either Social Security or public assistance or both. The two programs together account for approximately 21 percent of the proposed federal budget for fiscal year 1972. Since the programs are of this magnitude, affecting so many people and taking such a high proportion of public resources, it is clearly important to know something about them. Several major questions need to be answered, and several different kinds of statistics and analysis are useful: (1) How are these programs operating? (descriptive statistics); (2) How well are they meeting their objectives? (evaluative statistics); (3) How could these programs be improved? (statistics for analysis of alternative policies).

Several different groups of people are particularly interested in these questions and statistics: (1) program managers who must monitor the operation of the particular program; (2) beneficiaries and their representatives and lobbyists who would like a basis for proposals to increase or improve the programs; (3) policy makers in the executive and legislative branches of the government who need a basis for deciding how to change the programs; (4) students and scholars interested in learning how society works and in providing an analytical basis for policy recommendations.

To meet these various needs, a mass of statistics has been collected over the years about Social Security and welfare. Much of it has been analyzed and published. Some of it has proved useful, some of it has not; and there are many gaps in the data and in our knowledge about these programs and their effects. In the materials which follow these data are described and some of their uses and limitations are discussed.

For the most part, the Social Security and welfare systems are discussed separately because they differ in two major ways. First, the Social Security system is a federal program with records maintained at the national level; welfare, by contrast, is primarily administered by state and local governments with some federal financial contribution and some federal reporting requirements. Second, under Social Security, continuous records are maintained on the same person over his working life; but under welfare, the unit of statistical collection is the "case." Records are kept on cases until they are closed, but there is no procedure for keeping track of individuals as they come on and off the welfare rolls over their lifetimes. These program differences make for dissimilar problems of data collection and analysis.

SOCIAL SECURITY STATISTICS

The Social Security system operates like a huge national insurance company. It assigns each participant in the system a number (sometimes accidentally individuals end up with more than one number), and maintains an individual record for each person in the labor force over his working lifetime. A continuous record is kept of the amounts paid in on behalf of this person. If he dies, retires, or becomes disabled, computations are quickly made of the amount of benefit to which he is entitled. Once he (or his survivors) are established as beneficiaries of the system, records are kept of the amounts paid out to them over the years. Keeping track of all these transactions in a nation of this size is a massive operation which strains the capacity of even modern computers.

The major source of Social Security statistics is the system itself. Individual records are aggregated, and statistics are computed showing the characteristics of the beneficiary population, amounts paid out under different programs, the average size of benefits, the average size of contributions, and so forth. Many of these statistics are published regularly in the *Social Security Bulletin* and other sources.

For particular purposes, special samples are often drawn from the beneficiary population in order to answer particular questions. For example, one might be interested in the characteristics of recipients of minimum benefits or in what is happening to the average age of retirement.

Surveys of the population at large or segments of it (for example, the aged population) also yield information on Social Security beneficiaries and how they compare to nonbeneficiaries.

Descriptive Statistics and Their Use

Clearly, the managers of the Social Security program need to know something about the system for which they are responsible. They need to know how many claims are being processed in order to distribute the workload. They need to analyze past trends in order to project future costs of the system. Increasing longevity, for example, would tend to lengthen the period over which benefits had to be paid and make the system more expensive in the future. Declines in death rates during the working years, however, would reduce the expected future payments to survivors of insured persons.

Not only the program managers, but the general public and their representatives also, need an idea of where Social Security funds are going, how much is being collected, what the net fiscal impact of the system is on the economy and the federal budget, how many beneficiaries there are, what kind, and what benefits they are receiving.

The beneficiaries themselves and their organizations also need an idea of what is happening to average benefits. Are they rising as fast as the cost of living, for example? If they are not, the case for increases is more cogent.

Evaluative Statistics

Descriptions are indeed interesting but more importance attaches to evaluative questions: How good is the Social Security system? What proportion of the aged are covered and how adequate are their benefits? How many of those covered would otherwise be poor?

For these types of questions, the information generated by the Social Security system itself is often insufficient. It has to be combined with other information on the population as a whole or the aged portion. For example, a sample survey can be made of the aged population, as was done in 1962, and detailed information obtained by interview and questionnaire. When the information from the survey is processed, it is then possible to identify those receiving Social Security benefits and those not receiving them. The proportion of the population receiving benefits can be estimated and comparisons made between those who are covered and those who are not. Detailed data on sources of income permit estimates of the importance of Social Security in the total income of the aged. They also permit estimates of how many people would be poor if it were not for Social Security. These estimates, of course, should be interpreted with care. For millions of beneficiaries, Social Security is the principal or sole source of income in retirement. Not all of these people, however, would be poor if the system were abolished or had never been created. Some of them would have accumulated more savings through other means, would have continued working, or would have been absorbed into other nonpoor families.

Statistics for Analysis of Policy Alternatives

The question, "How good is the Social Security system?" of course, is a relative one. It can only be answered by looking at alternatives to the present system and seeing how much they would cost and how effective they would be in maintaining the income of beneficiary groups. One of the most important uses, therefore, of Social Security statistics is in estimating the costs and effects of changes in the system.

Sometimes these estimates are relatively easy to make. For example, estimating the cost of a 10 percent increase in benefit levels is fairly easy since the present structure of benefits is known. It is also possible to estimate how many more people would be lifted out of poverty by a 10 percent increase if fairly recent information is available on the joint distribution of income and Social Security benefits of various sizes in the aged population.

More difficult problems involve estimating the effects of changes in the system that are likely to alter the behavior of participants. For example, proposals often are made to lower the retirement age in the Social Security system. To evaluate the costs and effect of such a change, one would like estimates of how many people would take advantage of the early retirement possibility. It may be possible to extrapolate from past experience (other times at which the retirement age has been lowered), but one would not do this with great confidence.

Similarly, proposals often are made to increase the amount of income that beneficiaries are allowed to earn without losing their Social Security benefits (liberalizing the retirement test). Evaluating this proposal involves having a basis for estimating the extent to which retirees would actually take advantage of the opportunity to earn additional wages. Again, extrapolation from past experience is possible but not very reliable since wages, work opportunities, and attitudes toward work change over time. One might have more confidence in a national experiment—liberalizing the retirement test for a sample of beneficiaries and seeing what happened—but this type of experimental unequal treatment is generally not considered feasible in the context of the Social Security system.

Social Security statistics have proved useful in evaluating policy changes which have absolutely nothing to do with Social Security itself. The reason for this is that the Social Security records are a unique repository of work histories of individuals. The existence of the Social Security number makes it possible to match Social Security records with other official records such as tax forms or military service records. Matching these official records by means of a Social Security number has made possible some studies that never could have been done otherwise. For example, studies have matched military training records with Social Security work histories in order to determine the effect of military training on earnings and employment history of military personnel after they return to civilian life.

Useful as it is, the possibility of matching several official records on the same individual by means of his Social Security number is a frightening one to many people. They do not want to live in a society which maintains complete dossiers on all individuals. The Social Security Administration has, in fact, been extremely careful about the confidentiality of its records. It does not release these records to anyone in identifiable form. Nevertheless, the fear remains and has, in some instances, led to political opposition to use of the Social Security number. For example, for political reasons, Social Security numbers were not asked of respondents on the 1970 census. Thus, the possibility of matching census questionnaires with Social Security records was lost for this decade.

THE VALUE AND USE OF WELFARE STATISTICS

The Welfare System

The welfare system provides cash and in-kind assistance, social services, training and job referrals to a limited number of low-income persons through a variety of programs. The better known of these are the categorical forms of public assistance—Aid to Families with Dependent Children, Old Age Assistance, Aid to the Blind, and Aid to the Permanently and Totally Disabled—which were established under the aegis of the Social Security Act of 1935 or its subsequent amendments. Sometimes included in the term "welfare" are the Food Stamp Program which is administered by the U. S. Department of Agriculture (USDA), General Assistance (GA) which is a wholly state and locally supported cash assistance program, Medicaid and the other programs which pay for the medical care of the poor, and the entire panoply of job training programs.

Unlike Social Security, these programs do not operate uniformly throughout the nation. This is because the welfare system consists of a patchwork of similar—but not identical—state programs rather than a single federal system. While the states must establish and administer each program, a considerable degree of financial and administrative responsibility is shared by both the federal and local levels of government. The basic outlines of all but the General Assistance programs are specified by federal legislation which must be adhered to at least nominally to secure federal financial participation. Payment levels and most eligibility requirements are determined by the states which also are required by federal law to finance part of the costs of most programs. The actual decisions on whether assistance is to be granted to an applicant and the determination of the distribution of social services are usually the responsibility of the local or district welfare office. This office may be a division of local government in one state or a branch of a state welfare agency in another. In some states local taxpayers are required to share part of the financial burden of supporting welfare programs.

This complex division of responsibility and the lack of uniformity which it has spawned have had an important impact on the types of social welfare statistics that have been collected and their overall usefulness.

Welfare Statistics

All three levels of government—federal, state, and local—collect information pertaining to the welfare system. Due to the nature of this system the information flows from the bottom to the top—from local offices to the state agency and from there to the Department of Health, Education and Welfare in Washington. Only the data that are requested are transmitted upward. Since each successively higher level of government depends entirely upon the next lower level for its information, that which is not collected at the local level remains unknown at the top. The federal welfare statistics in a sense, therefore, represent the lowest common denominator of the types of information collected and aggregated by a diverse set of state and local welfare bureaucracies.

The federal agency whose responsibility it is to collect and aggregate social welfare statistics is the National Center for Social Statistics (NCSS). Most of the information it collects is published in one or another of its forty-one recurrent statistical reports. Unfortunately, these reports are relatively inaccessible since they are distributed almost exclusively to state welfare agencies. From 1963 to 1970, however, almost all of these data also were published in the statistical section of *Welfare In Review*. Moreover, a handful of the more basic statistics has been available in the *Social Security Bulletin* since 1938.

The welfare statistics published by the federal government can be grouped into three categories: those that indicate how the individual programs are operating, those that characterize the beneficiaries of these programs, and finally, those that seek to be useful in answering the many unanswered questions of policy makers endeavoring to evaluate or improve the welfare system.

The type of statistics included in the first category have been collected since the inception of the current welfare system in 1937. Among the indices of program operations that are currently available are:

1. The number of recipients and aid cases by program
2. The average benefit per recipient or case by program
3. The number of cases opened and closed by program
4. The primary reasons for case openings and closings by program
5. The number of applications for assistance acted upon and the number approved by program
6. The number of welfare recipients referred to manpower training agencies
7. The total amount expended for assistance payments, administration, services, and training
8. The sources of these funds (federal, state, and local)
9. The number of cases receiving social services

Of course, these by no means exhaust the list. Information also is published on the characteristics and cost standards of the various programs in each state, the staff and personnel levels of state Departments of Welfare, and so on.

Most of the information described above is available on a state-by-state basis. Since some states have chosen not to have certain programs there are understandable gaps in the data. The number of cases and recipients and the total amount of money payments for each of the cash assistance programs (AFDC, OAA, AB, APTD, and GA) are published for all counties in the nation once a year (February, Report A-8). Since local welfare jurisdictions generally follow county lines, federal data are available for cities only in those few instances where the cities and counties are coterminous (e.g., New York; San Francisco; St. Louis; Baltimore; Jacksonville, Fla.). In the late 1930s, however, monthly welfare figures for 116 cities were published in the *Social Security Bulletin.*

The data which have been described above are available at least on an annual basis. The basic program indicators (number of recipients and cases, and average payments) are published monthly. The reasons for opening and closing cases is published semiannually, while the data dealing with applications for assistance are available quarterly. The Appendix to this chapter contains a summary of the periodicity, geographic coverage, and sources of the most basic program indicators.

While the federal government has always maintained fairly good statistics dealing with the operation of individual programs, little has been known about the persons served by the welfare programs. This is not to say that such information was unavailable to welfare authorities. A wealth of detailed information on every case usually is contained on the welfare application forms and in the reports of caseworkers. With the trends toward self-declaration and protection of the privacy of the applicant, however, this is becoming less and less true. This information, however, has been squirreled away in the file cabinets of the thousands of local welfare offices.

To rectify this information gap the federal government initiated a series of individual surveys of the population receiving each type of public assistance. States were required to provide information on the social, demographic, and economic characteristics of a representative sample of their caseload. This information was taken from the files of local welfare offices, the memories of caseworkers, and from mail questionnaires. The volume of information in these surveys is tremendous. The following list from the test AFDC survey is typical of the types of data included.

1. Place of residence (size of city, urban, rural)
2. Race
3. Size and composition of family
4. Length of time on welfare and previous welfare history
5. Father's status and whereabouts with respect to the family, age, educational attainment, and birthplace
6. Mother's status and whereabouts with respect to the family, age, educational attainment, and birthplace

7. Child-care arrangements for mothers who are working or in training programs
8. Services provided to the family, receipt of food stamps, and participation in the Work Incentive Program (WIN)
9. Income of family from assistance and nonassistance sources

The surveys of welfare recipients have been conducted from time to time as follows:

Dates of Welfare Recipient Surveys

AFDC	1958	1961	1967	1969
OAA	1960	1965		
APTD	1962			
AB	1962	1970		

The relative infrequency of these surveys is not a serious limitation, however, since the turnover of cases in all but the AFDC program is fairly low. This means that the characteristics of the recipient populations probably change little from year to year.

The surveys generally contain tables giving the characteristics of the recipients for the nation as a whole, for the census regions and for each individual state. However, the cost of generating a representative sample for each state in the 1969 AFDC survey was deemed prohibitive and so information for only a dozen states is contained in this report. Such economizing severely limits the usefulness of the survey. This is because the national and regional data are difficult to interpret since they are the aggregation of data relating to similar but not identical state programs. Changes in the characteristics of all recipients from year to year may be the result of individual states changing the requirements and payment levels of their programs or the result of different rates of growth of the caseloads in the fifty states. Without state-by-state statistics it is therefore impossible to analyze why the characteristics of the welfare recipients are changing.

The welfare system has been subjected to increasing criticism over the years. Its detractors have asserted that it is inadequate both in terms of its coverage of the poor and in terms of its level of payments. They also have maintained that the current system rewards certain perverse behavior —that it reduces the incentive to work, it undermines family stability, it stimulates migration, and it destroys the dignity of the individual. In an effort to find out just how bad the current system is and what the effects of some of the policy alternatives might be, the federal government has initiated a number of social experiments. These have yielded additional data on the welfare system. One such experiment is described in the section "Income Maintenance Experiment."

State departments of welfare also publish information on welfare programs but the quality and quantity of these data vary greatly from state to state. At a minimum most have monthly statistical newsletters that indicate the number of recipients in each program and the average level of payments in each of the welfare districts in the state. Comparable yearly data usually are contained in the *Annual Report* of the state departments of welfare. Some states go much further. For example, Ohio and South Carolina also publish detailed figures on the number of applications completed, approved, and denied in each district. A handful of states try to publish a full complement of the data requested by the NCSS by welfare districts within the state.

Selected states have also published surveys of the characteristics of their welfare recipients (e.g., New York, Michigan, Illinois, and California). Usually the data in these publications were collected originally to provide the NCSS with information for its periodic surveys. In a number of instances, however, the states have conducted additional surveys. Using the information provided by these studies it is possible to determine the characteristics of the welfare recipients in a number of the nation's largest central cities (New York, Detroit, and Chicago), since these state surveys usually display separately the figures for their largest cities. This cannot be done from the NCSS sources.

Some local districts also publish data pertaining to their welfare systems. Usually they are the larger districts. Rarely do such publications pass beyond state boundaries, and often they are intended only for the eyes of local officials or those in the state welfare agency. The most comprehensive set of local statistics relates to New York City. Its published data parallel those of the NCSS and usually are shown by welfare centers. Reports are published monthly.

There have been a number of "surveys" or rather investigations of public assistance recipients in given localities that have yielded published data (New York; Washington, D. C.; Baltimore; Chicago). Usually these have been prompted by allegations of cheating or a concern over a rapidly rising caseload. The information contained in these reports is varied and often the methodology used to obtain it is open to serious question.

Income Maintenance Experiment

The policy debate over income maintenance and welfare reform which preceded the development of President Nixon's Family Assistance Plan provides a wealth of illustrations both of the usefulness and of the limitations of statistical analysis in formulating public policy.

By the mid-1960s, the level of concern about income maintenance programs was already high. The United States did not have an income maintenance "system" as such, but a patchwork of different programs mostly designed in the 1930s to protect certain types of individuals against certain kinds of income loss. The Social Security system was designed to insure contributors against income loss due to the retirement, disability, or death of the breadwinner. Unemployment compensation was designed to protect workers covered by the program from loss of income due to unemployment. Public assistance programs were a last line of defense, designed to protect certain categories of people who could not work and were not adequately covered by social insurance. Federal aid was provided to state programs of public assistance to the aged, the blind, the permanently and totally disabled, and to certain families with dependent children.

It was clear that this patchwork system was not solving the problem of poverty in the 1960s. Despite general prosperity and rising levels of employment, millions were still poor—about 38.9 million by 1966, using the Social Security definition of poverty. The poor fared unevenly under existing income maintenance programs, depending on where they lived and who they were. In general, public assistance benefits for the aged, the blind, and the disabled were more nearly adequate than for families with children, but benefit levels under all programs varied widely by states.

Hence, there was a fierce debate raging in and out of the government about the welfare system—what was wrong with it and what to do about it. Some of the differences among the participants in the debate simply reflected differences in values. Those who put a high value on the work ethic were against any solutions which might reduce the incentive for poor people to work. Those who put a high value on human dignity were against any programs which subjected the needy to means tests. Those who put a high value on states' right or local control were suspicious of federal solutions. Among the participants in the debate, some were emotionally more concerned with the plight of children, some with the problems of the aged poor, some with rural poverty, some with the tragedies of the urban slum.

But besides these differences in values, there were also genuinely different theories about the effect of the present welfare system on human behavior and real ignorance about how people would respond to a new kind of income maintenance system.

It was clear that the existing welfare system treated families with the same income very differently depending on where they lived and who was in the family. It seemed likely that these differences—besides being inequitable—affected the behavior of the poor, often in perverse ways.

For example, a mother with children and inadequate income received greater welfare benefits if she lived in the North than if she lived in the

South. This discrepancy created an incentive for families to migrate north in order to receive higher welfare benefits. But families migrate for a variety of reasons and no one knew how many families actually migrated from the South to the North in response to the welfare differential.

Under the existing welfare system, needy families headed by women generally were eligible for public assistance and those headed by men generally were not—even if they had the same income and the same number of family members. This discrepancy created an incentive for families to break up in order to get welfare benefits. A family headed by a man with little or no earning capacity would be better off if the man moved down the street and the woman and children went on welfare. But families break up for a variety of reasons and no one knew how many were influenced by the incentives built into the welfare laws.

Similarly, it was clear that the existing welfare system gave little incentive to work. Those who were covered by welfare were subject to high marginal tax rates on their earnings. Moreover, a recipient who took a job and got off welfare, but then lost the job might face a long wait before welfare payments were resumed. Nevertheless, work decisions are complex and no one knew how people were deterred from working by the structure of the welfare system.

Concern with the unequal treatment of the poor and the presumed perverse incentives created by this unequal treatment led to a search for a more general income maintenance system which would aid families and individuals because they were poor—not because they fell into a particular category—and would extend aid to the working poor without impairing work incentives. Several new approaches to income maintenance were being actively discussed. Serious consideration was being given to variations of a "negative income tax." This is a convenient term for a system under which all individuals and families would be guaranteed an annual sum of money (based on family size) and would have this grant reduced by some fraction of their earnings. For example, a family of four with no other income might be guaranteed $3,000 a year to be reduced by 50 cents for each dollar earned. Under such a system a family with no earnings would receive $3,000 from the government; a family with $2,000 earnings would receive $2,000 from the government for a total of $4,000; a family with $6,000 earnings would not receive any grant from the government. In this example, the guarantee is $3,000, the marginal tax rate is 50 percent, and the break-even point is $6,000. Negative income tax plans with various guarantees, marginal tax rates, and consequent break-even points were proposed.

A negative income tax was clearly an attractive proposal. It was simple in conception. It removed the categories in the welfare system and treated all families of the same size and income alike. It eliminated the perverse incentives associated with the categorical system.

A negative income tax would eliminate the unequal treatment of male- and female-headed families under the welfare system by extending aid to poor families headed by men. But the reason families headed by men had generally been excluded from welfare aid was precisely because it was feared that aiding men would impair their incentive to work. Opponents of a negative income tax claimed that such a program would induce men in low-income families to quit working or reduce their hours of work. But was it true? Would a negative income tax cause a significant exodus from the labor force? Would the level of the guarantee or the steepness of the marginal tax rate make a difference in working behavior?

The answers to these questions were essential to rational consideration of a negative income tax as an alternative to public assistance. No matter how one felt about the virtues of work, one needed some basis for estimating the effect of different negative income tax structures on working behavior in order to estimate the cost and effectiveness of the program. If a $3,000 guarantee caused men to drop out of the labor force, then the program would be more expensive and less effective against poverty than if they continued to seek employment at present rates.

Even rough answers seemed impossible to extract from existing statistics. Since present programs do not cover most able-bodied men, program statistics cannot be used to infer what behavior of men would be like if they were covered. Moreover, even where men are covered (as they are under General Assistance in some states) statistics relating payments to earnings would not tell what caused what.

In view of the importance of the questions and the difficulty of answering them from existing data, the Office of Economic Opportunity (OEO) decided to use an experimental approach—to try out several variants of a negative income tax on a sample of families in several communities and record the results. Interest centered mainly on the administrative feasibility of the program and the effect of alternative guarantees and tax rates on labor-force behavior. What followed is the best example of a social experiment supported by the federal government, namely, the New Jersey negative income tax experiment, officially known as the New Jersey Graduated Work Incentive Experiment, funded by the Office of Economic Opportunity. This project, begun in 1968, is an attempt to use the experimental method to answer some of the policy questions that arose during the debate over welfare reform in the mid-1960s.

Any experiment involving substantial payment to families was bound to be expensive. For example, if payments averaged $1,000 a year per family, an experiment involving 1000 recipient families would cost $1 million a year before any provision was made for costs of administration, data collection, or analysis. Clearly it was necessary to design the experiment carefully so that the most important information would be obtained.

There were basic design questions that had to be solved before the experiment could be launched. Should a national sample be used or should the sample be concentrated in a few communities? Should all kinds of low-income families be represented or only particular types of families? Which types? How many variants of the guarantee level and tax rate should be tried and which ones? Should other variations be introduced, such as differences in income accounting periods or in reporting procedures?

Use of a national sample was appealing because it would presumably give the best estimates of what might happen if a negative income tax were enacted at the national level. However, if a relatively small sample (say, 1000–3000 families) were spread over the whole country, one would expect great variation during the experimental period in their earnings, labor-force participation, and other behavior due to variations in local job availability, wage rates, and even weather. It would be hard to separate out the effects of the negative income tax from the effects of these local factors. Moreover, it would be far more difficult and expensive to keep contact with a national sample than with a sample concentrated in a few localities.

Including all types of low-income families in the sample was also appealing as a way of anticipating the results of a national negative income tax. But a varied sample would include a relatively small proportion of working-age males whose work behavior in the face of a negative income tax was of special interest.

Testing a wide variety of combinations of guarantee, marginal tax rate, and other special features of a negative income tax also seemed intriguing. If one tested only a few alternatives, one risked omitting some interesting options. But each additional option required dividing the sample into still smaller groups and reduced the chances that definitive results would show up.

The design decisions reflected the priority accorded to learning as much as possible about the effect of a negative income tax on the work effort of low-income families containing working-age males. Despite considerable public (including congressional) criticism, the sample was restricted to low-income families containing an able-bodied man aged 18-58. It also was decided that most would be learned from a sample concentrated in the poverty areas of a few neighboring urban communities. Three sites in New Jersey were chosen (Trenton, Paterson-Passaic, and Jersey City) plus Scranton, Pennsylvania. Scranton was added partly to pick up more low-income white families, since the initial sample turned out to be mainly black and Puerto Rican.

Four guarantee levels were chosen, all stated in terms of a percentage of the Social Security Administration's poverty line. Some families would receive a guarantee of 50 percent of the poverty line; others 75 percent, 100 percent, or 125 percent. Some of the families at each guarantee level were subject to a 50 percent tax on their earnings. Some of those at the two lowest guarantee levels were subject to a 30 percent rate, providing them greater incentive to increase their earnings. Some at the middle guarantee level were subject to a 70 percent tax rate, providing them less incentive to earn. Altogether eight different combinations of guarantee levels and rate schedules were chosen for the experiment. A control sample also was chosen which would be observed, but would receive no payment except for a modest inducement to provide information. The whole sample, including the control, consisted of 1350 families.

The experiment was run for three years. First payments were made in Trenton in August 1968. Other cities were added sequentially: Paterson-Passaic in January 1969; Jersey City in June 1969 and Scranton in September 1969.

At the time the experiment was conceived it did not seem probable that a negative income tax would receive serious consideration in Congress for several years. But events moved swiftly. In the summer of 1969, President Nixon announced that he was proposing the Family Assistance Plan (FAP). While not administered through the tax system, the FAP was in essence a negative income tax for families with children. It involved a guarantee of approximately 50 percent of the poverty line ($1,600 for a family of four) and a 50 percent marginal tax rate. There was an immediate demand for information on how FAP would work, especially how it would affect the earnings of the previously excluded working poor.

In a summary of the main results of the experiment (*The New Jersey Work Incentive Experiment*, 1974) David N. Kershaw and Felicity Skidmore conclude that:

1. "There was no widespread withdrawal from work on the part of the experimental group . . ."
2. For non-aged able-bodied males with family responsibilities, "the most important group for any national income maintenance policy . . ., the effect was almost undetectable."
3. "The employment rate for male family heads was only 1.5 percent less than for the controls." For hours worked per week "the difference was just over 2 percent." In respect of earnings per week the experimental group was "higher by 6.5 percent."
4. Wives in the experimental group did reduce their labor force participation, their hours of work and their average earnings. But with an average of four children this effect may be regarded as a social gain rather than a negative result.

5. Total family employment (husbands, wives and others) declined, as did hours worked, while earnings remained about the same. This result may also be regarded as socially desirable in enabling wives to devote more time to child care and household activities, and children to stay in school longer.

6. Ethnic differences were found. White males and wives diminished labor force activity the most; Spanish-speaking males and females diminished work activity less than white; Blacks showed no slackening in their work activity.

In the meantime, several other experiments have been started in Seattle, Washington; Gary, Indiana; and rural Iowa and North Carolina to test other types of income maintenance systems, coordination of income maintenance with other public programs (notably manpower and social services) and the behavior of other family types (especially female-head families and the rural poor). Out of these efforts should come a far firmer information base for improving our income maintenance system than we have ever had before.

There are, of course, some reasons for caution in extrapolating from any income maintenance experiment to a national income maintenance system. Since participants in the experiment know their good fortune is temporary, will they behave differently from the way they would behave if the change were permanent? Since only a few people have been singled out for the experiment, will they behave differently from the way they would behave if all their neighbors were also participants? Since participants in the experiment know they are being observed, will they buy different things or keep more honest records than they would if they were not observed? We do not have enough experience with social experiments to answer these questions. In a sense these income maintenance experiments test not only substantive questions but the validity of social experimentation itself.

The Users and Uses of Welfare Statistics

The use of social welfare statistics has been confined largely to four groups of persons, officials engaged in administrating welfare programs, legislators and politicians, welfare recipients, and students and scholars.

Welfare administrators have utilized statistics for three general purposes. The first of these is the maintenance of the smooth financial operation of the system. As was mentioned previously, financial responsibility is shared by at least two layers of government: federal and state. The amount contributed by the federal government is a function of the number of recipients in each program, the average payment per recipient, and the amount spent on service, training, and administration. Collection of these figures is, therefore, essential if the state is to be repaid for part of its expenditure.

Welfare statistics also are used to prepare cost estimates for future budgets. Federal, state, and local officials are all engaged in this exercise. Fairly crude procedures generally are followed. Often the existing rate of increase in the number of recipients is merely projected into the future. If unemployment is rising or falling, the rate of increase may be adjusted accordingly; if benefits are to be raised or lowered, another correction is made.

The final use the welfare official makes of the statistics he collects is informational. Public interest in welfare has grown consistently in the past decades especially as the tax resources devoted to public assistance have expanded. Current program statistics provide the public with some indication of why welfare costs are rising so rapidly. They have also been used to dispel a number of misconceptions concerning the characteristics of welfare recipients that continually threaten to undermine what little remains of the welfare system's popular support. For example, material taken from the recipient surveys has been used to show that most welfare recipients are white, that very few are employable, that recent migrants make up only a tiny fraction of the caseloads, and that most welfare families have no illegitimate children. Data from the financial statistics have been used to prove that the average American pays relatively little for support of the poor.

Legislators and politicians have used statistics of the caseload size as an index of the current location of the poor. It is not, of course, a good measure of this because not all poor receive welfare and the fraction of the poor who do obtain assistance varies greatly from jurisdiction to jurisdiction. As such it often is interpreted as a measure of the "need" a jurisdiction has for certain social programs such as public medical facilities, public housing, and job training programs. On occasion welfare indices have been incorporated into legislation. The distribution of educational grants for disadvantaged children (Title D) is based, in part, on the number of AFDC children in an area. The general revenue sharing formulas proposed include provisions for allocating funds among the localities partially on the basis of the number of welfare cases in the community.

For many politicians and legislators the number of welfare recipients or the percent of the population receiving assistance has become the single most significant index of the urban crisis. Newark's situation is dramatized by the fact that 30 percent of its residents receive welfare; former New York mayor John Lindsay's pleas for aid were given credence when he noted that 1.1 million of his constituents were on the welfare rolls.

Politicians and legislators have also made extensive use of the aggregate financial statistics pertaining to the welfare system. Such data are used to show the "inequitable" variations across states and localities in the amounts paid by taxpayers for welfare. The conclusion that usually is derived is that the federal government should assume total financial responsibility for income maintenance and other redistributive programs.

Organized groups of welfare recipients are a relatively recent phenomenon. Nevertheless, they have been avid consumers of welfare statistics. One use they have made of these statistics is as ammunition for attacking the current welfare system. Using data on payment levels they have publicized the low—or "starvation"—levels of support provided by public assistance. Payment levels and cost standards have been effectively contrasted with the size of the BLS's budgets for low and moderate living standards in various parts of the country. The wide variation from state to state in the benefit levels have also been criticized by the Welfare Rights Organization and other groups of organized recipients.

Groups of welfare recipients have used welfare statistics for organizational purposes. Data on the number of recipients is a handy index of the potential membership in any area. Activities can therefore be expanded in the most fertile localities.

The interest students and scholars have had in welfare statistics is of a more detached nature. In the main these consumers of welfare statistics have used them to try and answer questions concerning the operation of the welfare system and the behavior of welfare recipients. The following are among the questions that have been subjected to some analysis:

1. Why are welfare rolls increasing?
2. What factors determine the level of spending on welfare programs in the various states?
3. To what extent do welfare payments reduce the incentive to work?
4. Has the interstate variation in welfare payments influenced migration patterns of the poor?
5. Has marital instability been enhanced by welfare regulations?
6. Has illegitimacy been aggravated by the AFDC program?
7. Does welfare create permanent dependency?

The Limitations of Current Welfare Statistics

Welfare statistics have been collected, aggregated, and published primarily to provide insight into the operations of the various welfare programs and the characteristics of the recipients. Yet these data shed almost no light on some of the most important questions concerning the programs and their beneficiaries.

With respect to the programs, it is almost impossible to evaluate their success. One valid indicator of a program's accomplishments would be a measure of the fraction of the eligible population that was covered or reached. Unfortunately, it is not possible accurately to estimate the size of the eligible population for any of the cash assistance programs. This is because eligibility depends upon a vast array of complex economic and noneconomic criteria that vary considerably from state to state. No census or survey data are refined enough to classify the population by these characteristics. While a few hardy souls have attempted to estimate the size of the population at risk for the OAA and AFDC programs, their efforts were crude and depended on the infrequent data published in decennial censuses.

Another index for evaluating the success of public assistance is the percentage of the preassistance poverty gap that is eliminated by such programs. This can be—and has been—estimated for the nation as a whole from data contained in the Current Population Survey. The results of such a use of the data are contained in a 1967 report by Mollie Orshansky, "Counting the Poor: Before and After Federal Income-Support Programs," in *Old Age Income Insurance*. However, such estimates are not calculated regularly and data do not exist to make similar estimates for states or for the individual programs.

In an attempt to provide some comparable measure for evaluation purposes welfare officials have persistently published the welfare recipient rate for each program by state. These rates are rather meaningless ratios of the number of recipients in a program to a portion of the population (e.g., number of OAA recipients/population age 65 and over, number of AFDC/population under age 18). Obviously the recipient rate may change from year to year for a great number of reasons having nothing to do with whether there has been a change in the fraction of the eligible population receiving assistance.

With respect to the information available on the recipients of welfare, one big void relates to present ignorance on how they compare with the poor who are not receiving assistance. Are welfare recipients just a random sample of the eligible poor or are they generally worse off physically, psychologically, and socially than the rest of the low-income population? A sample survey of the low-income population that included information of past and present welfare status would be required to answer such questions.

Another type of information that is lacking on welfare recipients concerns their life when not receiving assistance. The recipient surveys give a snapshot of the characteristics of those currently obtaining assistance but they tell us nothing about how they lived before they got on the rolls. They do not answer the following questions: What circumstances led up to the decision to apply for welfare? How were they able to leave the rolls?

Where do they go once they have gotten off relief? Do they return to a life of assistance? Answers to such questions undoubtedly would enhance the nation's ability to design more efficient income maintenance programs for the poor and better job training courses to reduce dependency. Information like this could only be obtained, however, by keeping individual case histories of a sample of the low income population over a number of years.

A final gap in our knowledge pertains to the interaction between the welfare programs and the recipients. It involves determining how the poor react to the incentives inherent in any system of assistance and how their behavior would change with variations in the incentives. It is probable that such questions cannot be answered except by conducting carefully controlled social experiments of the type discussed previously.

The overall limitations of the current data are probably best illustrated by debate surrounding the development of an alternative to the existing public assistance programs. While there was universal agreement that the existing system was inequitable and often counterproductive, neither government officials, scholars, interest groups, or the organized recipients were able to quantify the magnitude of these deficiencies. The development of policy alternatives occurred without reliable knowledge on what would be their effect. Special surveys and models of the low-income population and the experiments mentioned above had to be commissioned so that policy makers could simply estimate the size of the welfare populations under alternative plans and the aggregate costs of the programs. In brief, the existing data were incapable of showing what was wrong with the current system or how it could be improved.

The Outlook for Welfare Statistics

For a number of reasons the availability and usefulness of welfare statistics may improve significantly. In the first place, if a welfare reform bill is passed, the overall welfare system could be markedly simplified and standardized. The patchwork of state programs could be replaced by a single federal system consisting of, at the most, three programs. Eligibility requirements and assistance levels could be standardized throughout the nation. Most of the noneconomic eligibility criteria could be eliminated. Such changes would mean that state and local data would be more comparable around the nation. It would also mean that indices of program success could be computed relatively easily.

Another factor that bodes well for the future is evidence of the increasing receptivity of Congress and the welfare establishment to experimentation. As the current experiments begin to yield their findings on the behavior of recipients and how it can be affected by changing incentives, there is a good possibility that more refined experiments will be funded.

Finally, the volume of useful data pertaining to welfare programs should increase if the federal government assumes full administrative responsibility for welfare as some proposed reforms suggest. The capacity and sophistication of the federal government's data-generating mechanism far surpass those of most states. As the size of the welfare budget expands under new reforms it is also likely that Congress and the taxpayers are going to demand and get more in the way of data that can explain the operation and efficiency of the welfare system.

CONCLUDING OBSERVATIONS

Statistical data relating to Social Security and welfare, unlike those in the preceding chapters, have their origin more in administrative records than in census or survey operations. The data are more restricted in circulation and, until recently, have been mainly used by program administrators, legislative bodies, and scholars. However, with the increasing trend toward organization of welfare recipients and the linkage of poverty and minority-group status, statistics relating to Social Security and, especially, welfare are being used by an ever-increasing proportion of the public for policy and program planning and evaluation.

The fact that the "welfare problem" is among the nation's major domestic problems, the solution of which will be neither easy nor quick, will unquestionably mean increased consideration of and debate about alternatives to the present chaotic welfare situation. Inevitably this will mean increased need for facts to guide policy and program. Statistics on both welfare and Social Security will, therefore, be expanded further; and they will undoubtedly also be supplemented by intensive studies and experiments such as that reported above on income maintenance. In respect to the increased experimentation which will undoubtedly develop, it is well to emphasize that the perception of the need for experiments and their design and evaluation will be in large measure dependent on the general statistics which have been described.

APPENDIX

Summary of Basic Welfare Statistics

Subject	Program	Periodicity	Geographic Area	Source
Number of recipients	AFDC, AFDC-UP, OAA, AB, APTD, GA Emergency assistance, institutional services	Monthly	State	NCSS A-2
	AFDC, OAA, AB, APTD, GA	Annual	County	NCSS A-8
	Medical assistance (by type)	Quarterly	State	NCSS B-1
	Social services (by assistance programs)	Semiannual	State	NCSS E-1 and E-6
	Work incentive (WIN)	Annual	State	NCSS E-5
	Food stamps (by assistance status of recipient)	Monthly	County	USDA Internal Report
Total benefit or average benefit per recipient	AFDC, AFDC-UP, OAA, AB, APTD, GA Emergency assistance, institutional services	Monthly	State	NCSS A-2
	AFDC, OAA, AB, ATPD, GA	Annual	County	NCSS A-8
	Medical assistance (by type)	Quarterly	State	NCSS B-1
	Food stamps	Monthly	County	USDA Internal Report
Source of funds (federal, state, local)	AFDC, OAA, AB, APTD Medical assistance (broken down into groups for cash assistance versus administration, training, and service)	Annual	State	NCSS F-2, F-3
Application, cases approved and discontinued	AFDC, OAA, APTD, AB, GA Medical assistance	Quarterly	State	NCSS A-9
Reasons for opening and closing cases	AFDC, OAA, APTD, AB, GA	Semiannually	State	NCSS A-5
Cost standards	AFDC, OAA	Annual	State	NCSS D-2

REFERENCES

Kershaw, David N., and Felicity Skidmore. "The New Jersey Graduated Work Incentive Experiment." Mathematica Policy Analysis Series: Comments and Papers on Current Research. Princeton, N. J., July, 1974 (mimeo).

Orshansky, Mollie. "Counting the Poor: Before and After Federal Income-Support Programs." *Old Age Income Assurance,* Part 2, *The Aged Population and Retirement Income Programs.* Compendium of Papers on Problems and Policy Issues in the Public and Private Pension System submitted to the Subcommittee on Fiscal Policy of the Joint Economic Committee, Congress of the United States, December 1967, p. 177.

Social Security Administration. *Social Security Bulletin.* Washington, D. C.: Government Printing Office, monthly.

The Welfare Administration. *Welfare in Review.* Washington, D. C.: Government Printing Office, monthly.

CHAPTER 8
On Delinquency and Crime*

THE DATA

The criminal and juvenile justice systems are made up of three parts—police, courts, and corrections. There is much overlap in these systems in the handling of adults and juveniles, but there is also in many jurisdictions separate machinery for dealing with adults and with most juveniles. Each of these systems produces statistics.

Like other outputs of these systems, their statistics are influenced by many factors. They are, most of all, the "bookkeeping records" of the work done by the official agencies. They tell us about complaints received, crimes known to the police, numbers of persons arrested, prosecuted, convicted, and disposed of in various ways by the courts, and about persons in correctional institutions and programs. They are gathered, processed, and distributed in many ways. They serve many purposes: administrative and other internal use; preparation and justification of budget requests; presentation to such audiences as "city hall," mass media, and taxpayers and other citizens' groups; and use by a variety of analysts, including journalists and social scientists. They are direct descriptions of the behavior of officials rather than of offenders. Thus, an increase in an arrest rate tells us that the police have made more arrests—it does not necessarily mean there are more crimes or criminals.

---

* Based on a memorandum by James F. Short, Washington State University.

Criminal and juvenile justice statistics are useful chiefly as indicators of agency activity (some would say of recording activity of these agencies), and of the ways in which those who are caught up in the justice system they represent are handled within those systems. Yet, they are used most often, as we shall see, as measures of the extent and nature of crime, criminals, and delinquents. They are useful for these purposes because the occurrence of crime and delinquency is *one* of the influences on such data. But they are neither a census nor a scientific sampling of all crime and delinquency or of all criminals and delinquents.

The Uniform Crime Reports (UCR) are the major source of police data for the United States. Published each year since 1930 by the Federal Bureau of Investigation, the UCR program has been the strongest force in the nation for more complete and accurate data on crimes known to the police. Based upon reports submitted voluntarily by police departments throughout the country, the UCR has grown from about 400 police agencies reporting in 1930 to approximately 8500 at present. These agencies, in 1973, represented 97 percent of the total United States population living in Standard Metropolitan Statistical Areas, 90 percent of the population in other cities, and 80 percent of the rural population. The combined coverage accounts for 93 percent of the national population (Kelley, 1974). The percentage of persons living in other cities and rural areas covered by the UCR continues to increase as a result of continued efforts by the FBI and state agencies.

Of equal importance to the extent of coverage of the UCR has been the influence of the system in establishing uniform definitions of offenses and standardized reporting procedures. This is an enormous task, in view of varying state and local laws, and the independence of local police departments. The President's Commission on Law Enforcement and Administration of Justice (the Crime Commission) concluded that the system is "as good as can be devised."

Even the most favorable judgments of the UCR, however, have been critical of some of its practices and of the system's limitations. Chief among these are variations in the extent to which crimes are reported to the police by victims and in the handling of such crimes as then come to their attention by the police. Others concern technical matters, such as the lack of uniform standards for classifying crimes and recording them, changing definitions within the FBI system itself, continuous change in the numbers of jurisdictions reporting data to the FBI, the practice of counting only the "most serious" criminal acts rather than all such acts committed when more than one crime is involved in the report of a victim, the failure to distinguish between attempted and accomplished criminal acts, the deficiencies of the "Crime Index" and the failure to relate changes in crimes reported to changing composition of the population, e.g., size, age, and degree of urbanization.

A most important "bias" in crimes known to the police data, as in all other criminal statistics, is that they are not routinely compiled for all crimes, and great secrecy surrounds such information as is collected for some crimes. Many crimes committed by persons of upper socioeconomic status in the course of business, for example (so-called white-collar crimes), are handled by federal regulatory agencies, such as the Federal Trade Commission, Federal Communications Commission, and the Securities Exchange Commission—and so are not recorded in the bookkeeping records of the criminal justice system. Legal technicalities of local, as well as state and federal, business regulations often require expertise beyond that available to police. Local police departments also are handicapped in their ability to deal with organized criminal activities which cross municipal and state boundaries. The secrecy surrounding data relative to organized crime and methods of investigating it has been justified on the grounds of greater efficiency in obtaining information and protecting information sources, and of necessity in "building a case" against organized criminal conspiracy and operation. The policy of secrecy has led to a system of "leaks" to reporters and journalists in the interest of providing public information, however, which is unsystematic and impossible to verify for accuracy or significance. The situation is similar with respect to the crimes of big business and other white-collar crimes. Because they are not included in any systematic public statistics, no accurate assessment of their extent and nature is possible. Clearly, this is an area in which systematic, objective "social indicators" are badly needed.

In part, as a result of limitations such as these, crimes covered by the Uniform Crime Reports are "used" to a greater extent than are data on other crimes. However, much local data from city police departments and prosecutors' offices also get utilized in communicating the "facts" about crime and criminals, delinquency and delinquents. Finally, information about individual cases often is used instead of statistics. This is true not only because of limitations of statistical data, but also due to the greater "human interest" which attaches to such case studies. Because of the limitations of available statistics, however, a good deal of misunderstanding of the nature of crime and delinquency is abroad, and abuses of the data are common and difficult to correct.

In the case of delinquency and crime, then, although considerable statistics are available, they are unquestionably defective. Nevertheless, they are used widely, often in ways that significantly affect public policy and programs, as is indicated in the materials which follow.

Statistics are available from the operation of the judicial and prison systems but they suffer from serious deficiencies. In appraising the state of American criminal statistics, the Task Force on Acts of Violence of the U. S. National Commission on the Causes and Prevention of Violence (Mulvihill and Tumin, 1969) noted:

> There are, in fact, no national judicial statistics today. The series begun in 1932 by the Bureau of the Census was discontinued in 1946.... Although the Children's Bureau of the Department of Health, Education and Welfare has collected and published data since 1940 on "Juvenile Court Statistics" (delinquency, dependency, and neglect cases are covered), there are several reasons why the series is not an appropriate indicator of the levels and trends of youth crime.... The present state of prison statistics, collected by the Bureau of Prisons of the Department of Justice and published as "National Prisoner Statistics," shows little improvement over the court situation....
>
> In addition to the information supplied by the Federal Bureau of Prisons, the Children's Bureau publishes annual statistics on juvenile institutions and occasionally produces special reports. A new classification system needs to be developed for these statistics. In general, the correctional statistics from both of these sources are of little or no use in measuring the levels and trends of violence (pp. 13–14).

The task force concluded that, in any case, *police* data were more useful for measuring the levels and trends of crime. The police system has first contact with the offense upon which the statistics are based, and there is considerable "mortality of information" from the time the offenses are recorded by police to the imprisonment of those convicted.

USES

Just as police, courts and correctional programs compile and use statistics concerning their activities for the purpose of presenting their needs and accomplishments to a variety of publics, so others use these statistics for their own purposes. The list of "others" is virtually without end, from the "man on the street" to international bodies such as the United Nations. This discussion is limited to users within the United States. For each category of users, discussion will center on (1) methods by which use of criminal statistics were determined; (2) types of statistics used; and (3) extent of use with examples.

In addition to statistics of the criminal and juvenile justice systems, special studies of self-reported crimes and delinquency, and of victimization, another type of data is important in assessing both the statistics and the problems they represent; that is, public opinion data. Polls have not inquired into the basis for the judgments and opinions surveyed, nor have they been systematically related either to statistics of crime and delinquency or to media coverage. Still, they are of interest in ascertaining the state of concern over these problems of the "general public."

The General Public

As revealed by public opinion polls over the past several years, the "man on the street" is much concerned about "law and order." "Polling Day in America," telecast nationally over the ABC network on January 13, 1971, provided such information. In response to the question, "Has law and order broken down in the country?" of 3000 adults interviewed over the country, 70 percent said "yes" and only 26 percent, "no" (4 percent were undecided). The same poll reported that 64 percent of the women interviewed said they felt unsafe walking the streets at night. Six out of ten respondents said they felt more money should be spent to restore law and order, 25 percent were satisfied with present levels of spending in this regard, while only 7 percent felt less expenditure was needed (8 percent were undecided).

The Gallup Poll has asked about "the most important problem facing this country today" since 1959. Over ten surveys the highest proportion who answered "crime and juvenile delinquency" was about 8 percent and in 1968 the proportion with this answer was less than 2 percent. In view of the rising crime statistics and the popularity of crime and juvenile delinquency in the media (in both news and entertainment) and in political campaigns, the percentage of people making this reply seems surprisingly small and consistent. When the question is changed to "What do you think is the most important problem facing this community today?" the percentage of crime and juvenile delinquency replies is somewhat higher, but still low, ranging from a high of about 11 percent to a low of about 4 percent.

While crime and delinquency may not be the most important problems facing the country or their local communities for most Americans, there can be little doubt that they are regarded as serious, and their concern about it appears to have increased in recent years. Results from two Gallup polls conducted in March 1965 and August 1967 may be compared with the January 1971 Harris poll. In response to the question, "Is there any area right around here—that is, within a mile—where you would be afraid to walk alone at night?" the percentage of women replying "yes" was 49.2 and on the earlier dates 43.8 compared to 64 percent in 1971. Fear levels and reported victimization are higher among blacks of both sexes according to these polls. Fear of walking the streets among women appears to be greater today than was the case three to five years ago.

Crime as News

The *New York Times* indexes "crime" as a news category. Every third column with a reference to "crime" for the year 1969 was examined in order to determine extent and types of statistical use. *Time* magazine similarly indexes "crime." Every issue of *Time* was examined for references to "crime" for the years 1962 and 1965 to 1968. All references to crime during these years were read and evaluated in a manner similar to that employed for the *New York Times*. In addition to these national news sources, most issues of *Time, Newsweek, U. S. News and World Report, The National Observer, Life,* and *Look* for 1969 and 1970 were examined, and local uses of crime statistics were obtained from sources "close to home," chiefly from the *Lewiston* (Idaho) *Tribune* and the *Spokane* (Washington) *Chronicle*.

Stephen J. Bahr (1970), in a paper titled "The Use and Abuse of Criminal Statistics in Minority and 'Hate' Literature," surveyed six magazines oriented toward black, radical left, and radical right constituencies in an effort to determine the extent to which such groups employ criminal statistics, and the nature of such use. *Time* magazine was analyzed as a "general news magazine" for comparative purposes. Black magazines studied were *Ebony, Black World,* and *Black Panther* (which also was classified as "radical left"). The other "radical left" magazine examined was *Activist. American Opinion,* official journal of the John Birch Society, and *The Conservative Journal* were chosen to represent the "radical right," in the absence of regularly published magazines from even more radical right groups such as the Ku Klux Klan and the American Nazi party.

Bahr's classification of articles using criminal statistics required "an explicit use of statistics related to crime or a specific reference to criminal statistics." This type of use was referred to as "numerical"; other references, nonstatistical, were labeled "literary."

Despite the lack of strict comparability in periods covered, certain conclusions are possible. First of all, it is clear that criminal statistics were not used very often in most of these magazines. "Radical right" magazines used criminal statistics to a greater extent than did magazines of the "radical left," or those addressed particularly to blacks and the general news magazine studied. Radical left magazines examined avoided altogether, possibly because they believed them to be biased, the use of crime statistics, and only *Ebony* among "black magazines" used "hard" (numerical) data.

Bahr's tabulation of the types of criminal statistics reported in these seven magazines reveals that the Uniform Crime Reports are by far the most commonly used source of crime data—hardly surprising since this is the most available and general source of information with the longest history of continuous operation. In addition, it is widely distributed and publicized by the FBI.

The general news magazine (*Time*) is the most consistent user of FBI data. The politically extreme magazines are most likely to use "other" and "unspecified" sources. Bahr's examination of the *content* of articles reporting or referring to criminal statistics suggests, also, that *Time*'s use of such materials is more objective and less often propagandistic and deliberately misleading than are the other sources, particularly those which are politically more extreme.

A study by William A. Hasten pointed out that "advertising's share of space" in newspapers has "steadily increased, and today it is not uncommon for it to fill up 70 percent of a paper. Of the remaining 30 percent, 'hard news' seldom occupies more than one-third of the paper (or 10 percent of total space)." One study of Sunday editions showed that while the average number of pages had increased from 118 in 1939 to 193 in 1959, the space allocated to news had actually decreased. The growth of special sections, particularly those devoted to leisure activities, together with increased advertising was responsible for this decrease (Lyle, 1969, p. 201). Crime as news accounted for a relatively small percentage of news and editorial space in a study of eight mid-western daily newspapers. Another study by Guido H. Stempel, III, found that crime ranked sixth out of ten news categories over all, with space taken ranging from 2 percent in one paper to 10 percent in the paper with the highest percentage of space devoted to crime (Lyle, 1969, p. 202). Statistics often are not used in crime stories and when used, are generally not documented as to source or reliability. Examples of several types of crime news stories follow.

Crime and Politics as News Crime has been a political issue, locally in many communities, and nationally for many years. New York City's 1969 mayoral campaign featured a good deal of talk and accusations concerning crime, but few statistics. Mr. Procaccino and other opponents of Mayor Lindsay stressed the law-and-order issue while attacking the record of the mayor. From the pages of the *New York Times,* Procaccino was quoted as saying, "I don't believe in a Fun City. I believe in a safe city." And again, "We cannot tolerate a society with a gun at its head," and "Lawlessness will be swept from the streets. Our streets are now avenues of terror." Former Mayor Wagner was pictured in a television commercial, standing in front of a theater, saying that he could not let his wife walk this street alone at night; and in another, telling voters that if they vote late, not to go to the polls alone. An advertisement in the *Times* by Wagner's running mate, Hugh Carey, pictured a murder victim lying on the street, with the caption, "Haven't you had enough?" Many more examples could be cited.

Occasionally, crime statistics are brought into political campaigns. On November 2, 1969, for example, the *New York Times* reported a clash over the interpretation of crime data between incumbent Mayor Kramer, of Paterson, New Jersey, and his challenger, former Mayor Graves. Each candidate claimed crime in Paterson had been more serious during the other's term in office. Uniform crime report data were bandied about in this exchange.

Politicians sometimes use statistics of unknown source and reliability. In the New York mayoralty campaign referred to above, Lindsay referred to "one-half of all our crime" as being committed by opiate addicts; and Mr. Scheur was quoted to the effect that "Only 1 percent of police manpower is concentrated on narcotics despite the fact that half the violent crime is committed by addicts. I would beef up the narcotics squad." The need for reliable and comparable statistics as a guide to public interpretation of political talk is clear. Good crime statistics could inhibit irresponsible charges and countercharges, and provide the public with sounder knowledge about crime.

News and the Politics of Crime Control Control of crime, as such, often becomes a political issue, in addition to affecting elections. Crime commissions and surveys, legislative committees, and campaigns for and against referenda related to crime control and to such issues as gun control use (and often abuse) crime statistics in many ways.

Thus, the New York State Joint Legislative Committee on crime held a public hearing in Harlem in February 1969. The *Times* reported that at the hearing Assemblyman Mart T. Southall, a Harlem Democrat, estimated that 85,000 to 90,000 Harlem residents used narcotics and that 70 to 80 percent of crimes committed in the area were attributable to addicts.

The reliability of such references—e.g., Assemblyman Southall's 70 to 80 percent, the "one-half of all our crimes" cited by Mayor Lindsay, and the "half the violent crimes" attributed to addicts by Mr. Scheur—is not known. The sources of these references, or the specific jurisdiction covered, or the definitions either of addicts or of crimes remain unspecified. Better statistics would not prevent their loose use by politicians, but they might at least provide a more reliable base for comparison of claims and counterclaims.

The politics of crime control took another twist in Mayor Lindsay's campaign for a "four-platoon" system of police patrol, in the spring of 1969. The mayor issued a fourteen-page booklet prepared by New York Police Commissioner Leary analyzing the incidence of crime in the city.

Mayor Lindsay was quoted as saying, on March 16, 1969, "Forty-seven percent of all violent personal attacks occur during the eight-hour period between 6:00 P.M. and 2:00 A.M. while only 15.6 percent occur between 4:00 A.M. and noon. Yet under the three-platoon system, the city has roughly the same number of police patrolling the streets at all hours in a twenty-four hour period." The proposed four-platoon system, it was said, would increase the number of police patrolling streets at night by 50 percent.

Five days later an advertisement appeared in the *Times*, paid for by a "group of concerned businessmen of New York City," citing some of these same statistics and others, and urging passage of the law which would create the four-platoon system. The bill was actively opposed by the Policemen's Benevolent Association.

The incidence of crime and problems of crime control often are linked in news stories. Under the heading, "Police Begin Times Square Cleanup," the *Times* discussed a "crackdown" on criminal activities in this area which had been ordered by Chief Inspector Sanford Garelik. The order followed a meeting between the police and union and management representatives of the *New York Times*. Union representatives had threatened a work stoppage because late-hour workers were afraid to walk the streets at night. Inspector Garelik protested that the problem was not one of more arrests, but rather of the permissive attitude toward crime and punishment and the breakdown in authority throughout society. He indicated that the first twelve persons arrested on a recent evening had been released for insufficient evidence in court.

A week later, this theme was elaborated as the controversy continued. Inspector Garelik was quoted to the effect that during a six-day period of intensification of the drive against crime in the Times Square area out of 292 arrests only 12 persons had been sentenced to jail. Figures cited were as follows: arrests—for loitering, 144; for disorderly conduct, 55; for public intoxication, 39; for prostitution, 21; miscellaneous, 29 (totaling 288). Inspector Garelik was reported as saying, "Demonstration of legal guilt in our society is becoming ludicrously difficult" as a result of restrictions imposed on the police by laws and the courts. Garelik cited figures related to the handling of those arrested in the most recent Times Square crackdown to demonstrate his point: in addition to the 12 who had been sentenced to jail, 109 of those arrested had been dismissed in court, two were being held in lieu of bail, 147 had been paroled on their own recognizance, and 22 were found guilty but unconditionally released. Garelik also was concerned about repeaters. He cited figures on February 13, 1969, indicating that all persons arrested on narcotics charges in the city in February 1968—563 persons—had been arrested previously. Of these, 142 had 5 or more arrests, 86 had 10 or more, 46 had 15 or more, 4 had 25 or more, and 1 had 46 previous arrests. These previous arrests included 10 for homicide, 146 for felonious assault, 124 for robbery, 168 for burglary, 80 for possession of dangerous weapons, 34 for rape, and 224 for larceny.

Crime as "Human Interest"

Many other examples of the use of local and national data on crime could be cited. The *New York Times* regularly publishes FBI Uniform Crime Report data, as well as more locally newsworthy items, such as Inspector Garelik's frustration concerning crime in the Times Square area and its handling by the courts. "Human interest" stories often feature crime and its relation to a variety of events, places and problems. The following is a sampling from the pages of the *Times* during 1969:

> January 5, under the heading, "Crime Taking Over Haight-Ashbury." Street robberies, numbering 64 in the first seven months of 1967, rose to 280 in the same period for 1968. A girl is quoted commenting on the fact that tourists now drive through the area with locked-up doors and rolled-up windows. "I don't blame them. This scene is too rough. There's not any love around here anymore. It's just a wild drug thing now."
>
> June 15. The Governor of Puerto Rico said in a speech that "the narcotics addiction problem here has reached such alarming proportions in the last 10 years that it now accounts for more than half the Island's crime." The Governor cited the following statistics: in 1960, there were 1600 addicts in a population of 2.4 million; in 1969 the population had increased by 10 percent but the number of addicts had risen to 11,000. Addicts were reported to spend $75 million per year on drugs. Crime—especially theft—has risen from 10,000 thefts in 1960 to 20,000 in 1968.
>
> October 24. "New Yorkers Find Familiar Ills After Moving to Mount Vernon." Burglaries are reported to have increased in this New York City suburb from 551 in 1965 to 714 in 1968, robberies from 56 to 96 during this same period. After extra patrolmen were put on duty during evening hours in 1969, the crime rate is reported to have dropped (but no figures are given). The article also reports that teachers and students estimated that between 30 percent and 50 percent of high school students in Mount Vernon are occasional users of marijuana, and the high school principal indicated that 12 students had been arrested in 1968 for possession of heroin.
>
> November 20. "The police attributed a sharp drop in reported crime last night and early today to the Apollo 12 moon landing and walk by Commanders Charles Conrad, Jr. and Alan L. Bean." A police lieutenant on duty was quoted as saying, "We should have moon walks more often.

It is a great deterrent to crime." No data were given, but the reference, one suspects, is to "ordinary" crime and to street crime, in particular.

Crime makes news and crime statistics are part of the news. To the extent that the crime statistics are defective, which they are, the news is distorted and the public is misled. The absence of reliable crime statistics does not seem to dampen the use of the defective data—with probably detrimental impact on public policy and practice.

Government

Government—at all levels—is at once the largest producer and, with the possible exception of the nation's lawyers and the press, the largest consumer of statistics on crime and juvenile delinquency. By its very nature crime is "political" since it represents action taken by a government agency, the state (again, at all levels of government), in defining certain conduct as criminal and in enforcing this definition by means of legal, that is to say, political means. This is also the case with juvenile delinquency, though, in a more technical sense, much behavior defined as delinquent is not considered criminal when engaged in by adults. Offenders may be called criminal or delinquent by other persons, and their behavior may be labeled criminal or delinquent, but without action by the state such labeling has no official meaning.

It is impossible fully to determine the extent to which governmental bodies which are responsible for the production of criminal statistics use them, or the extent to which such data are used by other governmental agencies, such as federal and state legislatures, executive departments, and various judicial bodies. The Legislative Reference Service of the Library of Congress gets many calls for information relative to crime and delinquency from members of the Congress of the United States, but no systematic information of the extent or nature of such uses is available. Other agencies, e.g., national commissions, often use this service through the offices of their members who are also members of Congress, or through other congressional connections. The data are used in testimony before congressional committees, e.g., in considerations of appropriations and other legislation and before other governmental bodies such as the Federal Trade Commission (see below, under "Consumers") or national commissions.

The most thoughtful and wide-ranging critiques of the statistics of crime and delinquency have come from the president's "Crime Commission" and the national "Violence Commission." These commissions were responsible, in addition, for major studies to assess the quality of official statistics and to utilize them more effectively for understanding crime and delinquency. The Violence Commission, responding to the Crime Commission's call for more investigation of the nature of the relationship between offenders and victims undertook "the first survey of national dimensions on victim and offender patterns of the four major violent crimes: criminal homicide, aggravated assault, forcible rape, and robbery." The survey, "a 10 percent random sample of 1967 offense and arrest reports from 17 large United States cities," concentrated on the characteristics of offenders and victims and the nature of their "interaction" in each violent "event" found in the police records. A sample of findings from the survey follows:

> Of the interactions in our survey concerning homicide in which the sex of the participants was known, 63 percent were male/male, only 4 percent were female/female, 16 percent were male/female, and 18 percent female/male. When race was known, 24 percent of all killings were between whites and 66 percent between Negroes. Six percent involved Negroes killing whites and 4 percent whites killing Negroes. The dominant age pattern was for individuals over 25 to kill persons in the same age category (47 percent of all interactions). Earlier studies of criminal homicides in specific locations have produced similar results.
>
> Similar sex, race, and age patterns occur in the aggravated assault category, suggesting that assault and homicide may differ only in the seriousness of the injury.
>
> . . . Ninety percent of the rapes where race was determined were intraracial. Thirty percent were white/white, 60 percent Negro/Negro, 10 percent white/Negro, and a negligible percent Negro/white.
>
> . . . Male/male interactions are the most frequent of armed robbery (84 percent). Females rarely robbed other females (1 percent) or males (4 percent), but males occassionally robbed females (10 percent). Unlike criminal homicide, aggravated assault, and rape, robbery is more interracial (49 percent), with Negroes robbing whites as the typical pattern (47 percent). Only 13 percent of the robberies were white/white, but 38 percent were between Negroes.
>
> . . . The leading combination of sex, race, and age was clearly Negro males 18 to 25 robbing white males 26 and over.
>
> . . . One in four homicides was between family members, and 9 percent involved other primary (intimate) group contacts. Thus, one-third involved primary (family or intimate) group relationships, while 46 percent involved nonprimary (other) relationships. About a fifth were miscellaneous or unknown. The proportion of family members in 1967 homicides, according to our sample survey, coincides with a complete tabulation made that year by the FBI, which found slightly under 30 percent within the family. Previous local city studies have reported roughly the same findings. However, they suggested relatively higher percentages in

the "other primary group" category and relatively lower percentages within the "nonprimary group." When all the available investigations are compared, the percentage of primary group relationships ranges from about one-third in our national sample up to about two-thirds in some of the previous more intensive but local surveys.

Organized Labor

Organized labor has been much concerned with social conditions associated with crime and delinquency, but references to them in their extensive research and publications programs are rare. Use of statistics of crime, delinquency, and police and judicial processes is rarer still. Thus, in response to the ghetto riots in the summer of 1967, *The American Federationist,* official monthly magazine of the American Federation of Labor and Congress of Industrial Organizations, for September of that year featured "A Program for the Cities" presenting excerpts from speeches, congressional testimony, and other statements of labor leaders on a variety of ghetto problems and programs related to their solution. The article begins with the following preamble:

America's ghettos are exploding. After the warnings of Watts came Newark. And then Detroit. And Atlanta. Birmingham. Chicago. Durham. Flint. Fresno. Grand Rapids. Kalamazoo. Lansing. Long Beach. Memphis. Mt. Vernon. Newburgh. Nyack. Phoenix. Pontiac. Portland. Poughkeepsie. Rochester. Saginaw. San Francisco. South Bend. Wilmington, Wichita. And then New Haven, model of urban removal.

The convulsions which have shaken some 80 cities this summer are signals and warnings of a social sickness. This has long been the view of organized labor, which has been fighting for many years for action and funds at every level to attack the root causes of poverty and despair.

The program of the AFL-CIO has stressed jobs, education, and housing among a wide range of remedies to equip people to solve their problems and master their circumstances. At the national level, labor has sought policies which would promote full employment, better education and good housing.

With the breadwinner and the family as the center of its concern, organized labor has developed policies aimed at aiding and strengthening the position of those most in need. Thus labor's programs range from the welfare of children to the health and security of the elderly. Labor's programs cover jobs, schools, housing, health care, welfare, the community's entire environment.

As better-off Americans are compelled to look again at the cities, they must see past the smoke and the ashes to the needs of people and create a unity of purpose to solve the problems of the ghettos. The following excerpts document labor's program and sense of urgency [AFL, 1967].

The article includes a speech of AFL-CIO President George Meany, on August 24, 1967, before a meeting of "over 800 mayors, and labor, business, and church and civil rights leaders," sponsored by the Urban Coalition. The speech stressed the need for "One Million Jobs—Now." Mr. Meany's opening statement was: "The course of a free society should not and must not be swayed by criminal acts—mob violence, arson, looting and murder. Neither should it be swayed by revulsion against these acts." The full article made reference, in addition, to "Full Employment," "More and Better Schools," "Model Cities, Decent Housing," ". . . and Fair Housing," "Protection for the Consumer," and "A Wider War on Poverty." This is fairly typical, as revealed by our examination of a sample of AFL-CIO publications over the past twenty-one years.

In August 1968, gun control, a subject often linked with crime and delinquency, was listed in *The American Federationist* among the most pressing "special and public needs." Discussion of the subject was limited and no data were mustered. "The absolute need for federal gun control legislation has been so clearly proven—both by testimony and the sad facts of political assassination in this country—as to make further argument unnecessary."

Business

Business is both victim and perpetrator of crime, and the business of protective devices and services against crime has become an important part of our economy; witness the many advertisements for burglar alarms and other protective devices cited below. One survey of business organizations and business-oriented publications included selected issues of *Fortune, Business Week,* the *Wall Street Journal* and the "Cumulative Index of NICB Publication, 1970," issued by the National Industrial Conference Board. Business advertising also was sampled from news periodicals such as *Time* magazine and the *New York Times.*

On June 26, 1969, the NICB held a conference at the Waldorf-Astoria Hotel in New York City, on "Crime and the Corporation." Three articles published in *The Conference Board Record* ("Reporting to Management on Business Affairs") for August 1969, impart much of the flavor of that conference. The quotation at length which follows is one of the best examples found of business use of crime statistics.

The keynote presentation at the conference was by Norman E. Cash, president of Television Bureau of Advertising, Inc., who spoke on "Crime and the Corporation." Mr. Cash laced his talk with statistics, some from FBI records, but most from unacknowledged sources. The following is a sampling of these data which shows not only the use of crime statistics but tells much about the nature of crime as it affects business:

> The percent increase in the rate of these crimes, 1960 to 1967, shows the trend of business' involvement. The more the crime concerns business directly, the faster its increase has been, from the 22 percent increase in the murder rate to the 88 percent increase in larceny-theft.
>
> Every form of crime has its impact upon business. Robbery costs business $77 million a year and employee theft costs $381 million. Compare the cost of robbery and of employee theft and it's clear that five times more money is lost to those *inside* the company than to those who come from outside. More robbers break out than break in. Bad checks cost businessmen another $316 million loss per year.
>
> Add to this list the cost of shoplifting—$504 million. In supermarkets pilferage can equal profits. In department stores they expand the definition somewhat and call it "shrinkage." It has been 2 percent of sales for the past few years. Much of the cost of this shrinkage must be added to the price of the items sold.
>
> Next in cost to business comes $813 million from vandalism. This is the crime of the amateur, of people within the company or the neighborhood or the family.
>
> To complete the list of the business costs of crime, add burglary at $958 million, with 58 percent of those arrested being juveniles.
>
> The estimated cost to business from all these crimes is some $3 billion a year. But this is far from the total business cost of crime. It doesn't include losses due to riot, though riot losses have put some businessmen out of business, making riots a business as well as a social concern.
>
> Nor does this list include the cost of *preventing* crime. The average supermarket may lose $28,000 from shoplifting a year, but it pays an additional $2,000 in the cost of the antipilferage equipment it buys. That's an 8 percent increase in crime's cost to business.
>
> To capture employees who steal, business hires 170,000 private policemen. And if the cost of this army isn't enough, it also pays for the electronic equipment used to catch our criminals. This is not equipment to protect the country from a foreign invader—it is to protect our companies from their own employees.
>
> The $3 billion cost of crime also does not include the cost of organized crime. How large is this? In April 1969, President Nixon asked Congress for $25 million *more* than President Johnson asked for—a total of $61 million to escalate the Federal war on organized crime—an important share of which business can expect to pay with its taxes. In 1968, Ralph Salerno, member of the President's Crime Commission, estimated the income of Mafia-controlled organized crime at $20–$30 billion annually

—a net of $6 million tax-free from gambling proceeds alone. At 5 percent interest, this means that since 1950 sufficient funds have been generated through just one activity to buy every share of common stock in this country's 10 largest corporations—with enough left over to buy AT&T.

With an estimated $20 billion a year to work with and little moral restraint, organized crime has started what's been called "Operation Shakedown"—the movement of organized crime into the world of organized business. The move has already started and the corporation may soon find it has a new competitor that doesn't play by the rules, or a new partner and there are only his rules.[1]

Robert M. Morgenthau, U. S. Attorney for the Southern District of New York, spoke to the NICB conference on "Equal Justice and the Problem of White Collar Crime." The absence of Mr. Morgenthau's presentation of statistics on "white collar crime" data such as Mr. Cash was able to cite concerning ordinary crime points to the inadequacies and biases in official criminal statistics. Morgenthau (1969) is quite clear on this problem.

[A] robbery, an assault, are easily identifiable crimes. They are frequently committed in the open and observed by witnesses. White collar crimes, on the other hand, often are not even discoverable without substantial investigation, and even when discovered, the trail of evidence is difficult, if not impossible, to follow. *It is essential, I submit, that law enforcement agencies do not follow the path of least resistance and concentrate their enforcement efforts only on crimes which are readily discovered—crimes which are generally committed by the poor* [emphasis added].

and again:

As one court has said: "In our complex society the accountant's certificate and the lawyer's opinion can be instruments for inflicting pecuniary loss more potent than the chisel or the crowbar."

I believe that the illegal use of Swiss bank accounts illustrates perhaps better than any other white collar crime what the poor would call a "rich man's crime" which frequently goes unpunished. It is a white collar crime whose dimensions and seriousness have only recently begun to be appreciated. Of all the white collar crimes it is probably the most difficult to investigate and uncover. *And perhaps most disturbing of all, we have discovered during the course of our investigation that the persons who illegally use these secret accounts are all too frequently highly respectable corporate executives, businessmen, brokers, accountants, and*

---

[1] From "Crime and the Corporation" by Norman E. Cash, in *The Conference Board Record* 2, August, 1969, 11–13. Reprinted by permission of the publisher.

lawyers—men who would be the first to complain about a robbery or a mugging in their neighborhood [emphasis added].

It is a deplorable fact that many businessmen tend to treat more sympathetically the banker guilty of tax fraud, the broker guilty of stock fraud, or the accountant who certifies a false balance sheet, than the poor man guilty of auto theft or the hijacking of a truck. We even find persons who publicly denounce crimes of violence while privately committing more "socially acceptable" white collar crimes. I recall in this connection recent publicity concerning the president of a large corporation of businessmen who complained to the New York City Police Department about a recent wave of hijackings in the garment district at a time when he was under indictment for paying a kickback in connection with obtaining a loan from a union pension fund—a crime for which he was subsequently convicted.[2]

Morgenthau, without indicating the time period involved, stated: "We have brought over 200 cases involving bribery of IRS (Internal Revenue Service) employees; about half the defendants are lawyers and accountants in private practice, and the balance are government employees who are also lawyers and accountants."

Especially disturbing is the lack of systematic data concerning organized crime, the topic of the third NICB conference paper by Will Wilson, Assistant Attorney General, Criminal Division, U. S. Department of Justice. His topic, "Corporate Vulnerability to Crime," specifically concerns vulnerability to organized crime and, in particular, to organized crime of the type associated with the so-called Mafia. No data are presented— a situation typical of both journalistic and social science treatment of the topic, despite mounting evidence from a variety of sources and considerable attention to the matter. A few quotes from Wilson's (1969) brief report are illustrative:

> ... it is sobering to reflect that substantial equity positions in key industries are being acquired with the proceeds of vice, gambling, extortion, narcotics and loan sharking, as well as from the illegal operations of legal business. An example of the latter is "skim" money from legal gambling casinos. . . .

> We know that investment in publicly traded securities by individuals with racket connections has preceded several spectacular market manipulations.

> Another specific instance of corporate vulnerability is the planned

---

[2] From "Equal Justice and the Problem of White Collar Crime" by Robert M. Morgenthau, in *The Conference Board Record* 2, August, 1969, 17–20. Reprinted by permission of the publisher.

bankruptcy or the so-called "scam" operation. This is one of the oldest of swindles and one of the most difficult for the honest businessman to cope with. The operation relies on good credit and speed. It begins when a racketeer gains control of a going business with a good credit rating, and begins to over-purchase inventory which is immediately resold in bulk. Suppliers deal with him because they do not know his credit rating is a sham. The proceeds are canceled and the company goes broke, often within two or three months. Creditors are left with no assets to reach in the ensuing bankruptcy proceedings. . . .

Payoffs either to corrupt labor leaders or corrupt politicians are another aspect of this problem. The employer's goal may be to buy labor peace. Despite the clear illegality of such an arrangement, management may seek to rationalize it as a fight-fire-with-fire measure, but in the end agreements with hoodlums can never advance the cause of good labor-management relationships.

The vast number of local unions are not under racket control, but there are locals, particularly in some of the big cities, which are dominated by racketeers. Corporations cannot submit to demands for side payments or other commercial advantages from these hoodlums. Once granted, the demands will never end. Instead, the appearance of mobsters in the guise of union officials should flash all the red lights. If one is not dealing with a bona fide labor organization, inside thefts are almost sure to increase.[3]

Business Products Related to Crime "Because of the rise in crime," says *U. S. News and World Report* for October 26, 1970, "a young industry is booming in this country. It makes electronic devices to protect homeowners and apartment dwellers from burglars and vandals." The article, complete with pictures, cites as the "big reason" for this burgeoning industry: "Burglaries more than doubled in number in nine years—up from 897,400 in 1960 to 1,949,800 in 1969. The loot taken in residential burglaries last year totaled 363 million dollars." Source of the data was the Uniform Crime Reports for 1969. Source of the only other data cited in the article is unclear, though the figure very likely comes from police statistics for the District of Columbia: "Eighty-nine percent of those arrested in Washington are under 21 years of age."

On June 11, 1970, the *Wall Street Journal* headlined an article: "Westinghouse to Offer Computer Controlled Burglar Fire Alarms; Firm

---

[3] From "Corporate Vulnerability to Crime" by Will Wilson, in *The Conference Board Record* 2, August 1969, 14–16. Reprinted by permission of the publisher.

Moves to Tap Household Fear Market; Manned Units will Monitor the Devices." The August 16, 1970, *New York Times,* under the headline, "Booming Burglar Alarm Industry Finds that Fear of Crime Pays," noted that "Sales ... are a direct reflection of rising crime rates, and the projections are for a continuing steep upward trend." The article continued, "Burglary or unlawful entry to commit a felony was the single most frequently committed crime last year, with 81 percent of the incidents listed as unsolved. Houses and apartments are prime targets. In Los Angeles, the city with the highest crime rate in the nation, the police reported 65,546 burglaries and attempts last year, against 36,256 in 1960. Single residences led the list with 21,968 burglaries, and apartments were second with 14,092." The *Times* article also noted "strident hawking of wares" in this field. A November 3, 1970, *Wall Street Journal* article also noted that 98 percent of the alarms set off by systems in Scarsdale, N. Y., a city where one out of ten homes are electronically "protected," were false. The article was headlined, "Home Burglar Alarms Keep the Cops Busy—Apprehending Dogs, Pets, Maids, but Few Crooks Set Off Scarsdale Systems; Three Squad Cars Crack Up."

Drug problems have been the subject of public concern, of businesses which advertise products related to such problems, and of "public service" type advertisements.

Figures relating to the extent of drug use occasionally are cited in public service ads, but their authenticity is questionable. Thus, *Newsweek*'s "Responsibility Series," reporting "Ten Facts Parents Should Know about Marijuana," cites the widely varying estimates as to the extent of marijuana use among young people "ranging to one estimate that as many as 80 percent of our young people have tried the drug." And *Time* magazine's Education Program, advertising the booklet, "Drugs and the Young," reports that "at least 5 million youngsters in this country have tried marijuana." The National Institute of Mental Health cites no statistics in its "Pot Primer for Parents," saying that more information on marijuana and other drugs is available from the institute.

Major advertising campaigns in behalf of stricter laws governing drinking drivers, aimed particularly at the drunk driver, have been launched in recent years by at least two large insurance companies, Allstate and State Farm Mutual Automobile Insurance Company. The Advertising Council and the National Safety Council often join in sponsoring these ads. Full-page and sometimes double-page ads appeared in several of the nation's news magazines citing statistics of the number of persons killed by "drunk drivers." Figures cited are not always consistent.

Consumers

Consumers—from the broad public appealed to by "public interest" advertising to homeowners, to specialized professions, as in medicine—are the target of advertising such as that cited. Information relative to consumer interests in crime is not easily separated from such information related to business uses, though the interests of the two parties vary somewhat in any given instance, and may be directly opposed. Costs of crime to corporations inevitably are largely passed on to consumers, and consumers are the targets of business advertising related to crime. Protection of consumers from deceptive advertising and from various fraudulent business practices has long been considered a responsibility of government. This responsibility has achieved high news value at various times and has led to such events as the National Consumer Protection Hearings, held by the Federal Trade Commission in November and December 1968.

The indexed transcript of the oral and written presentations at their hearings is a thick volume of 375 pages. Several of the witnesses dwelt on fraudulent commercial practices which victimize consumers. Statistics presented to indicate the magnitude of the problem include the following:

> Senator Warren G. Magnuson, Chairman of the Senate Banking Committee, in his book, *The Dark Side of the Marketplace,* reports that "Several billion dollars is stolen annually from consumers through fraud—more than all the auto thefts, burglaries, robberies, embezzlements, larcenies and forgeries combined."

> The President's Crime Commission reported that some $500 million to $1 billion is stolen from homeowners each year in home improvement frauds alone—in one year, more than all the damage to stores, inventories, and merchants' property in all of the riots that have ever occurred in the United States.

Earlier, David Rice, faculty member of the Boston University Law School, told the commission that his research had examined consumer complaints to Attorneys General Offices in "perhaps twenty-five or thirty states" and "that a very large portion of the complaints . . . received are found to be justifiable upon investigation. Estimates range, I think from my records, from about 50 percent to 90 percent." Professor Rice also indicated that his research found that consumer remedy in the case of fraud is most often "concluded by voluntary assurances instead of court actions." He defended this informal practice (which keeps the offending merchant out of the criminal, or even civil, court statistics) on the grounds that "when there is an innocent violation by the reputable businessman . . . there is no difficulty in rectifying that injustice," but recognized that such practices sometimes also protect the unscrupulous businessman complained of by other witnesses.

The "criminal statistics" cited in the hearings thus by and large were of unknown origin and reliability. The most important message of the hearings concerned the lack of proper statistics relative to consumer victimization and the contrast between the criminal sanction applied to crimes committed primarily by lower-class persons, in contrast to the noncriminal, and largely nonpublic nature of behavior by businessmen which results in far greater economic loss by consumers (many of them lower class). According to a "Newsletter" of the American Council on Consumer Interests, "State Attorney Louis J. Lefkowitz reported that nearly $700,000 was returned to consumers in money, goods and services and through the cancellation of alleged deceptive and fraudulent contracts as a result of action taken by the Bureau of Consumer Frauds and Protection during the first six months of 1970." This figure is a good example of a "criminal statistic" of the type which is only haphazardly made public and does not receive the enormous publicity accorded the Uniform Crime Reports.

Students, Educational Institutions, and Educators

Student concern with crime statistics probably occurs most consistently as a result of exposure in the classroom, since courses in social problems, criminology, and juvenile delinquency are among the more popular in college and university undergraduate curricula in sociology, police science and administration, and their counterparts in high schools and community colleges.

In the course of such academic work students are exposed to collections of readings and articles in professional and popular journals which criticize, analyze, or simply report statistics concerning crime. It is in this literature especially that special investigations by scholars concerning these matters are reported. There is, for example, a sizable literature concerning "self-reported" surveys of criminal and delinquent behavior, on observational studies in communities, on clinical studies, and on studies of victimization. Except for occasional special features and news releases, most of these studies rarely come to public attention. But they are the subject of intense discussion in thousands of classrooms throughout the country. And they are influential in shaping policies of such federal agencies as the United States Department of Justice and the Youth Development and Delinquency Prevention Administration. Such studies are also influential in the allocation of funds for continued experimental programs of delinquency prevention and for their evaluation, through the auspices of such organizations as the National Institute of Mental Health, chiefly but not exclusively through the institute's Center for Studies of Crime and Delinquency.

Student publications occasionally report crime problems on campus. Thus, for example, the December 9, 1970, issue of the *Daily Evergreen,* the student newspaper at Washington State University, reported the addition of floor walkers to the staff of the student bookstore in an effort to reduce the incidence of shoplifting.

The popular press often reports on crime and delinquency on college campuses and in secondary and elementary schools. An example is an article with the sensational title "Crime Invades the Campus" which appeared in the March 14, 1971, issue of *Parade,* a "Sunday Supplement" magazine distributed with many newspapers.

The scholarly literature on crime and delinquency rarely is cited in magazines aimed at elementary and secondary teachers and parents. Recent issues of *Counselor Education and Supervision, The Instructor, Journal of General Education,* and *PTA Magazine* were examined. Articles in these magazines occasionally concern delinquency, but hard data are rare indeed. The chief purpose of those which are cited appears to be to indicate the magnitude of the problem under discussion, rather than to contribute to understanding or solving the problem. Thus, an article in the August–September 1969 issue of *The Instructor* cited data from the California Bureau of Criminal Statistics as well as survey data to demonstrate that drug problems exist in elementary schools. The thrust of the article was to tell teachers how to identify drug users and to stress preventive action by the school. A September 1969 article in *PTA Magazine* referred to the number of student disorders in high schools throughout the country —the source was Allen F. Weston, director of the Center for Research and Education in American Liberties, Columbia University. This article attempted to develop guidelines for handling such problems. In February 1970, under the heading "Border War," a column in this same magazine cited statistics on the number of agents and expenditure of funds to control the illegal flow of drugs into the country. A month later, an article on "Early Steps Toward Preventing Drug Abuse" was accompanied by statistics on the number of deaths attributed to heroin in New York City for the year 1969. These and other articles and advertisements appear to be designed chiefly to muster support for drug education programs in local schools.

Minority Groups

Crime coverage in "black" magazines has been considered above. This section draws again from Stephen Bahr's paper on "The Use and

Abuse of Criminal Statistics in Minority and 'Hate' Literature," and supplements what has already been reported from that paper. It will be recalled that the "moderate black magazine," *Ebony,* cited more numerical data than did the "radical" *Black Panther,* and that *Ebony*'s sources usually were noted, whereas those utilized by the *Black Panther* were not. *Ebony* also used a greater variety of sources of data than did other magazines examined.

The scholarly literature has been much concerned with racial and ethnic differentials in crime and delinquency, and it is here that the more responsible efforts to understand such differentials are to be found. Scholars have employed virtually every technique in their bag of methodological tricks to generate new data concerning criminals and delinquents, as well as subjecting to careful analysis many sources of official data. The following summary of findings by two sociologists, Albert K. Cohen and James F. Short, Jr., may be taken as representative of scholarly efforts with respect to the analysis of racial and ethnic variations in crime and delinquency. Statistics do not appear in the summary, but the studies cited utilize statistics from every level of law enforcement, as well as national surveys and studies conducted in local communities:

> Racial and ethnic groups in the United States have widely varying rates of crime and delinquency. The rates for blacks, for example, are exceptionally high. Estimates range from about twice to about five times as many offenders as would be expected on the basis of the proportion of blacks in the total population. Puerto Ricans, Mexicans, and American Indians likewise have especially high rates, whereas Orientals and Jews usually have strikingly low rates.
>
> Differences such as these may be misleading, for numerous studies have found greater variation within these groups than between them. Furthermore, such intergroup comparisons are to some degree suspect because all the foregoing statements are based on *official* data, subject to all the qualifications of official data discussed earlier. Axelrad, for example, has found that black children were committed at younger ages, for less serious crimes, and with fewer prior court appearances and institutional commitments than were white children. Other studies have found that blacks are more likely to be arrested, indicted, and convicted than are whites who commit the same offenses, and that blacks have less chance than whites to be placed on probation, to be granted parole or a suspended sentence, or to be pardoned or have a death sentence commuted. When blacks are victims of crime, however, as they are in the vast majority of offenses committed by other blacks, official reaction has been shown to be less prompt and efficient in giving protection to the citizen. Still other studies find that blacks are much less positive in their evaluation of the effectiveness, honesty, and respect for citizens on the part of police, and in their attitudes concerning the efficacy of the system of law enforcement

and the administration of justice. Fear and distrust of the police by many black Americans has been a prominent theme in the literature concerning recent ghetto riots and related types of criminality.

Ethnic variations present a striking picture of change over time, reflecting very closely the flow of immigration to this country. As recently as 1930, for example, shortly after the sharp restrictions imposed on immigration in the mid-1920's, about one-half of the children coming to the attention of the courts were of foreign-born parentage. This is no longer the case, and recent studies indicate that neither the foreign born nor their children contribute disproportionately to delinquency rates.[4]

Women

Even the scholarly literature pays scant attention to female crime and delinquency, so heavily male is the population of greatest concern. Cohen and Short (1971) again summarize the relevant data from official and scholarly sources:

> Crime and delinquency rates for males are greatly in excess of rates for females; in all nations, all communities within a nation, all age groups, all periods of history for which organized statistics are available, and for all types of crime except for a few peculiar to women, such as prostitution, infanticide, and abortion. Ratios vary greatly by offense, however. Girls are typically brought before the court for sex offenses, as are their adult counterparts, and for "running away," "incorrigibility," and "delinquent tendencies," which often are euphemisms for problems related to sexual behavior.
>
> In recent years the ratio of boys to girls appearing before juvenile courts in the United States has dropped to about 4 to 1, probably the lowest ratio of any country. The figure represents a considerable decrease from the 50 to 60 to 1 ratios which obtained in this country around the turn of the century. The ratio in England and Wales is about 8 to 1, also a declining figure in recent years. Adult ratios tend to be higher than juvenile ratios, about 10 to 1 in the United States and 15 to 1 in England and Wales. These figures appear to have changed less than have those for juveniles.
>
> The extent to which male rates exceed those for females varies greatly from one cultural setting to another. In some traditional societies, such as those in Ceylon, Algeria, Tunis, and Japan before World War II, male criminals and delinquents came to official attention 3000 to 4000 times as frequently as females. However, in Japan and Turkey, where women

---

[4] From "Crime and Juvenile Delinquency" by Albert K. Cohen and James F. Short, Jr., in *Contemporary Social Problems* by Robert K. Merton and Robert Nisbet, copyright, 1961, by Harcourt Brace Jovanovich, Inc., pp. 108–110. Reprinted by permission of the publisher.

recently have become more nearly equal to men, as is the case in the United States and in Western Europe, marked increases in the proportion of female offenders have been noted.[5]

By 1969, "Juvenile Court Statistics," formerly compiled and issued by the U. S. Children's Bureau, now by the National Center for Social Statistics, reported that delinquency referrals of girls to juvenile courts accounted for 23.9 percent of all cases nationally, indicating a continued shrinking of sex ratios (number of males per 100 females). The percentage of girls referred to urban courts was higher (24.2 percent) than the percentage referred to semiurban (20.9 percent) and rural (21.4 percent) courts. As has been true in other reports for recent years, girls' cases increased more rapidly (by 19 percent nationally) than did boys' cases (up 7 percent). The remarkable decrease in sex ratios of crime and delinquency has attracted little scholarly attention. "Women's Lib" and the "unisex movement" among young people surely have important implications for the participation of females in activities defined as criminal and for the reaction of agents and agencies of social control relative to such behavior. The prediction clearly is that sex ratios of "official involvement" in such behaviors will be reduced further, perhaps to unity.

Some women have reacted to the perceived threat of crime—in which statistics probably have played some role—by arming themselves against possible intruders, learning to use guns, and taking other precautionary measures (e.g., karate lessons, purchase of home burglary alarms, etc.). These developments have been widely reported in the press and in such special interest publications as *The American Rifleman*, official magazine of the National Rifle Association.

Youth

Next to sex, age is the "categoric risk" most closely associated with criminal activity. In 1973, youths 16 years of age comprised the largest number of persons arrested for all crimes, with youngsters of 17 second, followed by 18- and 15-year-olds. It appears also that rates of serious crimes committed by young people have risen more rapidly than have these rates for older persons.

While they are not as likely as older persons to be involved in white-collar crime, professional theft, or organized crime, young people come to the attention of the police primarily for property crimes, for vandalism, and for specifically juvenile offenses such as running away and curfew violation. With the exception of embezzlement, fraud, forgery, and counterfeiting, which require greater finesse and higher social position, juveniles

---

[5] *Ibid.*, pp. 107–108. Reprinted by permission of the publisher.

account for a large percentage of all property-offense arrests. It is clear that arrests of young people have increased more rapidly during 1960 to 1973 than have arrests of older persons. And again, with few exceptions (including the two major violent crimes, murder and nonnegligent manslaughter and aggravated assault), arrests of females have increased more rapidly than have male arrests. Sex ratios remain higher for these major crime arrests than for juvenile delinquency referrals, but the gap clearly is narrowing. Extreme caution should be exercised in interpreting these data, since they do not take into account shifts in the percentage of the population in different age categories, and such other factors as increased urbanization.

Special Interest Groups

Concern with crime and delinquency has led to the formation of numerous organizations, lay and professional, which have as their mission some aspect of the control of these phenomena. The largest such private organization in the United States is the National Council on Crime and Delinquency (NCCD) which describes itself in various publications as follows:

> The National Council on Crime and Delinquency, with a membership of approximately 60,000 citizens and officials, organized in 1907 and incorporated as a national service agency in 1921, provides services to promote rehabilitation of juvenile and adult offenders. On a community, statewide, and national level, the Council works to develop effective juvenile, family and criminal courts, to improve probation, parole, and institutional services and facilities, and to stimulate community programs for the prevention, treatment, and control of delinquency and crime. The Council works with citizen and professional groups and with judges, probation and parole officers, correctional administrators, and other public officials.

NCCD does excellent work in reporting and analyzing official sources of statistics as well as the scholarly literature, and in bringing such information to the attention of lay and professional groups concerned with crime and delinquency. Since 1964 the council has published the *Journal of Research in Crime and Delinquency,* the editorial board of which consists of the Research Council of NCCD. That council, in turn, consists of leading research scholars in sociology, psychology, law and criminal justice, and occasionally others. The Research Council also advises the professional research arm of NCCD, located at Davis, California.

Dozens of professional associations, some with their own publications, are found, ranging from those which are primarily local in scope to national and international organizations. Most of these "use" statistics sparingly, though they constitute an important audience for scholarly research. Their primary goals are professional. Examples include the American Correctional Association which was 100 years old in 1970, the John Howard Association, the Osborne Association, various state correctional associations and academies of criminology, crime commissions, etc.

The United Nations has held congresses in this area and, especially at the London Conference held in 1960, paid a great deal of attention to statistics on juvenile delinquency. Comparative study of crime and delinquency has been severely hampered by the lack of statistics which are both reliable and valid in varying cultural contexts.

THE OUTLOOK

At the present time much crime and delinquency never reaches official attention; much that does reach such attention is handled in ways which are not recorded or, if recorded, are not reported in official statistics. This general situation has been speculated about but not systematically studied. We know, for example, that there is great variation in the extent to which victims of crimes report them to the police and in the extent to which the police file official crime reports and make arrests, and we know some of the reasons for such variation. Overall, from a national survey, it appears that only about half the victims actually report the crimes to the police and that the proportion of such reports varies from city to city. More serious crimes are reported more often than less serious crimes, but there are differences in the extent of reporting, even for the same offense. Most frequently, respondents indicated they had not reported a crime because they did not believe the police could do anything about it, that they would not catch the offender, or would not want to be bothered. Many victims wished to protect the offender, some did not want to become involved with the police, some simply did not wish to take the time or trouble to report an offense, and others were afraid of reprisal by offenders or their friends.

Still, the evidence suggests that underreporting of crime in official statistics is more often a result of police decisions than it is of the lack of citizen reporting.

It must be concluded, then, that current statistics of crime and delinquency are neither reliable nor valid within tolerable limits, whether the criteria of tolerableness be those of a science of human behavior or of social policy and its implementation. This, despite the good will and the best efforts of law enforcement officials and scholars alike. Improvements have been made, particularly in the gathering, reporting, and interpretation of police statistics. Especially noteworthy in recent years are the victim surveys initiated by the Crime Commission (Ennis, 1967), self-reported behavior studies (Reiss, 1974), investigations of police decision-making processes (Reiss, 1971), and studies which have provided more systematic measurement of the "seriousness" of criminal offenses as judged by citizens (Sellin and Wolfgang, 1964; Wolfgang, et al, 1972). But these efforts are beginnings only. The Violence Commission Task Force on Individual Acts of Violence concluded that "the most pressing support requirement behind our recommendations is for improved data on crime, criminals, and criminal justice system operations." The Violence Commission report went on to reinforce and add to recommendations of the Crime Commission and the Bureau of the Census in this respect. Attention to this area of the Bureau of the Census is particularly noteworthy, since the bureau has a most distinguished record of high-quality data gathering and dissemination in the public interest (for important beginnings in this respect, see United States Department of Justice, 1974).

The Violence Commission Task Force recommended that four procedural alternatives for the collection of statistics be included in a national system of criminal statistics, operating under the National Criminal Justice Statistics Center:

(1) Continuous collection for all persons, events, or operations (continuous census); (2) collection for all persons, events, or operations but at intervals (interval census); (3) continuous collection for a proportion of all persons, events, or operations (continuous sample); or (4) collection for a proportion of all persons, events, or operations at intervals (interval sample).

Given data requirements and a set funding level for statistical collection, the Center should decide which procedure is most desirable for each kind of data. Thus, for example, the great importance of police data surely dictates their collection as part of a continuous census, but special studies on community attitudes toward the police or victim-offender relationships can follow the interval sample approach. Mandatory local reporting of all census and continuous census data would be advisable, although it is not necessary for sample surveying [Mulvihill and Tumin, 1969].

The Task Force report goes on to recommend specific improvements in police statistics, arson, suicide, juvenile court, and prison data, and initiation of new statistical programs on criminal justice system workload volumes, administrative characteristics, and pretrial operations. Concerning the latter:

Few pre-trial statistics are maintained, even at the local level. These are required to cover the operations and workloads of prosecuting attorneys; the composition, characteristics, and decisions of grand juries; the requirements for effectiveness of bail; and the operations, facilities, staff, prisoner intake, and detention periods of jails [Mulvihill and Tumin, 1969].

Special recommendations are also made with respect to court data, probation and parole data, and data on violent auto fatalities, organized and professional crime, juvenile gangs, group and mass protests, and, finally, provision for sample surveys and other special studies, e.g., periodic victim surveys and self-reports of behavior and attitudes relevant to crime and delinquency and various aspects of criminal justice operations.

The need clearly is great. Statistics of crime and delinquency are used and abused in many ways by many groups and in many contexts. Their improvement should have high priority in any national "social accounting" system.

The imbalance of data concerning the crimes of different groups in our society has been noted. It is important, therefore, to add to the recommendations of the Violence Commission the point that statistics on white-collar crimes stand in need of great improvement. This is especially important in view of the rising political self-consciousness of those groups who are at once the perpetrators and the victims of most of the "ordinary crimes" on which traditional police and other statistics are most systematically gathered and disseminated; that is, the young, the poor, and the black (and in some parts of the country, other ethnic groups, e.g., Puerto Ricans, Latin Americans and Chicanos, and native American Indians).

A more well-rounded picture of the crimes of members of those groups which have had the power to protect their own interests would at least provide the basis for greater understanding of the nature of crime and delinquency in our society and for more effective control. As of this writing, little progress can be reported toward this end. Greater progress appears to be in the offing toward comprehensive coverage and standardization of reporting "ordinary" (blue-collar) crime than white-collar crime. The gap thus appears to be widening and the discrepancies in reporting are likely to produce more "heat" and less "light" on inequities within our society. In the long run, as less powerful groups achieve power, this situation may change. If it does, the change will be much more profound than will appear in the tables of statistical reports, for it will itself reflect fundamental changes in the social order, as much as it will permit measurement of heretofore neglected aspects of social accounting.

REFERENCES

AFL-CIO. "A Program for the Cities, Jobs, Education, Housing." *The American Federationist*, 74, September, 1967.

Bahr, Steven J. "The Use and Abuse of Criminal Statistics in Minority and 'Hate' Literature." Paper presented for a graduate seminar in Criminology at Washington State University, 1970.

Cash, Norman E. "Crime and the Corporation." *The Conference Board Record* 2, August, 1969, 11–13.

Cohen, Albert K., and James F. Short, Jr. "Crime and Juvenile Delinquency," in Robert K. Merton and Robert Nisbet (eds.), *Contemporary Social Problems*, third ed. New York: Harcourt Brace Jovanovich, 1971.

Ennis, Philip H. *Criminal Victimization in the United States: A Report of a National Survey, Field Surveys II*. The President's Commission on Law Enforcement and the Administration of Justice. Washington, D. C.: U. S. Government Printing Office, 1967.

Kelley, Clarence M. *Crime in the United States: 1973 Uniform Crime Reports*. Washington, D. C.: U. S. Government Printing Office, 1974.

Lyle, Jack. "Contemporary Functions of the Mass Media," Appendix II-B in David L. Lange, Robert K. Baker, and Sandra J. Ball, *Mass Media and Violence: A Report to the National Commission on the Causes and Prevention of Violence*. Washington, D. C.: U. S. Government Printing Office, 1969.

Morgenthau, Robert M. "Equal Justice and the Problem of White Collar Crime." *The Conference Board Record* 2, August, 1969, 17–20.

Mulvihill, Donald J., and Melvin M. Tumin. *Crimes of Violence: A Report to the National Commission on the Causes and Prevention of Violence*. Washington, D. C.: Government Printing Office, 1969.

National Council on Crime and Delinquency (NCCD). *Journal of Research in Crime and Delinquency*. New York: NCCD and the Center for Youth and Community Studies, Howard University, semi-annual.

Reiss, Albert J., Jr. *The Public and the Police*. New Haven: Yale University Press, 1971.

———. "Surveys of Self-Reported Delicts," in Albert Biderman (ed.), *Crime and the Public: A Symposium*. New York: Naiburg Publishing Co., 1974.

Sellin, Thorsten, and Marvin E. Wolfgang. *The Measurement of Delinquency*. New York: Wiley, 1964.

U. S. Department of Justice. *Uniform Crime Reports for the United States*. Washington D. C.: U. S. Government Printing Office, 1973.

———. *Crimes and Victims: A Report on the Dayton-San Jose Pilot Survey of Victimization.* Washington, D. C.: Law Enforcement Assistance Administration, 1974.

Wilson, Will. "Corporate Vulnerability to Crime." *The Conference Board Record* 2, August, 1969, 14–16.

Wolfgang, Marvin E., Robert M. Figlio, and Thorsten Sellin. *Delinquency in a Birth Cohort.* Chicago: University of Chicago Press, 1972.

CHAPTER 9

On Consumption and the Consumer*

THE CONSUMER SECTOR

Economists divide the domestic economy into three sectors: households, businesses, and the government. The sum total of the output of the sectors is called gross national product, the largest part of which consists of the expenditures of households or consumers. From a different point of view, the activities of households may be seen as falling either in the area of acquisition or in that of allocation of income, people being engaged in work, or in consumption and leisure. How consumers budget the time as well as the funds available to them—how much they work and how much they either spend or save, what they buy and how much they pay for things purchased—represent decisions important for the individuals as well as for the economy as a whole.

In a subsistence economy the great majority of families spend their entire income to gratify their minimum requirements for food, shelter, and clothing. When earnings advance people spend more; when they decline people are compelled to be satisfied with less than they think is necessary. Under these conditions, consumption is a function of income. In today's affluent society, as it has developed first in the United States, the majority of families have considerable choice. Their income exceeds what they must spend on keeping body and soul together. Therefore, they also spend money

---

* Based on a memorandum prepared by George Katona, University of Michigan, and articles by Helen H. Lamale of the U. S. Bureau of Labor Statistics.

on what they would like to have; that is, they make discretionary expenditures. To be sure, there still exists a sizable poverty sector, although it is much smaller than in earlier years when only a thin upper class had great freedom of choice.

The role of the consumer sector in today's American economy is different from what it was 100 or even 50 years ago. The automobile industry, which caters to consumers, is the largest of all industries, both in terms of the value of its output and the number of people it employs for the production, maintenance, and use of cars. Consumers buy cars, overwhelmingly, not because they must have them due to the breakdown of their old car or because they do not have a car, but because they want a newer or better car or they want a second car. This transition from a "needs" to a "wants" or "aspirations" economy, which could be illustrated by numerous examples beyond that of the automobile, has made the consumer a very important factor in the structure and growth of the economy. Consumers' decisions are based not only on their ability to buy, but also on their willingness to buy, and they influence economic trends such as upswing and downturn or inflation.

While traditionally economists have considered business investment in plants and machinery as the major force generating capital or wealth, today a very large part of national wealth is in the possession of the household sector. About two-thirds of American families live in one-family homes which they own. Consumers' enduring possessions—cars and other durables—likewise have substantial value. Most important, human capital—the sum total of people's investment in education, skills, and health—represents a very important national asset. Both businesses and consumers frequently borrow in order to acquire goods. During the last twenty-five years consumer debt has grown to a much larger extent than business or government debt.

GOALS OF STATISTICS ON CONSUMERS

The previous discussion makes it possible to summarize the goals which are served by statistics on consumption and the consumer. They range from contributions to economic and social theory to practical needs of business firms. Statistics on consumption and the consumer make the following possible:

- To understand changes in economic and social processes
- To detect and document problems of public policy
- To predict economic trends
- To guide opinion leaders in their consideration of public as well as private affairs

- To display consumer needs and dissatisfactions
- To guide organizations in helping consumers to plan their financial affairs and resist exploitation
- To assist business firms—manufacturers of consumer goods, the retail trade, and firms providing services to consumers—in their policies

ECONOMIC STATISTICS AND SOCIAL STATISTICS

As has been indicated, economic or business statistics and social statistics sometimes are viewed as representing two independent or even unrelated areas. This view is especially untenable if applied to statistics on consumption and the consumer. Statistics on changes in consumer incomes, in prices, and even in amounts spent on various types of goods (e.g., alcohol) have social significance and are also useful for the purposes of business firms and consumer organizations.

Nevertheless, there are differences in emphasis among statisticians and there are statistical data which would hardly be collected in great detail except for their usefulness for business. In this chapter some of the latter kind of statistics will also be mentioned, but attention will be focused on consumer statistics of social significance.

AVAILABLE STATISTICS

Considered next are the major types of statistics on consumption and the consumer which are collected at present in the United States by public or private agencies. Needless to say, the enumeration that follows is far from complete.

The most comprehensive single source of statistical data on consumption is the Office of Business Economics in the U. S. Department of Commerce. It collects and publishes annual, quarterly, and monthly data on the components of GNP. Most relevant in the present context are statistics on the amounts of total personal income, consumer expenditures for durable goods, expenditures for nondurable goods and services, and some additional subdivisions of consumer expenditures. The monthly issues of the publication *Survey of Current Business* contain voluminous statistics on the expenditures of all consumers on food, clothing, housing, household operation, transportation, etc.

The U. S. Bureau of Labor Statistics is the major source of data on the prices of things on which consumers spend money. The monthly Consumer Price Index (CPI), commonly called the cost of living index, indicates the changes in the average cost of a market basket of goods and services, typically purchased by the urban wage earner and clerical worker. The index is subdivided into major subgroups such as food, housing, health, recreation, etc. It is based on monthly surveys of retail stores and on occasional Consumer Expenditure Surveys, the purpose of which is to determine the proportionate share of each item in the market basket.

Surveys of consumer expenditures which collect data on incomes and savings were made as early as the 1880s. Widespread use of the data, however, especially by business for marketing purposes, did not begin until after the 1935–1936 survey. In 1950 the survey was limited to urban places including ninety-one metropolitan and urban areas. The 1960–1961 survey, conducted as was the 1935–1936 survey with the cooperation of the Department of Agriculture, covered urban and rural areas and provided representative data for all American families—urban, rural nonfarm, and rural farm. The information collected, in addition to detailed annual expenditure, income, and savings data, included data on one week's purchase of food items for urban and rural nonfarm families, on many family characteristics, on their living arrangements, and on an inventory of selected household desirables.

The U. S. Bureau of the Census is the source of monthly data on the number of employed or unemployed persons in the American labor force (see Chapter 6). These data are based on surveys conducted with large samples of the population. The Census Bureau also conducts annual surveys on the distribution of income by size and on housing, and quarterly surveys on buying intentions for durable goods.

The Federal Reserve Board collects from lenders monthly data on consumer debt (or personal debt), its various forms and sources, and the extent of debt incurrence and debt repayment. The flow-of-funds statistics of the Federal Reserve Board provide information on the financial assets of consumers and the amounts saved by consumers. (Savings data also are collected by the Securities and Exchange Commission and, as the difference between consumer expenditures and income, by the Commerce Department.)

Turning to private organizations which provide regular information for the country as a whole on matters reflecting consumer activities, mention may be made of data on housing contracts awarded for residential construction, collected by the F. W. Dodge Division of McGraw-Hill (see Chapter 10), of data on automobile registrations collected by R. L. Polk and Company, and of data on the ownership of common stocks collected by the New York Stock Exchange.

While the data of the Commerce Department on consumer expenditures are not shown for different population groups—e.g., the rich and the poor, the young and the old, etc.—survey data do provide such information. In addition to some surveys carried out by the Bureau of Labor

Statistics, a survey by *Life* magazine may be mentioned. Based on a large sample interviewed by Alfred Politz Research, Inc. (1957), the *Life* magazine study presented background data for marketing decisions. A large number of consumer expenditure categories were shown by the income, occupation, education, age, and color of the household head and the location of the household. Such data are continuously updated by marketing magazines.

The Survey Research Center of the University of Michigan began its annual surveys of consumer finances in 1946 and its periodic surveys of changes in consumer attitudes and expectations in 1952. (Since 1960, the periodic surveys have been conducted at quarterly intervals.) Sample surveys are carried out in order to obtain information on (1) the distribution of income, major assets, debts, and purchases of cars and other durables among American families, and (2) consumer attitudes toward purchases and consumer expectations and aspirations, as well as the reasons for changes in attitudes and expectations. An Index of Consumer Sentiment is published at quarterly intervals. The survey findings are reported in press releases and in annual monographs entitled *Survey of Consumer Finances*.

Many private agencies, some of which are affiliated with advertising or marketing firms, engage in marketing research. Business firms are supplied with information, often of confidential nature, on such topics as the composition and characteristics of their customers, preferences for various products, and the extent of store and brand loyalty.

MACRO VERSUS MICRO STATISTICS

The primary concern of economics is with trends in the economy as a whole, for which aggregate data provide the best indications. However, for some major purposes of economic and social policy as well as for an understanding of the dynamic forces in the economy, statistics on such broad aggregates as GNP, personal income, or total consumer expenditures do not suffice. What macro and micro statistics are and why the former need to be supplemented by the latter may be best understood by presenting a few examples.

Macro statistics compiled by the Commerce Department inform the student of economic trends as well as the business world and the consumer that in a given year the total income of all households increased by, say, 5 percent against the previous year. But an increase of the average income of households or of the average per capita income by 5 percent does not mean that the income of every household rose by 5 percent. There probably will be some households with very much larger income increases as well as households with stable and with declining income. It is of crucial importance to find out how many households have had different income changes and who these households are—the young or the old, the poor or the rich, the majority or minority groups. Possibly, for instance, a small proportion of households with fairly high income made substantial gains, while the majority of households had stable incomes. In that case the change in median income—the income of the middle family—would differ greatly from the change in average (mean) income. Such a finding would have social implications (e.g., "the rich are getting richer") and would have an impact on forthcoming trends because people with or without income increases behave differently in that the former are and the latter are not stimulated to undertake certain transactions. The distribution of income changes can only be obtained by determining the income, in two successive years, of all households or a representative sample of households. Such data relating to individuals rather than broad aggregates are called micro data.

Information on the number of the poor calls for micro data that emerge from the size distribution of income and delineate the proportion of families or individuals whose income and assets are below a limit deemed necessary (see Chapter 7). Similar considerations apply to the other side of income inequality, the degree of concentration of income or assets among the top income receivers or asset holders. Changes in the rate of concentration emerge from micro statistics only. Finally, micro data supply information on the share of various population groups in total income, assets, debts, and major transactions.

DATA FROM RECORDS OR FROM SAMPLE SURVEYS

A few decades ago it was generally true of economic statistics that they originated in records kept for legal or practical purposes. For example, data on foreign trade or on corporation balance sheets, collected for legal or practical reasons, were reworked by statisticians so as to provide information necessary for an assessment of economic trends. The same is true in the consumer sector, for instance, of records on the number of cars sold or the changes in financial assets. Most of the data derived from records are macroeconomic, but information derived from Social Security or income tax records may yield micro data.

Surveys are the only possible source of information for a variety of statistics on consumption and the consumer. This statement is particularly true of information on the interrelationship among different sets of data. Take, for example, bank deposits. Banks and savings and loan associations do not have information about the income, age, education, etc., of those who maintain large or small deposits in their savings accounts. Therefore, statistics derived from bank records may tell how much money households have added in a given period to their savings accounts, but not whether the additions were made primarily by upper income, older, or minority group families. Similarly, data from records of automobile registrations, or of sales of one-family houses, are deficient with respect to a characterization of owners and purchasers.

The inadequacy of records may be illustrated further by a reference to the life insurance industry. The voluminous sets of records maintained by this industry do not disclose the number of American families who carry life insurance. The number of policyholders is known from the records, but only through surveys is it possible to disentangle duplications resulting from the fact that many people carry several policies, often with different life insurance companies. The question of great importance for an assessment of the adequacy of available life insurance protection, namely, whether people with rising income—the great majority of Americans—do or do not step up the amount of insurance they carry corresponding to income and price increases, can only be answered by conducting surveys.

Turning from an old established industry to a newer one, the aviation industry may be mentioned. Private and public records disclose the number of passenger miles flown and their changes over time. But some people never fly, while some others travel by plane several times a month. Therefore, the number of people using commercial aircraft for travel, as well as their characteristics (income, age, etc.) and their purposes (for business, vacation, etc.) are known only from surveys.

Surveys have the great advantage that they are tailor-made for the purposes chosen. The questionnaires are prepared according to the needs of the users of statistics by researcher or statistician. In addition to data on economic magnitudes expressed in dollars—on the respondents' income, assets, purchases, etc.—demographic and psychological data may be collected in the same surveys so that a variety of relationships will be available for the same respondents.

But surveys have significant disadvantages as well. Data that are derived from samples are subject to sampling errors and yield information on the order of magnitude of variables rather than exact figures. Because of faulty recollection and even intentionally incorrect information given by respondents (due to modesty, pride, etc.), surveys are subject to reporting errors. In contrast to sampling errors, reporting errors are not as easily measurable even though good survey methods tend to reduce them. But there is often justification to assume that reporting errors are fairly constant in two successive surveys that use the same questions and the same methods. When this is the case, then the most relevant data on changes in the frequency of variables are subject to lesser error and bias than one-time data.

USES

The major users of consumer statistics are scholars, opinion leaders, government agencies, business firms, and consumer organizations. Scholars and opinion leaders make use primarily of statistics which reflect the impact of consumer behavior on economic trends. Government agencies—the Council of Economic Advisors to the President, the Commerce Department, the Treasury, the Federal Reserve Board, as well as agencies of some state governments—make use of the same statistics; occasionally their interest extends to data on the consumption of specific goods. All these users are greatly concerned with consumer statistics relating to the poverty sector.

For a very large number of business firms, consumer statistics are indispensable. Production and marketing strategies may, of course, be established on the basis of subjective notions or the intuition of business leaders who claim to know what their customers want. Over the last few decades especially, large business firms have turned, however, to a scientific underpinning of their policies and forecasts. Needless to say, much remains to be done in this respect. The observation still has some validity that businessmen make use of statistical data only when they are in accord with what they personally believe has happened or will happen. Spending money on the collection of statistical data by business firms appears to be more common in periods of expanding rather than contracting sales, although the need for data may be greater during unfavorable conditions.

The recent movement of consumerism, whether on the part of private groups or federal or state agencies entrusted with consumer protection, is conspicuous in its failure to collect or even make use of available statistics. Information on the extent of consumer dissatisfactions and grievances and on fraudulent business practices that hurt consumers is mostly anecdotal rather than based on sample surveys. Needless to say, there are immense problems confronting the collection of reliable data that would shed light on major questions such as whether the quality of goods and services supplied to consumers has or has not deteriorated during the last few years.

Attempts to educate consumers undertaken by scholars, writers, and consumer organizations often make use of consumer statistics. The need for planning and budgeting on the part of individual families, and especially the necessity of considering alternatives when purchasing life insurance or incurring mortgage and installment debts, have frequently been explained and illustrated by statistical data in books on consumer economics.

Consumer Price Index

The uses of the Consumer Price Index have been mounting under the impact of inflationary pressures. Geoffrey Moore, former commissioner of the Bureau of Labor Statistics, in a letter to the author has summarized some of the major uses of the CPI in the statement which follows:

> One of the most important uses of the CPI is as a guide to broad economic policy. It is one of the most widely used measures of inflationary pressures and plays an important role in the government's efforts to maintain stable wage-price relationships and to judge the advisability of alternative economic policies.
>
> Widespread use of the CPI is made in wage adjustments and collective bargaining agreements. The number of workers covered by contracts which employ CPI data for wage escalation was approximately four million in 1971. The CPI is also used as a means of maintaining constant purchasing power for such things as royalties, pensions of government and nongovernment workers, welfare payments, rental contracts, and occasionally alimony payments. For example, adjustments to Federal civilian and military retirement annuities and social security benefits to compensate for changes in purchasing power of the consumer dollar are based upon the CPI.
>
> In addition to these uses, components of the CPI are used to convert estimates of the gross national product to dollars of constant purchasing power. Changes in real wages are also derived by adjusting money wages for changes in the CPI. The Bureau receives about 100,000 inquiries a year concerning the CPI from persons all over the United States.

The CPI is given for individual Standard Metropolitan Statistical Areas and cities. It is shown for "all items" and for commodity groupings including food, housing, apparel and upkeep, transportation, health and recreation, all sources, and special groupings such as "all items less shelter," "all items less food," "all items less medical care," and for durable and nondurable commodities. The CPI together with "standard budgets," discussed below, and intercity indexes provide statistical measures of the levels and standards of living of American families.

Consumer Expenditure Survey

A major use of the consumer expenditure data has been in the improvement of other government statistics including the Consumer Price Index. The data obtained provide the weight and pricing lists used to calculate the CPI. In this way the index, when it is constructed, can reflect changing prices for actual expenditure patterns of the family types.

Although the requirements of the CPI provided the basic official reason for the survey, the data obtained have a wide range of other significant economic and social uses.

Relation to Other Statistics and Agencies Perhaps the most important single contribution of the Consumer Expenditure Survey lies in its revelation of the level of living of the population—past, present and prospective. This is why such surveys were conducted shortly after the founding of the Bureau of Labor Statistics in the 1880s. The information obtained played a vital role in efforts to raise wages and living and working conditions. Thus, the information collected is used to define "standard budgets" for a city worker's family of four persons and for a retired couple. Budgets developed include a "lower budget," an "intermediate budget," and a "higher budget." These budgets provide a basis for preparing comparative indexes of living costs. Although the standard budgets are prepared for urban workers as indicated above, work has been done on "equivalence scales" for calculating budgets for other family types. In brief, this use of the Consumer Expenditure Survey data provides basic information on what is happening to the level of living in the United States.

The survey information feeds basic statistics to other important statistical measurements. It has contributed much to the development of the household sector of the National Income and Product Accounts of the Department of Commerce. Similarly, it has contributed greatly to the Department of Agriculture's development of agricultural price indexes and consumption.

The survey data provide insights into specific categories of expenditure which permit assessment of the specific areas studied and provide a basis for remedial policy or action as may be indicated. For example, the report, *Expenditure Patterns of Low-Consumption Families* (BLS, 1965), based on the 1960–1961 data, describes the level of living of the poor and provides a basis for the government's definition of poverty.

The report, *Food Expenditures of Urban Families, 1950 to 1960–61* (BLS, 1965), presents the changes in spending for food and factors out the increase attributable to price change. It permits an appraisal of food expenditures of single consumers with those of families and indicates the factors which account for decreasing expenditures. The report, *Contrasts in Spending by Urban Families: Trends since 1950 and Variations in 1960–61* (BLS, 1965), analyzes broad changes in expenditures, income, and savings in relation to other economic and social changes. The Department of Agriculture makes similar analyses for rural farm families. For example, in March 1965, the *Family Economics Review* of the Agricultural Research Service was devoted to articles on low-income families.

The consumer expenditure statistics are used by many government and private agencies in relation to their operating problems. The Bureau of Internal Revenue, for example, uses the data to compile its sales tax tables as a guide to taxpayers in preparing their income tax returns. Assistance agencies and counselors use the data to help solve the financial problems of individual families and to establish guidelines for fees for social services. An example of the former is *Guide to Family Living Costs* (United Community Services of Metropolitan Boston, 1963). An example of the latter is *Guidelines to the Measurement of Ability to Pay for Health and Social Services* (New Jersey Welfare Council, 1962).

The results of the survey are widely used for basic socioeconomic research and for teaching, especially in home economics. Research uses are contained in the *Socioeconomic Research Abstract Series* of the U. S. Office of Education (1939 and 1940); and in the article, "The Future of Home Economics Research" (Leverton, 1965).

Marketing The consumer expenditure data serve many marketing uses. They are used to estimate the total size of the market for specific goods or resources; to calculate the share of a given enterprise in the market; to establish sales quotas; to organize or reorganize sales territories; to plan advertising; to determine where to test new products; to determine outlet locations; and to forecast increased market potentials.

An interesting use of the data was afforded by Andrew F. Brimmer of the Board of Governors of the Federal Reserve when, as deputy assistant secretary of commerce, he gave a talk on "Economic Trends in the Negro Market."

The consumer expenditure data also are used to lay plans for the development of new products and services. For example, the 1960–1961 survey results were used to study demand for passenger transportation in the Washington-Boston corridor in relation to the feasibility of high-speed railway facilities and the demand for supersonic transport. The data also were used to estimate the potential competitive position of electric automobiles as compared with combustion-engine vehicles. The Division of Marketing Research of the Life Insurance Agency Management Association was interested in variations in life insurance expenditures of families with varying levels of housing costs. F. G. Adams and D. S. Brody at the University of Pennsylvania used the survey data, back to 1918, to trace the diffusion of new durable goods among different types of consumers, as well as their impact on consumer spending.

Although rather substantial general-purpose tabulations are made available, the BLS receives numerous requests for special tabulations of the data for a variety of uses. One type of special tabulation much in demand by market analysts shows, for each metropolitan area surveyed, average expenditures for individual items, or classes of goods and services, by families subdivided as below or above the median income for the area. Such a tabulation for New York City in 1950 was used by the Research Department of the *New York Times* to develop a market profile entitled "New York's 19¼ Billion Dollars—Who Spends It and How." This publication served as a guide to advertisers and advertising agencies.

Such special tabulations are made by the BLS on a reimbursable basis. In addition, within the limits of confidentiality provisions forbidding disclosure of information about individual enterprises, the BLS has prepared a general purpose tape sold on a restrictive contract basis to the private sector; and has also provided six other federal agencies (in addition to BLS and the Department of Agriculture) with master tapes for special tabulations.

Special tabulations were also made for the National Industrial Conference Board with the understanding that the data would be made generally available. Some examples of the uses made by the NICB were published under the sponsorship of *Life*. In October 1969, in one of a series of bulletins entitled *Consumer Markets* on "Home Ownership: 1980," Fabian Linden of the National Industrial Conference Board, Department of Consumer Economics, presented projections of home ownership in the year 1980. These projections, significant, of course, to all businesses concerned with and related to home ownership, were based on census statistics showing the characteristics of the population which owned homes. Such data included the age of the household head and income. The statistics showed that home ownership increased with the age of the household head and with income. Using this information along with census projections of changes in the nation's age structure and anticipated changes in income it was possible to show potential markets for home ownership.

Similarly, the same writer (Linden, 1970) in a reprint from the *Conference Board Record* showed the market potential for "appliance ownership" by 1980. Estimates were made for "white goods"—refrigerators, washing machines, and dryers; for "luxury appliances"—room air conditioners, dishwashers, and color TV. Equivalent estimates were made for the "household durables market" in 1975 including home furnishings and automobile ownership, which included the used-car market and the second-car market.

Comparable projections using census age structure data, income statistics, and consumer purchase data were made by Leo J. Shapiro and Associates, Inc., of Chicago on behalf of Foley, Warendorf and Company, a member of the New York Stock Exchange, for the detailed list of items in the Bureau of Labor Statistics' Consumer Expenditure Study using the study and the National Industrial Conference Board report "Market Profiles of Consumer Products" (in *Changing Patterns of Consumer Spending in the 1970s*).

Projections of this kind, needless to say, serve as guidelines to producers, distributors, and investors, and, to the extent that they increase efficiency in allocation of resources, production, and distribution, contribute to the high consumption levels which characterize life in the United States.

Consumers The consumer as well as the business enterprise is making increasing use of the survey data. Consumer advocates, family counselors, and families themselves use the expenditure and savings information in relation to consumer protection practices and to improve family financial activities. In 1963, for example, the Agricultural Research Service issued a report, *Helping Families Manage their Finances* (Home Economics Research Report 21). In 1966 the Pittsburgh National Bank instituted a service called "Family Money Profile." In response to confidential information obtained from the family, the bank provided it with spending patterns for similar families in the Pittsburgh area and made available a computer analysis as a guide to family spending and saving. In April 1967, the Kiplinger magazine, *Changing Times*, initiated a similar nationwide service. In response to questionnaire information made available by the family, *Changing Times* provides a "Spending Yardstick." This enables the family to compare its expenditure pattern with the average for families with the same characteristics. A sales manager of one company asked the Kiplinger organization for 150 copies of the questionnaire for its employees as part of the company's consumer education program.

Finally, the Consumer Expenditure Survey, by strengthening of the Consumer Price Index, indirectly provides the consumer with current information, the trends in prices of the total basket of goods for which the index is calculated, and for specific categories of goods and services as indicated above. Especially under inflationary pressures, these statistics have political implications which lead to government policies and programs designed to protect the consumer.

Consumer Attitudes

Sometimes the contributions of surveys to a collection of statistics on consumption and the consumer are disparaged by being dubbed "nose-counting." Although answers to the questions of "how many" and "who" are of great importance, it is true that they need to be supplemented. A crucial question is: Why have certain changes occurred? To some extent, procedures of nose-counting do supply answers to this question. Assume, for instance, that surveys disclose that vacation travel by low-income people is done overwhelmingly via the family car or the bus, while high-income people mostly use the airplane. A substantial correlation between income and travel modes would shed light on causation. Similarly, correlation between education and certain types of expenditures permits inferences on causation because, obviously, expenditures of adults do not influence the number of years they have spent in school.

Nevertheless, it is possible and necessary to go further. Surveys can obtain information on changes in motives, attitudes, and expectations. Some statistics of this type have already been mentioned when discussing purposes of travel (business, vacation, visiting relatives, etc.), or may be illustrated by studies of purposes of saving (for a "rainy day," for retirement, for the purchase of durable goods, etc.). Extensive additional use of statistics on psychological data has been made over the last twenty years in order to predict probable economic trends that are dependent on consumer behavior.

Such studies began toward the end of World War II by inserting questions on intentions to buy in population surveys. Expressed plans to purchase houses for owner-occupancy, automobiles, and household appliances, the frequency of which is determined in one sample survey, do not give reliable indications of forthcoming actual purchases. Some people may buy with a very short planning period, without having indicated buying plans at an earlier time. Some buying plans may not be carried out because of changed circumstances. But an increase or decrease in the frequency of buying plans over time indicates rising or falling demand and yields valuable information.

On the basis of theoretical considerations about variables intervening between stimuli and responses, the Survey Research Center of the University of Michigan proceeded to collect survey data on changes in consumer attitudes and expectations. The collection of various measures of consumers' willingness to buy led to the compilation of an Index of Consumer Sentiment, consisting of information on attitudes toward personal finances, expectations about business trends, and attitudes toward supply conditions and prices. The index proved to have predictive value for major changes in consumers' discretionary expenditures. This was the case, for instance, in 1955 when sharply rising automobile demand was indicated by a substantial improvement in consumer sentiment in 1954. Similarly, deterioration of sentiment was noted much before the onset of the recession of 1958. Finally, data on a substantial worsening of consumer sentiment in 1969 anticipated the slowdown in consumer demand that occurred in 1970.

The Survey Research Center's quarterly surveys of changes in consumer attitudes and expectations also are concerned with the study of reasons for changes in consumer sentiment. An analysis of people's attitudes toward inflation, unemployment, and higher or lower taxes or interest rates contributes to an understanding of economic fluctuations, as well as to the prospects of several major industries. The greater the importance of the consumer sector, the greater the need of policy makers to understand what motivates the consumers and to obtain information on the probable response of consumers to policy measures. Finally, that part of market research which is called motivation research supplies business firms with information relevant to their marketing and advertising endeavors; information on why consumers buy and why they do not buy certain products, even if incomplete and preliminary, has proved helpful to many business firms.

LOOKING AHEAD

Recent extensive discussions of social indicators often begin with the assertion that economic indicators are available and the time has come to prepare an extensive set of different indicators relating to changes in the quality of life and including matters of health, pollution, crime and violence, sex, etc. (see Chapter 16). Yet a comprehensive set of social indicators must also include changes in satisfactions and dissatisfactions with material well-being as well as data on changes in economic motives, incentives, expectations, and aspirations. Some such consumer statistics are available but they need to be expanded and integrated with what is called social indicators.

Consumer statistics appear to be least complete with respect to leisure-time activities (see Chapter 12). Because expenditures for these purposes, which have become increasingly important during the last two decades, involve both goods and services, few reliable data exist on how much different families spend on vacation travel. Similarly, there are no adequate statistics on the maintenance or repairs of homes. Statistics on home expenditures are complicated further because home repairs often are done by the home owners themselves, who do not assign monetary value to their own time.

An extension of consumer statistics is needed regarding the seamy side of affluence. Presently available statistics are woefully insufficient to answer questions such as the following:

> Does the impatience of many consumers in obtaining the constantly growing number of goods and services they desire contribute to excessive borrowing and to inflation?

Have the expectations of the American people regarding material well-being grown to such an extent that they are bound to be disappointed?

Does the growing affluence of many enhance dissatisfaction and alienation of those who do not participate in the affluent society?

Is it true that an increasing proportion of young people tend to say "no" to the consumer economy and to believe that rising production represents a threat rather than a benefit?

Answers to these and similar questions point to the need for additional data, including attitudinal data, to provide a better basis for understanding and dealing with the problematic aspects of consumption and the consumer.

In Chapters 10 and 12 attention is focused on two significant areas of consumption, housing and outdoor recreation, which, apart from being important areas of expenditure, have wide-ranging social as well as economic implications.

REFERENCES

Agricultural Research Service. *Family Economic Review*. Special Low Income Issue. Consumer and Food Economic Research Division, U. S. Department of Agriculture. Washington, D. C.: Government Printing Office, March 1965.

Guide to Family Living Costs. United Community Services of Metropolitan Boston, 1963.

Guidelines to the Measurement of Ability to Pay for Health and Social Services. New Jersey Welfare Council, 1962.

Leverton, Ruth M. "The Future of Home Economics Research." *Journal of Home Economics,* Vol. 57, No. 3 (March 1965), 169–172.

Linden, Fabian. "Consumer Markets Appliance Ownerships." *The Conference Board Record,* Vol. VII, No. 6 (June 1970), 57–59.

———. "Home Ownership: 1980." *Consumer Markets*. National Industrial Conference Board, October 1969.

Politz, Alfred, Research, Inc. *Life Study of Current Expenditures: A Background for Marketing Decisions*. 4 Vols. New York: Time, Inc., 1957.

Shapiro, Leo J., and Associates. *Changing Patterns of Consumer Spending in the 1970s*. New York: Foley, Warendorf and Co. (member New York Stock Exchange), 1971.

Survey Research Center. *Survey of Consumer Finances*. Ann Arbor: University of Michigan, annual.

U. S. Department of Agriculture. Agricultural Research Service. *Home Economics Research Report No. 21. Helping Families Manage Their Finances.* Washington, D. C.: Government Printing Office, 1963.

U. S. Department of Commerce. Economic Analysis Bureau. *Survey of Current Business.* Edited by Lara S. Collins. Washington D. C.: Government Printing Office, monthly (with a weekly supplement *Business Statistics*).

U. S. Department of Labor, Bureau of Labor Statistics. *Contrasts in Spending by Urban Families: Trends since 1950 and Variations in 1960–61.* BLS Report 238–8. Washington, D. C.: Government Printing Office, 1965.

———. *Expenditure Patterns of Low-Consumption Families: Survey of Consumer Expenditures, 1960–61.* BLS Report 238–10. Washington, D. C.: Government Printing Office, 1965.

———. *Food Expenditures of Urban Families, 1950 to 1960–61.* BLS Report 238–9. Washington, D. C.: Government Printing Office, 1965.

CHAPTER 10
On Housing and Construction*

Housing and construction statistics considered in this chapter are defined rather broadly. The statistics cover the following general areas: the inventory of housing; housing programs operated by the federal government and by state and local governments; the construction and repair of housing; the volume of nonresidential buildings and other nonresidential construction; measures of construction prices; requirements for construction materials; and the Census of the Construction Industries. A variety of data relating primarily to other fields are not dealt with even though they provide information important for housing and construction. Thus, excluded are statistics on labor, though they relate to construction labor. Likewise, financial statistics relating to housing and construction finance generally are treated as outside the scope of the present discussion though some reference is made to such data in the section on "Government Housing Programs." Statistics on construction labor compiled in the Census of the Construction Industries, and on housing finance available from the Census of Housing are, however, included in the discussion. Also excluded are the data on residential rents compiled as part of the Consumer Price Index (see Chapter 9), data on expenditures for new plants and equipment, and the data on the construction industry available from income tax records.

---

* Based on a memorandum by Samuel J. Dennis, formerly of the U. S. Bureau of the Census.

The volume of statistical material available on construction and housing is extensive. The summary which appears below cannot undertake to be a comprehensive listing of the available data nor a complete description of the statistics. However, it does attempt to list at least the principal types of statistical data on housing and construction which are available and to sketch in skeleton terms the major characteristics of the selected series.

INVENTORY OF HOUSING

The primary source of information on the inventory of housing is the Census of Housing, conducted by the Bureau of the Census. The Census of Housing was established as a part of the 1940 decennial census and has been included as a component part of each of the decennial censuses since that time. In addition, in 1956, the Census Bureau carried out a rather large-scale sample survey under the title of the National Housing Inventory. The Components of Change portion of the 1956 survey produced the first set of definitive statistics measuring basic changes in the housing inventory, such as losses due to demolition, destruction by fire and storm, or mergers, and additions stemming from new construction and conversions. Initiation of the Census of Housing in 1940 had been preceded by a series of smaller-scale local surveys beginning about 1934. Prominent among these local surveys, which were undertaken as work-relief projects, were the Real Property Inventory of 1934 and the series of local real property surveys which followed during the next several years.

The housing census undertakes to provide information on the number of housing units, with considerable detail on the characteristics of those units, their tenure, and other aspects of their use. The information on characteristics includes details on the plumbing facilities within the housing unit (see Chapter 1) and, in years prior to 1970, on the physical condition of the unit. Data also are included on the number of housing units within the structure, the age of the structure, the extent of overcrowding as measured by the number of persons per room, the number of rooms, the value or rent, and a number of other characteristics, such as the source of water, presence of air conditioning and other household appliances and facilities, the nature of the fuel used, etc. As an adjunct to the housing census, the Survey of Residential Finance provides detailed financial statistics on mortgaged and nonmortgaged homeowner and rental properties.

Housing census data are available in great geographic detail. Abbreviated tabulations are published for individual city blocks; somewhat more detailed tabulations are available for census tracts; and still greater detail is published for incorporated places, counties and states, and metropolitan areas. Summary statistics appear for regions and divisions as well as for the United States as a whole.

In addition to the decennial programs, the Census Bureau provides quarterly statistics on rates and characteristics of housing vacancies, and annual statistics on characteristics of occupied housing units.

GOVERNMENT HOUSING PROGRAMS

All of the federal government agencies which operate housing programs of one kind or another maintain statistical records of their accomplishments. The most voluminous of these records are those which have come historically from the programs of the Federal Housing Administration (FHA) and the federal agencies responsible for the program of federally assisted publicly owned housing. Other agencies such as the Veterans Administration, the Farmers Home Administration, and the Federal Home Loan Bank Board have also maintained statistics on their operations. At the present time, the principal federal housing programs—and the related statistics—are centralized in the Department of Housing and Urban Development. Some data are also available from state and local government agencies which operate rather limited housing programs independent of the federal programs.

In general, these housing program statistics tend to start at the beginning of a specific program and continue as long as that program is in operation. Thus, many of the statistical series on the operations of the Federal Housing Administration date back to the middle 1930s when FHA was established. Similarly, many of the statistical series having to do with publicly owned housing date back to the beginning of the low-rent public housing program at the same time. The frequency with which such data are available varies from program to program and series to series. Some of the major series are available monthly for the entire period. Other series may be available less frequently, perhaps only annually. The major types of data provided by these series are shown in the Appendix to this chapter.

The geographic detail in which information is available differs widely from series to series. Sometimes, as in the case of projects built by local housing authorities with the assistance of the federal government, information is available on each project individually. In the case of other series, data are available by metropolitan area or by state. In general, however, a large proportion of the program-type information is national or regional rather than for smaller local areas.

CONSTRUCTION AND REPAIR OF HOUSING

An extensive body of statistics is available on housing starts, housing completions, residential building permits, housing sales, and expenditures for alteration and repair of residential structures. The present source for all of these data is the Bureau of the Census. Some of these statistics are old; others represent developments of the last decade. The series on the number of housing units started and the series on the number of housing units for which building permits have been issued extend back into the nineteenth century. At the other extreme, information on the completions of all housing units has been available only beginning in 1968. For further information, see the Appendix to this chapter.

The basic data on housing construction are available monthly. Greater detail on the characteristics of what is built is presented quarterly or annually.

Nonresidential Construction

Three principal statistical series exist which provide information on the volume of construction other than housing: the series on the value of new construction put in place, the series on building permits for nonresidential buildings, and the construction contract series. Details on the data obtained are given in the Appendix to this chapter.

Measures of Construction Prices

Indexes of construction costs or prices are prepared by a number of private businesses and by a few government agencies. Most of the private compilers are construction companies, which develop indexes to summarize their cost experience, or appraisers or cost estimators who need such indexes to carry on their work. The government agencies involved are generally large purchasers of construction or engaged in construction grant programs.

The existing indexes are of several types. A few are indexes which measure changes in the price of the output of construction, for example, the price of constructing highways or the price at which new one-family homes are sold. Most of the construction cost indexes are developed from the prices of construction inputs, representing a weighting together of the wage rates or hourly earnings with material prices. In some cases, the indexes simply are weighted averages of such wage and material prices; in other cases some attempt is made—usually through the exercise of judgment—to account for changes in productivity or changes in the methods and materials used.

Most of the existing construction cost or price indexes are national though a few are available for individual cities. Most are available monthly, some only quarterly or annually. Many extend back to World War I or earlier.

Requirements for Construction Materials

Although a great deal of work is undoubtedly done in attempting to measure the requirements for materials used in construction, the only continuing organized published work which is available is that carried on in the studies of labor and material requirements made by the Bureau of Labor Statistics. In these studies, data are derived for very small samples or projects on expenditures for each of a number of materials (or groups of materials) per thousand dollars of construction cost. These studies have been made for a number of individual types of construction over the last ten years. Some of the studies have shown regional data. So far in only one or two cases have studies for individual types of construction been repeated during the last decade.

Census of the Construction Industries

The statistical work dealing with the volume and characteristics of construction outlined above has related to all of construction, irrespective of the mechanism by which it was produced. Thus, the statistics on housing construction and other construction activity, as well as those on prices, material requirements, and housing programs have related to both the work done by the construction industry as such and to construction done in other ways.

The first Census of the Construction Industries was taken by the Bureau of the Census covering the year 1929 and was followed by somewhat similar censuses covering 1935 and 1939. After 1939, however, the Census of the Construction Industries was discontinued and was not resumed until the year 1967. Information collected in the 1967 census is shown in the Appendix.

USES

Statistics on construction are used by a wide spectrum of the general public, business firms, government, nonprofit organizations, and others. It is difficult in all cases to identify either the user or the use which he makes of the data. The following discussion attempts, however, to summarize these users and uses to the extent that they are known or may reasonably be assumed. Major emphasis is placed on uses other than by business, though the use by business is in its scope a very important one.

The General Public

Most broadly stated, construction and housing statistics are used by the general public to establish a factual base for understanding many matters of major public concern. This factual base, in turn, becomes the foundation for public opinion underlying support for or opposition to specific proposals having to do with broad issues of public policy. Examples are provided by the formation of public opinion with respect to public housing, subsidized housing, monetary policy, control of water quality, the attitude toward a national land-use policy, the ramifications of land-use policy at the local level, etc.

Obviously, the use of any particular series of housing or construction statistics by the general public for these purposes is impossible to demonstrate. However, public opinion is in some manner formed on matters such as those enumerated, and one of the key elements in its formation must be the factual information (accurate, partially accurate, or inaccurate, as the case may be) which has come to the general public concerning the matter on which its opinion is being formed. Thus, the development of public opinion with respect to the necessity of a housing program in general or a specific housing program in particular has included in its background —among other things—information on the quality of the existing housing supply, the numbers and characteristics of people who are now inadequately housed, the rate and characteristics of housing construction both public and private, and the scope and nature of operations under present housing programs. It is impossible to say, of course, to what extent the general impression on which public opinion is based has been derived from any specific statistics or group of statistics. However, many of the basic statistical data do filter into general understanding through the various news media and do, in fact, form a part of the basis on which judgments as to public policy are made.

Construction and housing statistics are increasingly important to the public as voters. Specific examples of the kinds of issues presented to voters in which statistics play an important role are referenda on the establishment of a local housing or redevelopment authority, or on approval of a particular public housing project. Broader issues of overall city or county policies respecting zoning and development also face the voter (and the public generally) from time to time, though the voter's role in such issues is usually—though not always—expressed through his influence on his elected representatives rather than through a referendum.

In addition, various voters' groups, such as the League of Women Voters, which are concerned with the education of the citizen and voter on matters of public policy, specifically make use of construction and housing statistics, along with many other kinds of statistical and nonstatistical materials, in their analyses of, and statements on, the various issues which they present to the voters. In those cases where groups of this sort take formal positions on matters of public policy and on political candidates, the statistics enter specifically into the decision as to the type of position to be taken.

The Federal Government

The use of housing and construction statistics by the federal government can be classified under several designations.

Housing Policy The development of national housing policy, as expressed in a long series of legislation enactments, has depended very heavily on the analysis of available statistics relating to housing and construction. The reports of congressional hearings are filled with these statistics, presented both by government and private witnesses. Congressional committee staffs have made intensive use of these data. In fact, the whole process of legislative consideration of housing measures has proceeded within a factual framework to which these statistics have made the major contribution.

In the Housing Act of 1968 formal housing goals were established for the United States. The decision to establish these goals can be attributed in large part to housing statistics. These statistics provided information on the quality of the existing housing and the way it was being used, as well as information on the rate of change in the existing inventory of housing and on the volume of new housing construction. They thus contributed to recognition of the housing problem and provided the information necessary to reduce the problem to quantitative terms. They made possible the calculation of the amount of new or rehabilitated housing needed, the portion of the total which could be provided through the operation of the normal market, the portion which required assistance or subsidy, and the general levels of subsidy required. In the absence of statistics measuring the situation as it existed and measuring changes in that situation with the passing of time, it would have been impossible to establish meaningful housing goals in quantitative terms, and fruitless to have attempted to do so.

It was recognized, of course, that housing goals could not be established in isolation, without reference to their impact on other national objectives or the economy as a whole. The feasibility of the desired housing goals thus was subject to examination. For this purpose, statistics on labor and material requirements in housing construction were used as the basis both for estimating the total demands on the labor supply and on supplies of materials, and for judging whether resources could reasonably be made available to accomplish the desired goals with respect to housing.

Once the housing goals have been established it becomes necessary to measure progress in meeting the goals. This progress requires statistical information on the housing inventory, the quality of the housing inventory, new housing production, housing units withdrawn from the inventory, and other changes in the existing stock of housing. Since the annual report on housing goals required by the Housing Act of 1968 must be made formally by the president, the housing goals thus require that the president himself nominally make use of a variety of housing statistics. (In practice, of course, the housing goals report is prepared in the Department of Housing and Urban Development on the president's behalf.)

Within the framework of the housing goals, it becomes necessary to consider what specific housing programs are needed in order to achieve the stated goals. For this purpose, it is necessary to know what new housing is being produced, how much is being produced by the official housing programs and how much independently of any of those programs, the characteristics of the current housing output, and what additional official programs are needed to produce the housing which is required. It becomes of particular interest to know the characteristics of the purchasers and renters of new housing provided under the various housing programs, and outside of them, in order to identify the groups which are being served. Both the executive branch and the Congress are faced with the policy question, and both require a broad factual background as the basis for their consideration.

When a specific new housing program has been established, it is also necessary to know what that program accomplishes. Thus the requirement exists both for broad summary information and for detailed reports on operations of the specific programs from the federal government agencies responsible.

General Economic Policy A second major use of housing and construction statistics by the federal government is in connection with the establishment and revision of monetary and fiscal policy. In considering monetary and fiscal policy, housing and construction as a whole play a double role. First, current and expected future developments in construction are important in determining what broad economic policy is needed. For purposes of general economic analysis, it is necessary to know what is happening in housing and the remainder of construction. Construction is a substantial component of the current total of all economic activity. Construction is also important because it is a principal element in capital formation, and thus has a powerful influence on future productive capacity. Finally, economic analysis must take cognizance of the effect which expenditures on capital goods such as construction tend to have on the economy as a whole.

Second, in the last several decades at least, the production of new housing has been particularly susceptible to influence through the exercise of monetary and fiscal policy, particularly the former. Thus, housing has operated as one of the balance wheels in the economy, though—somewhat incongruously—the effects of monetary and fiscal policy on housing have sometimes been different from those which might have been sought by housing policy itself. Thus, the managers of the economy are confronted with the delicate problem of operating monetary and fiscal policy in such a way as to achieve the overall objectives sought and at the same time to achieve as nearly as possible the specific housing objectives. Where these two objectives are in conflict with each other, economic policy has the task of seeking the best compromise of inconsistent objectives.

In all of these operations, close attention must be paid to the statistics on housing production and the value of new construction work put in place, as well as to the volume of funds required for the financing of new construction, repairs and improvements, purchase of existing properties, and repayment of existing indebtedness. Data on the trend in housing vacancies also are considered. Because of the nature of the use, the primary users are the Council of Economic Advisors, the Bureau of Economic Analysis, the Federal Reserve Board, and the Department of the Treasury.

Operation of Housing Programs The operation of some of the federal programs themselves necessarily depends upon a variety of statistical information. One of the best examples of this type of use may be drawn from the experience of the Federal Housing Administration. Historically, decisions as to the volume of mortgage insurance to be provided in a particular locality, for a particular type of structure, and for a particular price or rent level, have been made in the light of the best available information as to the market for the type of construction involved in that locality. The necessity for organized factual information of this type has long been recognized in the Federal Housing Administration where an extensive series of local housing market analyses has been prepared and brought up to date from time to time, primarily for use by the FHA itself. As described by the FHA, the purpose of these analyses is to provide assistance and guidance to the FHA offices "in resolving market problems in the operation of mortgage insurance programs. Basically, these problems are concerned with the quantity and quality of additional housing which a local housing market can absorb satisfactorily over a reasonable period of time." These local market analyses are now available to the public, and are used widely by lenders, builders, local government agencies (particularly planning commissions), and many others. They draw upon all available statistics having to do with housing supply and demand in the locality and with the local economy as a whole. They would be impossible without substantial statistical information specifically on the local inventory of housing and the history of additions to the supply through new construction.

Another example is provided by the limitations on rents, incomes, sales prices, mortgage amounts, rent-income relationships, etc., established for the various federal housing programs. These limitations, which may be uniform throughout the United States or may provide for local or regional variations, are in many cases written into the enabling legislation. Selection of these limits is influenced directly both by the operating statistics for related programs in the past and by the more general statistics providing information on these items for all housing, whether or not provided through government programs.

Policies with Respect to the Construction Industry Construction statistics also are needed in the development of specific construction policies within the federal government. Major problems of current concern are those of inflation, of the seasonality of construction operations, and of an apparent inadequate rate of technological development in construction. All of these require statistical information as the basis for both development and execution of the necessary government policies. This necessity has been clearly recognized. The Cabinet Committee on Construction, appointed by the president in 1969 to concern itself with questions of construction policy, promptly appointed a Subcommittee on Construction Statistics for the purpose of identifying needed improvements in construction statistics, and preparing recommendations for achieving them. The Cabinet Committee evidently believed that improvement of construction statistics was necessary in order to permit it to cope effectively with the specific policy problems with which it had to deal.

Inflation has continued as one of the most urgent of these problems. Available statistics appear to suggest that for many years the rate of inflation in construction, and particularly the rate of wage increases for construction labor, have been appreciably greater than the rate of inflation in other major industries. The first use of statistics, of course, is to establish this proposition. Statistics then measure and to some extent pinpoint the price changes that occur and help to identify the outstanding areas of trouble. They thus help to point out those areas in which specific action needs to be taken, such as the February 1971 action by President Nixon in suspending the Davis-Bacon Act, or the appointment in March 1971 of the Construction Industry Stabilization Committee. In addition, some of the specific methods proposed for dealing with individual aspects of inflation require a specialized statistical base. For example, one of the proposals has been temporarily to defer federal or federally assisted construction in counties or other local areas where the demand for construction is currently outrunning the capabilities of supply. Such a measure would require statistics (not now available in the required detail) to identify areas where public construction should be deferred, together with information on the volume of public construction before and after the deferral.

Another area to which special attention has recently been given by the federal government is that of the wide seasonal fluctuations in construction activity and employment. This is an important matter not only because of its social impact—through the lack of jobs for construction workers during the winter—but also because of its impact on the costs of construction and therefore on the rate of inflation in construction. A formal study of this matter was made in 1969 by the Departments of Labor and Commerce in response to specific legislation. Such a study necessarily rests on statistics in order to describe the size and characteristics of the problem as a prelude to identifying solutions. The same statistics are required in order to appraise proposed solutions and to study their actual applicability and their effect. Similarly, once a program has been placed into operation, statistical measurements would be necessary to know how effective it has been.

Available construction statistics have contributed to the general conclusion that construction is backward in technology and that the rate of productivity improvement in construction has been markedly behind that in other industries. This conclusion rests in part on the available indexes of construction costs. Many of these construction cost indexes, however, appear to be seriously deficient not only in their methods but in the accuracy of their measurement. If the existing indexes of construction cost have overstated increases in costs in recent decades, they would have resulted in underestimating the increases in construction productivity. In any event, the judgment does exist that the construction industry is technologically backward. As a result, federal programs such as Operation Breakthrough have been initiated. Operation Breakthrough was set up by the Department of Housing and Urban Development in 1969 to encourage and help finance the development of new, more efficient, and less costly methods of construction, and improved planning and design, with the objective of providing new housing at substantially lower cost. In planning or in operating such a program, statistics are needed to indicate accurately the state of technology in the industry, to measure the rate at which it changes, to provide a measure of the several components of cost and thus identify the most promising areas for cost reduction, and to measure the effects of the program. Many of the statistical series needed for this purpose do not now exist.

A final example of federal government use of statistics in connection with construction policy may be found in the legislative proposals considered several years ago with respect to the reservation of certain federal government construction projects for small businesses. The necessary definition of a small business requires data on the size distribution of construction companies. A second type of information necessary is statistics on the extent of subcontracting from large contractors to small ones on government jobs. Neither of these types of information was then satisfactorily available, and it was necessary to make the best use possible of those statistics which did exist. The Census of Construction Industries has subsequently greatly increased the knowledge both of the size of construction operations and of the behavior of construction contracting. Nevertheless, even the statistics available today are still not adequate to answer fully the kinds of questions necessary to establish and maintain a program for the reservation of specific construction projects for small companies.

Budget Planning and Review Indexes of the price or cost of construction are needed not only as bases for measuring changes in productivity but also in their own right for various purposes within the federal government. Price indexes are needed to provide the past history as the basis for estimating the cost of future planned construction projects. They are, therefore, important in budget planning. Similarly, they are important in budget review, both for federal projects and for the federal government in administering grant-in-aid programs. Actual use of the available price and cost indexes for these purposes has been handicapped by the poor quality of much of the data. However, the existing indexes are being used to the extent possible, and a real need exists for far better statistical material in order to meet this particular requirement.

Calculation of Gross National Product Statistics on the value of construction put in place contribute to the larger aggregate of the national accounts. In fact, the construction statistics are used with little change as one of the component elements in the Gross National Product calculation. Thus, statistics on construction contribute indirectly to all of those uses to which the GNP aggregate itself is put. This includes not only general economic analysis of the type mentioned above but a wide variety of studies stemming from use of the GNP. Important among these are all of the studies dealing with the overall allocation of our national resources and with the question of national priorities. From the narrower statistical standpoint, the interindustry study—conducted as one of the components of the national accounts calculations—depends upon information from construction as well as from all other parts of the economy. Preparation of the interindustry table requires not only the total series on construction value put in place but also information concerning the requirements of individual materials for use in individual types of construction.

State and Local Governments

In general, the uses of housing and construction statistics by state and local governments are different from those of the federal government. In some few states, however, the development of housing policy and the establishment of housing programs is now a matter of major state government concern and in those cases the uses of statistics for those purposes are much the same as they are in the federal government.

A major use by local and regional governmental bodies is that for comprehensive land use and community development planning. Such planning necessarily begins with a knowledge of the existing development of all types within the area covered by the plan. In an urban area, housing is one of the principal, or perhaps the principal, land use. At decennial intervals, the Census of Housing provides a measure and a quantitative description of the inventory of housing, not only for the area as a whole but also for very small subareas, down to the city block in size. Comparison between successive censuses shows trends in the location of growth, and indicates areas of improvement and of decay. The census statistics are thus indispensable in the process of delineating neighborhoods, assessing their relative quality, and preparing long-range plans for their future development. Other types of housing and construction statistics available on a local basis—particularly building permits, reports on inspection of existing houses, and data on the processing of subdivision applications—are used to bring the decennial census data up to date. Building permits are of special importance in preparing small-area estimates of population, since where adequate local tabulations are made the building permit information identifies the specific location of new construction and therefore of the population which it houses. The locally available information also sheds some light on current changes in the density of use and the quality of housing in existing neighborhoods. Changes of this nature may require the adaptation of long-range plans or immediate administrative action on such matters as the development of code enforcement programs or the scheduling of inspections.

Housing and construction statistics are also important from the metropolitan areawide standpoint in the analysis of the location of housing need within the area, in comparison with the location at which new residential construction is actually taking place. Results of this analysis are useful to state or metropolitan housing agencies (where they exist) in their program planning, and contribute to discussion of the broad policy question of the desirability of creating such agencies where they have not been established.

In the whole planning process, the housing and construction statistics play a double role. They enter directly into planning for housing—for clearance of substandard residential areas, for provision of housing for residents of the areas to be cleared, for conservation or improvement of most existing residential areas, and for the development of new residential districts. Housing statistics also enter into almost all other aspects of the comprehensive plan, partly because housing uses so much of the total land, but more importantly because the location and characteristics of housing determine so much of other land uses. The location of housing creates a demand, for example, for shopping centers. Similarly, housing determines to a considerable extent the need for schools, highways, hospitals, and other public improvements. Thus, the nonhousing portions of a comprehensive plan, like the housing portion, depend heavily on the factual base provided by housing and construction statistics.

These same data also enter importantly into the comprehensive planning for highway purposes required within major urban areas under the federal highway aid program.

Within the framework of general plans, the formulation of housing action programs is similarly dependent upon the same kind of information. Housing statistics provide much of the basis for the calculation of the quantitative need for new (or rehabilitated) housing within a locality, both in total and for special groups, such as the elderly. These data also aid in establishing some of the characteristics of the required housing, such as the distribution of new units by number of bedrooms.

It is recognized, of course, that the actual development of specific projects in accordance with a general plan requires considerably more information, more of a case study nature, than broad statistics such as those provided by the housing census or the current series on construction. Nevertheless, the statistical base is essential as a foundation for the initial steps, and it continues to have important uses even at the developmental stage.

In connection with proposals for clearance of areas of substandard housing, statistics from the housing census have specific application in estimating the dimension and nature of the problem of relocating the occupants of the buildings to be demolished. As of the date of the census, they give both an indication of the numbers and characteristics of the households to be rehoused, and some measure of the availability of vacant housing in the community into which these people might be moved. Even when the census data have become somewhat out of date, they may still be useful as the basis for preliminary estimates.

Another of the very specific uses of housing and construction statistics by state and local governments in their development of specific programs and projects is the preparation of applications for assistance under a number of federal programs. Extensive statistical information (including important housing and construction statistics) is required as part of these applications. This information is designed to enable the federal government to evaluate the needs of the applicant most effectively and to make sound judgments on the allocation of federal assistance. To qualify for certain federal housing and community development programs, a community is required to have a "Workable Program for Community Improvement," which cannot be prepared without statistical data on the housing characteristics of neighborhoods, past construction trends, and the need for additional housing. For other federal programs, the application is required to include information on such matters as the amount of standard and substandard housing, overcrowding, tenure, vacancy rates, and new construction.

Local and, to some extent, state governments also use construction statistics in making estimates of current additions to the property tax base. Statistics on building permits appear to form the primary basis for current estimates of this sort. These estimates are required for short-term purposes in calculating the yield of current tax rates and in estimating what tax rates will be necessary to provide required revenues in the forthcoming year.

Finally, potential use at the local government level is appearing in the efforts which have gotten under way in the last few years to develop the capacity to bring together many kinds of information from many different sources on very small areas, or even for individual properties or parcels. With this information it will be possible to prepare tabulations for very small areas (blocks, block faces, census tracts, operating districts of local government departments, areas used in local transportation studies, etc.) comparing, for example, construction and housing statistics with other related data such as information on tax assessments, land use, zoning, various kinds of local government activity, highway construction, results of special surveys, and the like. These "urban information systems" could mean the development of statistics of a new kind, or at least of a new level of detail, which will make possible the examination of relationships among many different kinds of statistics for which such relationships cannot now be studied in the necessary detail. This increased body of knowledge, in turn, should lead to better informed and more effective operation of many kinds of government activity at the local level. For example, better factual information will be available as an aid in reviewing proposals for changes in zoning, or in identifying the land most suitable for needed industrial uses. Planning of sewers can be carried out more effectively. And many of the local government's social programs can function with a clearer understanding of the total environment within which they operate.

Labor Unions

The national labor unions have long been concerned with the adequacy of the housing of families of low and middle income. They were early advocates of a national public housing program, and have paid close and continuing attention to the development of housing policy and programs over the years. The unions have been active in proposing and supporting related legislation, and their representatives have regularly appeared to testify before congressional committees on housing matters. In all of these activities, they have depended on available housing and construction statistics to demonstrate the adequacy or inadequacy of the housing inventory, to show how much new housing was being built and for whom, and thus to provide the background for conclusions as to necessary legislation and administrative action. The same information has been used by local unions in their contacts with their representatives in the Congress to furnish the factual basis supporting the union-advocated course of action.

The cost of housing has been a matter of special interest to the unions. They have felt it necessary to defend themselves against the frequently repeated claim that labor is responsible for the high cost of new housing and for its consequent inaccessibility to a large proportion of the total population. To this end, therefore, unions have used available statistics on the subdivision of the total cost of new housing, to show labor's contribution to the total and to demonstrate how labor cost as a percent of total cost has changed over time.

In several hundred communities, labor unions have established local housing committees. These committees direct their attention primarily to the local housing scene. They are concerned initially with state legislation or local ordinances establishing housing agencies or programs, and subsequently with the local operation of those programs. They continuously bring their news to the attention of mayors, local governing bodies, and local housing authorities, using all available statistical data on the housing situation and local needs to support their position. They have found the local housing market analyses prepared by the Federal Housing Administration to be of substantial value for this purpose, and—at decennial intervals—they make extensive use of the housing census results.

Some local unions have also become the sponsors of individual nonprofit housing projects. In the planning and justification of these projects, they require much the same type of statistical information on the local housing market and the local housing supply as is needed by public agencies in planning specific housing programs and projects.

Other union uses of housing and construction statistics have arisen in connection with analysis of specific problems. One example is provided by studies of the seasonality of construction employment; another by a study of technological changes in construction and their prospective impact on construction labor and the construction unions. The process of collective bargaining makes some limited use of housing and construction statistics, largely data on housing costs in different areas which have a bearing on local or regional wage differentials. Housing statistics have also been used by national unions in their relationships with international organizations of trade unions and with agencies of the United Nations, both in responding to requests for information and in the preparation of recommendations on housing matters.

Business

Businesses of all types make some use of construction and housing statistics in their general economic analysis and forecasting. The considerations of business firms are very much the same as those of the federal government in this regard. Because construction is an important component of the Gross National Product and represents a large part of total capital investment, it is important in the general analytical and forecasting work which business firms must do.

Producers of construction materials use construction and housing statistics not only for purposes of their general economic analysis and forecasting but also in connection with specific policy decisions which must be made for their particular operations. In the first place, production policies must be set and production schedules established. For this purpose, construction material producers make extensive use of statistics on housing starts, building permits, the value of new construction put in place, construction contracts, and the survey of residential alterations and repairs, in order to gauge the future levels of demand for their products as a guide to proper production scheduling. Business firms also are aided in the measurement and projection of market demand by housing census data—for such items as age of structures, types of plumbing and heating equipment, rents, values, and the relationships of these latter items to occupant's income—which can be used as the basis for estimates of the current situation.

Producers of materials also use construction and housing statistics in their long-range planning for capital expansion. They need to know what has happened in the past in order to forecast the long-run demand for their products in the future as a basis for determining what capital expansion is necessary. In many cases, where sales are made to local rather than national markets, data on the geographic breakdown of construction are used in determining where a particular capital expansion should take place and what the size of the capital expansion in any area should be.

These statistics are also important in connection with marketing—in defining sales territories, determining sales organization, establishing sales quotas, and controlling the sales operation. The assessment of a particular salesman's ability can be facilitated by statistics on his sales in relation to the total market in his area in comparison to the sales of other salesmen in relation to the total market in their areas; such an analysis obviously requires detailed statistics on construction. In a broader sphere, the data are used in measuring the market share of the company as a whole in a particular product in relation to the market shares of other companies. It is thus possible to appraise the performance of the company in relation to its competitors and to develop judgments as to changes in the company's operations which are necessary to maintain its competitive position. Construction statistics also are used in connection with establishing advertising programs and in determining what kinds of advertising media should be used, the extent and nature of the advertising program, the audience to which it should be addressed, etc. For their part, construction trade publications call upon statistics in describing the market on which they form and in estimating their coverage of that market.

Utility companies, most prominently perhaps the telephone companies, draw upon construction statistics for local areas in connection with their continuous planning for expansion of their facilities. By close attention to these data, they are able to keep track of historical trends, particularly in housing construction, and of the volume of new building currently under way. Thus the factual basis is provided for projections of demand into the future, and for the development of the necessary capital expansion programs to meet the demand as it appears.

Lending institutions which provide construction financing look to construction and housing statistics to determine their general lending policies. As usual, these policies are not established solely in terms of such statistics but the facts on housing and construction are important, along with other information, in deciding what a lending policy ought to be at a particular point in time. Uses by lending institutions may be of national statistics, where it is a question of determining overall national lending policies, or they may be of statistics for regional or local market areas in order to know how to proceed in particular localities.

Developers of shopping centers and other types of new commercial projects take advantage of housing and construction statistics in the market analyses that underlie the decisions to proceed with their projects. These statistics provide both an indication of the absorptive capacity of the market in the past and a measure of the competition to be faced from other new projects currently under construction. They are useful in preparing estimates and forecasts of population changes resulting from the current volume of residential construction; such estimates and forecasts may become of crucial significance since the total population in the market area, and the characteristics of that population, are important determinants of the market for store or office space.

Construction companies themselves have, in the past, made relatively little use of construction statistics, except for a few of the larger apartment developers and home builders who have the kinds of marketing problems outlined above for the builders of shopping centers and office complexes. At the present time, however, a potential clearly exists for the use of the data from the construction census by contractors to compare their own operations with those of the industries of which they are a part. While little actual use of the construction census information has so far been made for this purpose, it is known that at least some of the larger construction companies plan to use the data in this way.

The results of the construction census are also of use to trade associations in the construction field for the very specific purpose of providing a measure of the total potential association membership and thus giving an indication of whether the association is serving its constituency as effectively as possible. One of the larger national construction trade associations has purchased special tabulations of the results of the 1967 census so that it may know more about the characteristics of its members, as well as the characteristics of nonmember firms in the same industry. The association will then be in position to analyze the kinds of changes it might make in its own operations to be of maximum value to its members. It will also be able to make better judgments as to the possibilities of expanding its membership and as to the approach to take in attracting additional members.

A broad policy use for construction and housing statistics also exists within trade associations representing the home-building and construction industries. This policy use is recognized by some of the larger associations, but less well recognized by others. Almost any one of these trade associations is confronted continually by an assortment of policy issues affecting its industry—ranging from legislative proposals to actions or proposed actions by the federal executive departments and extending to wage negotiations with labor unions. In the same way as construction and housing statistics are used in the development of policy within the federal government, they can also be used within trade associations in the development of policy positions to be presented to the federal executive agencies, to the Congress, and to the public.

Educational Institutions and Educators

Several different kinds of uses of construction and housing statistics in educational institutions can be identified. In some cases, educational institutions maintain general economic models in which housing and construction, because of their importance in the total economy, are very likely to enter as individual items. In other instances, educational institutions maintain economic models relating to the housing market alone, necessarily drawing on a variety of housing data for the purpose. In addition, many types of housing and construction statistics are used for various analytical studies conducted by faculty members and research workers at educational institutions. Such research work has dealt, for example, with the housing market, the prices of capital goods (including construction), etc. In addition, in many instances students are assigned as part of their educational program the task of preparing papers or theses on some aspect of housing or construction, which, in many cases, requires the use of statistics.

Other Research Organizations and Nonprofit Institutions

The broad diversity of the nature and purposes of nonprofit research organizations and other nonprofit institutions gives rise to a corresponding diversity in their reliance upon statistics on housing and construction. The Committee for Economic Development, the National Bureau of Economic Research, the National Planning Association, Resources for the Future, the Twentieth Century Fund, and the Urban League are all examples of the kinds of organizations which draw upon these data from time to time.

Some of the uses made by these organizations are in connection with general economic analyses, or arise in the preparation of recommendations on broad economic policies or specific policies with respect to housing or construction. For these purposes, the uses are generally similar to the corresponding uses by the federal government described above.

Other requirements for construction and housing data become evident in the examination of very specific research or policy questions. One of the organizations listed above, for example, studied the location within metropolitan areas of new nonresidential construction, for the purpose of comparing the location of new job opportunities (in suburbs or central city) with the place of residence of the labor supply in general and of that portion of the labor supply most in need of new jobs. Out of such a study could come both an understanding of the facts of the present situation, and policy recommendations concerning housing, transportation, and perhaps even the structure of urban growth as a whole.

Nonprofit organizations established for the purpose of promoting specific policies and actions, especially with respect to housing, and engaged in related educational and propaganda activities or in lobbying, necessarily make extensive use of the housing and construction data. These statistics provide the factual background essential for effective presentation of the organization's point of view, and are carefully marshaled in support of the programs which the organization espouses.

FUTURE PROSPECTS

The scope of statistics on construction and housing has expanded considerably over the past decade. Meanwhile the quality of many of the available series has been substantially improved. Prospects for the immediate future are that this extension of scope and improvement in quality will continue. The changes that have taken place, and the further changes in prospect, appear to reflect a rather general feeling on the part of statistical users that the data on construction and housing are, and continue to be, in substantial need of elaboration and improvement. This belief in large part stems from the increasing importance of many of the uses to which these statistics have been and are being put.

Decisions made in the management of the economy become increasingly critical. Development and operation of new housing programs have resulted in bringing increasing proportions of the housing market more or less directly under federal government influence or control, so that the decisions with respect to these programs loom continuously larger in the total housing picture and, in fact, in the economy as a whole. Local governments, beset with more and more insurmountable urban problems, turn increasingly to statistics in an attempt to understand the origin of these problems and perhaps to help find solutions. The apparent tendency for companies engaged in home building to grow larger in size, and the possibility that increasing proportions of the construction process may be shifted from the site of construction to manufacturing plants, mean that the potential business users of statistics of a size large enough to provide for intelligent and informed data use are likely to increase substantially in number.

Thus, it seems probable that the trends of the recent past will be continued, that the scope and quality of housing and construction statistics will widen and improve, and that increasing reliance will be placed on these statistics by even greater numbers of users for uses of steadily growing importance.

APPENDIX

Statistical Resources on Housing and Construction

Government Housing Programs

The major type of data provided by these series for any program consists of measures of the size and progress of the program. Many of these series, therefore, represent counts of housing units covered by a program, money figures summarizing the amounts of money which have been spent or committed on behalf of the program, or the financial status of the program. In addition, information is available on the characteristics of the housing constructed or otherwise aided, and on its financing. In some cases, also, information is provided on the characteristics of the buyers or renters of the units built under the various programs.

Data on the characteristics of the units covered by the programs include information such as the sales prices of units which are sold, the rents of units which are rented, the financing costs of units which are covered by mortgages, and information on physical characteristics such as number of rooms, square feet, etc.

Construction and Repair of Housing

For housing starts, data are available on the number of housing units started, with a classification by type of structure (in terms of the number of units in the structure). Similar statistics are available for housing completion. For housing units for which building permits have been issued, the available statistics show both the number of housing units and the permit value, with a classification by type of structure. For sales of new one-family homes, data show the number of units sold and the price at which sold, and provide information on the characteristics of the homes sold, including the types of financing. Similar data on other new one-family homes (those built on contract for a lot owner and those in which the owner does some or all the work himself) also are published to provide comparable information on the characteristics of all new one-family homes. For new multifamily buildings, data are prepared on the rate at which the newly completed units are being rented. For both new homes and newly built apartments, periodic surveys obtain information on the characteristics of the families and persons who occupy them. Statistics on alterations and repair expenditures show detail on the type of work done.

In the case of housing starts, housing completions, housing sales, and alterations and repairs, the geographic detail available is limited, with figures for four regions being the greatest geographic detail available. Statistics on the number of housing units for which building permits have been issued, with detail by type of structure, are published for each of 13,000 permit-issuing places and are summarized for each metropolitan area, for states, divisions, and regions. Statistics on the value of housing units covered by permits are available for metropolitan areas, for states, and for larger geographic areas.

Value of New Construction Put in Place

The series on the value of new construction put in place is an old series. Data exist on an annual basis back to 1915 and on a monthly basis since 1939. To a considerable extent this is an analytically derived series. Though it rests in part on data collected on actual value put in place, it is derived in large measure from data of other types from which the estimates of value put in place are calculated by various analytical estimating devices. This series provides estimates of the dollar value for new construction actually put in place at the site of construction, by type of construction, in both current and constant dollars. Only national totals are available. This series is compiled monthly by the Bureau of the Census.

Nonresidential Construction

Data are available in value terms for building permits issued for nonresidential buildings. This series has been compiled in one form or another back in the early years of the present century. The data relate to the steadily increasing numbers of permit-issuing places, reflecting the gradual spread of the area in which building permits are required and the gradual extension of reporting by those places to the federal government. The data show the value as stated in applications for building permits, sometimes as edited or revised by the permit-issuing authorities. In general, however, the stated value is less than actual construction cost. The data as currently tabulated cover private construction only, since much public construction takes place without the issuance of a building permit. At the local level, these figures frequently are tabulated and published by an individual permit-issuing place for itself, and in many individual areas the series is available over a long period of time. Summary statistics are, at the present time, published nationally and for four regions and approximately twenty-three individual metropolitan areas. Only overall totals are published for states. The summary data are compiled monthly by the Bureau of the Census, and published by the Bureau of Domestic Commerce.

Construction Contracts

Statistics on construction contracts are compiled by the F. W. Dodge Division of the McGraw-Hill Information System Company as a by-product of the Dodge Reports on individual construction projects. Information for these reports on individual construction projects is gathered for sale to a variety of users who wish to know about the initiation of individual projects for the purpose, in turn, of selling their services in connection with their projects. For purposes of statistics, the data on construction for individual projects are summarized, together with some data derived from building permits, to provide the series of Dodge Construction Contracts. This series was established in the early years of the century for a relatively small number of states and has been continuously expanded. At the present time, it covers forty-eight states, excluding only Alaska and Hawaii. The data shown are in terms of the number of projects, the value of contracts, number of square feet (of buildings), and for residential buildings the number of housing units. Great geographic detail is tabulated, though much of the geographic detail is available only through special purchase. Data are compiled and issued monthly.

Census of Construction Industries

The 1960 census covers establishments engaged primarily in contract construction (i.e., both general contractors and special trades contractors), together with operative builders and subdividers and developers. For establishments in these industries it provides information on receipts, on the kind of work done, on the location (by state) of the work, on employment and payrolls, on the amount of work subcontracted to other establishments, on total payments for materials and supplies, on payments for rental of machines and equipment, on capital expenditures, and on "value added." Information, in terms of the location of the establishment, is provided for each state and for divisions, regions, and the United States. At the present time, the latest data relate to the year 1967.

CHAPTER 11

On Metropolitan Transport and Land Use*

Transport statistics are of value in many ways which extend far beyond information relative to transport per se. In order to understand the ways in which transport statistics can be utilized to gain insight into social issues and problems, it is necessary to consider briefly the nature of transport and, incidentally, also of communications.

Transportation and communication constitute two forms of what may be termed "spatial interaction," or the overcoming of the friction represented by space or distance. Spatial considerations, therefore, are primary in the use of transportation and communication statistics. Transportation—the movement of people and goods—and communication—the movement of ideas—together make it possible for various areas to have specialized functions. This is evident in the specialization of land uses and the localization of activities.

Every place on earth has certain unique characteristics. These characteristics are utilized by man in the development of economic and social activities. Transportation and communication make such area specialization in man's use of the earth possible.

Any phenomena which differ from place to place are capable of being mapped. The map is a vital method of representing area statistics and their complex interrelationships. The definitions of areal or spatial units are important in gathering, compiling, and interpreting statistics on the

---

* Based on a memorandum by Harold M. Mayer, University of Wisconsin, Milwaukee.

movement of people, goods, and ideas to, from, and among places. Unfortunately, there seldom is a standard area unit for statistical studies, or even a multipurpose unit. Area statistics, therefore, often leave much to be desired.

It is very difficult to generalize about the availability and value of spatial statistics involving transportation and communication; the criteria, areal units, accuracy, and detail vary from country to country, from time to time, and from local place to local place. They vary, furthermore, with respect to the type of transportation or communication, reflecting, among other things, the extent to which each type is owned or operated by the public or by private interests, the extent to which the various types may be regulated, and the attitude of the public agencies and private interest toward issues of commercial competition and public security.

TRANSPORTATION STATISTICS

In the United States, the regulation of the various forms of transportation is a major factor in the availability of statistical information. Transportation data are in some instances pitifully inadequate and in other instances there is an embarrassment of riches. As in most statistical fields, the availability of electronic data processing has stimulated a proliferation of data, some much more useful than others. In the United States, because the various types of transportation data differ, it is necessary to consider each form of transportation separately, and then to discuss some of their more significant interrelationships.

In respect to transportation within the United States, one of the major data problems arises from the fact that movement is handled by common carriers, contract carriers, and private carriers. Private transportation of both people and goods is rapidly increasing relative to common and contract transportation. Since private transportation, obviously, is not regulated as to routes, frequencies, and costs, data are relatively scarce with relation to such movements and much of the information must be inferred.

In this chapter attention is restricted to the consideration of highway transport and transportation and land use in metropolitan areas. Rail, maritime, and air transport are, of course, essential ingredients of the transportation system which links the economy of the nation with significant social as well as economic implications. Comprehensive treatment of these transportation modes, however, fall beyond the scope of this chapter. The material on highway transport is, in summary form, included because of its increasing importance and special implications for circulation of goods and people within, as well as between, metropolitan areas.

Highway Transport

During the twentieth century, highway transportation within the United States has become the dominant multipurpose mode. It is the only type of transport which is virtually ubiquitous, with door-to-door access to almost every household and business establishment. It furnishes overall transportation for between 85 and 90 percent of the mileage of person movement, over one-fifth of the ton-miles of intercity goods movement, and, in addition, it is the originating and terminating mode for most intermodal movements involving transfer with or without break-of-bulk among the several types of transport.

Automobile and Truck The private automobile, being unregulated as to routes and services, produces many difficulties in statistical study, and much data must be derived by inference rather than directly. Motor trucking, like many other types of goods transportation, is divided into common carriers, contract carriers, and private carriers; intercity mileage is about equally divided among the three, and, of course, statistics are most readily available for common carriers. The principal source of statistics for highways, automobiles, buses, and motor trucks is the U. S. Bureau of Public Roads, Federal Highway Administration, Department of Transportation. Regulated carriers by highway are also the subject of statistics, generally comparable to the railroad statistics, published by the Interstate Commerce Commission in many series, especially the *Annual Report on Transport Statistics in the United States, Part 7, Motor Carriers.* As in the case of railroads, it is virtually impossible to ascertain specific origins and destinations or routes.

Aggregated statistics for the nation and by states, including numbers and types of trucks and the nature of their employment, are compiled and published annually by the American Trucking Association in *American Trucking—Trends,* a very useful compendium.

Since a significant proportion of truck trips are in cities and metropolitan areas, it would be very useful to have detailed knowledge of the patterns of such movements, together with the commodities moved. Such knowledge is not systematically compiled, however, except for the infrequent comprehensive urban and metropolitan transportation land-use studies, discussed below. It is not easily possible, therefore, to establish continuous time-series, or to make intercity comparisons of truck trips or truck utilization. We know very little about the flows of goods within cities and metropolitan areas; certainly the knowledge of personal travel, by both automobile and mass transportation, far exceeds our knowledge of goods movements. In 1970, two international conferences were devoted to the subject of urban goods movement, one in Paris and one in Warrenton,

Virginia, and it is hoped that these will stimulate interest in the systematic collection of data on the flow of goods—which is principally by truck—in urban areas.

Bus Intercity bus transportation has been holding its own in total passenger volume during the past two decades, but its proportion of total intercity travel, other than by automobile, has been declining, from nearly 38 percent in 1950 to about 16 percent in 1970. It is anticipated that the completion of the interstate highway network, the abandonment of most intercity rail passenger service with the advent of Amtrak in early 1971, and the "use it or lose it" policy of the Civil Aeronautics Board which is resulting in the loss of airline service to many small communities will produce a resurgence of intercity bus service.

In addition, most bus operators also are in the business of transporting small parcels on their vehicles, a business which the railroads have largely abandoned, and which has in part been diverted from the postal service because of decline in the quality of that service. One nationwide operator is responsible for about half of the intercity bus traffic of the United States. Estimates of bus mileage are compiled for such carriers, and the intercity common and contract carriers submit to the regulatory agencies the usual statistics, comparable with those of other types of transport, and, as with most other modes (except airlines), it is very difficult or impossible to ascertain point-to-point traffic. Aggregated statistics, in addition to those in official governmental reports, are summarized in *Bus Facts,* published by the National Association of Motor Bus Owners; these statistics cover the regular intercity carriers.

Highways Statistics on the highways themselves are generally much more numerous and available than are statistics on the carriers which use them. All highways, of course, are depicted on maps, with which every motorist is familiar, as they are probably the most widely used maps of any type. States and counties publish, usually annually, official maps of the highways in their respective territories, classified by type; most cities, as well as counties and states, publish traffic-flow maps, based upon periodic or continuous counts. Statistics on highway use, including flow maps, and on the extent and financing of highways in the United States, are found in various publications of the U. S. Bureau of Public Roads, and are summarized in *Statistical Abstract of the United States.*

The monthly *Public Roads* published by that agency includes statistics on the status of the highway system of the nation, and frequently the center spread is a map showing the status of the National System of Interstate and Defense Highways, the 42,500-mile system which is scheduled for completion in 1976. Many of the state highway departments publish detailed statistics on their respective systems, in annual reports and otherwise. The Highway Research Board, a part of the National Academy of Sciences-National Research Council, sponsors much research on highways and highway use, not only from an engineering viewpoint, but also on traffic flows, regulation, and highway economics, and also publishes many monographs and other reports. A useful journal, frequently containing statistics not available elsewhere, is the *Traffic Quarterly,* published by the Eno Foundation for Transportation.

URBAN AND METROPOLITAN TRANSPORTATION STUDIES

Movement of people and goods in cities and metropolitan areas involves, from some standpoints, rather different considerations than movement between cities, and the availability and applications of statistical data, consequently, are different.

The major trends in the twentieth century, relative to transportation of both people and goods in urban areas in the United States (and to a lesser extent in Canada, and in other "advanced" nations to some degree) has been away from mass transportation to private transportation, by automobile and private truck. Both offer door-to-door service, free from constraints of schedules and fixed routes, but at the same time have certain inherent inefficiencies. The proliferation of private vehicles also has contributed substantially to congestion, air pollution, and other urban problems. At the same time, private transportation, with its flexibility, has intensified the handicap of relative immobility suffered by many disadvantaged people: the poor who cannot afford private transportation; the young, old, and infirm who cannot drive an automobile; and the suburban families living in locations where inadequate public transportation makes necessary the expenditure of a disproportionate share of the family's resources on the maintenance and operation of multiple cars. All of these conditions are appropriately the subject of investigation, but not until very recently have even the most fundamental data bearing upon these considerations become available.

Except in a few of the very largest cities, mass transportation has declined precipitously since before World War II, being revived only temporarily during wartime restrictions on automobile use. Furthermore, most urban and suburban passenger transportation has shifted from status as regulated privately owned utilities to public ownership or subsidy, with a much greater degree of public control. Whereas the mass carriers—the rapid transit subway and elevated lines, streetcars, trolley coaches, and buses—were previously the basic all-purpose urban transporters of people, they have become, where they survive at all, highly specialized carriers. They bring people to and from very concentrated traffic-generating areas, principally central business districts, and meet, though inadequately, the transportation needs of the young, old, infirm, and economically disadvantaged.

The decline of urban mass transportation is largely the result of a combination of circumstances, which can be documented in part by studies of historical traffic patterns in combination with analyses of shifts in urban land use. Among the changing circumstances are an increasing affluence, and the scale economies of motor car production which brings them within economic reach of most people. Moreover, the spread of urban development at ever-lower densities reduces the traffic density to below the point at which continuation or extension of mass transportation is feasible. Consequently, the proliferation of highways and motor vehicles and the decreasing population densities produce the result that traffic generation, with few exceptions, is too thin to justify high investments in mass transit.

The highway, including the expressway, has the advantage that it does not necessarily involve a change in mode between origin and destination, and it can cumulate traffic from a large area, thereby building up the requisite traffic density. It is a continuing cycle. Because of the intimate relationships between the patterns of transportation in cities and metropolitan areas on the one hand and the general geographic patterns of population distribution, residential densities, and traffic-generating nodes such as commercial, industrial, and institutional areas on the other hand, it is almost impossible to separate urban transportation data from other closely related data on many aspects of city and region. Urban transportation studies, therefore, have through the years increasingly converged toward related demographic, economic, and especially land-use studies.

The electric street railway, as the dominant form of transportation in the latter years of the nineteenth century and until World War I, inspired a proliferation of studies of routes and traffic generation areas. Hurd's famous study of the patterns of urban land values shortly after the turn of the century, for example, was based largely upon the street railway patterns, and inspired several of the later models of urban structure and growth, such as Hoyt's sector model which placed the high-density, high-value areas along the main transportation radials. A noteworthy prototype of a transit traffic study, analogous in some respects to the curent transportation land-use studies, was the Chicago traction study of 1916, which not only was concerned with routes, but also with origins and destinations of trips, subclassified by time and by trip purpose.

With the advent of the automobile, the science of traffic engineering developed, and the necessity for traffic-flow data became evident. Until the mid-1930s the principal statistical studies involved data on the volumes of vehicular, and occasionally person, flows on the route sectors of road and street networks. Later, empirical principles were evolved from such studies which were analogous to those used by hydraulic and electrical engineers. The traffic counts were made at designated points along route segments, and various automatic counting devices usually were employed. Surveys were either 100 percent complete, or based on samples taken at representative times. The results typically were maps, in which bands proportional to traffic flows on the various route segments were represented.

Meanwhile, parallel studies of urban land use were being made, while the bridge between traffic and land use continued to be nonexistent. Urban planning moved from the "city beautiful" stage of the early twentieth century to the preoccupation with housing conditions characteristic of the New Deal activities of the 1930s. Zoning, which entered the picture in 1916 and which was firmly established by a Supreme Court decision in 1926, was adopted by most municipalities and later by counties. This necessitated comprehensive inventories of land uses, existing and projected.

With the proliferation of urban planning agencies in the 1930s, and with the stimulus of the various federal housing and work-relief programs, techniques were developed and applied in several hundred cities, for comprehensive land-use surveys and real property inventories. Perhaps somewhat unfortunately, they were largely residentially oriented, and the inventories of commercial and industrial land uses and establishments—which, of course, are the major traffic-generating nodes—were much less than adequate. However, for the first time, a large number of American cities produced detailed land-use maps, with many cross-tabulations, by blocks, census tracts, community areas, and other subcity areal units, of data on housing and other physical and occupancy conditions which, prospectively, could be utilized in traffic studies.

World War II began before commercial and industrial land-use data comparable to the residential data were developed. The surveys, furthermore, generally were confined to individual municipalities, since prospective local agencies of metropolitan scope were rare, and the federal government required official local sponsorship, with some local funding.

Typical of these surveys, although larger than most in areal coverage, was the Chicago Land Use Survey, sponsored by the Chicago Plan Commission, and conducted between 1937 and the time it was aborted by World War II. This survey, at a cost of $3 million, employed 3600 people at its peak, with a total employment during its duration of about 10,000, most of whom were on relief, and whose tenure was limited to eighteen months. Thus, training and indoctrination activities were responsible for a large share of the cost and effort. The survey covered 20,000 city blocks, over a million parcels of land, and an area of about 212 square miles. It produced data on punch cards for every land use, every dwelling unit, and every commercial and industrial establishment in the city.

The land uses were classified into several categories; the residential units were described and tabulated as to the nature of the building construction, the style of building, the age and condition of the structure, location in the structure, duration of occupancy or vacancy; whether owner or tenant occupied; the value or rental of the unit; the nature of heating and plumbing; the age, sex, race, and relationships of the occupants; and many other bits of information. Two large volumes of maps and tabulations were produced, as well as 75 volumes of cross-tabulations by community areas, and seventy-five volumes of census tract tabulations, one volume for each of the seventy-five community areas into which the city had been previously divided. For the first time, an accurate base map of the city was compiled and drafted, in 238 square-mile equal-area sheets, with streets and alleys proportioned to actual widths, and both with and without boundaries of the individual parcels. On these maps, many statistical series were plotted by means of overlays, and a large variety of data maps were published. The individual sheets were joined at various scales and reproduced; these maps, continuously revised, still constitute the official base map of the city and are used for most planning studies, including traffic planning.

But it soon became evident that neither land-use surveys nor traffic-flow studies produced adequate insights into the role of transportation in the cities; something more was needed. What was most lacking was a conceptual scheme of the relationships between circulation and the other elements of the city pattern.

A major step forward toward bridging the gap was the development of the Origin-Destination (O-D) survey during the mid-1940s, primarily by the U. S. Bureau of Public Roads.

These O-D surveys consisted of several parts. An internal survey, usually conducted with a scientific sample of dwellings, produced responses by members of the household relative to all trips made on the previous day (a normal weekday, or a weekend if desired in special cases), with information as to time of day, purpose of the trip, mode of travel, and age, sex, race, income, and occupational status of the persons making the trips. The internal survey covered the area within a cordon which was designated at the periphery of the study area. Trips crossing the cordon, both inbound and outbound, were surveyed by questionnaire at "external stations" along the routes crossing the cordon, and were tabulated with respect to both internal and external zones of origin and destination. A third portion of the O-D survey generally involved responses from "fleet" operators, such as taxicab companies, while concurrent surveys were made of mass transit travel crossing the cordon, and truck movements, based upon trip logs, within the cordon.

For purposes of tabulation, the area of study was divided into several orders of zones and subzones (commonly four), and all origins and destinations in the sample were coded and tabulated by zones of origin and destination, so that almost any degree of geographical detail could be studied. In low-density areas near the cordon, zones might be a square mile or more in area, while in the central city core zones might be as small as large individual office or apartment buildings. Screen-lines were established across the study area to insure accuracy of the survey sample.

These surveys, however, lacked several essential ingredients; most importantly, they had no information relative to the land uses which, in fact, generated the traffic. A noteworthy book, *Urban Traffic: A Function of Land Use* (Mitchell and Rapkin, 1955), pointed out this deficiency, and led directly, in the following years, to the development and application of much more comprehensive surveys, generally known as metropolitan transportation land-use studies, which have now become virtually mandatory. These surveys, finally, bridged the gap between the earlier land-use surveys on the one hand and the O-D surveys on the other. They contain most of the elements of both types of surveys, and they develop the interrelationships between land uses as traffic generators and the patterns of urban and metropolitan circulation.

During the mid- and late 1950s, several concurrent and successive surveys of this type each contributed new concepts and techniques. Notable were the early Detroit study, the Chicago Area Transportation Study which conducted its field work in 1956, the Pittsburgh Area Transportation Study, and the Penn-Jersey Study. In most instances, senior staff and survey directors transferred from one city to another, and thus, experience was cumulative, and the results facilitated intermetropolis comparisons.

USES

City and Metropolitan Planning

Transportation statistics have become an integral element in city and metropolitan planning. Since 1965, the federal government, acting through the Department of Housing and Urban Development (HUD) and the Department of Transportation (DOT), has required that in all metropolitan areas, a recognized coordinating agency be operational in carrying on continuous planning. This is to be accomplished by referral of all projects of metropolitan concern involving any one or more of a wide variety of federal assistance programs to such an agency. If the project is acceptable, the agency then certifies that it is in conformity with a comprehensive metropolitan plan. Thus, effectively for the first time, metropolitan areas are officially recognized as appropriate planning units for transportation and other interrelated elements. In many instances, the planning agency is a metropolitan council of governments and in other instances, is designated as a metropolitan or regional planning commission. In the spring of 1971, the Tri-State Transportation Commission, covering the New York region, became the officially recognized Tri-State Regional Planning Commission, and the movement from ad hoc to comprehensive metropolitan planning was completed, at least in theory.

Chicago Area as an Example In order to be concrete, the agencies and their evolution in metropolitan Chicago will be described as they involve the collection, analysis, and application of transportation data to the process of comprehensive metropolitan planning. In most other metropolitan areas of the United States (and to a major extent also in Canada) the complex of agencies and procedures is similar.

In the Chicago region, there had been a long tradition of city and metropolitan planning, although, as in most urban areas, it had been largely intuitive, with only a limited amount of data constituting inputs to the process. Throughout the city of Chicago and in nearly all other portions of the metropolitan area, the principal transportation consisted of a radial pattern of railroad lines, supplemented since the 1880s by a series of concentric-belt railroads, permitting interchange among the main lines and developing industrial concentrations with neutral railroad access. The highway and street system had been platted as a rectangular grid, in accordance with the federal land survey of 1785 and the Northwest Territories Ordinance of 1787, which provided for section-line roads a mile apart in each direction. Later urban platting provided interior streets in each section conforming to this grid. However, a few major diagonal roads, most commonly conforming to topographic features, antedated the grid system and continued to carry relatively heavy traffic. Density of the grid bore no relationship to traffic demands, but the convergence of the major diagonals, both highway and rail, "anchored" the core of the region, downtown Chicago.

Many subsequent features resulted from conscious planning but most were not based on the results of research. Olmsted in 1869, for example, laid out a semicircular and continuous belt of parks, connected by boulevards, along the then outer periphery of the city's built-up area. In 1893 the World's Columbian Exposition indirectly led to publication of the

Plan of Chicago (Burnham and Bennett, 1909), with its emphasis upon symmetry and a monumental civic façade. The plan, however, directly resulted in the creation of two agencies which subsequently played a major role in the development of a statistical and quantitative basis for comprehensive metropolitan planning, in which transportation constituted the main connecting element.

One of these agencies was the Chicago Plan Commission, created in 1909, which for three decades promoted the individual elements of the Burnham and Bennett plan within the municipal limits of the city of Chicago. This commission, reorganized as a quasi-official city agency in 1939, sponsored the Chicago Land-Use Survey, previously mentioned. It was subsequently twice reorganized, and eventually became the city's Department of Development and Planning, charged with responsibility for a comprehensive plan for the city (published in 1966) and an annual public improvements program by which most of the physical features of the city plan are scheduled.

The second agency was the Chicago Regional Planning Association, a quasi-official and largely voluntary agency, which promoted the features of the plan in the suburban portions of the region outside of Chicago. The latter agency was noteworthy for its promotion, in the 1920s and 1930s, of the metropolitan highway network, but, characteristic also of the era, its planning was not based upon quantitative data to any real extent.

At the beginning of World War II, the principal data utilized by the planning agencies in the city and region consisted of a primitive (by present standards) traffic survey, the Chicago Land-Use Survey within the city, and a comprehensive series of monographic, although nonquantitative studies of the region produced mainly in the 1920s at the University of Chicago for the Chicago Regional Planning Association. Additionally, there were a number of substantive studies of individual social areas within Chicago, and the familiar zonal model of the city, as well as studies of special topics, produced mainly in the Sociology Department at the University of Chicago. This research interest led eventually to the establishment of the Chicago Community Inventory, and the Population Research Center, for nearly three decades the principal nonofficial agency for collection, collation, and interpretation of quantitative data on the city and metropolitan area. But the latter organization has not been especially concerned with transportation or traffic data. Nor, in fact, was the Chicago Plan Commission; its principal publication was the *Master Plan of Residential Land Use of Chicago* (CPC, 1943), which largely overlooked the role of transportation in conditioning the physical structure of the residential areas of the city.

The most notable trend in development of statistical applications to transportation planning in urban and metropolitan areas during the postwar period was probably the comprehensive transportation land-use studies, previously mentioned. The Chicago area benefited greatly from the operations of the Chicago Area Transportation Study (CATS) which conducted its field operations in 1956, continued as a permanent research agency under local, state, and federal support, and updated its survey in 1970. The study was, in its time, probably the most comprehensive of its type undertaken, and it still constitutes a prototype for metropolitan transportation land-use studies in many other metropolitan areas, not only in the United States, but also in other nations.

The O-D study technique was incorporated as an integral part of the CATS study. In addition, alternative land-use schemes for the metropolitan area were tested, by means of analog computers, in which traffic generation formed the basis of projections of volumes and patterns of movement resulting from each of a number of alternative patterns of urban growth in the metropolitan region. The results were published (1959–1962) in three volumes covering the survey findings, data projections, and the transportation plan, respectively. Close liaison was maintained, largely unofficially, with the major local and regional planning agencies in the survey area and in adjacent territory. This was particularly the case in northwestern Indiana, where a somewhat similar survey was undertaken. There were some difficulties, however, in reconciling the data due to different dates and other differences, particularly with regard to projections.

Meanwhile, several organizational developments were taking place in the Chicago region which affected the application of the study results and which were not atypical of comparable developments in other metropolitan areas. In 1957, the state of Illinois created the Northeastern Illinois Metropolitan Area Planning Commission, later shortened to Northeastern Illinois Planning Commission (NIPC). Its area of operation embraced the six counties of the Illinois portion of the metropolitan area, corresponding to what became the 1960 delimitation of the Chicago Standard Metropolitan Statistical Area. This was designated by the state as the coordinating agency for comprehensive planning for the region. Shortly thereafter, the quasi-official Chicago Regional Planning Association, which had embraced a somewhat larger area in Illinois and adjacent states, was merged into NIPC; the latter, however, did not extend its area of primary concern beyond the state line. Comparable regional planning agencies later were established in the contiguous regions in the two adjacent states: the Lake-Porter County Transportation and Planning Commission in Indiana and the southeastern Wisconsin Regional Planning Commission, whose area included the Kenosha, Racine, and Milwaukee SMSA's. These contiguous planning regions, in effect, recognized the existence of a continuous urbanized complex extending for about 200 miles along the southern and western shores of Lake Michigan.

In the early 1960s with the publication of the CATS report, it became clear that close cooperation between the planning agencies was essential. Especially urgent was the setting up of a mechanism for coordinating the research and planning operations of the city of Chicago's Department of Development and Planning, NIPC, and CATS. Various overlapping official and staff groups were set up, and the preparation of the respective comprehensive plans of the city of Chicago and of NIPC involved frequent interagency consultations, in which major inputs from CATS were included.

Effective July 1, 1965, the federal government, as a prerequisite for federal aid for a wide variety of programs including most public mass transportation and highway projects, required that each metropolitan area have an official regional planning agency. Furthermore it called for all projects of metropolitan concern proposed by any local unit of government within the area and which would involve federal assistance to be submitted to the regional planning agency for certification as to conformance with the comprehensive regional plan.

Funds were provided, under section 701 of the National Housing Act, to assist the agencies in preparing comprehensive plans. The state of Illinois designated NIPC as its official agency for the Chicago SMSA, and work on the comprehensive metropolitan plan was expedited. NIPC, furthermore, agreed that CATS would be relied upon for the transportation aspects of the comprehensive plan. Frequent consultations were held between city of Chicago and NIPC personnel as the respective city and metropolitan plans proceeded in order to ensure compatibility.

When the *Comprehensive Plan of Chicago* was published in 1966 by the city's Department of Development and Planning, it contained a chapter on "Metropolitan Development." A major feature of the city plan was the proposal for intensive development along radial "corridors of high accessibility," served by the principal express highway, rapid transit, and commuter railroad lines, where the maximum amount of trip generation would take place. This propsal was for essentially an intensification of the status quo, reinforced by additional transportation facilities. Some, such as the Dan Ryan and Kennedy Expressway rapid transit lines, were subsequently built. These were also compatible with the earlier CATS proposals, published in 1962. Finally, NIPC, after more than a decade of work and a series of public hearings, adopted a comprehensive plan for the "northeastern Illinois counties" in April 1968. It had as a dominant feature a series of "fingers" extending radially outward from Chicago along the major transportation corridors, the inner portions of which constituted the "corridors" of the Chicago comprehensive plan.

In development of both the Chicago and the regional plans, CATS data played a vital role. In its earlier studies, that agency had worked out from projections of its 1956 data a series of proposals which emphasized express highways, in a radial pattern (then already largely committed), and additionally a grid, consisting of expressways spaced about three miles apart in highly urbanized portions of the region and about six miles apart in the less developed outer portions. The current prospective "crosstown expressway" in Chicago would be in conformance with such a grid.

Later, when NIPC proposed a series of alternative schemes for metropolitan development, CATS, utilizing data which it had previously developed empirically as a result of its 1956 survey and projecting it upon each of NIPC's alternatives in turn, generated on an analog computer the assignment of traffic that would result from each of the alternatives. This involved consideration of such variables as the character of land uses, their distances apart, projections of trip purpose and frequency by socioeconomic status, etc.; the result was a series of movement assignments to optimal networks which would serve each of the alternative schemes. The alternates were then placed in rank order in accordance with the relative costs of providing for the projected patterns of movement which each would generate.

Fortunately, and perhaps not entirely coincidentally, the "finger" plan of NIPC (which also subsumed the major features of the Comprehensive Plan of Chicago insofar as transportation was concerned) proved to be, by a slight margin, the most efficient among the alternatives from the viewpoint of economy of providing the necessary transportation routes. NIPC then could adopt that particular plan with greater confidence.

There are, however, several additional complications. Federal requirements dictate cross-referrals among the regional planning agencies where a project in a metropolitan planning area may have a bearing upon planning in adjacent metropolitan areas. To accommodate this requirement, NIPC has developed a mechanism for regular communication with its counterpart agencies in the two adjacent states. Interregional cooperation in planning thus is facilitated in such intermetropolitan concerns as regional airport locations, highway development, and air and water pollution control, all of which depend upon an adequate informational base and which involve aspects of transportation.

Traffic Planning

Origin-Destination surveys provided an informational base as elements in comprehensive city and metropolitan planning. It is instructive, however, to observe the way in which such data were used specifically for traffic planning.

The O-D surveys, as the name indicates, were concerned not only with traffic flows, but more especially with where they would occur, given existing patterns of land use and projected traffic generation, if suitable routes were available. By comparing the pattern of so-called desire lines between areas of origin and of destination of trips with the existing network and its theoretical capacity, deficiencies could be identified. Desire lines are straight lines between origins and destinations, with weights proportioned to traffic volume, independent of existing routes. Desire lines could be cumulated along routes of prospective major traffic arteries, thereby indicating needed capacities, based upon existing, or projected, land uses. Thus, existing and potential bottlenecks could be identified and remedial action planned. Implicit in this procedure, of course, was the assumption that the patterns of traffic generating activities and land uses would be constant; alternative assumptions made possible revisions in the projections of traffic demand. But such traffic studies were generally inadequately related to studies of other aspects of urban and metropolitan development which utimately would generate the traffic.

The O-D surveys, covering many cities and metropolitan areas, quickly became established as standard inputs into the urban transportation planning process. Results usually were published in the form of reports containing descriptions of the areas and maps of desire lines, subclassified into various combinations of times, modes, trip purposes, and other variables. They also included matrices of zone-to-zone trip data in considerable detail and, usually, maps and tabulations of major directional desire lines, which often formed the basis for planning of networks of expressways and major arterial streets.

Port Cities

An important, but specialized, aspect of transportation is the study of ports. Many agencies in the United States are concerned with ports. The Corps of Engineers conducts studies of ports relative to harbor improvement projects, authorized and prospective. The Maritime Administration conducts studies of port traffic and of methods of cargo handling. The Coast Guard is concerned with studies of port operation from the viewpoint of cargo and personal security and safety of vessel operation. The Department of Defense conducts studies of port efficiency and protection, etc. Port research projects are proposed and frequently evaluated by the Ports and Cargo Systems Committee of the Maritime Transportation Research Board.

Port research has long been of special interest to city planners and others. There are several reasons for this interest, all of which involve considerations of the availability of statistical data. Ports are gateways to their respective hinterlands and, by analysis of traffic flows through ports, much can be learned of the economic and social development of the respective hinterland counties and regions, and of the interregional and international relations involving transfers of goods, and also of people (immigration). Since nations must of necessity maintain records of international flows, statistical data on port traffic are much more adequate in most instances than are data on flows through inland points, which are subject to the constraints discussed earlier.

Many basic research concepts have emerged from studies of port traffic. Among them is the idea of the nested hierarchy of tributary or trade regions in competitive hinterlands. This idea was extended to all so-called central places by Walter Christaller (1933) in his classic formulation of "central place theory." Delimitation of port hinterlands has furnished much experience in data analysis for determination, using analogous methods, of retail and other trade areas and service areas.

At the local scale, planners and others are interested in waterfront land requirements and statistics on volumes of cargoes of various types handled per lineal foot of berthage and per acre of port land. Such data, taking into account various degrees of mechanization and in view of the trends in vessel size, are indispensable in determination of the allocation of waterfront land, a scarce resource, among the various competing users. In many cities, port use is declining in the central waterfront areas, with shifts toward peripheral areas. More adequate space for port terminals, port-associated industries, and landward access is available. Without statistics to identify and determine the magnitude of peripheral versus central land requirements, it would not be as feasible to work out renewal plans for central waterfronts, or to identify suitable areas for port-associated terminal and industrial developments.

THE OUTLOOK

Several considerations permeate virtually all aspects of transportation statistics, and should receive attention in the future.

1. Aggregated statistics are much more readily available than are localized statistics. It is impossible, in most instances, to utilize such aggregated statistics in local or regional planning at a subnational scale. Possibly the principal exception is the infrequent, but reasonably comprehensive transportation land-use studies in metropolitan areas. In these studies a systematic, but formalized and stereotyped, procedure is virtually mandatory as prerequisite for federal assistance in a variety of programs—over 200—involved in the effectuation of comprehensive urban and metropolitan plans. There is a need for more adequate localized infor-

mation on traffic flows, not only for metropolitan areas but for regions of all sizes and types. Such data would be meaningful in constructing models and in analyzing individual situations relative to the relationships between transportation and regional development.

2. There is a need, which gradually is being met, fortunately, for greater uniformity in classification of commodities and traffic flows. There is a trend toward uniform classification of commodities based upon the Standard Industrial Classification, and for greater uniformity of documentation among the various transportation modes, nationally and internationally. These developments will permit gathering and processing more adequately the commodity-flow statistics. One set of applications resulting from uniformity would be a better comparison of the relative efficiencies, and hence costs—whether defined as out-of-pocket or fully distributed—among the various forms of transportation. Such comparative data would be of material assistance in the determination of policy at all levels for treatment of each form of transportation and would be useful for partial or complete regulation, freedom or restriction of entry, subsidies, etc.

3. Eventually, it is hoped, it will be possible through uniform classification of commodities and uniform record keeping among the various forms of transportation to trace movements from ultimate origin to ultimate destination. This could be done through all intermediate transfer points, and through all changes in form as components are processed from raw material *in situ* to final consumer.

REFERENCES

American Trucking Association. *American Trucking—Trends*. Washington, D.C.: American Trucking Assn., annual.

Burnham, Daniel H., and Edward H. Bennett. *Plan of Chicago*. Chicago: The Commercial Club, 1909.

Chicago Plan Commission. *Master Plan of Residential Land Use of Chicago*. Chicago: The Chicago Plan Commission, 1943.

Christaller, Walter. *Die zentralen Orte in Süddeutschland; eine ökonomisch-geographische Untersuchung über die Gesetzmässigkeit der Verbreitung und Entwicklung der Siedlungen mit städtischen Funktionen*. Jena: G. Fischer, 1933.

Eno Foundation for Highway Traffic Control. *Traffic Quarterly: An Independent Journal for Better Traffic*. Sangatiok, Conn., 1947–.

Interstate Commerce Commission. *Annual Reports on Transport Statistics in the United States.* Part 7, Motor Carriers. Washington, D. C.: Government Printing Office, annual.

Mitchell, Robert A., and Chester Rapkin. *Urban Traffic: A Function of Land Use.* New York: Columbia University Press, 1955.

National Association of Motor Bus Owners. *Bus Facts.* A publication of facts and figures of the motor bus industry. Washington, D. C., annual.

U. S. Bureau of Public Roads. *Public Roads.* Washington, D. C.: Government Printing Office, monthly.

CHAPTER 12

On Outdoor Recreation*

BACKGROUND

An increasingly important element of family expenditures and consumption is leisure time activity. With greatly increased productivity and per capita income over the years, hours of work have diminished and free weekends and extended vacations have made play and recreation assume great importance in the life style of the American people. Moreover, the commercialization of various forms of play and recreation has generated into a major economic activity indicated by consumer expenditures of some $39 billion for recreation in 1970.

In consequence, there has been a growing demand for information about recreation by government—federal, state, and local; by business; by various research bodies; and by the public at large. The materials which follow constitute a case study of the development of statistics on one aspect of recreation, outdoor recreation, and of their utilization as a recent and still vigorous development.

What are the questions one might ask about recreation and for what purpose might one ask them?

1. Is recreation good for a person? (So as to justify participation.)
2. What forms of recreation will people pay for? (So as to guide recreation investment decisions by both public and private sectors.)

---

* Based on a memorandum by Abbott L. Ferriss, Emory University.

251

3. How much recreation do we have now and how much do we need? (So as to plan for it.)

These are some of the questions that federal and private statistics try to answer about recreation.

The good that recreation does for a person is not the subject of a major statistical program. Instead, social science and medical research attempt to relate recreation and sports to a limited aspect of the person's welfare—physical and mental health. Particularly, such research tries to find out how various forms of recreation help to maintain or restore health and physical well-being. Except for a question on health in the first National Recreation Survey (1960), mass surveys sponsored by the federal government have not included questions on the relation of recreation to health. On the other hand, a great many experimental studies relate recreation and exercise to various physical and mental outcomes.

The second question posed above is asked by business and commerce. These interests are concerned with supplying the means to engage in the recreational activity—the equipment, the clothing, the advertising, the travel to the recreation site, and so on. More specifically, equipment is required to make the activity possible (such as the machine to make snow for skiing; clothing is needed for warmth or exposure, for the feet and the head, for exhibition, or for survival); advertising is needed to incite the participant to want to travel by ship, air, dune buggy, snowmobile, or motorboat, as well as to provide knowledge about recreation sites in the mountains, on the seashore, or in foreign countries. The reason for all of this is that recreation, and all of the complex associated with recreation, involves large expenditures by consumers. Questions relating to the supply of and demand for recreation, then, generate a need for much data.

The third question posed—how much recreation do we have and how much do we need?—is a bookkeeping and planning question, functions that our society more and more allocates to government. While government pays some attention to the second question (supply and demand), it concentrates on the third, surveying the public to find out how much recreation people engage in, how much the people want that they do not have, their preferences, etc. These data, then, combined with future population forecasts and future estimates of consumer income, and the like, go to form the basis for planning and for estimating "the demand" for recreation in the future.

AVAILABLE DATA

Statistics relating to recreation have been increasing as national interest in and attention to its role in contemporary life have broadened. Recognition of the growing importance of recreation in the life style of the

American people was highlighted in the creation by the Congress of the Outdoor Recreation Resources Review Commission (ORRRC) in 1960–1961. Under the aegis of this commission, twenty-seven study reports were published (available from the Superintendent of Documents, U. S. Government Printing Office), which covered many significant facets of outdoor recreation. Among these studies was a volume based on the National Recreation Survey of 1960.

The National Recreation Survey

The National Recreation Survey was conducted in 1960 and 1965, respectively, by the ORRRC and the Bureau of Outdoor Recreation (BOR), Department of the Interior. The data were collected for each by the U. S. Bureau of the Census. Each survey presents participation rates for twenty or more outdoor recreational activities. Neither treats indoor recreation. For further details, see the Appendix to this chapter.

The National Travel Survey

A National Travel Survey was part of the Census Bureau's proposed plan for the first Census of Transportation, scheduled by law for 1952. However, Congress did not appropriate funds for that census. The survey again was proposed for the next census (scheduled for 1957) but again funds were not appropriated. In the meantime, the bureau conducted a "pilot" National Travel Survey in 1957 under the sponsorship of the National Association of Travel Organizations. Subsequently, a larger travel survey became a major element in each of the censuses of transportation (1963, 1967 and 1972).

The purposes of the survey were:

> (1) to analyze travel patterns, (2) to compute the apparent statistical relationships between travel and socioeconomic conditions, (3) to develop factors for projecting the 1963 data into the future on the basis of estimated (or assumed) changes in travel patterns or socioeconomic conditions and (4) insofar as feasible, to integrate relevant information from other sources with the Travel Survey data to support analyses of travel in greater depth and in broader areas than would be possible by using data from only a single source.

The results of the survey are available from the Bureau of the Census (see the Appendix).

National Survey of Fishing and Hunting

A National Survey of Fishing and Hunting was made in 1955, 1960, 1965, and 1970, providing information on participation in these two sports and on expenditures (see the Appendix). While minor changes have been made over time, the data are essentially comparable. The sample includes only those with a "special interest" in either of these sports, and omits those who participate only rarely. This survey in 1965 estimated 33 million anglers and hunters, while the more comprehensive National Recreation Survey estimated 50 million. However, the 33 million accounted for 95 percent of the recreation days and 99 percent of expenditures for these sports. The National Survey of Fishing and Hunting, thus, includes only the "real" sportsmen! The studies based on these surveys are available from the Fish and Wildlife Service of the Department of the Interior.

Current Population Survey

This monthly survey of the employment characteristics of the non-institutional population identifies the number of people in the labor force who are not at work during the week of reference of the survey. It asks the respondent the reason for not being at work. One of the reasons is "on vacation." Because the resulting estimate excludes the nonlabor-force population and because of the possibility that some of the not-at-home sample were on vacation during the week of the interview, the resulting data were not comprehensively representative of the population, but the data nevertheless provide an indicator of vacationing. Results are published in the *Monthly Report on the Labor Force* by the U. S. Department of Labor. They provide a systematically collected indicator of the trend in vacation experiences of the population.

Hunting and Fishing License Holders

Annually, the Bureau of Sport Fisheries and Wildlife, U. S. Department of the Interior, assembles information from each state on the number of hunting and fishing licenses sold, and publishes the information by state. The cost of a license varies from one state to another and some states may exempt persons with certain characteristics from purchasing a license. The data are published annually as a news release by the bureau.

Public Land Statistics

An annual compilation by the Bureau of Land Management, U. S. Department of the Interior, includes information for the year on the various types of land holdings of the federal government and statistical data on the Bureau of Land Management's program on outdoor recreation and wildlife. In addition to resource information, the data include estimates of the volume of visitors or family units, by states, and the visitor days by activity. The data are obtained through reports from subordinate units within the bureau.

The Bureau of Land Management has responsibility for 452 million acres of federal land. Within the Department of the Interior, other landholding agencies include the National Park Service, the Fish and Wildlife Service, and the Bureau of Reclamation. Some 24 percent of federal land is managed by the Forest Service, U. S. Department of Agriculture. While these agencies do not assemble precisely comparable visitor information, the data nevertheless reflect a vast segment of recreation. Some of these are illustrated below.

The National Park System, comprising some 283 units, is administered by the National Park Service, U. S. Department of the Interior. The volume of visits and overnight stays at most of these facilities are reported monthly, by park. Detail is presented for the month, the cumulative total on a calendar-year basis (with the annual totals thus represented in each December issue), and annually for fiscal-year totals (in the July issue). The July issue also shows the fiscal-year totals for the different categories of areas administered by the National Park Service, each park being classified as primarily a natural, historical, or recreational area. The trends in visits according to these different areas, as well as the total volume of tourism, provides an index to the changing interests of tourists. In addition to the visitor data mentioned above, the National Park Service also issues in mimeographed form information by park showing other details on visitors, such as camper days in tents or trailers, patronage of commercial accommodations in the parks, etc.

The Forest Service, U. S. Department of Agriculture, manages about 187 million acres of lands and waters for resource production, including recreation opportunities. This agency has a modern automated data system for recreation information management. The information system is referred to by the acronym RIM. It provides capability for storage, maintenance, and retrieval of recreation information used in the forest service planning, budgetary, management and other decision-making processes.

Both the measured and estimated recreation use of national forest developed sites such as campgrounds, picnic grounds, swimming and boating sites, winter sports sites, etc., as well as for dispersed areas is recorded in the Forest Service RIM system. Such recreation use information is categorized further as to a broad range of recreation activities such as camping, hunting, fishing, horseback riding, skiing, foot travel, and motorized travel. Also, information about the numbers of facilities (stoves, tables, etc.) and their condition is included, as well as directory information to assist the public in locating specific recreation sites and areas.

The Forest Service RIM system will be expanded in the future to include an inventory of the recreation characteristics of lands and waters for potential recreation opportunities and some capability for deriving origin-of-visitor information.

The Forest Service information system for recreation is designed to aggregate information on a state and county basis as well as by national forest administrative and management units (ranger districts, national recreation areas, national system of trails, units of the national wilderness preservation system, etc.). All data are reported as part of the administration of the National Forest system and the reporting follows a long-established administrative routine.

Other Government Sources

Other agencies of government also provide outdoor recreational data as they relate to their activities or jurisdictions. These include the Bureau of Reclamation, Department of the Interior; the U. S. Army Corps of Engineers; the T.V.A.; the Federal Power Commission; and the U. S. Coast Guard. The Bureau of Outdoor Recreation of the Department of the Interior also collects data by state on areas in state parks, estimated visits, and state expenditures on those facilities.

Private Recreational Enterprises

Private outdoor recreational enterprises were identified through nationwide sample surveys conducted in 1960, sponsored by ORRRC, and in 1965 by a survey sponsored by the Bureau of Outdoor Recreation and conducted by Chilton Research Service of Philadelphia.

The 1965 survey was a sample of 256 counties. It collected information on the use and overuse, the types of facilities offered by the private enterprise, the years the enterprise had been in existence, the proximity to other enterprises that might be competitive, and other items. Special state surveys were made of Maine, California, Oregon, Washington, Tennessee, and Georgia.

Some private organizations also provide statistics on outdoor recreation. These include the Athletic Institute, the (nongovernment) National Recreation and Park Association, and the American Automobile Association.

USES

Users

The Bureau of Outdoor Recreation, U. S. Department of the Interior, has methodically logged the requests it has received for information on recreation. The volume and variety of requests from the public in the United States and from foreign countries is great, and the ability of the bureau to find and deliver the answers to these questions leads one to admire the devotion of our government's bureaucracy. Discussed first is the apparent uses to which the requested information will be put and, then, the types of information sought by the public.

By far the most frequently expressed purpose was that of preparing a magazine article or a research study on some recreational topic. Some requests mentioned that a speech was being prepared.

The second most frequently mentioned purpose was for business, finance, and commerce. This purpose appeared to come from all economic levels of business, from a farmer considering the economic advantage of leasing his land for hunting or fishing to an investment analyst who was fathoming the future of the recreation industry. Assessment of a market, determining prospective demand for recreational goods or services appeared to be this predominant use of the data.

The third most frequent source of requests was from other units of government, other federal agencies, and state and local planning and service agencies.

Another type of user is found in foreign governments and agencies. The Bureau of Outdoor Recreation has fielded nearly reciprocal requests for information from every continent except Antarctica regarding its role in nationwide planning for outdoor recreation.

Finally, there were many requests from teachers and students who were studying some aspect of recreation.

Thus, the users of recreational statistics cover a wide variety of interests—researchers and writers, business, government agencies, foreign governments and agencies, and teachers and students. No doubt a comprehensive listing of all users from all sources of information, though not feasible, would disclose many other types of interested persons and agencies.

Information Requested

Information on almost all aspects of recreation is widely sought from the data sources. Leading among the requests received were those for data on the number of persons participating in various forms of recreation and the rates of participation. Data on recreational resources appeared as the second most frequently sought type of information. Financial information on recreation and information on expenditures was also often in demand. There were, also, many requests having to do with equipment used in recreational activity. Finally, there were many requests for information on the organizational or institutional aspects of recreation.

Rates of participation or the numbers participating were requested for "popular sports," for water skiing, snow skiing, hunting, and bicycling. The number and socioeconomic characteristics were asked for of participants in golf, tennis, and other sports that use equipment.

Information was requested on visits to national and state parks, attendance at federal recreation areas, visits to rural recreation areas (of interest to a manufacturer and distributor of waste disposal equipment), the volume of visitation to state and country parks. Information was requested on numbers of campers and picnickers, the number of occasions they took part in, and the number of public camps and picnic sites in a particular geographic area of the United States.

The variety of data requested on resources almost equaled that requested on participation. Information was wanted on the number and the acres in public and private swimming beaches, the number of bodies of water closed to recreational use because of pollution, the miles of ocean and Great Lakes shores, the number of marine resources and the extent of their use, the number and location of recreation ponds, and the number of miles of shoreline. There also were questions on trends in resources: trends in the number of ski areas, in the number of campsites (for highway planning), and projections of the number of campgrounds.

The information requested on recreation equipment concerned the number of the various items in use and potentially in demand: the use of automobiles in recreational activity, the use of camping and other recreational vehicles, the number of outdoor motors, snow ski equipment, camping utensils, and motorcycles.

Financial data on outdoor recreation were requested on consumer expenditures for recreational goods and services as well as information on the capital invested in recreational "enterprises" of various kinds. What is the dollar volume of recreational expenditures? How much is spent for hunting and fishing? How much is spent by tourists? How much do consumers spend while at their second homes? How many dollars are spent on recreation?

Other questions related to the volume of business of various segments of the recreation industry. What is the dollar volume of the skiing industry? What are the total dollar sales of recreation vehicles? What are the annual dollar sales of sporting goods? What is the annual income of operators of overnight camps? What are their expenditures?

Another set of questions concerned investments—the amount spent by the federal government on outdoor recreation, the amount of federal expenditures on marinas and the amount of private investment in marinas. Estimates also were requested on the costs of developing various types of campgrounds, and requests were received for an assessment of the economic impact of recreational boating.

Many requests were for trends, future forecasts, or projections. What is the projection of recreation participation in 1980 and 2000? What is the trend in the number of skiers? What is the forecast of the number of tennis players? What are the trends in the distance traveled for recreational purposes? What are the projections of recreational activity used in the nationwide plan of the Bureau of Outdoor Recreation? How many campers will there be in 1980?

Many specific questions were asked, such as: How many campers are there? How many canoeists, backpackers, pleasure drivers, swimmers? How many ice skaters? How many hunters and fishermen are there, by region and by income? How many birdwatchers are there and how many have the hobby of photographing wildlife? What is the extent of playing outdoor games and sports, of hiking, of archery, of mountain climbing? What is the extent of horseback riding? How much leisure time does each person have in a month?

Some questions, of course, were outside the scope of our present knowledge: How many people are there in cities who are denied recreation because they do not have automobiles to reach outdoor recreation sites? What is the demand for recreational facilities by county?

Governmental Planning

The Land and Water Conservation Fund Act of 1965 (Public Law 88-578) authorized the secretary of the interior to stimulate the states to develop comprehensive plans for outdoor recreation. For the development of these plans, the federal government through the Bureau of Outdoor Recreation (BOR) provides funds to the states. The plans then are used as the basis for developing the recreational resources that are needed, now and in the future. The information that goes into the plans, and the interpretation made of the information, thus bears a direct relation to the process of acquiring land, developing recreational facilities, enacting enabling legislation by the state, manning the facilities, and taking other necessary steps to provide the public with outdoor recreation opportunities.

In developing a comprehensive outdoor recreation plan a state is largely on its own, although the bureau provides "guidelines" and other suggestions. Consequently the state plans differ from one another. Some differences arise from the varying types of recreation afforded by the resources, climate, and interests of the state's population and the importance accorded outdoor recreation in relation to other problems. Other differences arise from the varying information base for developing a plan; some states, such as Florida and California, have a great deal of information, and others have little. Finally, differences among the comprehensive statewide plans for outdoor recreation arise from genuine differences in the orientation to recreational planning, the appropriate information to use, and the validity of one or another theoretical position. As the result of these differences, the use of statistical data varies among the state comprehensive plans. While no list of informational items in a plan will be entirely complete, the items of information in some of the state plans will illustrate the use made of data for this very important public purpose.

Two items of information prominently employed in state plans are activity participation rates and resources inventory information. Shortly after work on state plans was initiated the only such data available were current as of 1960, having been produced by the Outdoor Recreation Resources Review Commission. In 1965, however, the inventory was updated and a second National Recreation Survey was conducted. These two sources then were used in state plans. Some states, however, realized a need for participation rates reflecting the state's unique participation patterns, and special surveys of the states' populations were conducted to provide information on activity days per person in various kinds of outdoor recreation. Inventory information, however, continued to come from its primary source: the federal, state, or local agency administering the recreational resource, for governmental resources and for private recreation, from a special 1965 survey conducted for BOR by Chilton Research Services.

Plans include information on the current participation in recreation in a state and estimates of demand, including projections of future demand for recreational activity; and information on proposals for augmenting or developing the supply to meet the demand in the future. The scope of such an undertaking suggests that a very wide variety of information is needed.

A second type of important statistical data on recreation used in comprehensive state plans is an inventory of recreational facilities: number of parks and acres in them; number of facilities, such as picnic tables, swimming pools, boating piers, and so forth; acres of water; miles of access roadways; acres of wilderness; miles of trails; family units of camping positions; and so forth, through the entire gamut of resources that are used for recreation. Federal agencies supply the information on resources under their administrative supervision; state and local agencies do likewise. Obtaining information on recreational resources offered by private sector enterprises is more difficult but the Bureau of Outdoor Recreation (1965) had assembled such information on a sample basis for the nation as a whole. This information is presented as the "supply" of recreational resources and may be translated into potential "user" days just as participation rates can be translated into demand for recreational facilities. The latter is accomplished by the use of "standards," to be reviewed shortly, which translate activity days into a "requirement" for facilities.

Another important item of information entering into comprehensive state plans is a projection of the population to future target dates, such as 1980 and 2000. Estimates must be for each of the planning districts of the state and for some states must be according to rural or urban categories. For states such as Florida, whose recreational resources are used extensively by people from elsewhere, the volume of tourists expected in the future also is projected.

Comprehensive plans thus use a great deal of statistical information. An examination of some of the informational items entering into Florida plans will illustrate this use.

The Florida Example The plan developed for the state of Florida includes such information as the number of registered boats, the number of campers who use the state parks, and the number of licenses sold for fishing and for hunting. It includes estimates of the number of tourists coming to the state, information Florida can supply with considerable accuracy since the state in the past has sponsored a number of tourist surveys. Trends in statistical indicators of recreational use also are used in the Florida plan: trends in attendance at parks, in the number of hunting and fishing licenses, in per capita income, in the total resident population, classified by residential location of the population, etc.

The Florida plan, also, includes an inventory of recreational resources. The state is delineated into areas and, within each, estimates are made of the wildlife populations.

To measure demand, estimates are made of the resident and visitor population for future years. The state developed participation rates per capita for some thirty-two recreational activities by conducting a survey of its own. With these factors estimates of recreational "demand" for the years 1970, 1975, and for the year 2000 were developed.

The extent of the demand in the Florida plan rests upon the concept of "design demand," which is an estimate of the required recreational resources for an activity based upon the demand on a peak day. In user occasions this peak day demand then is converted into facility requirements. Many assumptions must be made in this step, as one might imagine, but these assumptions are quite specific and are set forth as standards. For example, the demand for beach activities is converted into a statement of the physical resources required by applying the "standard" of 100 square feet of beach per person. In another example, the demand for boating in fresh water is converted as follows: one ramp is assumed to be required for every fifty boats per day of use and ten acres of water are assumed to be needed for each boat. Such standards as these are based upon observational studies which show the capacity of a resource to satisfy an activity-need under assumed levels of satisfaction to the participant and upon other logical considerations.

Parenthetically, the problem must be met of whether to plan upon the basis of meeting the "peak day" demand, which would represent the maximum demand; or the expected average demand during the season for a particular outdoor activity; or the year-round average demand; or upon some other basis. If the plan accommodates the maximum demand inevitably the resource is underused much of the time; if, on the other hand, the plan accommodates the minimum demand, overcrowding and overuse occur on peak weekends. As one of the assumptions implied in the "standards," then, such policies have rather significant impact upon the eventual plan.

The Florida plan also enumerates resources for recreation within its borders, some of the information coming from federal sources and other information from its own accumulations of data. Resources are categorized according to ownership: (1) federal/state, (2) local, (3) private commercial, (4) private noncommercial, (5) quasi-public.

The above list of data used in the Florida plan is, of course, incomplete, but it provides a general picture of the vast range of data required to prepare a comprehensive plan for the development of outdoor recreation resources in a state. Great investments of money may result from such a plan, so there is an extreme compulsion to make the information accurate and adequate to the decisions which will rest upon the plan. The plan, of course, leads to justification to purchase particular sites of land and develop them into specified types of recreational uses.

Other states also made use of recreational data in planning recreational facilities. Among them were South Carolina, Alabama, and Minnesota.

Travel Survey

The primary uses of the Travel Survey data were to analyze travel patterns and to predict future ones—each use being relevant to decisions and planning by the travel industry.

"Travel Expectancy Tables" have been developed which make possible estimates of the number of person-trips during a year, based upon the experience of one of the surveys, for persons of given socioeconomic characteristics. By extension, it is planned eventually to develop forecasts of future travel, given future estimates of certain socioeconomic characteristics of families.

The National Travel Survey information on recreational travel has been used by federal and state agencies with responsibility for travel and tourism and by business and commercial interests offering products or services in travel and tourism.

Uses among states center in the travel promotion, planning, and development agencies. The states of Virginia, Washington, Maryland, New York, and Florida are examples. The data on travel are used as background information on the volume of travel, the purposes of the trip, the length of stay, the areas from which tourists come to the state, and the like. States plan their promotional advertising campaigns upon the basis of such information. The information helps to evaluate the geographic areas from which tourists to the state originate, the travelers' socioeconomic levels, their mode of travel, and related information that is useful in planning advertising and identifying appropriate media for the advertisements. The information also is useful in state decisions relative to development of the state's recreational resources: whether to develop natural resources for recreational purposes, to invest in improvement or restoration of historical monuments and sites, and the like.

Another use made by state governments is that of estimating income from out-of-state travelers within the state. The New England states, for example, have estimated that the travel industry is the second largest producer of income for the region. (Paul Hendrix, consultant, has made these estimates for the New England governors for several years.)

Other examples of state use follow:

Data from the 1965 National Fishing and Hunting Survey were used by the Maryland Department of Game and Inland Fish in its testimony before the Maryland General Assembly to show the impact a proposed gun control law would have on the hunters of Maryland.

In 1959, the same Maryland department reported its use of information from the 1955 survey, which included a state survey of Maryland in that year, to support an increase in the cost of fishing licenses during the 1957 session of the Maryland General Assembly.

In 1959, the counterpart state department in Michigan reported: "We found the 1955 data extremely helpful in impressing upon the Legislature and the public the importance of hunting and fishing in our State economy and believe that another survey in 1961 will further strengthen the findings of the 1955 survey."

In 1959, the counterpart agency in Hawaii reported: "we have still found the data obtained through the National Survey as an invaluable aid in determining general trends in recreational fishing and hunting, particularly in our dealings with the State legislators."

Among federal agencies, the National Forest Service, the National Park Service, and the Department of Transportation have made systematic use of the data in developing policies and programs. The Department of Transportation has sponsored a continuing monthly assessment of the Washington-Boston corridor of travel since 1967 as a basis for measuring the consequences of the fast train service from Washington to New York and Boston. Of course, the agency is interested in all travel, rather than recreational travel alone, and uses information from other sources as well as data from the monthly travel survey in the corridor area.

Special tabulations have recently been prepared by the Bureau of the Census for use by a consultant in evaluating the travel potentialities of the V-STOL (vertical or short take-off and landing) plane. The information is considered useful in assessing the potential market for such a plane, and identifying the city-pairs between which the traffic of such a plane might be generated, the population of such cities, etc.

Each new publication of the survey is distributed to members of Congress and "some of the individual congressmen in turn have requested additional copies" to distribute to their constituents.

In the opinion of officials responsible for the National Travel Survey the uses made of the information by consultants and other commercial interests may surpass the direct applications and analyses made by state and federal agencies, but such uses are often more difficult to document. This is because business interests analyze the data and reach conclusions or recommendations which affect the competitive market and they usually are not anxious to describe the decision-making process nor to reveal the basis for their decision. Consequently, the variety and magnitude of uses of the National Travel Survey recreational travel information by commercial and business interests can only be inferred by the volume of requests received by the Bureau of the Census, which, in its usual penchant for service with anonymity, preserves even the source of these requests.

Foreign Governments

Some examples of uses of recreational data by foreign governments and agencies follow. Information was requested by Argentina's *Direcion Nacional de Turismo* on travel and recreation; by Bolivia's municipality of La Paz on recreation park planning; by France's *Ministère de l'Agriculture* on suburban forest econstaging; by an Australian city engineer on study-tour planning; by Japan's Municipal Planning Research Center on federal recreation management; and by both governmental and private agencies of the Netherlands on problems of recreation, physical facilities, open spaces, and town planning. A request was received concerning major outdoor recreation planning issues from the Latin American Committee on National Parks of the International Union for the Conservation of Nature and Natural Resources (Morges, Switzerland). Also received, via airgram to the United States secretary of state from eighteen U. S. embassies, were requests for information regarding national outdoor recreation planning from other countries.

Information from the National Hunting and Fishing Survey has been exchanged with the public recreation and fish and game departments of Canada, and the Food and Agricultural Organization in Rome. Data from the 1960 survey were used by George Beall, an American citizen living in France, in a study in which he attempted to extrapolate the results of the United States survey to the French economy in order to show how much amateur fishing contributed to the French economy.

There has been active interchange of travel information—especially with respect to methods and other technical aspects—with foreign countries, such as Canada, Great Britain, Australia, and France. There appears to be a trend toward increased compatibility of definitions, especially with Canada, which is mutually beneficial because of the substantial volume of travel across the border.

Business

It is, of course, impossible to list all of the types of uses of recreational data by the business community. Many of the uses, however, can be inferred from the kinds of requests received for the statistics. Examples are given below:

A land development company was interested in the number of parks, the number of recreation vehicles in use, the number of boats in use, and the number of participants in camping, water skiing, snowskiing, and the recreational aspects of retirement living. Participation in these activities evidently had some bearing upon land development decisions of the company.

The number of participants by age in archery, amateur ice hockey, and baseball, and how these fit into the overall sports market, was requested by a market research group.

Leisure information was requested for investment purposes, for use by security analysts: amount of money spent on an activity and the number of various kinds of resources, such as marinas.

The number of water-based recreation areas in the United States was requested by a private manufacturing company. It was interested in estimating the size of the market for floating docks.

A shoe manufacturing company was interested in information on the number of participants in sports activities by each sport, its purpose being to produce sports footwear for the market.

Projections of the extent of participation in various outdoor sports, by the activity, are used by a national safety organization to forecast the number of accidents.

Trends in the rates of participation in various outdoor recreational activities, based upon surveys conducted in 1960 and 1965, were of interest to the program manager for business development of a large corporation, for use in production planning.

A carpeting manufacturing company requested information on the number of recreation motels.

A company was interested in the amount of leisure time and the disposable income of consumers, for use in assessing the market for snowmobiles and motorcycles. Information on the number of parks, the automobile traffic in parks, and the outlook for an increase in park areas was requested by the same company.

One "requester" was preparing advertising copy, a car rental agency was making some plan for "tapping" the recreation market, a travel agency was focusing upon the direction of tourist travel, and another entrepreneur was planning to develop a campground. Production planning by manufacturing industries also required recreational data.

In one instance a nationally known company sought printouts for purposes of determining whether to diversify their product lines to include the manufacture of fishing tackle.

The magazine, *Outdoor Life,* obtained special tabulations to determine the expenditures of sportsmen in 1965 who subscribed to magazines and those who did not. Finding that the sportsmen who subscribed to sports magazines spent eleven times more on fishing and hunting equipment than those who did not subscribe, the magazine used the information in February 1967 to promote advertising in its pages.

Many of the uses of the National Hunting and Fishing Survey by commerce and business can be inferred from the requests received for the information. As reported by Mr. William M. White, chief of the Division of River Basin Studies, in a personal communication to Abbott Ferriss (dated October 30, 1970): "We have answered written and telephoned requests for our survey data from large nationally known marketing and public relations companies, recreation consultants, news media (newspapers, magazine, radio, and TV stations), chambers of commerce, tire and boat manufacturers, etc."

Much information about the uses of recreational statistics by business and government are based on the results of research which involve intensive analysis of the data, often in relation to other data involving broad policy or theoretical considerations. Research use of recreational information is considered next.

Research

A number of studies have been conducted both national in scope and focused upon particular regions or river basins, including "economic impact" studies. The latter attempt an assessment of the economic contribution of the recreational resource on the local, state, or national economy. Sociological and other social science studies also are contributing to increased knowledge about outdoor recreation and its correlates.

Economists make estimates of the primary benefits to be derived from investment in a recreational facility. A statement of anticipated benefits in relation to the costs of the investment is used to justify budgets proposed by governmental agencies, by financial institutions to assess the feasibility of a capital investment, and by business organizations to gauge the economic feasibility of entering the production of a recreational item—everything from fishing tackle to a Disneyland.

The economic framework for examining recreation has been set forth most completely by Clawson and Knetsch (1966). With respect to a facility the total cost of a visit is related to the total annual number of visits. The general idea is that the cheaper the cost, the larger will be the number of visits. Such demand curves may be generated for the several socioeconomic classes, based upon annual income. Other elements of demand include the average length of the work week, the type of road leading to the facility, and certain managerial and "attractiveness" features of the site. In each of these instances a relationship is postulated to the total cost of the visit.

Other relationships may be established between the number of visits arising from a population in relation to the distance of the population center from the recreational site. Economists also are interested in the effect of the entrance fee upon the number of visits to the site. In addition to these uses that economists make of recreational data, they also make use of population estimates and projections, information on the amount of leisure time, information on modes of travel to a site, and information on income of the population.

A general theoretical orientation to the economics of the development of a site for outdoor recreation has been written by Ivan M. Lee and published by the Outdoor Recreation Resources Review Commission. The same publication also includes articles that are concerned with the evaluation of the economic benefit of outdoor recreation and the problem of establishing an appropriate price or valuation on the experience. While some of these analyses employ numerical data relative to recreation at particular sites, the primary purpose of the analyses is to present a theoretical economic framework for the examination of recreational data.

Economists, also, have examined the supply and demand of outdoor recreation as it is revealed through mass surveys. Two of these are cited below and the general use to which such data are put is discussed in connection with the National Recreation Survey. The per capita use of recreational resources in relation to personal background and socioeconomic factors is viewed as an expression of demand and a basis for the prediction of the future demand. Earlier studies of the same phenomena were conducted at the University of Michigan and were published by the Outdoor Recreation Resources Review Commission.

Some studies focus upon particular river basins or regions of the country. Sielaff's 1963 study analyzes available data on the outdoor recreation industry in the Upper Midwest. Local data on acreage in parks, visits, and estimates of expenditures are included along with other resource and participation data for the states in the area of the study. Comparable data also are presented by county where available. Generally the supply-demand orientation is employed and there are some thirteen supplementary essays, some dealing with recreation in individual states, presented at the Upper Midwest Recreation Resources Institute, held at the Duluth Campus of the University of Minnesota in 1962. In addition to data from national sources, the report incorporates the results of a number of studies at several universities, by a department of the state of Minnesota, some of them conducted through the cooperation of associations and state departments.

A planning study of the environmental aspects of a river basin involves assembling a very wide variety of information on the river, farmland, wooded land, hills and mountains, towns and cities, industries and agricultural uses, income, population, recreational participation, and projections of demand factors into the future. Almost all of this information is found in surveys, censuses, studies, or archives of state and federal governments. Economic, recreational, engineering, industrial, demographic, and other aspects of the present and the probable future use of the river are discussed. Such a composite, many-faceted approach to river basin planning is necessary if all of the elements affecting the resources are to be considered, as they must. Much of the information is placed on maps. Some of it is interpreted aesthetically in terms of landscape architecture, and much of it is interpreted in terms of future conditions and future demand for recreational uses.

Economists and others also have conducted a number of "economic impact" studies. In some cases the study assesses the contribution likely to result from the development of the site, as might be the case of a dam being installed on a river. While chiefly local data are used in such studies, often average values from national studies, such as the National Travel Survey, are employed in making economic estimates.

The economic significance of travel is viewed as measured by the amount spent by the tourist in connection with a visit to a site. In addition to expenditures, the contribution of salaries of business enterprise employees, of governmental employment, etc., is included. Trends in employment within a metropolitan area or a county and data from the state employment security records also are used. While information in impact studies comes from a variety of sources, the studies generally fall into two types: (1) those depending entirely upon federal, state, and local statistical information, including, of course, visitor information from the recreational facility, and (2) those using available federal, state, and local data plus surveys of visitors to the facility. The latter type provides a much more comprehensive assessment of the impact of the recreational visitor to the site.

Research has also been conducted on the sociocultural aspects of outdoor recreation. Such research is focused largely around various theories that attempt to explain play and recreation. Examples of such studies are given in the References. Sociological and psychological research will undoubtedly accelerate with present trends in recreation and growing interest in its implications and consequences.

THE OUTLOOK

Ample evidence, then, exists of extensive use of recreational statistics. They provide information for legislation at the federal and state levels and the development of public policy; for decisions by businessmen and financiers concerning investment and production; and for research leading to the increase in knowledge, particularly through economic analyses and research in the interest of planning. It may be anticipated, as the population continues to grow and exert greater pressures on outdoor recreational resources, that the demand for and use of recreational statistics will continue to increase.

APPENDIX

On Outdoor Recreation Surveys

The National Recreation Survey

The 1960 survey consisted of four seasonal surveys and the one in 1965 reflected primarily that summer's outdoor recreation participation, but included estimates by the respondent for other seasons. The 1960 survey provided detail by the four major census regions, while the 1965 survey, being a larger sample, provided detail by the nine census divisions. Measures of summer recreational participation, by activity, are included in both surveys; these measures include the days, the average number of days' participation by activity for the population, and the population participating. The respondent also named his three favorite seasonal outdoor recreation activities in the 1960 survey but only his favorite in 1965. The extent of outdoor recreation on vacations, trips, and outings was obtained in both surveys, while trip expenditures were obtained in 1960 but not 1965. The 1960 survey obtained information on equipment ownership and the amount of leisure time spent on outdoor recreation but the 1965 survey did not obtain this information. However, the 1965 survey obtained estimates of outdoor recreation participation during the three seasons other than the detailed information obtained on the summer months, thus making possible a partially valid comparison of annual recreational participation between the two periods. The plan to conduct a comprehensive national survey every five years was interrupted in 1970 because of insufficient funds for the study. The 1970 Survey of Outdoor Recreation Activities, however, provided some data on participation in about twenty activities.

The National Travel Survey

The 1957 survey was partly experimental. Sampled households were a subsample of the Current Population Survey, and provided sufficient detail for tabulations by region of origin. It provided estimates of the number of trips and the purpose of the trip, the mode of travel, and the distance and region of destination of the trip. Tabulation of trips included income of the family, season of the year, number of days on trip, the age of travelers, whether or not the trip originated in a Standard Metropolitan Statistical Area, and whether the destination was the same state, adjacent state, or beyond adjacent state. Tabulations of these characteristics were by the purpose of trip. Thus, trips to visit friends and relatives were tabulated separately from trips for other pleasure, etc.

The 1963 survey included the above items of information, with some refinement, and an increase in the number of tables released. For example, location of the traveler's residence included additional detail as to whether the residence was within or outside the central city for SMSA residents and, for non-SMSA residents, whether residence was a farm or nonfarm.

The 1967 survey was conducted by mail in order to reduce costs and "to satisfy requests for estimates of travel by states and regions in addition to national aggregates." It consisted of a panel of 12,000 households who were asked to respond to a mail questionnaire at three-month intervals for a year. The purpose of the trips on which reports were obtained included outdoor recreation [hunting, fishing, entertainment (theater, spectator sports), sightseeing, and visiting friends and relatives] in addition to purposes other than recreation.

The National Survey of Fishing and Hunting

This survey includes details on the "different types of fishing and hunting by the money and recreation days spent, the number of trips, place of residence, income, occupation, and license status." The 1955 data were collected by Crossley S-D Surveys, Inc., but the remaining surveys were performed by the Census Bureau. Each was sponsored by the Fish and Wildlife Service, U. S. Department of the Interior. The surveys provide certain estimates by the nine census divisions. While much of the survey is devoted to expenditures of sportsmen by type of expenditure for each major type of sport (fresh-water, salt-water, Atlantic Coast salt-water, Gulf Coast salt-water, Pacific Coast salt-water fishing; and hunters by big game, small game, waterfowl), tables are presented for size of city, sex, age, and place of residence, in addition to the other characteristics already mentioned. Salt-water fishing, also, is classified as surf, bay and sound, tidal river and stream, and ocean. The number of times the sportsman engaged in the sport and the miles traveled is presented in some detail. There is an estimate of the number of licensed and unlicensed fishermen and hunters and classifications by occupation, education, and income.

REFERENCES

Clawson, Marion, and Jack L. Knetsch. *Economics of Outdoor Recreation.* Baltimore, Md.: Johns Hopkins Press, 1966.

Sielaff, Richard O. *The Economics of Outdoor Recreation in the Upper Midwest.* Duluth: University of Minnesota, 1963.

U. S. Bureau of Outdoor Recreation. *Private Sector Study of Outdoor Recreation Enterprise, 1965.* Washington, D. C.: Government Printing Office.

U. S. Department of Labor. *Monthly Report on the Labor Force.* Washington, D. C.: Government Printing Office, 1942–1965. (From Jan., 1966–June, 1969, the report was titled *Employment and Earnings and Monthly Report on the Labor Force.* Since July 1969 it has been called *Employment and Earnings.*)

U. S. Outdoor Recreation Resources Review Commission. *Economic Studies of Outdoor Recreation.* Reports to The Outdoor Recreation Resource Review Commission. Contributors: Marion Clawson, Arthur L. Moore, Ivan M. Lee. Washington, D. C.: U. S. Government Printing Office, 1962.

CHAPTER 13

*On Governments**

THE DATA

Public services in the United States are provided by more than 80,000 separate governments. These include, in addition to the federal government and the fifty states, many thousands of municipalities, counties, townships, school districts, and other special-purpose districts.

Particular kinds of public services are reflected by data in such subject fields as education, transportation, social insurance and welfare, and health. However, the most comprehensive overall measures of government are provided by the "government statistics" program of the Bureau of the Census. Like bureau programs in other fields, this one involves a census that supplies relatively detailed data at periodic intervals (in this case, for years ending with "2" and "7"), and the reporting of more summary statistics on an annual and quarterly basis. The information thus reported deals mainly with state and local governments, although figures for the federal government also are included, especially in the presentation of nationwide totals.

Periodic Censuses

Some governmental statistics were gathered and published in conjunction with each of the decennial population censuses in the latter half

---

* Based on a memorandum prepared by Allen D. Manvel, formerly of the U. S. Bureau of the Census.

of the nineteenth century. The early emphasis was on "taxation, public indebtedness, and 'taxable wealth,'" but for 1880 there was also some treatment of public expenditures, and by 1890 the census reporting of governmental data ran to nearly 1700 pages.

From 1902 on, the governmental census (prior to 1942 cited as the census of "wealth, debt and taxation") was taken separately from the decennial population census, and generally covered years ending with "2." Significant new features were included in the 1902, 1913, and 1932 censuses (1932 was the first year when county-area totals of local government revenue and expenditure were reported), but the 1922 census involved a severe cutback from earlier censuses, and the 1942 census (the first to be termed "census of governments") was even more limited. In one important respect, however, the 1942 census broke new ground: it provided benchmark data on numbers and types of local governments, thus supplying a precedent for the reporting on local government structure that has since been a major feature of this periodic census.

In 1950, Congress passed the "Census of Governments Act," which required that such a census be taken at five-year intervals, beginning with 1952. However, no appropriation was made for a 1952 census other than for "advance planning and preparation," which supplied only an updated inventory of governmental units. There have since been four such censuses, respectively for 1957, 1962, 1967, and 1972. Each of these supplied about 7000 pages of published reports.

Current Statistics

Annual reporting on the finances of city governments began in the 1890s, and has been maintained with only two interruptions (1914 and 1920). Annual reporting on state government finances has been continuous since 1915, except for 1920, 1921, and 1933 through 1936. Separate annual reports on state tax revenue have also been issued since the 1940s. With the development of sampling methods, annual sample surveys on governmental finances and employment became feasible. This led to the reporting of nationwide totals of governmental debt beginning with 1940, of governmental revenue beginning with 1945, and then of governmental finances more broadly (dealing with expenditure and financial assets as well as revenue and debt) beginning with 1952.

Current census reporting on governmental employment and payrolls dates from 1940, but did not reach its present form—to include detail by function and figures on "full-time equivalent" employment, as well as other measures—until 1953.

Since 1958, annual sample surveys have provided state and local financial data by states as well as nationally, and since 1965 local finance amounts have been reported annually for each of the thirty-eight largest metropolitan areas and their component county areas. Since 1959 there has also been a separate annual series on the finances of employee retirement systems.

Three series of quarterly reports also are issued: on state and local tax revenue (since 1962), construction expenditure of these governments (since 1963), and assets of their major retirement systems (since 1968).

Data Classification

The conceptual framework employed for the reporting of current governmental statistics has been maintained with only limited revisions since 1951. However, the reporting pattern applied from 1937 to 1950 involved quite different treatment of some aspects of governmental finances, and that in turn differed from the classification framework which had applied before 1937. To deal with the resulting problem of historical noncomparability, the Census Bureau prepared a number of special studies in which certain earlier-period figures were recast and presented in terms of the classification framework that was initiated in 1951. These studies are cited and drawn upon in *Historical Statistics on Governmental Finances and Employment* (U. S. Bureau of the Census, 1968). The introduction to that report also summarizes major differences between the various classification systems mentioned above.

Published and Unpublished Data

Published statistics are available on a quarterly, annual, and quinquennial basis. The information contained in the publication is given in the Appendix to this chapter.

Many of the sets of published data represent selective summations drawn from far more detailed underlying figures. This is especially true of the current statistics on local government finances and employment, which appear mainly in the form of national, state, and metropolitan-area aggregates but are based on information gathered from several thousand individual governments. Even in the periodic census, however, financial and employment data are published for only about one-tenth of all the individual governments canvassed. And, especially in the reporting of financial statistics, another kind of compression also is involved—the combination of various detailed items to arrive at a feasibly limited number of figures to be actually published.

Such compression is necessary mainly because (1) the "financial statistics" actually involve several subjects—revenue, expenditure, indebtedness and debt transactions, and financial assets, and (2) cross-classification is needed—especially to deal with expenditure amounts both by function (schools, highways, hospitals, etc.) and by character or object (current operation, purchase of equipment, intergovernmental payments, etc.). As a result, the Census Bureau's basic framework for recording of financial data for individual governments includes provision for several hundred separate items or cells of information—far more than could be specifically published for any considerable number of areas or governments.

Unlike the information that the Census Bureau gathers from individuals and private business firms in most of its other surveys and censuses, these detailed figures about particular governments do not require confidential handling, but can be made available for unrestricted reference and research use. Accordingly, informational needs that are not adequately met by the published statistics can often be served through special tabulations, or by providing duplicate detailed tape records from which the interested researcher can develop the particular groups or comparisons he requires. The Census Bureau's regular *Catalog* describes the various computer tape records which are available for duplication or the preparation of special tabulations on a contract-cost basis. Also, as it did even before these governmental statistics were "computerized" in the early 1960s, the government's division of the Census Bureau is prepared to make underlying survey reports and records available for reference use under appropriate circumstances.

USES

General Public

Many of the specialized uses of census data on governments that are described in later sections are intended to influence public attitudes about such issues as the cost of government, levels of taxation, particular expenditures, tax or borrowing proposals, pending federal or state legislation affecting intergovernmental relations, and—though less often—proposals for adjustments of governmental structure. The general public thus tends mainly to be exposed to the data on a selective and piecemeal basis, as particular figures are cited in editorials or policy statements by various public figures, civic organizations, or interest groups.

Opportunities for a broader public exposure are provided by some other occasional presentations. For example, background or "analytical" reports in news magazines or major newspapers may review evidence of the rapid growth in state and local debt or in taxes; or they may trace trends in public employment, or in governmental spending for particular purposes, or in federal grants to state and local governments.

Some relatively limited groups of the "general public" are also more fully informed through educational institutions and educators (see below), and by the League of Women Voters, the National Municipal League, chambers of commerce, and various other civic or taxpayer groups.

The Federal Government

The federal government itself draws heavily upon census statistics regarding governments, using such data (1) as part of the input for other broader sets of statistics; (2) in the formulation of policy through legislation and otherwise; (3) and in the specific administration of various programs.

Input for Other Statistical Series Three examples of such usage may be mentioned. The government statistics program supplies much of the basic background for the "state and local government" component of the statistics on national income and product which are developed regularly by the Office of Business Economics. The census data on public employment and payrolls especially contribute to the state-by-state series on personal income, and to the calculation of the "implicit price deflator" for governmental purchases.

Statistics on "public debt" published regularly by the Treasury Department draw upon census findings as to the debt and asset holdings of state and local governments.

Similarly, the Bureau of Labor Statistics uses annual census data on public employment as benchmarks for its more frequent summary estimates of public employment, nationally and for certain smaller areas.

Policy Formulation This kind of federal usage is widespread, but hard to quantify or document except by illustration. The difficulty results both because of the vast range of federal interests and activities and because information about state and local governments is likely to be only a part of the background affecting policy attitudes and decisions.

Insofar as legislative action is concerned, some idea of the significance of this part of the background is offered by the frequent references that show up in the congressional debates and committee hearings to state and local government conditions. Especially in debate regarding federal fiscal policies, federal personnel arrangements (including pay rates), and legislation involving grants-in-aid or other types of intergovernmental relationships, there are frequent and sometimes quite detailed citations of data on such matters as trends in state and local revenue, debt, and expenditure; relative "tax burdens" in various states; public pay rates; and the extent to which state and local governments use particular kinds of taxes.

The background governmental data thus surfacing at the legislative stage are assembled by the staffs of individual members of the Congress and of various committees, by the Legislative Reference Service, by interest-group organizations, and by various federal executive agencies.

Particularly where the data have been assembled by an executive agency, the census-source figures are likely to be only part of a presentation that also (or mainly) supplies information drawn from the agency's own source records. This resembles the usual practice in the annual federal budget presentation regarding grants-in-aid. In that presentation annual grant amounts for recent years are shown in relation to census-reported totals of expenditure and own-source revenue of state and local governments, as background for the budget-recommended amounts of prospective grants.

Especially extensive policy-related uses of these governmental statistics have appeared in studies sponsored by the Joint Committee on the Economic Report (for example, its Ninetieth Congress hearings on *Revenue Sharing and Its Alternatives: What Future for Fiscal Federalism?* reported in three volumes), and by various special commissions.

An example of the latter was the National Commission on Urban Problems, headed by former Senator Paul H. Douglas. Part IV of its six-part final report dealt with "government structure, finance, and taxation," and drew heavily upon census governmental data in describing problems on those subjects and offering various proposals for public action.

Even more varied examples of the relevance of these governmental statistics to the formulation of public policy are offered by the reports issued since 1961 by a continuing agency, the Advisory Commission on Intergovernmental Relations. Having a membership drawn from all three levels of government as well as the general public, and with a modest-sized research staff, this body has developed recommendations for governmental action on various subjects.

Many of the commission's proposals have been directed toward state or local governments, but others contemplate federal legislative or administrative action. Following are some of the subjects which have been examined intensively in one or more commission study for which the Census Bureau's governmental statistics supplied an important part of the background:

> Governmental structure in metropolitan areas—dealing with the typical proliferation of local governments in such areas, with attendant duplication of effort, lack of coordinated planning, public disinterest and dissatisfaction, and governmental incapacity.
>
> Issues concerning "special district" governments—similar to the foregoing,

but considering also problems resulting from increasingly atomized and "irresponsible" local governments in rural as well as metropolitan areas.

Problems of "fiscal balance" nationally and within states and metropolitan areas—tracing marked disparities in the government-financing capability of various areas, and governmental efforts (especially through grants-in-aid) to limit the damaging effects of such disparities. The commission's study of these matters led it to recommend a system for federal revenue sharing with states and major cities and counties—one feature of the "Intergovernmental Revenue Act" introduced in 1969 by Senator Muskie and other members of Congress.

State aid to local governments—reviewing the amounts and nature of state grants for schools, other particular functions, and "general government support," as background for commission policy recommendations on this subject.

Strengthening of the property tax—using census findings about this tax as background for numerous commission proposals. Some cited facts: the property tax provides the bulk of local government tax revenue, or about two-thirds as much as all state taxes combined; the task of property valuation is scattered among many thousands of local assessing agencies, most of them far too small to afford competent professional staff or modern data-processing equipment; and there is evidence of gross inequities of property valuation in many parts of the country.

Investment of "idle cash balances"—examining the revenue potential of interest earnings on fund holdings of state and local governments.

State controls of local government debt—reviewing the influence of legal limitations on local borrowing upon the amount and nature of local public indebtedness, and offering recommendations as to state policy in this regard.

Measures of relative fiscal capacity and effort—intensive research studies (issued in 1962 and early 1971) that deal with methods for gauging the relative government-financing capability of various areas, so as to provide measures needed for state and local policy makers who usually are interested in keeping fiscal burdens in their respective communities reasonably in line with those elsewhere, and by the federal government and states in trying to design equitable grant-in-aid arrangements.

Administration of Federal Programs A large and increasing variety of federal activities involve collaboration with or assistance to state or local governments. Typically, much of the data base needed for such programs is generated directly in the course of their administration, but the agencies involved in many cases also consider such information in the context of the Census Bureau's broader governmental data. For example, in reviewing budget plans of the states' employment security operations (which are federally reimbursed), the responsible federal agency considers the relation of proposed pay rates to those of other employees in the respective states, as recorded through census surveys.

Again, an agency administering a grant-in-aid program is likely to face a difficult problem of "rationing" when the amount appropriated is considerably less than the total of grant requests and (as is the case for most federal-local grants) the distribution is on a specific project basis rather than according to a detailed formula. In this instance, comparisons based on census-reported data may help the administrator to decide which applicant governments should receive priority or, at least, may help him to appraise the reasonableness of allegations made in support of competing requests. Especially because the structure and functional assignments of local governments differ widely from one part of the country to another, such uses of the comparative figures must be made cautiously. However, the recent multiplication of federal-local grant programs has no doubt considerably expanded administrative uses of the data.

The Omnibus Crime Control and Safe Streets Act adopted by Congress in 1970 presages even more explicit use of census data in governmental finances for administration of the federal grant program. Under this act, the portion of each state's allocation that must be passed along to local governments will depend on the census survey findings as to the relative state-local proportions of expenditure for public safety purposes within the state.

A similar approach is contemplated in various proposals for federal revenue sharing, under which the amount of money allocated to particular state and local governments would depend partly on their own tax or revenue effort as calculated by reference to comparative census data.

The governmental listings available from the Census of Governments often are used to assemble information needed in connection with the administration of particular federal programs, either through surveys conducted directly by the agency concerned or on its behalf by the Bureau of the Census. Recent examples of the latter have included the following:

- Surveys for the Department of Agriculture, concerning school lunch operations in the public schools
- Surveys for the Department of Defense, concerning operations of civil defense agencies
- Surveys for the National Commission on Urban Problems, concerning types of land use in major cities, and the zoning and building control activities of local governments
- Surveys for the Department of Justice, to identify local agencies engaged in various kinds of public safety activities, and to gather facts about the nature and condition of local jail facilities

- Surveys for the Labor Department, concerning pay rates and fringe benefits for certain types of public employees
- Surveys for the Federal Reserve System, concerning the debt-issuance operations of selected major governments
- Surveys for the National Science Foundation, concerning research and development activities of state and local governments

State Governments

Underlying many differences of detail, there is basic similarity across the nation in many aspects of state and local government. For example: public schools are everywhere the most costly public function; all states delegate considerable responsibility to local governments; and in most states the property tax is the largest single source of local government financing. These and many other items illustrate that the state governments, despite their legal independence of one another, have always been interested in the experience of other states and have often tended to be influenced by one another.

In an increasingly interdependent society, the interest of state policy-makers in practices and conditions elsewhere has multiplied. Elective officials especially have found themselves politically vulnerable to the charge that their particular area is seriously "out-of-line" with some others elsewhere. Although this kind of issue is most commonly heard about tax burdens, it also is raised about particular governmental functions, such as the quality of schools or standards of health or welfare services.

It is not surprising, then, that state policy makers—governors, legislative committees, and administrators—make many applications of the Census Bureau's comparative governmental statistics. Such uses show up widely in governors' budget transmittals or other messages to legislators, where census-based comparisons with the past, with other neighboring or comparable states, or with nationwide averages, often are used to provide background in support of particular recommendations. Sometimes the data cited pertain only to state governments; in other instances, they relate to state and local amounts. Following are some of the subjects that thus surface in governors' transmittals to legislatures:

The scale of governmental activity (in expenditure or employment terms) for particular functions or in total

Proportions of total governmental spending devoted to various functions

Levels of taxation, or governmental debt

The extent to which charges are used to help finance certain services, such as state universities or hospitals

Particular aspects of state-local relations, such as proportions of local school financing provided by state grants

Public personnel practices, especially as to pay rates and retirement protection for governmental employees

Less visible than such presentations, but perhaps at least as important from a policy-making standpoint, are more intensive research uses made by state budget and revenue staff agencies. For example, the budget examination of requests for a particular function (such as state universities and colleges) may include comparative review of census-reported amounts of expenditure and related receipts involving this function in a number of states.

State's efforts to gauge their future financial prospects are likely to involve differing kinds of research effort. The simplest case, predominant in the regular budget process, calls for estimating the yield in the next year or two from taxes that are already in use. Interstate comparisons are unlikely to be involved; rather, the task is to relate the particular state's collections to actual and prospective trends in pertinent measures of economic activity. Background for such efforts has been provided for many years by conferences on revenue estimating sponsored annually by the National Association of Tax Administrators, at which economic prospects and estimating techniques are discussed.

But interstate comparisons do sometimes enter into important tax-yield research even where no legal change is being anticipated—for example, in efforts to measure the probable effect that a change in the size of tax enforcement staff would have upon the "completeness of collections" of a particular tax. In this case, actual yield amounts in various states generally are compared with estimates of potential yield based on other economic measures, and the results are related to measures of tax-enforcement staffing. Such comparative studies have sometimes been used by tax administrators to justify requests for larger auditing staffs and to defend their estimates of prospective resulting revenue gains.

Interstate comparisons are also crucial for another kind of state revenue-estimating effort, where the problem is to gauge the potential yield of a new tax. In most such instances, the development of a yield estimate is likely to rest heavily upon, or at least to take account of, the revenue experience of one or more other states that already have the particular type of tax anticipated. In many instances also, interstate comparisons are used to anticipate the likely effect on yield of prospective changes in the rate or scope of a particular tax. This is done by considering the experience of other states which have recently enacted similar changes or the apparent effect of important differences in the scope of a particular tax upon its yield in various states.

A third type of revenue projection effort is still more demanding, and is practically certain to include heavy reliance upon comparative census data. When looking beyond merely the next year or two, a state attempts to gauge its financing requirements further ahead, usually as part of a major "tax structure" study, the census data are crucial. Such studies have been carried out in many states during recent years, reflecting the fact that state and local expenditures have been increasing about twice as rapidly as the rate of growth in the economy as a whole. A minor part of the resulting "financing gap" has been filled by increased federal grants, but the bulk has been met by borrowing and especially by new taxes and tax-rate increases. The Advisory Commission on Intergovernmental Relations has estimated that only about half of the sizable growth in state tax collections in recent years is traceable to economic gains, with the rest coming from additional taxation.

Tax-structure studies carried out recently in various states have ranged widely in coverage and intensity, but have generally gone well beyond the scope of annual state budget issues to consider longer-range prospects and local as well as state revenue sources. In this broader context, attempts have also often been made to project the state's expenditure needs several years ahead, so as to determine the amount of "financing gap" that must somehow be closed.

A particularly ambitious effort of this kind was carried out in the mid-1960s on a nationwide basis under the auspices of the Council of State Governments. Using as a background historical census data for each state, in relation to various other demographic and economic measures, the study developed state-by-state projections of state and local government expenditures, overall and for various functions, and of the prospective yield of the state and local revenue system in effect at the time of the study.

Background for state legislation and policy making is developed not only in connection with the budgetary process but in many other ways. Most states have a standing legislative research agency, and all of them create various special study commissions at each legislative session. Some states draw heavily on university bureaus of governmental research. Grist for legislation and policy making also comes from planning or development agencies, offices for local government, and various functional line departments.

The studies or recommendations coming from such sources often draw in part upon the comparative experience of other states. As one aid to such interchange, the Council of State Governments issues a quarterly *Legislative Research Checklist,* citing various publications that bear upon state problems and issues. Each issue of this bibliography lists numerous studies citing census governmental data—for example, in dealing with particular governmental functions or activities (health services, public assistance, parks and recreation, local colleges, municipal utilities, etc.); with particular aspects of local government structure; with public personnel practices, including pay rates and retirement system arrangements; with state grants-in-aid or other aspects of state-local relations; and with property taxation, including assessment arrangements and tax exemption provisions.

Local Governments

At least three rather different kinds of applications of census governmental statistics by local governments can be recognized. One of these involves the development and defense of policy positions with regard to prospective federal or state legislation that would affect local government. Such usage of the data shows up in studies, conferences, and statements of such nationwide bodies as the National League of Cities, the U. S. Conference of Mayors, the National Association of Counties, and the National Education Association, as well as regional or state affiliates of these organizations. In particular, reported census figures on local and state government finances often are cited in connection with proposals for federal revenue sharing, changes in the present public welfare system, the tax treatment of municipal bonds, and other matters of intergovernmental concern. At the state level similar citations of the census figures commonly appear in connection with pending legislation on such matters as state-local grants, debt limitations, property taxation and other revenue measures, and public personnel arrangements.

A second kind of local government usage (served partly through the regular publication of various census figures in the *Municipal Yearbook* issued by the International City Management Association) includes reference by local officials to summary or comparative data that may help them gauge how their particular jurisdictions compare in various respects with those elsewhere. Such analysis may provide background local officials need for dealing with budgetary, revenue, or personnel issues. This resembles some of the states' applications of census data to deal with policy-oriented issues. However, efforts at interlocal comparison are subject to certain handicaps that do not apply, or are less serious, for *interstate* comparisons.

In particular, (1) statewide governmental data can be related to various other kinds of measures, such as annual estimates of population and of personal income, which are not available on a current basis for individual cities; and (2) the scope of assigned responsibilities of individual cities or other particular types of local governments differs considerably. For example, most municipalities underlie a county government that also plays an important role but some are composite city-counties; and the provision of public schools is in some cases a responsibility of the municipal government, elsewhere of the county government, but more commonly of separate school districts. The assignment of responsibility for some other functions also frequently varies as among particular kinds of local governments and the state. These variations especially hamper efforts to compare particular units located in different states, but important assignment differences sometimes appear even within a single state. For example, a few large cities in New York directly administer their local school systems, even though independent school systems prevail in the rest of that state.

Differences of this kind make it particularly hard to appraise intercity differences in overall measures, such as the total revenue, expenditure, debt, or employment of individual municipalities. However, more meaningful comparisons can often be made of detailed figures—e.g., concerning municipal expenditures or employment for police protection, fire protection, sewerage, or other functions that are typically handled in city areas solely or very largely by the municipality rather than by some overlying government.

Variations in functional scope are far less serious when the attempted comparison involves all-local government aggregates for entire counties of metropolitan areas, but even such figures may be affected by important differences in state-local patterns (for example, public welfare assistance is administered by local governments in some parts of the country but directly by the states elsewhere). Furthermore, local area aggregates of local government finances are reported annually for only the thirty-seven largest metropolitan areas and their major component counties; only the periodic governmental census supplies local finance aggregates for other metropolitan areas and counties, or any local-area aggregates of local government employment and payrolls.

The third kind of data usage by local governments is more intensive and detailed, and likely to draw not only upon information available from the Census Bureau in published form but also upon its underlying unpublished record sources. Such applications occur when an in-depth examination is made of the structure of local governments, or their fiscal conditions and prospects, in some particular county or metropolitan area. This is typified by a set of parallel studies of local financing problems as they are in ten metropolitan areas, under the sponsorship of the National League of Cities. Each study was carried out by an "urban observatory" group involving collaboration between a local university and the metropolitan central city. As part of their background, these studies will utilize not only published census figures but also computer-tape records from the past two governmental censuses and more recent annual surveys, and worksheets reflecting in detail the Census Bureau's handling of financial data for the metropolitan central cities and counties.

Labor

Organized labor, as various other groups concerned with public programs and policies, frequently draws on governmental statistics to explain or defend its positions. For example, in arguing against new or increased sales taxes on grounds of their regressive tendency, labor has often cited census figures which indicate that this kind of tax is already the principal revenue source of many state governments. In recent years, with spreading unionization of governmental workers, various unions have utilized census statistics reflecting the level and trend of public pay rates as part of the background for their negotiations with particular governments and public agencies.

Business

It seems probable that relatively few business firms have had occasion to make much direct use, on their own account, of the governmental statistics reported by the Census Bureau. However, certain important exceptions may be noted. The several firms that develop grade-ratings for bond issuances of state and local governments use the census data as part of the background they need for this purpose. And in a number of important lawsuits, various railroads have cited findings from the Census of Governments concerning assessment levels in particular areas in seeking relief from apparently excessive assessments for their property holdings. The National Association of Railroads has similarly used the census data in arguing for federal legislation to prevent discriminatory property taxation of railroads.

Chambers of commerce, trade associations, and other business-oriented groups frequently cite comparative governmental statistics in commenting to congressional or state legislative committees on pending legislation. Traditionally, such groups have been especially concerned with issues of taxation, but in recent years they have shown increased interest in matters of governmental organization, including the layered and fractionated nature of local government in metropolitan areas. The Committee on Economic Development, in several major studies, has drawn heavily upon census data to develop proposals regarding this and other long-range aspects of local and state government. The U. S. Chamber of Commerce has distributed informational materials on such subjects to its local and state affiliates, and has urged their active participation in efforts toward the updating of governmental institutions.

Voters

As previously indicated, the "general public" typically is exposed to governmental statistics in only selective and piecemeal fashion. Aside from general news stories, this exposure often is provided by candidates for office or by interest groups in expressing their points of view, especially on budgetary or tax issues of concern to particular states or local areas. It is not unusual in this connection to find the same set of figures being cited on behalf of opposing policy positions. For example, an incumbent governor running for reelection in a state which shows up from census findings as a relatively "low tax" area may cite this as a situation designed to promote sound economic growth, while groups seeking more generous support of public schools, higher education, welfare, or other public purposes may use similar comparisons to argue that the state could meet the needs they desire without getting seriously out of line with others elsewhere.

Such argumentative uses of the data probably tend in many instances to provide lopsided or oversimplified "information" to voters about particular governmental questions. It seems likely, nevertheless, that the many citations tend altogether to enlarge the horizons and add to the background of the electorate. For example, few voters worrying about recent or prospective increases in their own local or state taxes can hardly be unaware that similar trends and problems are found in many parts of the nation.

Students

At least two quite different levels of intensity appear in the use of governmental data by students. One of these occurs through the citation of the statistics in textbooks and reference volumes—to some extent in high school texts on civics and American history, but far more in texts and supplementary sources used in connection with college and postgraduate courses relating to government, public finance, and public administration. Practically all general textbooks in these fields draw upon census data regarding state and local governments, and often the citations are extensive and varied. For example, a recent volume on *The 50 States and Their Local Governments* (Fesler, 1967) includes more than a dozen tables and nearly as many charts directly based on governmental census statistics, and draws heavily on the data especially in dealing with such matters as the functions of states and their subdivisions, intergovernmental relations, governmental structure in metropolitan areas, and problems of financing and personnel management.

Such textbook usage of the data for educational purposes is obviously handicapped by the pace of changes that have been occurring in some aspects of American government and public finance. Given the considerable timelag usually involved in the writing and publication of such a volume, many of the illustrative figures cited are likely to be seriously out of date by the time of their appearance. This problem is often offset in college course work by supplementary reference use of articles in professional journals or other sources where later statistics appear.

The second application of governmental data by students is in connection with studies they undertake on particular topics, from course papers to masters' theses and doctoral dissertations. These range widely in subject matter and scope, and there is no one reference source that would identify all or even the more significant documents of this nature. Some of them, of course, are reflected in articles appearing in various professional journals, particularly in the fields of political science and economics.

Educators

As indicated above, census statistics on governments are utilized for classroom instruction in colleges and universities, particularly in courses relating to American government and public finance. They also are drawn upon by scholars for various types of research studies, ranging from those concerned with specific localized governmental problems to more abstract or theoretical kinds of analysis. Examples of the former kind of "applied research," made by or with the aid of university economists or political scientists, include studies of fiscal problems and tax structure which have been carried out under official state government auspices in many parts of the nation during recent years; similar studies of local fiscal problems and arrangements; and studies of local government structure in various metropolitan areas, often as background for the development of proposals for revised organizational arrangements (e.g., the development in recent years of new city-county governments in Nashville and Jacksonville).

More abstract or "pure research" applications of the data are reflected in scholarly works and professional journal articles concerning many subjects. Sometimes the census data are a primary resource; for example, in the foreword to his volume, *Economics of the Property Tax,* Professor Dick Netzer (1966) observes that one main reason for undertaking the study was the availability of extensive basic data on this subject from the 1957 Census of Governments.

The recent availability of more and better statistics on governmental finances has also encouraged widespread attention by economists to "determinants of public expenditures"—especially including efforts to see how governmental spending in total and for various purposes seems to be influenced by such things as the level of personal income, income distribution, population size, urbanization, rate of growth, and other variables. A recent review of significant scholarly writings counted sixty-six items on this subject up to early 1967, of which only a few antedated the 1960s and most drew mainly or entirely upon Census Bureau sources for their government finances data.

Many of these studies include efforts to go beyond the summary of statistical findings to draw inferences bearing on important issues of public policy, such as prospective trends in governmental spending, the probable effect of federal or state grants upon the spending or "revenue effort" of aided governments, and the influence of local government structure upon public financing in metropolitan areas. In fact, some of the more ambitious and sophisticated efforts to project future fiscal "requirements" in certain states have drawn upon the methods first explored in these scholarly studies.

Some political scientists have explored similar problems, as illustrated by Professor Ira Sharkansky's (1967) volume, *Spending in the American States*, which examined the historical consistency of expenditure patterns, and the apparent influence of various demographic as well as economic variables. The results supplied a background for more detailed consideration of apparent departures from "normal" or "expected" budgetary developments that showed up in a number of states.

The foregoing examples related to studies that rest heavily or even primarily upon the Census Bureau's governmental statistics. Far more numerous and diverse are scholarly writings or research efforts for which such data are, directly or indirectly, only one of various sets of input. This may be illustrated by a half-dozen recent issues of *The National Tax Journal*. These included four articles based mainly upon the census statistics, but at least nine others that also made some incidental use of them. The four primary-use articles dealt with the following subjects:

The fiscal capacity and welfare expenditures of states

City-suburban differences in local government "fiscal effort"

Trends in the apparent "unit costs" of various local public services

Relative rates of "automatic growth" in state and local tax yields and in expenditures for various purposes

The other nine articles dealt with a far wider variety of subjects, ranging from legal limitations on local debt to the effect of city-suburban migration upon city government's revenue potential.

Home Owners and Renters

The periodic Census of Governments, and especially that part concerned with "taxable property values" is of great potential significance to home owners and renters—even though relatively few of them have probably had occasion to make direct use of the reported statistics.

This significance arises (1) directly, from the information provided about such matters as the proportion of the property tax base represented by housing, comparative rates of residential property taxation in various areas, and the extent of departure from a uniform level of property valuation in various areas; and (2) indirectly, by stimulating other efforts at property tax research and "reform." The volume by Netzer (1966) is one example of the latter sort. Other examples include property tax studies and recommendations by the Advisory Commission on Intergovernmental Relations; a research report on housing taxation prepared by Dr. Netzer for the National Commission on Urban Problems; and property tax studies undertaken in various states, including some assessment ratio surveys that incorporate methods used in the Census of Governments.

The general intent of many such "reform" efforts has been to make the property tax—which is by far the largest single revenue source of state and local governments—a more equitable and less economically damaging fiscal device. Especially in states where the census data show a relatively high level of property taxation, the figures have been cited in behalf of proposals for even more drastic changes, such as "property tax relief" offset by greater use of state income or sales taxes.

THE OUTLOOK

As indicated at the outset, major gains have been made during the past two decades in the content, coverage, and timeliness of the Census Bureau's governmental statistics. Not surprisingly, this has encouraged a great expansion in the amount and variety of data applications.

Looking ahead, it is possible to observe both encouraging and discouraging prospects as to the availability and effective use of government statistics.

Favorable Elements

On the plus side are both "internal" factors—those affecting the ability of the Census Bureau to assemble informative and reliable data—and "external" factors pertaining to the interpretation and application of such statistics.

From the standpoint of data reporting, the Census Bureau is now far better equipped than it was a few years ago to operate effectively. Here, as in other fields, it has benefited by increased know-how with regard to sampling, and by the availability of computer processing methods that permit more sophisticated handling of data (especially including options for cross-classification that were lacking with primitive tabulation methods). It has developed directory records and historical background records that can be used effectively in planning additional studies or surveys. It can draw upon improvements that have been made by some governments in their own accounting and statistical records. Furthermore, although the resources applied to that subject field are still very small in relation to the total for all Census Bureau reporting, and even smaller relative to all federal statistical operations, these resources are less obviously inadequate than in the past. It would be hard to imagine the Congress again, as it did in 1951, refusing on grounds of "economy" to provide any funds for the conduct of a periodic Census of Governments. The lessening of budgetary constraints has come partly through funds provided by other federal agencies for special surveys, studies, and tabulations. An example is given by the Department of Justice which arranged for data needed in its dealing with law enforcement activities of state and local governments. Especially as the federal government becomes increasingly involved with functions that have traditionally been dealt with mainly at "lower" governmental levels (e.g., with regard to protection of the environment), such specially focused efforts are likely to grow and to supply additional resources for and place increased demands upon the Census Bureau's governmental statistics work.

On the user side, some important gains can also be noted. In particular, there are many more scholars, students, and governmental researchers actively concerned with this subject field than was the case a few years ago. This development can be traced in considerable part to the availability of much more statistical information, though also, no doubt, in part to the growth in scale and complexity of government in the United States and to the difficulties that governments have experienced in keeping pace with increased urbanization and rising public service needs and expectations. The more sophisticated data users can and do draw upon computer technology and other methodological improvements to carry out kinds of research and analysis that would have been impracticable only a few years ago.

Unfavorable Elements

It is possible, however, to observe various factors that are likely to limit severely both the ability of the Census Bureau to accommodate many expressed needs for governmental statistics and the effectiveness with which data in this field actually are interpreted, analyzed, and used.

From the data-assembly standpoint, one such factor is the great diversity in record-keeping practices of states and especially local governments, and the lack of any effective sanction to promote increased standardization of such practices. Given the degree of state sovereignty inherent in our federal system, and with local governments existing as political subdivisions of the states, the assembly of "uniformly classified" statistics from and about particular governments has traditionally rested upon completely voluntary reporting rather than—as in the case of other periodic censuses—being backed up by enforceable requirements for the canvassed individuals or establishments to provide the information called for as well as possible. The kind of information that can be sought in such other statistical operations is also, of course, inherently limited by the widespread availability of certain underlying records, but the mandatory reporting sanction undoubtedly provides additional leverage not available for the governmental statistics program.

Progress toward more standardized record keeping has been made through official state requirements in some instances and also through educational and promotional efforts by such organizations as the Municipal Finance Officers Association and the National Association of Assessing Officers. However, there is still so much diversity that certain kinds of desirable detail cannot be acceptably obtained, and for a very large proportion of some kinds of governments (especially counties) acceptably "uniform" financial data can only be obtained by the arduous compilation of detailed amounts from official local records. This is a method of data assembly which has traditionally also been applied to financial statistics for state governments and many large municipalities.

Another limitation, related to the foregoing, involves the increased use of computers for financial record keeping by many large governments. Where the basic concepts and classifications they apply substantially parallel those needed for census reporting, such installations, when fully in operation, have sometimes eased or accelerated the collection of data. But where or to the extent that different classifications are applied, computerization has often worked in the other direction. Types of detail that traditionally could be found at least in underlying records have sometimes become "invisible" and thereby not available unless possibly by specially negotiated tabulating results.

A third development which has made it more difficult to assemble meaningful governmental data is the proliferation of special districts and other kinds of local government instrumentalities. The nationwide count of special districts nearly doubled (from 3712 to 7207) between 1952 and 1967, and in the same period thousands of new "semiautonomous" local agencies also were set up. As noted below, these developments have greatly complicated the task of the analyst concerned with interarea comparisons.

Finally, other complexities have been added by the proliferation in number and types of intergovernmental grants-in-aid, and the development of new types of joint intergovernmental or public-private efforts. Many of these are based on the well-founded premise that various public services which seek some common objective should be planned and conducted in concert. An example lies in specifically relating certain efforts to minimize crime through activities that involve law enforcement, dealing with juvenile delinquents, drug control, and the reduction of poverty. Nonetheless, in breaking down traditional lines between various governments and public or private agencies, the resulting arrangements often tend to blur functional distinctions that have traditionally provided a framework for "uniform" or "comparable" statistics. From the standpoint also of those who wish to analyze and apply governmental data, some increasingly difficult problems become apparent.

Statistics in this field have always been especially subject to abuse or misinterpretation, both because of the complexity of government in the United States and because so many attempted uses of the data involve an effort to defend some particular position with regard to public policy. Increased journalistic concern for "the urban crisis" and other governmental problems has not been matched by greater capacity or willingness of commentators to delve deeply enough into the available data to limit the possibility of their drawing unwarranted inferences. And some of the developments of governmental structure and relationships mentioned above have made it increasingly difficult for even the most conscientious researcher fully to understand and make proper use of the statistics in this field.

Sometimes these problems arise because a limited-effort attempt is being made to obtain "answers" to measurement questions that simply cannot be answered from available basic data, but require supplementary research or estimation. A prime example involves efforts to derive meaningfully "comparable" figures on the costs of local government in various cities. As previously noted, the number of local governments involved ranges upward from one in a few cases to a considerably larger number in many cities. And since one or more of the overlying local governments typically serve a larger area than just the city, estimates of the city's allocable share of their finances must somehow be built into the comparison process. Moreover, if the target is to make intercity comparisons that also take account of interstate differences in the relative roles of state and local governments, there is a further need for estimated allocation of the city's share of statewide totals.

This is not a new problem. However, it has become more serious with the increased complexity and layering of local government in many parts of the country, and of greater consequence as interest in interarea comparisons has grown.

Another long-standing problem or limitation arises from the fact that the Census Bureau's governmental statistics deal mainly with "inputs" for public services—revenue raised, persons employed, amounts expended, etc.—and provide no information about governmental "outputs" (unless the reporting of public school enrollment in connection with the Census of Governments might be so viewed). The reason for this disparity in subject coverage is obvious. Inputs for various functions lend themselves to measurement in common denominator terms—people and money—that can be compared and summed, while this is not the case for the vast array of services provided by government. These call for measures tailored to the specific nature of various functions and activities. It is not surprising, therefore, that to the rather limited extent that statistical measures of governmental output or workload exist, they have generally been developed by agencies concerned with particular functions (e.g., the Public Health Service, Office of Education, Public Roads Administration, Social Security Administration). The same is true for efforts to measure apparent "needs" for particular public services, except as these are sometimes inferred from more general statistics, such as data on school-age population or on numbers of poverty-level households.

It would be most helpful if additional and better measures of governmental "output" could be developed. It seems likely, however, that progress in this direction is going to depend more upon particular functional agencies than upon steps initiated by the Governments Division of the Census Bureau.

That division is facing increased needs for the maintenance and strengthening of its more traditional reporting work, in the periodic Census of Governments as well as in recurrent and special surveys. In particular, the prospect that its annual financial data may be increasingly used as a formula element in a system of federal revenue sharing with states and local governments will probably require more exacting statistical standards than have previously been necessary. Depending on the nature of the actual formulas enacted, revenue-sharing legislation may also require an expansion in the coverage of individual governments in annual census surveys of governmental finances.

APPENDIX

Statistical Information Provided by Periodic Evaluations on Governments

Published Data

On a quarterly basis:

Nationwide totals of state-local tax revenue, by type of tax

Nationwide totals of state-local construction expenditure, by function

Revenue from selected types of state taxes in each state

Property tax collections in the thirty-eight largest SMSA's and in counties of at least 250,000 population

On an annual basis (along with national totals):

Data on finances of state governments and of individual municipalities of 50,000 plus

Data on employment and payrolls of state governments and of individual municipalities of 50,000 plus

State-by-state data on state and local government finances, by level of government

State-by-state data on public employment and payrolls, by level and type of government

Data on local government finances of each of the eighteen largest SMSA's and the counties of 100,000 plus in those SMSA's

Statistics on employment and expenditure for "criminal justice"—police protection, correction, courts, and defense of indigents

On a quinquennial basis—The Census of Governments:

Data for more than 8000 individual governments (all counties, municipalities, and New England-type townships of 10,000 plus, school districts having at least 8000 pupils, and "large" special districts

Local government data in various degrees of detail for individual states, regions, metropolitan areas, and county areas, as well as for size-class groups of counties and metropolitan areas nationally and by states

Aggregates for the several major types of local governments, by size-classes, nationally and by states.

The periodic census also provides information on subjects not reported on a current basis. This includes a volume on "governmental organizations," which summarizes the types of local governments authorized in each state and provides data nationally and for states, regions, metropolitan areas, and counties as to numbers of local government units, together with related information about their characteristics, such as population or enrollment size, or (in the case of special districts) functional class.

The periodic census also provides a major report on "tax valuations," supplying the following:

Data on assessed valuations for property taxation, in various degrees of detail, nationally and for states, counties, and major cities

Data on numbers of places of realty subject to property taxation by type, nationally and for states, counties, and major cities

Measures of the level of assessment (the relation between assessed and market value indicated by sample "measurable sales") for various types of taxable realty in each state and for single-family houses in major counties and cities

Data on residential property tax rates for major counties and cities

Other subjects dealt with solely in the periodic Census of Governments include the following:

Numbers and types of elective local and state government officials

Pay-rate distributions of full-time employees of state and local governments

Retirement coverage and other "fringe benefits" of public employees

Characteristics of particular state programs for grants-in-aid to local governments in each state

The subject matter of recurrent state reports concerning state and local government finances (a bibliographic study)

Some kinds of information are published on a *one-time* or *intermittent* basis. Subjects thus handled in recent years have included the timing of governments' fiscal years; local areas for assessment administration; historical trends in assessed valuations and sales ratios; and state governments' sales-ratio studies.

REFERENCES

Fesler, James W. (Ed.). *The 50 States and Their Local Governments*. New York: Knopf, 1967.

International City Management Association. *Municipal Yearbook*. An authoritative resume of activities of statistical data of American cities. Chicago: ICMA.

National Tax Association. *The National Tax Journal*. Chicago: National Tax Association, quarterly.

Netzer, Dick. *Economics of the Property Tax*. Washington, D. C.: The Brookings Institution, 1966.

Sharkansky, Ira. *Spending in the American States*. Chicago: Rand McNally, 1967.

U. S. Bureau of the Census. *Historical Statistics on Governmental Finances and Employment*. Vol. 6, No. 5, *1967 Census of Governments*. Washington, D. C.: Government Printing Office, 1968.

U. S. Joint Committee on the Economic Report. *Revenue Sharing and Its Alternatives: What Future for Fiscal Federalism?* Hearings before Subcommittee on Fiscal Policy, 90th Congress, 1st Session, 2 parts (November 7–15, 1967), 1968.

CHAPTER 14

*On Elections**

THE DATA

Statistical data for the study of American politics abound in the United States, both in terms of historical experience and of current availabilities. But the abundance is not uniform in either quality or in geographic distribution, and the portfolio of material must be examined in detail to know just what is at hand.

The simplest form of electoral data are the state-by-state figures for the selection of presidential electors. Available from official state sources back to the earliest days of the Republic, these have been assembled in Petersen's (1963) *A Statistical History of the American Presidential Elections* and they represent the official figures in the National Archives. But they naturally are limited. The universe for this type of statistical presentation are the various states (plus, since 1968, the District of Columbia). While the statewide figures are obviously important, they are of little value per se in analysis and capable of only the broadest sort of interpretation.

Next in level come the collections of county-by-county data, again in the voting for president. These begin with Burnham's (1955) *Presidential Ballots,* running the data from 1836 through 1892, and are continued in the two volumes by Robinson: *The Presidential Vote, 1896–1932* (1934), and *They Voted for Roosevelt* (1947), which brings the earlier

---

* Based on a memorandum by Richard M. Scammon, director, Elections Research Center, Washington, D. C.

Robinson work down through the 1944 voting. The publication of *America at the Polls* (Governmental Affairs Institute, 1965) provided a county-by-county pattern from 1920 through 1964, giving some overlap of the Robinson studies and carrying the data through the Lyndon Johnson-Barry Goldwater contest. A later edition of *America at the Polls* is planned to extend the earlier book by the inclusion of data for 1968 and 1972.

All these surveys of the presidential vote present the figures on a county basis, with raw vote normally divided between Republican and Democratic candidates with provision for an "other" column or two. The earlier studies give the vote only; *America at the Polls* also provides plurality figures and percentage data.

The University of Michigan Survey Research Center has been developing in recent years a historical accounting of county-by-county figures going back to the Jackson period, not only for president, but for governor, senator, and Congress as well. These data will be published during the 1970s in a total work of ten volumes, and should provide the basis for a great amount of historical research into our American political process, especially in the nineteenth and early twentieth century.

In the current field, there remains no formal, official governmental source of elections data on the national level. The Bureau of the Census tried once to produce such a volume, but economy measures in the early postwar period cut off the work, and only limited publication has been undertaken since then. The office of the Clerk of the House of Representatives does issue each two years a tally of voting for presidential electors (when applicable), senators, and congressmen, but these are gross totals and apply to the federal level only.

The gap in current data has been filled in the past few years by the Governmental Affairs Institute's *America Votes,* published biennially with county-by-county figures for voting for president, governor, and senator in each state, plus congressional data, and also detailed ward figures in selected large cities. This study is now in its ninth volume, and serves as the major reference source for printed data, with cards and tapes of the Michigan Survey Research Center able to supply the specialized user needs of members of the University Consortium which that center serves.

In addition to the *America Votes* series, a number of special research efforts have been undertaken in recent years in specific states to pull together data on a time and/or geographic base for elections in the individual states concerned. Such works have included *Indiana Votes* (Pitchell, 1960; Francis, 1962), *Florida Votes* (Hartsfield, 1963), *How Wisconsin Voted,* (University of Wisconsin, 1962), *Illinois Votes* (Gone, 1958), *Kansas Votes* (Cade, 1957), *North Carolina Votes* (University of North Carolina, 1962), *Montana Politics Since 1864* (Waldron, 1958), *Kentucky Votes*

(Jewell, 1963), *California Votes* (Lee, 1963), *Oklahoma Votes* (University of Oklahoma, 1964), and *Michigan Votes* (White, 1958). The basic character of these research studies is in the *America Votes* pattern, but often with special addenda of interest in the state concerned. Finally, mention should be made of the biennial reports of *Congressional Quarterly*, in which voting for president, governor, and senator is given by congressional districts.

Beyond these statistical efforts, there have been ephemeral studies of varying types and utility. Perhaps the best known (and most useful) were the several volumes of the *Gallup Political Almanac* brought out in the late 1940s and early 1950s. These volumes contained a great deal of useful electoral statistical material. Their publication stopped some twenty years ago, however, and has not been resumed, given the appearance of the *America Votes* volumes.

Finally, a great deal of data about elections, some of it in much detail, may be found in the regular (and sometimes irregular) publication of state legislative manuals and state "blue books." An invaluable guide to the data contained in such volumes may be found in *State Manuals, Blue Books, and Election Results* (Press and Williams, 1962).

All the states have some sort of statement of the vote for statewide primary and general elections. These will vary from a simple page or two of county-by-county figures (in Arkansas, Utah, Idaho, North Dakota), to detailed, precinct-by-precinct returns for primaries and general elections for most offices (in New Hampshire, New Mexico, Nevada, Alaska, Hawaii). Primary results will normally be less easy to find than general election totals; though in some states the two types of elections are treated equally well and substantial data are at hand, others appear to regard the primary process as less worthy of statistical attention than the general election voting. In all cases, available election figures may be requested from the various secretaries of state, or, in a few cases, from the State Elections Board (as, for example, in Virginia and Oklahoma).

Most of the state reports are simply statements of the votes cast, by counties, for a certain number of offices filled at the election. While a few include state legislative figures, many do not. Some, either as individual publications or in the election sections of state manuals, will provide registration data and a few publish percentage figures as well. Some states add special embellishments of their own, as in Illinois, where the number of counties carried by each candidate is carefully recorded, or in California, which makes a special count of absentee and "new resident" votes. Very occasionally whimsy will prevail and an elephant or donkey will parade across the report. But this is rare. Mostly the state canvass documents are simply straightforward listings of counties and votes.

One great difficulty with all this, of course, is that it is geared to reporting by counties. A few states will also list results of statewide races by congressional districts (Tennessee has done this, for example, for some years, and Connecticut and California have recently followed suit). In California reporting is also available by assembly districts, senatorial districts, local county districts, and by incorporated cities. In New England, reporting is available by cities and towns, and in Ohio and New York a special break-out of cities is offered in addition to the usual county-by-county report.

But the basic reporting unit continues to be the county, while the basic counting unit in every state is the precinct (called variously by that name or "box," "division," "ward," "district," or some other locally applicable designation). Statewide publication of precinct data does exist, especially in the smaller states, and it is even available in some large states such as New York for small precincts which are themselves whole minor civil divisions. In Ohio the state has printed statewide by precinct from the secretary of state's office, but economy moves in recent years have stopped this practice, as they have stopped it in Pennsylvania, where similar precinct figures used to appear in the biennial *Pennsylvania State Manual.* In Missouri and in Michigan *some* precinct figures appear, but larger cities usually are reported by whole wards, each including a number of precincts.

This does not mean that reports are not available by precinct. They are, and in some cases, as indicated above, they are available for a whole state in a single printed state document. But above all the individual county data are at hand in the counties themselves. This means that a truly national collection of precinct data must be put together from the 3000-plus counties of the nation. All have the data in one form or another, for all have had to consolidate their precincts in a county canvass report which has then gone forward to the state capitol to become the basis for the final, official statewide vote canvassing operation.

But the data are available in countless forms. Some are nicely printed, as in the New York City *Record,* in which a thick volume of precinct data used to appear in December to detail the voting a few weeks earlier. Unfortunately, the material in the *Record* has been overtaken by the economic facts of contemporary New York City government, and the figures are no longer so printed.

At the other end of the scale may be a rural county in the Far West, with only a few precincts, which may respond to a request for data with a hand tally on the back of the requesting letter. In between are all sorts of mimeographed statements, Xerox and photostatic copies of canvass sheets, newspaper returns printed in the local county's official newspaper of record, and printouts. For Los Angeles County, for example, the printout for the thousands of precincts in that jurisdiction makes a very weighty tome indeed.

The value of these precinct returns is constantly increasing, of course, as life in America metropolitanizes. The number of counties in which one may find half the nation's population becomes smaller and smaller, and these counties themselves have constantly increasing numbers of voting precincts (except for situations in which consolidation of precincts is possible due to mechanization of voting). The contribution of the rural county to the total vote becomes less, and the county itself is less important as a measuring unit of politics. Conversely, of course, the county retains its importance because it remains, relatively at least, an unchanged geographic unit.

The most sophisticated kinds of electoral analysis lie in the use of statistics at the precinct level, as indicated below, and these figures are available, but they must be dug out, often with considerable difficulty, from local county offices of varying degrees of cooperation orientation. Some will supply material freely, some are reluctant; some will make a small service charge for their work, others will engage in a copying exercise which obviously takes much time but make no charge at all. Some will suggest the requester come in and copy the data himself; some just do not cooperate at all. But the precinct returns are there, and for the most part they are available.

Like the states, most local jurisdictions report just votes. Sometimes registration is added, and very occasionally an office will use its computer machinery to add percentages to the totals, or to give other information such as male-female turnout, but that is about all, though it should be added that in one county (Bexar, in Texas) local officials have also added an ethnic report for each precinct, indicating the group in the precinct which is largest—Anglo, Latin-American, or Negro—and their estimate of its percentage share of the voters.

One other problem in the use of precinct data, of course, is mapping. Since the lines of the precincts do change, and sometimes change regularly, some sort of map availability is essential to use the data to maximum advantage. In only one case—and this is also the only case of a privately printed collection of precinct data—are maps made available along with the voting figures. *Texas Precinct Votes* (Tarrance, 1967) does present precinct data (with percentages and maps) for the larger counties in the state, representing about three-quarters of the state vote. But so far no other state is served with this kind of reference document, and work with precinct figures in any detail implies also reference to appropriate map sources.

Two final problems should be cited in the matter of American electoral statistics—those dealing with primary elections and with elections at the local level. It has been mentioned that statistics of primary elections tend to be rather more ephemeral than those of general elections. This is not so much the case in the North as in the South, where primary elections sometimes still have a quasi-private character, with returns not infrequently canvassed by the party rather than the state. And what may be said of primary elections can be said as well of municipal and county voting. Some jurisdictions have detailed returns going well back in time. Others, areas in which archival awareness may be somewhat limited, have little to offer the enquiring scholar, journalist, political leader, or just plain ordinary interested citizen.

But though these types of electoral data are often harder to acquire, and may be more difficult to use, they *are* available, at least at a time not too far removed from the holding of the election with which the data deal. With care and attention they can be localized and, if the effort is undertaken promptly, they can be assembled in good order.

USES

Basically, electoral statistics are reference statistics. They are employed immediately to declare official winners in elections, but they are referential from that point onward. They are not used to guide wage discussions or to fix an increase in Social Security benefits; they do not trigger economic defense measures against imports nor determine locations of poverty relief programs. They are for reference only. They are the kind of statistics of which it is sometimes said: "Get it out of the *World Almanac.*"

Use of electoral statistics can be grouped under three general headings: use by academicians and scholars in research and in teaching; use by political journalists and political analysts in newspaper, magazine, book, and radio-TV work; and use by political parties, political personalities, and political and quasi-political groups. Under this final grouping would be found business, labor, and consumer interests; minority groups; age, sex, and ethnic groupings; and a whole variety of special interest organizations—ecologists, hunters, religious groups, and the like. Beyond all of these would be the citizen who simply has an interest in politics and uses statistics to illuminate his interest much as a baseball fan would use batting and pitching averages.

In all consideration of electoral statistics and their usage, moreover, it should be understood that voting data frequently are employed in connection with other kinds of figures. It is true they can stand alone as, for example, in working out historic patterns of voter loyalty to political party labels, or in establishing a relation between voting for congressional incumbents and voting for party nominees for other offices in a given election. But it is also true that these figures often are used in connection with demographic data (Negro population, ethnic characteristics of an area), income-and-education data (to measure socioeconomic characteristics and voting patterns), religious data (insofar as available), and the like. In such circumstances, of course, the electoral data are only a part of the overall statistical treatment developed in analytic work.

Political Uses

For political people, including parties and candidates, managers, and private groups interested in influencing public policy, electoral statistics are the track record of the people with whom they are constantly doing business. From the earliest days of politics, when "clout" was expressed in such a phrase as "the friends of Henry Clay had a majority of 500," the statistics which measure political success and failure have been the warp and woof of political planning and action.

Where has this candidate been strong, and where has he been weak? Where should money and time and candidate effort be invested to get more support? Which possible nominee does the track record show to be the stronger for a future test? How do the statistics of a particular state, congressional district, or county indicate the best moves in the interests of the group?

Perhaps as good an example of any in this category is the present effort of the newly formed black caucus in Congress to evaluate the circumstances of each congressional district in which Negro voters are a substantial (or even moderate) minority to determine how black interests in Congress may be served by concentrating on the electoral circumstances indicated by the voting patterns in those districts. Another, and older, example would be the listing, at the beginning of each Congress, of those seats held by each party which the other party considers marginal and an appropriate target for special effort the following year. Usually the figure applied here is 55 percent, and those Congressmen who have won with less than 55 percent of the vote become themselves an electoral statistic for the attention of friend and foe.

What applies to the parties applies just as much to a trade union political effort, to a business interest group, to a teacher federation, to a Super Sonic Transport (SST) lobby (or an anti-SST lobby). The electoral statistics show who is vulnerable and who is strong, to whom pressure may be usefully directed, to whom such pressure would be meaningless or even possibly counterproductive. Naturally, many other considerations come into play in the commitment of political influence by interest groups, but certainly the track records of the contestants—actual and potential—as revealed in the electoral statistics are of prime importance.

Academic Uses

For the teacher-academic-scholar-student group, the use is both contemporary and historical. In the research category a number of uses can be cited. Among the more interesting are efforts to relate voting patterns in New York in the 1840s and 1850s to census data on ethnic origin (especially Irish) and to numbers of persons whose occupation was reported as "mechanic." Examples of this sort are numerous and may be expected to increase as the Survey Research Center project develops in the 1970s, particularly in study areas involving county voting patterns, census data, and voting patterns in Congress.

In the more current field, the whole study of voting habits comes basically to consideration of two types of material—the "hard data" of specific voting situations and the "soft data" of survey research, or public opinion polling (see Chapter 15). In recent years there has been a bit more attention paid to the latter in published research. The data, condensed from polling questionnaire forms onto cards and tapes, are easier for the analyst to handle than the raw "hard data" of voting, and the breadth of opinion survey work often gives the researcher a wider view of attitudes and of attitude formation than may be available from voting figures. This is especially true in situations in which the researcher is operating away from the field and may be less aware of local circumstances than otherwise.

Nonetheless, the frequent references to the *America Votes* series in recent academic literature lead one to the view that the "hard data" side of scholarly analysis is not being neglected. Research based on precinct data is less readily observable and here the work of journalists is more likely to be notable than that of scholars.

Within the academic community, however, both precinct and county data are used as teaching tools in beginning and advanced course work in the political process. Since the county data are readily available and can be reproduced with greater ease than can precinct figures, the former tend to be used in teaching behavior courses in time and space considerations and in combinations of the two.

For example, an instructor may assign students to study the voting patterns of a given state for a single election, noting variations in turnout and participation ratios, the appeal of various candidates running on the same party label, voter fatigue with long ballots, failure to vote on referenda and constitutional questions, and the like. Or the teacher may have students use the "hard data" to do time series studies of changes and shifts in voting patterns in the state over time. Or he may do both.

Finally, the teacher may ask his students to consider farm employment as a percentage of total employment and relate this to voting behavior; to work out religious factoring in behavior patterns of voting; and to develop rationales for countertrend voting. These last, in such a circumstance as identifying the "un-Kennedy belt" in 1960, are particularly valuable as teaching tools. The student, in this example, is asked to take a county-by-county outline map of the United States, then to mark in those counties in which Republican candidate Richard Nixon polled a higher percentage of the county's presidential vote in 1960 than had President Eisenhower in his 1956 reelection campaign.

While these teaching usages of the data are normally developed with county-level figures, they can be done with state-by-state statistics, to introduce the student to the employment of this kind of material, or they can be done at the local level within the student experience of local circumstances. For example, the voting patterns of a Chicago ward with perhaps seventy-five precincts are just as capable of this sort of analysis as are the patterns of a state with seventy-five counties, with only the caution that for a time-series it must be remembered that precinct lines are changed with much greater rapidity than county boundaries.

In sum, the greatest use of electoral statistics in the academic world is in backstopping scholarly research in popular voting patterns and in the teaching of the political process at the various levels of academic work.

Journalism

The electoral data-use pattern in the world of political journalism varies in some ways from the academic usage and is similar in others. In a sense the political journalist, whether writing against a newspaper deadline, preparing a magazine article, writing a book, or doing radio and TV work, is *both* a researcher and a teacher. He is trying to explain a current situation to his readers/auditors/viewers and teach the techniques of what he is doing at the same time, so that his audience will follow him and his analysis. Depending on the depth of his effort, he uses the electoral data available to detail past performance and postulate future developments, often, as with the academician, in terms of the additional material at hand in census counts or public opinion surveys.

For example, the newspaper writer will speculate about how many voters a Democratic candidate will "need" in Cook County to carry the state of Illinois, drawing upon the electoral data to provide him with the historical evidence from which to draw a figure. Similarly, a writer on Pennsylvania politics may speculate about the turnout of voters in Philadelphia, and their possible political orientation, in writing an evaluation of a gubernatorial contest in that state. In his postelection work, either immediately on election night or for a later issue of his newspaper, much will be made of what the electoral data may have shown about Jewish voting patterns, upper-income area defections from Republican candidates, black voters and those for whom they have cast their ballots, blue-collar worker loyalties and the like, all drawn from specific county, ward, and even precinct figures. Typical language would be: "and voters in all-black precincts 17, 18, and 20 supported the Democratic candidates by margins of from five-to-one up to twenty-to-one."

The work of the magazine writer can take more time than that of his newspaper colleagues and can permit more careful study of the results, especially more careful than may be possible on election night. But the nature of the work remains journalistic scholarship or scholarly journalism, depending on the quality and depth of the effort undertaken. In any event, much of the basic data for the analysis made comes necessarily from electoral statistics, from the voted opinions of the electorate at the moment of political choice.

The book writer is a further extension of the magazine and newspaper writer. The work involved in such a study as *The Emerging Republican Majority* (Phillips, 1969); the various studies of Theodore White (1960, 1964, 1968, 1972) and Sam Lubell (1965, 1970); *Where are the Voters?* (Friedheim, 1968); *Five States for Goldwater* (Cosman, 1966); *The Real Majority* (Scammon and Wattenberg, 1970) are all examples of this sort of undertaking, frequently embodying census data and survey research as well as electoral data.

In the electronic media (radio and television) the use of data tends to be related more to reporting of specific elections. The requirement is for immediate relevancy and the time allocated is even less than that available to the newspaper writer. For preelection roundup programs there is some time and for postelection comment there is more time, but the largest audience for analytic material in radio and television is the audience lending its eyes and ears on election night.

For this audience, producers and commentators in radio and television have specific usages of electoral data based upon the need to identify leading and winning candidates as quickly as may be prudently possible and to tell why this or that candidate won or lost. Naturally much of the material used on election night comes from prepared references and from the commentator's own view of the general political circumstances of the election contest; but much relies also on the analyses of hard data. In some instances this may come from random samples of voting precincts, in others from the selection of (and quick reporting from) so-called tag precincts designed to "tag" the voting pattern of, say, black voters, Jews, upper-income areas, and the like. For example, in the April 1971 election of a mayor in Chicago it was possible to indicate an enlarged voting percentage for Mayor Daley in blue-collar white areas and to indicate Daley support in certain preselected high Republican precincts (that is, high Republican in national and state voting).

Prediction of Elections

Perhaps the most interesting use of election statistics is that by Dr. Louis H. Bean, a statistician formerly in the Department of Agriculture, who used historical election data as a basis for predicting elections. Beginning his analysis of election results for predictive purposes as a hobby, Dr. Bean, in a series of publications following an initial discussion of his results in 1936 at an annual meeting of the American Statistical Association, compiled an enviable record as a forecaster of election outcomes. Dr. Bean, with remarkable accuracy, greater than that of the polls, predicted the Roosevelt landslide in 1936, the outcome of the 1938 congressional elections, and the unexpected victory of President Truman in 1948.

Dr. Bean's analysis of past election results in relation to economic and social developments, supplemented by public opinion and preelection polls, constitute a manual not only for predicting elections, but much more important, a guide to political leaders on the factors that may determine election victory or defeat. The use of such knowledge like any other may, of course, be for good or for evil. That is, the politician may use this knowledge to help him win elections without regard as to whether his stand on significant issues is or is not for the public good. In any case, even if the knowledge is used in a manner inimical to the interests of the public, it would be absurd to argue that less knowledge is to be preferred to more. One can only hope that increased knowledge can also be used by the general public as well as by the politician so as to protect the public interest.

The emergence and proliferation of public opinion polls and preelection polls has added a new dimension to political behavior. Current and continuing information on public attitudes, opinions, and perceptions of events and their significance may, in relation to election statistics, make possible a much better understanding than was ever obtained in the past of the political process, and may provide a mechanism for more comprehensive and timely interaction between leaders and the public, leading to more responsive and responsible government. Although preelection polls are not dealt with in depth in this volume, public opinion polls concerned with substantive issues are considered in Chapter 15.

THE OUTLOOK

Finally, as to the outlook for the development of electoral data, precinct figures are replacing the once dominant county and state figures, the more so as perhaps half our population may be found in the top hundred or so counties. Computer treatment of electoral data should make these precinct data easier to obtain and handle, though sad experience shows that this does not always happen. Mapping remains the major obstacle to proper use of precinct figures.

Probably little change will occur as to usage, except that computerization of precinct data may permit more precise efforts in research, in teaching, in analysis, and in political use of data.

REFERENCES

Burnham, Walter Dean. *Presidential Ballots, 1836–1892*. Baltimore, Md.: Johns Hopkins Press, 1955.

Cade, June G. *Kansas Votes: National Elections, 1850–1956*. Lawrence: Governmental Research Center, University of Kansas, 1957.

Cosman, Bernard. *Five States for Goldwater: Continuity and Change in Southern Presidential Voting Patterns*. Norman: University of Oklahoma Press, 1966.

Francis, Wayne L. *Indiana Votes: Election Returns for U. S. Representatives, Returns for State General Assembly, 1922–1958*. Bloomington: Bureau of Government Research, Indiana University, 1962.

Friedheim, Jerry. *Where Are the Voters?* Washington, D. C.: Washington National Press, 1968.

Gallup, G. *Gallup Political Almanac* (1946–52). New York: B.C. Forbes (title varies).

Gone, Samuel Kimball. *Illinois Votes, 1900–1958: A Compilation of Illinois Election Statistics*. Urbana: Institute of Government and Public Affairs, University of Illinois, 1958.

Governmental Affairs Institute. *America at the Polls: A Handbook of American Presidential Election Statistics, 1920–1964*. Washington, D. C.: Government Printing Office, 1965.

———. *America Votes: A Handbook of Contemporary American Election Statistics*. Washington, D. C.: Government Printing Office, biennial.

Hartsfield, Annie Mary. *Florida Votes, 1920–1962: Selection Election Statistics*. Tallahassee: Institute of Governmental Research, Florida State University, 1963.

Jewell, Malcolm E. *Kentucky Votes*. Lexington: University of Kentucky Press, 1963.
Lee, Eugene C. *California Votes, 1928–1960: A Review and Analysis of Registration and Voting* (with 1962 supplement). Berkeley: Institute of Governmental Studies, University of California, 1963.
Lubell, Samuel. *The Future of American Politics*, 3rd ed. New York: Harper & Row, 1965.
———. *The Hidden Crisis in American Politics*. New York: Norton, 1970.
Petersen, Svend. *A Statistical History of the American Presidential Elections*. New York: Ungar, 1963.
Phillips, Kevin. *The Emerging Republican Majority*. New Rochelle, N. Y.: Arlington House, 1969.
Pitchell, Robert J. (Ed.). *Indiana Votes: Election Returns for Governor, 1952–1956, and Senator, 1914–1958*. Bloomington: Bureau of Government Research, Indiana University, 1960.
Press, Charles, and Oliver Williams. *State Manuals, Blue Books, and Election Results*. Berkeley: Institute of Governmental Studies, University of California, 1962.
Robinson, Edgar Eugene. *The Presidential Vote, 1896–1932*. Palo Alto, Calif.: Stanford University Press, 1934.
———. *They Voted for Roosevelt: The Presidential Vote, 1932–1944*. New York: Octagon Books, 1947.
Scammon, Richard M., and Ben J. Wattenberg. *The Real Majority*. New York: Coward-McCann, 1970.
Tarrance, Lance, Jr. (Ed.). *Texas Precinct Votes '66*. Precinct analysis and maps. Austin, Texas: Politics, Inc., 1967.
University of North Carolina, Political Studies Program. *North Carolina Votes: General Election Returns by County for President of the U. S., 1868–1960; Governor of North Carolina, 1868–1960; U. S. Senator from North Carolina, 1914–1960*. Chapel Hill: University of North Carolina Press, 1962.
University of Oklahoma, Bureau of Government Research. *Oklahoma Votes, 1907–1962*. Norman: University of Oklahoma Press, 1964.
University of Wisconsin, Bureau of Government. *How Wisconsin Voted, 1848–1960*. Madison: University of Wisconsin Press, 1962.
Waldron, Ellis Comp. *Montana Politics Since 1864: An Atlas of Elections*. Missoula: Montana State University Press, 1958.
White, John Patrick. *Michigan Votes: Election Statistics, 1928–1956*. Ann Arbor: Institute of Public Administration, University of Michigan, 1958.
White, Theodore H. *The Making of the President, 1960*. New York: Atheneum, 1961.
———. *The Making of the President, 1964*. New York: Atheneum, 1965.
———. *The Making of the President, 1968*. New York: Atheneum, 1969.
———. *The Making of the President, 1972*. New York: Atheneum, 1973.

CHAPTER 15

*On Public Opinion Polls**

Among the statistics of which the general public is most aware are those emanating from the public opinion polls. Especially in presidential election years the preelection polls engage the attention of the American people with heightened interest as an important element in electioneering and political debate. Political leaders in all political parties—despite denials of the relevance of the data particularly on the part of the candidates with poor showings—watch the preelection polls closely and, undoubtedly, adjust the conduct of their campaigns in response to them and, also, in response to polls on specific issues of significance at the time. Although there is invariably some discussion of the impact of the polls on the public's actual voting behavior, and diverse stands are taken by the various candidates involved, there can be little doubt that whatever their impact may be the preelection polls on anticipated balloting and on specific issues are not ignored either by the candidates or by the public at large.

In between presidential elections the attention that the public opinion polls receive varies in intensity, undoubtedly reaching intermediate peaks in the congressional election years and in respect to specific issues on which there is widespread concern and emotional response. Moreover, during election intervals political leaders in the executive, legislative, and even the judicial branches of government on the federal, state, and local levels are

---

* Based on a memorandum by Rita J. Simon, University of Illinois.

313

mindful of public opinion as reported in the polls. Certainly over the past several decades, since the abortive experience of the *Literary Digest* in its effort to predict the outcome of the 1936 presidential election, the public opinion polls have commanded increased respect by both government officials and the public at large and have become essential ingredients in the working of our political system. In recognition of this fact, national poll data from 1936 to 1970 are reviewed on selected domestic and international issues. In the nature of things it will be difficult to trace the specific uses of the data either by public or by government officials and other policy makers and administrators. But there can be little question that the impact of public opinion polls has been a significant one and that it will increase further. In the summary of the results of the polls, the indication from time to time of subsequent developments points to the powerful influence that they must have exerted in the political sphere. Also apparent in the presentation is the way in which political action has influenced public opinion.

SOURCES AND RELIABILITY OF DATA

The polls reported in this volume have been obtained from three main sources: the periodicals, *Public Opinion Quarterly, Gallup Monthly Report,* and the Roper Public Opinion Research Center in Williamstown, Massachusetts. From these sources it was possible to obtain data from surveys run by the National Opinion Research Center, the George Gallup American Institute of Public Opinion, Louis Harris Associates, and any other major polling agency that conducted national surveys from the late 1930s to 1970. Not all of the national surveys conducted during that period have been analyzed here. However, all those reported in the polls section of the *Public Opinion Quarterly,* from 1937 on, and more recently from the *Gallup Monthly Report* have been received. For specific topics, such as civil rights, aspects of foreign policy, trade unions, and Social Security, the Public Opinion Research Center was good enough to make the data available.

In the early polling experience time and cost considerations led the pollsters to use sampling procedures of questionable scientific merit that were a large factor in accounting for early misses in their preelection surveys. In recent years, however, the major polls use sounder sampling procedures and, also, more sophisticated questionnaires and analytical methods.

The typical sample size for a national survey is 1500 respondents. With a sample that size, there is a .95 probability that the results obtained are no more than three percentage points off the figure that would be obtained if every adult in the country was interviewed. However, to shave even one point from the percentages that are obtained with a sample of 1500 to come even closer to reproducing the universe, about twice as many people would be required. It would thus be extremely expensive and time-consuming to increase substantially the sample size, and the rewards for doing so would be minute.

One often hears exclamations from persons who question the validity of the polls to the effect that they have never been interviewed by a polling organization. Although this is an understandable reaction, it is a matter of simple arithmetic to ascertain that with a sample of 1500 persons the chances of being interviewed by a representative of a polling organization in any survey, given a total population of 200 million, is only about 1 in 133,333. With such odds it is quite likely that the proportion of the total population that would actually be polled would remain quite minute, even over a lifetime. The failure of any given person to be interviewed, therefore, cannot be used as a basis for questioning the accuracy of polls. The fact is that modern mathematical statistical procedures make it possible to obtain reasonably reliable information about a population as large as that of the United States from a scientifically selected sample of only 1500 persons.

It is important, also, that something be said about the validity of the verbal responses called "public opinion." In this context, validity means the likelihood that the verbal responses will serve as predictors of behavior. Opinions in this context are useful mainly because they tell us what the public wants and does not want of its government, and hopefully, what the public is likely to support and not to support when it goes to the ballot box.

In the literature on voting, there is ample evidence that voters' verbal choices *before* they go to the polls to cast their ballots and the election results match very closely. Even in those dramatic and important instances in which the pollsters picked the wrong man to win (their choice of Dewey over Truman in 1948 and of Harold Wilson over Edward Heath in the British elections in 1970) they were off by only a few percentage points. Not since the *Literary Digest*'s prediction that Alfred Landon would defeat Franklin Roosevelt in the 1936 presidential election have the pollsters been off by more than three or four percentage points. Of course, in the case of the events cited above, those points can and did make all the difference. But for the problems discussed here, if the opinions reported predicted behavior as well as verbal preferences for presidential candidates and indicated how the respondents were likely to vote, the validity of those responses would be assured.

Another area in which the public's verbal preferences or attitudes and behavior match closely is in market research. A high proportion of the time, products that people say they want, like, or will buy turn out to be the ones they do, in fact, purchase. Having found a good deal of consistency between verbal expressions and overt behavior in voting and consumer behavior, it is just as likely that if and when people are given a choice to act on the opinions reported in this study, their behavior would be consistent with their opinions a great majority of the time. One can therefore use their opinions about allowing their children to attend a school where a majority of the pupils are black, or their willingness to go into business with a Jew, or permitting their church to be used by a "peace group," as proxies for how they would behave should a similar situation arise.

Results of national polls are easily accessible to the public as well as to groups or institutions or government agencies that may have special interests in the responses to particular topics. Newspapers, weekly news magazines, and professional journals such as the *Public Opinion Quarterly* and the *Gallup Monthly Reports* carry national poll results about major or particularly controversial issues as a regular feature.

SELECTIVE REVIEW OF NATIONAL POLL DATA

Socioeconomic Issues

A scanning of the topics about which the public was queried most often in the second half of the 1930s reveals something of the public's mood during that period. The polls describe a nation almost wholly concerned with questions of economic policy and social welfare. There were no polls about civil liberties or civil rights and hardly even a single item concerning Negroes and their place in American society. If Negroes were the "invisible minority" during the depression years, this was not true of the Jewish community. Tapping attitudes toward American Jews and feelings of anti-Semitism were very prominent themes in the period that saw the development and enactment of a policy of genocide on the part of Nazi Germany vis-à-vis European Jewry. It turns out that on social welfare and policies and proposals for economic recovery the public either anticipated or prompted governmental action. Eight months, for example, before the passage of the first Social Security Act, the public was asked whether it favored government old-age pensions for needy persons. Eighty-nine percent answered "yes."

Paul Douglas, author of *Social Security in the United States* (1936) commented about the public role in the recently enacted legislation as follows:

> ... the federal security act is the result of a very sharp change in public opinion. Prior to the great depression, the consensus of public opinion was that American citizens could in the main provide for their own old age by individual savings. So far as unemployment was concerned, the articulate American public predominantly believed either that unemployment was being reduced to very narrow limits by "the stabilization of industry" or that unemployment insurance was a debasing "dole" which subsidized men for being idle and hence led them to shun work [p. 3].

Between 1936 and 1940 the public was asked on several occasions whether it supported government-financed old age pensions. Each time between 90 and 94 percent answered that it did. In 1938 and 1943, 72 and 64 percent, respectively, indicated a willingness to extend benefits to household help, farm hands, and employees in small shops [from the American Institute of Public Opinion (AIPO)]. Yet in 1948, we heard President Truman in his address to the Democratic convention chastise the Congress for its failure to extend Social Security payments:

> Time and again I have recommended improvements in the social security law, including extending protection to those not now covered, and increasing the amount of benefits to reduce the eligibility age of women from 65 to 60 years. Congress studied the matter for two years but could not find the time to increase the benefits. But they did find the time to take social security benefits away from 750,000 people, and they passed that over my veto [Bernstein and Matuson, 1966, pp. 151–152].

Even in the 1950s when much of the public was no longer hungry or unemployed or fearful of its economic future, it strongly supported expansion of the Social Security program (68 and 74 percents in the surveys conducted) so as to allow people who were over 65 and who worked full time to receive benefits (AIPO). In 1940 and 1947, when asked whether it thought the government ought to provide for all people who have no other means of obtaining a living, 65 percent and 73 percent answered "yes" [*Fortune* (FOR)].

The area of government-financed medical programs is another in which public opinion anticipated and preceded government action on this issue by two and a half decades. In 1938, for example, 81 percent said that they thought the government should be responsible for providing medical care for people who are unable to pay for it (AIPO). Fifty-nine percent said they would be willing to pay higher taxes to support such a program (AIPO). In 1943, during the war, 74 percent believed that "medical care for anyone who needs it" should be one of the programs for which the federal government should collect taxes (AIPO).

But, unlike the Social Security and old age pensions issues, about which the public never wavered in its support, after the war and in the 1950s the public did lose interest in, and to some extent changed its mind about, government-financed health programs. For example, in 1949 only about 56 percent said they had any familiarity with the national health insurance program that President Truman was trying to get through the Congress (AIPO). When asked to choose between Truman's comprehensive health program and the plan submitted by the American Medical Association which was private and voluntary, the latter received about one and a half times as much support (AIPO). By 1949 one and a half times more people had come to believe that a government-financed scheme would not provide as good medical care as a private program (AIPO).

A dozen years passed between the time Truman's proposals were defeated in the Congress and the public was asked again for its opinion about a government-sponsored health program. By 1961 public opinion had shifted so that two-thirds of those queried said they favored a government program (AIPO). In the subsequent four years between 1961 and the passage of the Medicare bill during the Johnson administration, the public continued to support the principles embodied in the health insurance program that was eventually enacted.

The adoption of minimum wage standards and the level of payment for employees in industries covered by those standards is still another socioeconomic issue about which public opinion preceded official enactment. When the public was first asked whether it supported the principle of a minimum wage standard (before the passage of a particular bill) over 60 percent said it did (AIPO). The level of payment favored by most people was 40 cents an hour compared to the 25 cents enacted into law in 1938. Over the next three decades the issue of what the minimum wage standard ought to be was before the public at least half a dozen times and on every occasion the public recommended a higher minimum standard than either the existing one, or the one under debate, or the new standard that was adopted most recently.

Under the Nixon administration, a new concept in welfare was proposed by the president's adviser on urban affairs, Patrick Moynihan. The idea was that the government would guarantee employment, rather than direct financial subsidies, to families whose income is below the $3,200 minimum set for a family of four. This specific proposal was embodied in a larger welfare package that failed the Congress, in part because the administration's interest in its passage diminished. But the public appears ready and willing to support the principle of guaranteed employment as witnessed by the fact that on two occasions (June 1968 and January 1969) over 75 percent said that they favored the Moynihan plan.

There is at least one issue that falls within the domain of socioeconomic policy, however, on which public opinion hardly ever precedes or prompts the government to act. That issue is whether or not the personal income tax should be raised in any given year. While the public does not always oppose tax increases or support tax reductions, for example, when the former is sought in the name of national defense or the latter in the name of helping to balance the national budget, it never believes that existing tax burdens are too low, and usually feels that they are too high. Table 15.1 traces public opinion about the personal income tax over a twenty-year spread following World War II.

Table 15.1. Do you consider the amount of federal income tax which you (your husband) have to pay as too high, too low, or about right? (AIPO)

Year	About Right	Too High	Too Low	No Opinion
		(percentages)		
1948	38	57	1	4
1949	52	43	1	4
1950	40	56	—	4
1951	43	52	1	4
1952	26	71	—	3
1953	37	59	—	4
1957	31	61	—	8
1959	40	51	1	8
1961	45	46	1	8
1962	43	48	—	9
1966	39	52	—	9
1967	38	58	1	3

The figures in Table 15.1 are especially interesting in light of the fact that the public's knowledge about what the personal income tax burdens are, and its standard about what they ought to be, are consistently off base. For example, the public consistently *underestimates* the amount of money that people who earn more than $10,000 a year have to, or should, pay. The public also errs, but in no consistent direction, about the amount of money people who earn less than $10,000 ought to pay. These errors of judgment and ignorance are illustrated by the figures in Table 15.2.

Civil Liberties

Next examined are issues relating to civil liberties and civil rights. In this context, the former concerns the extent to which public opinion supports government actions that promote or secure individual freedom versus government actions and policies that endanger freedom of speech,

Table 15.2. What the public thinks the taxpayer does pay, should pay, and what he actually pays (AIPO)

Head of Family Earnings (Family of 4)	What Public Thinks He Pays	What Public Thinks He Should Pay	What He Actually Pays
		1938	
$ 5,000	$ 100	$ 150	$ 90
10,000	400	500	590
100,000	9,000	9,000	40,000
		1941	
3,000	30	60	0
5,000	100	200	130
10,000	300	600	720
100,000	5,000	10,000	46,000
		1947	
3,000	200	50	131
10,000	1,000	900	1,720
50,000	9,000	2,500	24,000
		1949	
2,500	54	—	0
5,000	340	—	350
50,000	5,400	—	16,000
		1961	
3,000	—	46	65
5,000	—	216	420
10,000	—	617	1,372
50,000	—	7,250	18,294
100,000	—	25,000	51,192

assembly, etc. The civil rights topic focuses on white opinion about the status of blacks in American society. It is to be noted first that civil liberties has not been a topic about which the public has been polled with any great frequency. The 1930s and early 1940s saw many polls directed at assessing the public's opinion of religious prejudice; and in the 1950s and 1960s civil rights and social justice vis-à-vis black Americans were topics about which the public was polled regularly. But civil liberties has never attracted the same degree of attention during any of the three and a half decades of national polling. There have been times when interest increased somewhat —for example, during periods of national emergency (i.e., during World War II) and of heightened political tensions (i.e., during the McCarthy era or during the past few years as a result of increasing resistance to the Vietnam war). But in periods of relative stability and quiescence, interest in civil liberties is almost nonexistent.

There is a consistent theme that pervades the public's reactions to rights of dissident groups who wish to express their beliefs, to the principles embedded in the Bill of Rights, to the protection of the freedoms contained therein, and to an executive order or legislation that seeks to limit those freedoms. The theme is that when questions pertaining to the above issues are posed abstractly or when they are posed as theoretical or academic matters, the public responds in such a way as to be almost unanimous in its support of freedom and the right of dissent.

For example, in 1938 and 1940 when asked simply, "Do you believe in 'freedom of speech'?" over 96 percent said "Yes" [Office of Public Opinion Research (OPOR)]. But when that question was followed by, "Do you believe in freedom of speech to the extent of allowing radicals to hold meetings and express their views in the community?" the proportion who supported that interpretation of the free speech amendment dropped to 39 and 22 percent respectively (OPOR and AIPO).

In 1938 and 1940, there seemed to be a great many radicals around on both the right and the left, and fears of subversion and a takeover of the system were deeply felt by a lot of people. The German American Bund was still active, as was the Communist party, and there was much talk about the ties both groups had with powerful foreign powers and the willingness of those groups to serve the interests of those foreign powers. But even when the danger of internal subversion was not at issue, and the free speech principle was merely placed in a more concrete or realistic setting, public opinion veered sharply from expressions of a consensus to that of a near fifty-fifty split. For example, when it was asked in 1940 and 1941, "Do you think that in America anybody should be allowed to speak on any subject any time he wants to, or do you think there are times when free speech should be prohibited or certain subjects or speakers prohibited?" only 49 and 44 percent supported free speech any time [Roper Research Associates (ROP) and OPOR]. Crossing the intervening decades quickly, to 1970, we find that when the public is queried concerning its support for free speech, again in a context that suggests that the exercise thereof is not likely to result in laudatory remarks about one's government or the state of the nation, there is the same rather low level of support, namely 42 percent.

The war in Vietnam is one of the less popular wars in which Americans have been actively involved. Sentiments against the participation of the United States have been loud, insistent, and on many occasions disruptive. A good test of the extent to which the American people support the rights of free expression, guaranteed by the First Amendment to the Constitution, may be seen in their respect for the rights of those who protested the war and government policy in Southeast Asia. Between 1965 and

1970, the public was queried at least five times on the issue of whether people have the right to conduct peaceful demonstrations against the war in Vietnam [Louis Harris Associates (HAR)]. The percents who have supported that right are shown below:

Year	Support Right to Dissent
1965	59%
(July) 1967	61
(December) 1967	54
1969*	38
1970	21

* In 1969, the item read, "Do you feel that *students* have the right to make their protests or not?"

Even if we assume that the public may feel students should have fewer rights than adults, there is still the sharp drop in public support between 1967 and 1970 that cannot be explained by its attitudes toward any one group in the population. We see that in 1970 over 75 percent of the public did not approve of organized peaceful protests against government policy.

We remember that in 1940, 76 percent opposed the right of radicals to hold meetings and express their opinions. If we were to examine the interim period in any detail we would find that the public has rather consistently supported those governmental actions that would set restraints and limits on the interpretation of the free speech amendment. Illustrations of this support may be seen in the public's reactions to the activities of the late Senator Joseph McCarthy of Wisconsin. When asked in the summer of 1950 whether they thought Senator McCarthy's charges were doing the country more good than harm, 39 percent thought they were doing "more good," 29 percent thought "more harm," and the others did not have an opinion (AIPO). The item was asked of the 84 percent who said in a previous item that they had heard of Senator McCarthy. When queried further as to whether they approved or disapproved of the senator's charges, 31 percent said they approved, 10 percent approved but with some qualifications, while 20 percent disapproved. The others had no opinion, and 22 percent had not heard of the specific charges. On both items there was more support for or approval of McCarthy's actions and charges than there was disapproval.

On all of the national polls conducted in the 1950s and 1960s that queried the public about the activities and rights Communist party members should have, more of the public supported placing restrictions upon them than did those who favored allowing them to work at their jobs, to speak openly, or to operate as a political party. Perhaps the strongest expression of the public's support of restraints may be seen in the way in which it responded to these three issues:

> Do you favor or oppose revoking the citizenship of admitted Communists? (AIPO)
>
> Do you believe that anyone who admitted he was a Communist ought to be put in jail? (AIPO)
>
> Do you think it is a good idea for people to report to the Federal Bureau of Investigation any neighbor or acquaintance whom they suspect of being Communists? (AIPO)

Seventy-seven percent favored revoking the citizenship of admitted Communists, 57 percent thought they ought to be put in jail, and 73 percent favored reporting neighbors or acquaintances to the FBI.

It seems difficult to conclude anything from this review except that the civil liberties provided for and protected by the federal and state constitutions and federal statutes do not enjoy widespread popular support much of the time, and that if they were not protected from recall or revision by enormously complicated mechanisms, such statutes might indeed be in jeopardy. But perhaps one could argue with this interpretation and claim instead that the American public feels free to express punitive and repressive sentiments vis-à-vis the civil liberties of political minorities or dissenters because it understands implicitly that their rights to free speech, assembly, etc., will not be seriously endangered by such largely "expressive" opinions. In the absence of supporting data for the latter interpretation, the former interpretation appears to be more consistent with the facts, pessimistic and fearsome as it might sound to those who are concerned with preserving constitutionally guaranteed rights.

Civil Rights

The thrust of the discussion of public opinion about civil rights is directed at answering the question: Have there been significant shifts in the attitudes of whites toward blacks over the past three decades? Earlier it was noted that it was not until the United States had become an active participant in the war against Nazism and Fascism in the 1940s that questions concerning the lack of congruence between the observed and the ideal status of Negroes in American society were given much attention by national polling agencies. The beginning of the 1940s was the first time that items appeared on national polls that probed the discrepancy between the constitutional rights of Negroes and their observed treatment, and the legitimacy of the policy of segregation. Since that time, the mass media, the polls, the government, and civil rights organizations have polled, tested, instructed, and propagandized the public about their beliefs and behavior vis-à-vis blacks. We will look at a few key issues: schooling and relative intelligence, social distance, and assessment of responsibility and blame for discriminatory treatment.

The item that reflects the greatest shift in white attitudes is about the intelligence of blacks compared to whites. In 1942, this item appeared for the first time on a national survey: "In general do you think Negroes are as intelligent as white people, that is, can they learn just as well if they are given the same education and training?" Forty-two percent answered "Yes." [National Opinion Research Center (NORC)]. Between 1942 and 1963 this same item appeared on at least five national polls. By 1963, 76 percent answered "Yes, Negroes are as intelligent . . ." and each time the item appeared a higher percentage had answered in the affirmative.

But the public's changing perception of the relative intelligence of blacks was far ahead of its willingness to support the integration of black and white children in the same schools. For example, in 1956, only 49 percent approved of Negro children attending the same school as whites (NORC). At this same time 75 percent said they thought Negroes were as intelligent as whites. Northern support for having their children attend a school where a majority of the pupils are Negro never attained even the 50 percent level. Moreover, between 1954—the year that the Supreme Court rendered its decision in *Brown* v. *The Board of Education*—and 1966, the public became less, rather than more supportive of the doctrine of integration with all deliberate speed (AIPO).

The busing issue, which of course has subthemes and complexities to it that extend beyond the matter of integrated or segregated schools, has never had widespread popular support. As late as eight years after the Supreme Court destroyed the legitimacy of the segregated school system, over 75 percent of the American public continued to oppose the busing of school children in order to achieve a better racial balance (AIPO).

If the details were filled out or more of the nuances concerning the public's opinion on the school issue were examined, the major theme that would emerge is that in principle a big majority (about two-thirds) supports the idea of an integrated school system. But the closer to home, and the more personal the implications of a fully integrated system, the less willing are white Americans to support the programs and policies implied by such a principle.

Indeed, this theme of white support for integration or equality in principle, or on matters that do not affect one's family, or do not involve contact of a personal or intimate nature can be generalized beyond the school issue to all areas of white-black relations. Table 15.3, from the article, "Attitudes Toward Desegregation," describes the various facets of white opinions about blacks and the extent to which whites desire contact and interaction with blacks as social equals (Hyman and Sheatsley, 1956).

The responses reported in Table 15.3 show that in the more formal and institutionalized spheres, most whites accept the principle of equality. But there is a big gap between believing that Negroes should have equal job opportunities and welcoming Negroes as neighbors, friends, and possible mates.

Table 15.3. Guttman Scale of Prointegration Sentiment, 1963

The Responses from a Guttman Scale	Percent Giving Prointegration Response*
1. "Do you think Negroes should have as good a chance as white people to get any kind of job, or do you think white people should have the first chance at any kind of job?" ("As good a chance.")	82
2. "Generally speaking, do you think there should be separate sections for Negroes in street cars and buses?" ("No.")	77
3. "Do you think Negroes should have the right to use the same parks, restaurants and hotels as white people?" ("Yes.")	71
4. "Do you think white students and Negro students should go to the same schools, or to separate schools?" ("Same schools.")	63
5. "How strongly would you object if a member of your family wanted to bring a Negro friend home to dinner?" ("Not at all.")	49
6. "White people have a right to keep Negroes out of their neighborhoods if they want to, and Negroes should respect that right." ("Disagree slightly" or "Disagree strongly.")	44
7. "Do you think there should be laws against marriages between Negroes and whites?" ("No.")	36
8. "Negroes shouldn't push themselves where they're not wanted." ("Disagree slightly" or "Disagree strongly.")	27

* The properties of a Guttman scale are such that if a person rejects one item on the scale, the chances are at least nine in ten that he will reject all items below it. Thus, those who reject the top item—equal job opportunities for Negroes—are highly unlikely to endorse any of the other items on the scale and may be considered extreme segregationists. At the other end of the scale, the 27 percent who disagree with the proposition that "Negroes shouldn't push themselves where they're not wanted" are extremely likely to take a prointegration position on all seven of the other items.

[Source: This table was reprinted by permission of *Daedalus,* Journal of the American Academy of Arts and Sciences, Boston, Massachusetts. Winter 1966, *The Negro American*—2.]

The 1960s was a decade of social protest, violent rhetoric, and collective action. After the summer of 1967, which in retrospect was the climax of the most serious urban race riots the country had ever experienced, the public was queried about whether it thought "most or only a few Negroes supported the riots." Eighty-three percent of the whites and eighty-five percent of the blacks said they thought that only a minority of the blacks supported the riots (HAR). While there was almost complete agreement between whites and blacks that the riots did not have widespread support within the black community, there was little agreement between them as to the reasons why the riots broke out. Sixty percent of the whites placed the blame on outside agitators, ignorance, and laziness on the part of the blacks. Eighty percent of the black respondents, on the other hand, explained the riots by pointing to the lack of jobs for blacks, to the conditions in the ghettos, and to the prejudice and broken promises of the white community (HAR).

The white respondents' explanation for the riots generalized to their beliefs about responsibility for the overall status of the black community in the larger society. In 1968 when asked, "Who is more to blame for the present conditions in which Negroes find themselves, white people or Negroes themselves?" more than twice as many, 58 to 22 percent, answered Negroes (AIPO). Further confirmation of this attitude is reflected in whites' overall evaluation of how Negroes are treated in the country. Note the absolute level of responses to the two questions shown below and the lack of change over time:

1. Do you think most Negroes in the United States are being treated fairly or unfairly? (NORC)
2. In your opinion, how well do you think Negroes are treated in the country—the same as whites are, not very well, or badly? (NORC)

Year	"Fairly"
1944	60%
1946	66
1956	66
	"Same as White"
1967	72%
1968	70

Most white people believe today, as they did almost a quarter of a century earlier, that Negroes are treated fairly and are not special targets of discrimination. One might argue that these responses are defensive manifestations of guilt feelings. To acknowledge the guilt would also involve acknowledgment that important and extensive changes need to be made in American society, and those changes would be likely to have direct repercussion on their own status in the society. But the more obvious conclusion is also the more valid. Namely, that white Americans perceive that the social and economic conditions under which most blacks live are not as attractive or as healthy or as stimulating or as comfortable as those under which most whites live. But they do not believe that they, or the white community, are responsible for those conditions, or that they *owe* it to the blacks to improve them. The white community does not blame itself for the blacks' poorer living conditions, their slower occupational advancement, or their fewer years of schooling. Given these perceptions, it is not unexpected that most whites did not agree with the conclusions reached by the President's Commission on Civil Disorders in 1968 that "our nation is moving toward two societies, one black, one white—separate and unequal." Of the respondents, 52 percent disagreed, 32 percent agreed, and 16 percent had no opinion (AIPO).

The major theme that emerges from even this brief overview of public opinion about civil rights and black status is that most white Americans do not accept the conclusion that the United States is a racist society, that blacks are treated unfairly, and that separateness and inequality in social matters is a basic dimension of American life. Instead, they focus on the institutional changes that have occurred in such areas as public transportation, housing, education, employment opportunities, etc., and argue on the basis of those indices that Negroes have been integrated into American society, and that therefore the riots, demonstrations, and protests are not justified. Most whites do not believe that Negroes are treated "unfairly." Lacking such a feeling, there is not much basis for optimism that in the foreseeable future blacks will become first-class citizens in American society in contexts and behavior that go beyond "formal" equality and institutionalized integration.

Foreign Policy

The issue of how much the public knows about the foreign policy of this government is as much a topic of concern as is the content of that knowledge and the convictions the public holds about the government's policies. The traditional view, which was discussed earlier, is that the American public is largely ignorant of important themes in American foreign policy, and compared to domestic issues, more apathetic to changes and fluctuations in the management of that policy.

One compelling theme that has persisted throughout this period of three and a half decades is the public's sentiments about the wars in which it has been asked to serve. How much support has there been for American involvement in World War II, Korea, and Vietnam? How much does it evaluate its government's policies prior to the commitment of American troops? How much faith does it have in the alliances its government has made with other foreign powers in the conduct of those wars?

First, looking farthest backward, there were misgivings that were widespread and long lasting about the wisdom of United States participation in World War I. In 1937 and 1939 when the public was queried on this issue, 64 and 59 percent, respectively, said that it had been a mistake for the United States to have entered the world war; and 95 percent said that the United States should not take part again, if another world war were to develop in Europe (AIPO). Even as late as 1941, 39 percent were still saying United States participation in the world war had been a mistake compared to 42 percent who did not think so (AIPO). The others were on the fence. On the second point—whether the United States ought to involve itself again—over 79 percent said "no" when queried between March 1939 and as late as October 1941 (AIPO).

The public has not been queried during the decades following the end of World War II about the merit of United States participation in that war. It was asked in the years immediately following the war (1946, 1947, 1948) whether entry had been a mistake, and more than two-thirds said it did not think so (AIPO). It is quite likely that if asked today, or in the past half dozen years or so, the proportion who considered it a mistake would be considerably greater; but probably not as high as the percent who felt our entry into World War I had been a mistake. But World War II was a special war, not only because of the enormity of it and the stakes involved, but because of the principles and the issues over which the war was presumably being fought.

Five years after it was over, when President Truman ordered American troops into combat in defense of the territorial integrity of the Republic of South Korea, there was only a brief period during which the public felt it was not a mistake to have done so. In August 1950, right after the action had been taken, only 20 percent thought it was a mistake. By February of the following year, the proportion had more than doubled to 50 percent, and it remained at about that level until the end of the fighting (AIPO). Vietnam is still too recent to assess fully; but, in looking at the public's responses between August 1965 and May 1971 as to whether our participation in Vietnam was a mistake, a similar pattern may be noted. At the outset, 24 percent thought it a mistake; two years later in July 1967, 41 percent thought so; and four years later the figure had increased again by 50 percent to 61 percent (AIPO). Disillusionment about the Korean war set in sooner than it did about Vietnam but that is probably because in the Korean war there was no preliminary stage. There was no long period in which the United States sent technical assistants or advisers, and then later followed that action with combat troops.

In retrospect then, the data that are available suggest that the American public does not have a uniform response to the most significant of its government's foreign policy acts—that of committing the lives of its young men to war. It is not known, in the absence of comparable information from other countries, how similar or different the American public is from the Russian or the French or any other on this matter. Comparable data about another country—Israel—show that the public there has demonstrated a much higher level of support for all of its recent wars—1948, 1956, 1967—than the public in the United States has shown for all but World War II. Whether the American public is more or less enthusiastic or antagonistic about its participation in armed conflicts is not interpretable from these statistics. But it is evident that wars are responded to differently, that some have more support than others, and that the level of support is not a direct function of the number of American soldiers involved but is probably more related to the issues about which the war is being fought.

In a discussion of this type, in which foreign policy is one of several aspects of national policy under review, it is necessary to be extremely selective about the particular topics or events that are singled out for discussion. By even the most stringent of those criteria public reaction must be considered to the news of the atomic bomb and to subsequent policy issues concerning use of nuclear weapons and nuclear tests.

Within days after the atomic bombs were dropped on Hiroshima and Nagasaki, a national poll asked the public whether it approved or disapproved of the action. Of the respondents, 85 percent said it approved of the extraordinary action, 10 percent disapproved, and 5 percent had no opinion (AIPO). That only 5 percent would say they had no opinion is what is so unusual about the distribution of these responses. An event without precedent in the history of the world had just occurred. For practically all Americans it must have come as a complete surprise. There could have been no preparation for absorbing the enormity of the act. Yet, only days after the event, when it is fair to assume that most people still did not understand its consequences, or indeed the factors that were involved in the decision to use the bomb, only 5 percent said "no opinion." The fact that there was almost consensus in the public's mind about the wisdom of the act, speaks to the extent of the endorsement that the public gave to its government for its policies in conducting the war. It is probably also a reflection of the strength of the public's enmity toward the Japanese.

In the years that followed, most of the public maintained a high level of support for the development and stockpiling of nuclear weapons. While the proportion who thought that it was a good idea that "we develop the bomb" was not as high as the support expressed initially for its use, it represented at least twice as many respondents as those who had second thoughts and opposed its development (AIPO). The public also continued to favor nuclear tests and when asked in 1950 for its opinion about the hydrogen or H-bomb, 85 percent said that it had heard or read about such a bomb and 69 percent approved of the already publicized government decision to try and make such a bomb (AIPO). An additional 9 percent qualified their approval by saying, "make it but don't use it."

The public, however, did not support a proposal recommending use of an atomic bomb in the Korean war—28 percent said we should, 60 percent said we should not, and 12 percent had no opinion (AIPO). It said, at that time, that it would condone the use of an atomic bomb if the United States were to find itself in another world war—77 percent said "yes" under those conditions which are admittedly more hypothetical than a war one is fighting at the time (AIPO).

A year earlier, when asked in effect to choose between two strategies as the best alternative for keeping peace in the world, "try to make the United Nations organization strong enough to prevent all countries including the United States from making atomic bombs" or "try to keep ahead of other countries by making more and better atomic bombs," the first alternative was favored by more than a two-to-one margin (AIPO).

As the years passed, and Korea was settled and Vietnam did not directly involve the United States, public opinion shifted more decisively into supporting international control and the banning of tests. By the time the Nuclear Test Ban Treaty was about to become a *fait accompli,* the American public supported United States participation—63 percent supported, 27 percent opposed, and 10 percent had no opinion (AIPO).

One could most accurately sum up the state of public opinion on this issue of nuclear policy by noting that to a very large degree the American public was informed and knowledgeable about a highly technical and morally complex problem. Unlike its stance on domestic socioeconomic issues about which public opinion tended to precede and prompt the government for more and quicker legislation, public opinion was more likely to follow official policy on the nuclear power issue. But the public's opinion and expression of support followed very closely behind the formulation of that policy, and indeed in its response probably helped put into law some of the administration's proposals.

One more foreign policy topic that demonstrates public concern and interest about major issues is the response that the public has shown to the job of rebuilding Europe and Asia following World War II. This problem, in its way, embarked the United States on almost as new a path as did the development of nuclear weapons. The United States had some limited experience in international aid following World War I, but very soon after the fighting was over a mood of isolationism and a desire to retreat into one's own borders and interests dominated American politics. This did not happen right after World War II; and although there have been some voices suggesting such action recently, it has not happened in the more than two decades since the end of the war.

One manifestation of this difference in public and governmental moods between the two postwar eras is the decision of the United States not to join the League of Nations on the one hand, and its strong and consistent support for the United Nations on the other. Another is the massive foreign aid program that the United States initiated in the form of the Marshall Plan and the Point Four Program in the years shortly after World War II.

When President Truman went before the Congress in December 1947 and asked it to enact the Marshall Plan, he said:

> The people of the United States have shown, by generous contributions since the end of hostilities, their great sympathy and concern for the many millions in Europe who underwent the trials of war and enemy occupation. Our sympathy is undiminished, but we know that we cannot give relief indefinitely and so we seek practical measures which will eliminate Europe's need for further relief.
>
> Considered in terms of our own economy, European recovery is essential. The last two decades have taught us the bitter lesson that no economy, not even one so strong as our own, can remain healthy and prosperous in a world of poverty and want [Bernstein and Matuson, 1966, p. 266].

Between 1947 and 1950 the public was queried about its knowledge of and support for the Marshall Plan at least a dozen times. When first asked about the plan only half the respondents said they had heard or read about it, but within two years, that figure increased to 82 percent. As knowledge grew, so did support, although not nearly as dramatically. But starting from slightly below the 50 percent level, public support increased steadily over a three-year period until it reached the 60 percent mark.

Support for the Point Four Program which was directed at less developed countries was even greater. When the American public was asked on three polls conducted between 1949 and 1950: "In general do you think it is a good policy for the United States to try to help backward countries to raise their standard of living, or shouldn't this be any concern of our government?" (NORC), between 72 and 75 percent answered that it was a good policy.

What assurance do we have, however, that public support for America's responsibilities to the rest of the world had not burned itself out within a few years after the war, that the American people had not grown tired or disillusioned or indifferent to their international commitments? The opinion about the importance of the United Nations described earlier is one piece of datum that they had not. But a look at the public's response to this straightforward but comprehensive policy question: "How do you feel about foreign aid—are you for or against it?" (AIPO), reveals that from 1958 to 1966 between 30 and 35 percent of the public were against it, 51 to 58 percent favored foreign aid, and 10 to 16 percent had no opinion. These figures do not describe a public that is apathetic toward, ignorant of, or opposed to the involvement of its government in the affairs of the world on a broad and extensive basis.

The final major issue in American foreign policy about which the state of public opinion is assessed is the China question. And it is on the China issue that the public's opinion fits more closely the traditional model that combines a large portion of ignorance, mixed with a heavy dose of rigidity, which in this case has resulted in a consistently echolike affirmation of official policy. Just prior to the toppling of the Nationalist Chinese government, the public was queried about its opinion of Chiang Kai-shek and the support that it thought ought to be given him. The results showed two things. First, the public was more unfavorable than favorable in its attitudes toward Chiang and more unwilling than willing to help his regime even if it meant that the Communists would take over all of China. Second, at least one-third, and on some of the items, more than 40 percent said it did not know or had no opinion about the topic in question (AIPO).

A few months after Mao Tse-tung became premier the public was asked whether it thought the United States should recognize the new government in China that was being set up by the Chinese Communist party. More than twice as many opposed as favored recognition, but, as on the item mentioned previously, some 40 percent said they were unfamiliar with the problem or had no opinion about it (AIPO). This was the period in which Senator Joseph McCarthy was accusing the administration of housing large numbers of Communists in the government, and allowing them to concentrate, particularly in the State Department, where they were, according to McCarthy, determining our foreign policy in various sensitive areas, one of which was China. It was also a period when the administration was working out its strategy for engaging in a cold war with the Soviet Union and her allies, of which the Communist regime in China was clearly the newest and most prized possession. When only 20 and 16 percent of the public in November 1949 and June 1950 said they favored recognition, they were probably accurately reflecting the state of official opinion on that issue.

Over the next two decades from 1950 through most of the 1960s, the American public heard little about what was happening inside China but it was queried regularly on two issues that seemed to represent the cornerstones of government policy toward China: (1) whether China should be admitted into the United Nations, and (2) whether the Chinese Communists should replace the Nationalist government in the Security Council. Both of those issues have recently been resolved in favor of the Communist government.

Of all the nations that have played significant roles on the international stage following World War II, the stance that the American government adopted toward the "new" China was the most monolithic. The United States was the only major power that did not recognize the new government and even at the time of writing, relations between China and the United States are not normal, although the situation has eased considerably following President Nixon's visit in 1972. The shift in government policy quickly was reflected in a significant warming trend in public opinion, just as the earlier policy had also carried over and seemingly determined public opinion. The public's responses to the two standard items asked from 1950 through 1971 concerning China policy graphically describes public opinion, as is shown in Tables 15.4 and 15.5.

Table 15.4. Replacement of Nationalist with Communist China on the Security Council (AIPO)

Month	Year	Favor	Oppose	No Opinion
September	1950	11%	58%	31%
August	1954	8	79	13
June	1955	10	67	23
July	1956	11	74	15
February	1957	13	70	17
February	1958	17	66	17
September	1958	20	63	17

Table 15.5. Favor Admission of Communist China to United Nations (AIPO)

Month	Year	Yes	No	No Opinion
July	1954	7%	78%	15%
July	1955	10	79	13
July	1956	11	74	15
February	1957	13	70	17
February	1958	17	66	17
March	1961	20	64	16
February	1964	15	71	14
March	1965	22	64	14
January	1966	22	67	11
October	1966	25	56	19
February	1969	33	54	13
October	1970	35	49	16
May	1971	45	38	17

May 1971 was the first time in almost two decades that a higher proportion of the American public favored rather than opposed the admission of the Peking regime into the United Nations.

Public opinion vis-à-vis China fits much more the mold described by Almond (1950), Key (1961), and other political scientists about the public's interest and knowledge of foreign affairs (see below). But it is not a good weather vane for measuring or predicting how interested or knowledgeable or independent of government policy public opinion is likely to be on other major issues affecting our relations with the rest of the world, assuming—and this is an important assumption—that the government is willing to inform and keep the American public posted on what is happening on any given issue. This strategy of involving the public through information campaigns seemed to have been adopted by the administration in the late 1940s in the area of foreign aid and economic development, and as witnessed by the level of awareness the public claims it had on these issues, and by the support it has shown for these programs, the strategy seems to have been effective.

USES

General

The review of the findings of public opinion polls on selected issues summarized above included references to subsequent developments which appeared to be influenced by the polls. It included references also to government policy decisions, especially in the realm of international relations, which influenced public opinion. The effect of government policy and actions in influencing public opinion may, of course, be regarded as important use of the polls. That is, the polls can be interpreted to show the impact of government policy and actions and thus keep potential leaders informed on the public support or lack of support of their policies and programs.

In the complex and interdependent society that constitutes contemporary United States, public opinion polls are playing an ever increasing role in the conduct of political affairs. The poll may well be viewed as a mechanism for facilitating interaction between the public and political leaders to replace the function of the town hall meeting in "the little community" which in the historic past characterized this nation. It is in order to examine the views of key political scientists who have attempted to assay the role of public opinion in a democracy.

Public Opinion in a Democracy

Many political scientists who have written about the relationship between popular sentiments or public opinion and democratic governments have argued that most policy decisions are made under circumstances in which extremely small proportions of the general public have any awareness of the particular issue. Four decades ago John Dickinson wrote that, "the task of government . . . is not to express an imaginary popular will, but to effect adjustments among the various special wills and purposes which at any given times are pressing for realizations. . . . These special wills and purposes are reflected in the small cluster of opinions that develop within the larger uninformed and inattentive public."

V. O. Key (1961) agrees essentially with Dickinson's view that most people have no opinions or preferences on specific issues, but asks: "What characteristics of the interaction between government and public opinion can be invoked to convert such a condition into government by, or in accord with, mass preferences?" Key's explanation is that broad popular sentiments are indirectly controlling. His argument assumes that while the public may have no position on specific issues or questions of policy, vague sentiments of "fairness," "justice," and "policy propriety" are widely held among the general public, and government officials are guided by these inchoate public attitudes in deciding day-to-day questions. Key also argues that there exists between the general public and the government a "layer of political activists or influentials" (composed usually of lobbyists or heads of pressure groups or professional organizations), and this layer interacts most closely with government officials on specific matters of public policy. It is this layer of political activists that in turn influences and mobilizes public or mass opinion on crucial issues. On matters of major policy, the basis for the public's reactions are likely to be the "fairness," the "justness," and the "appropriateness" of the governmental decision.

Samuel Stouffer (1955) analyzed the public's response to "McCarthyism" and its potential threat to civil liberties by emphasizing that the issues that have the greatest relevance and importance for most Americans are those that affect their day-to-day lives. Americans, Stouffer claimed, are intensely involved in private matters affecting their pocketbooks, their jobs, their children, and their health.

Gabriel Almond (1950) observed that "there are inherent limitations in modern society on the capacity of the public to understand the issues and grasp the significance of the most important problems of public policy. This is particularly the case with foreign policy where the issues are especially complex and remote." Almond argues that because under normal circumstances the American public is indifferent to foreign policy, when an event occurs that is perceived as a threat to national security, the public tends to "over react." He warns that the volatility and potential explosiveness of American opinion must constantly be kept in mind if panic reactions to threat are to be avoided. This observation does not mean that the American public is more or less interested and/or knowledgeable about foreign affairs than are publics of other societies. But, Almond stresses, "a lack of information on foreign policy problems among the American public may affect policy more significantly in the United States than in foreign countries."

One may continue along this same theme and note that ignorance and indifference on the part of the American public may have greater consequences for the rest of the world than an indifferent or ignorant public would have in a less powerful nation or one whose government was less responsive to the public's mood. Also, given the American public's varied ethnic composition and the special "loyalties" to foreign countries that different groups are likely to have, relative indifference or ignorance by much of the public may provide the opportunity for special ethnic interests to exercise greater influence on the course of foreign policy generally, and particularly in relation to certain countries, than would probably happen if the public as a whole was more aware of foreign policy. The claim here is not that such influence is, in and of itself, pernicious, or, on the face of it, necessarily against the best interests of the United States. It is argued that such influence may commit the United States to friendships or policies that do not reflect the underlying mood of the American public.

Having contrasted the public's greater interest in bread-and-butter type domestic issues against a lesser interest in matters pertaining to foreign affairs, it is also important to stress that any assessment of the American public's interest or involvement in international affairs must recognize that the rude awakening the public received in 1941 from its isolationist sleep of twenty years could not help but deeply affect its perception of the role the United States ought to play on the world stage. Perhaps, simply because its government did have star billing since at least the middle of World War II, the American public has consistently supported and advocated that the United States maintain an activist stance and a leading role in world affairs. National polls, for example, that have queried the public concerning its support for and interest in active participation of the United States in the United Nations show a high degree of public commitment to international affairs. For example, between the decade 1947 and 1957, when the public was asked: "Are you in favor of the United Nations Organization?" over 75 percent said "Yes" (AIPO). When asked on three occasions between 1947 and 1961 how important it was that the United States try to make the United Nations a success, between 79 and 82 percent answered "Very important" (AIPO). In 1967, less than 15 percent said they thought "the United States should give up its membership in the United Nations."

Whatever misgivings and disappointments the public has voiced concerning Vietnam, there are no significant signs that the public wishes to return to its pre-World War II isolationist position. On major issues of foreign policy over the past three decades (for example, the Marshall Plan, policy vis-à-vis nuclear weapons, and the United Nations), the public has been more informed and more opinionated than the traditional model of public awareness of foreign policy would have led one to expect. While foreign affairs and policy concerning its management has not assumed, and may never assume, the importance that certain bread-and-butter issues —such as farm policy, taxes, welfare programs—do on the domestic scene, the characterization of the public's traditional apathy or indifference to it may no longer apply. Contrary to many views which have been expressed, the evidence indicates that the American public is more informed about, more involved in, and more committed to the formulation and implementation of national policy than professional observers have described it as being. On domestic issues, particularly those of a bread-and-butter variety, the public is not only reasonably well informed and prepared to express an opinion, but has on many occasions led or prompted the Congress or the president toward passage of a program that might otherwise have been delayed for months or years. Welfare legislation concerning minimum wages, Social Security, and medical programs are examples of issues on which public opinion has preceded and prompted government action.

Civil liberties and civil rights, on the other hand, are issues about which public opinion has either lagged behind government policy or tended to support measures that are repressive of constitutional rights. Since the mid-1950s the Supreme Court and, to a lesser extent, the executive branch of the government have led both the Congress and the public in interpreting and formulating policies and perspectives on civil rights which were more progressive than those shared by the latter groups. In the area of civil liberties, the Congress and the president have quite consistently been able to depend upon the public to support actions and legislation that would contain dissent, that would limit the activities of dissident political groups, and that would control expressions of opposition and disagreement with official policy. The public's opposition to deviant political groups and its support of policies that reward conformity were manifest in the 1930s against both the right and the left and in the 1950s and 1960s most especially against the left.

The traditional view that the American public is largely ignorant of and indifferent to foreign policy has not been substantiated by this review of the national polls. However true such a characterization may have been in the era following World War I, it does not apply today and has not applied since the end of World War II. The American public experienced a profound lesson about the dangers of isolationism and the relative advantages of participation in international politics. Its commitment to American participation in and support for the United Nations, its backing of foreign aid programs and nuclear test ban treaties, all are illustrations of the public's change of mind and role.

Political scientists and other professional observers may still be correct in their belief that domestic policy, particularly issues that affect pocketbooks, safety, and health, are more salient and more interesting to the American public. But the image of an ignorant, indifferent public who neither knows nor cares about the commitments that its government is making, or the image that it is projecting to the rest of the world, is also without empirical basis. In summary, then, public opinion in national affairs is a more positive and a more active force than has previously been assumed, and this conclusion, based on the review of public opinion polls, in itself constitutes an important use of the polls.

REFERENCES

Almond, Gabriel. *The American People and Foreign Policy*. New York: Harcourt Brace Jovanovich, 1950.

American Association for Public Opinion Research. *Public Opinion Quarterly*. New York: Columbia University Press.

Bernstein, Barton J., and Allen J. Matuson. *The Truman Administration: A Documentary History*. New York: Harper & Row, 1966.

Douglas, Paul H. *Social Security in the United States*. New York: McGraw-Hill, 1936.

Gallup, G. (from 1965–May 1966: American Institute of Public Opinion). *Gallup Opinion Index*. Princeton, N. J., monthly. (Titles varied.)

Hyman, Herbert, and Paul Sheatsley. "Attitudes Toward Desegregation," *Scientific American*, Vol. 195, No. 6 (December 1956), 35–39.

Key, V. O. *Public Opinion and American Democracy*. New York: Knopf, 1961.

Stouffer, Samuel. *Communism, Conformity and Civil Liberties: A Cross-Section of the Nation Speaks its Mind*. New York: Doubleday, 1955.

CHAPTER 16

On Social Indicators*

The review of selected areas of social statistics in the preceding chapters and discussion of their various uses makes it clear that social statistics already play a significant role in the operation of our society. Yet, especially to those familiar with economic statistics, it is apparent that there is no systematic, additive way in which social statistics can be summarized simply to portray the state of our society in the same manner as the gross national product measures the state of our economy. GNP, as a measurement of the money value of all goods and services produced, despite a number of limitations, in general can be interpreted as a measurement of economic health. One reason this is so is that various forms of economic statistics to which money values can be attached, as, for example, consumer or government expenditures, can be added into a single aggregative figure.

Thus, it is known that the decline of GNP from $103.1 billion in 1929 to $55.6 billion in 1933 was an overall measurement of the impact of the depression on the state of the American economy. Or that the increase in GNP (in constant dollars) from $720.0 billion in 1971 to $739.4 billion in 1972 constituted an economic advance.

Can the same be achieved in the social realm? Is it possible to aggregate some combination of the types of social statistics which have been

---
* Teresa A. Sullivan, candidate for the Ph.D. degree in Sociology at the University of Chicago, assisted in the research and writing of this chapter.

discussed to produce a single figure comparable to GNP as a measurement of the state of our society? Is it possible to achieve such an aggregative index which would enable us to conclude that social affairs, as distinguished from economic affairs, are improving or worsening?

Another relevant question concerns the relationship between social indicators and social statistics. In what respects are they similar and in what respects different? Both social indicators and social statistics are facts about society in quantitative form. But social indicators involve not only quantitative measurement of an aspect of the social but also its interpretation in relation to some norm against which the statistic represents advance or retrogression. The interest in social indicators may, therefore, be understood as evidence of the growing usefulness of social statistics and, more specifically, as evidence of the growing concern about the social problems that afflict society and the desire to obtain measurements of their improvement or worsening.

Although interest in social indicators has heightened in recent years, undoubtedly in response to manifestations of intensifying social problems such as those embodied in the urban crisis, the quest for social indicators is by no means a new one. Efforts to obtain measurements on the state of society have taken many forms both on the domestic and international scene. Before the term "social indicators" achieved widespread usage, the same type of interest was expressed in such language as "levels of living" or "quality of life." In addition to "economic" considerations, efforts to obtain their measurement have also involved, as is elaborated below, concern with "social" considerations.

EARLY DEVELOPMENTS

In the United States perhaps one of the earliest antecedents of the current interest in social indicators was the monumental study of *Recent Social Trends* commissioned by President Herbert Hoover in 1929 and directed by Professor William F. Ogburn. Thirty aspects of American living were examined in 1568 pages. Although the depression and World War II interrupted the projected annual follow-up reports, the subsequent research in economic areas influenced the development of economic indicators.

On the international front the United Nations, charged in its charter with the promotion of "higher standards of living," undertook activities, in response to a Resolution of the General Assembly (527, VI) in 1952, that are relevant. Prior to that year, in 1949, recommendations relating to improved measurement of standards of living were independently made by the Social Commission of the Economic and Social Council, the Seventh International Conference of Labor Statisticians of the International Labor

Organization (ILO), and the rural welfare panel of the General Conference of the Food and Agricultural Organization (FAO).

On July 25, 1952, the Economic and Social Council, noting the action of the General Assembly, requested the U.N. secretary-general, Dag Hammarskjold, "to convene a small group of experts to prepare a report on the most satisfactory methods of defining and measuring standards of living and changes therein in the various countries, having regard to the possibility of international comparisons, to obtain the comments and recommendations of the Statistical Commission and the Social Commission thereon and to report to the Economic and Social Council at an early date" (Resolution 434B, XIV). The report of this Committee of Experts convened by the secretary-general of the United Nations jointly with the ILO and the United Nations Educational, Scientific and Cultural Organization (UNESCO), which the writer served as *rapporteur,* will be discussed below.

CURRENT DEVELOPMENTS

Twenty years later, the United Nations continues its interest in improving social data. The United Nations Research Institute for Social Development (UNRISD), in particular, is continuing research on measurements of levels of development which can be compared across nations and which include indicators of social, as well as of economic, concern. The countries belonging to the Organization for Economic Cooperation and Development (OECD) are developing a standard set of social indicators for international comparison. The member nations of the OECD, including the United States, have also begun collecting social data in more or less regular fashion. Some of these developments are summarized below.

Great Britain's official contribution to the growing body of social indicator research is an annual volume which is issued from the Central Statistical Office and which is entitled *Social Trends* (Nissen). Its purpose is to bring together some significant statistical series relating to social conditions. As befits the word "trend" in its title, most of the data are presented in time series, although some tables show cross-sectional differentials. The tables are grouped by government function as a service to policy makers and administrators. Short summary articles provide an overview of significant areas—for example, prisons, the labor force, and high school dropouts. Much of the British data come from the General Household Survey, which began in October 1970. The survey provides raw data on both individuals and groups at frequent intervals.

In 1957, the Danish Parliament established a National Institute of Social Research to collect and publish social data. Similar data are collected in France by the government's Planning Commissariat.

Japanese social scientists have embarked on an ambitious research program, developing social indicators to augment the national income accounts. Their goal is a measure of "net national welfare." The Economic Planning Agency of Japan has published the *Report of National Life in 1972*, a comprehensive set of data about social concerns in Japan.

In the United States, a great deal of research into social indicators has progressed in both the public and private sectors. The volume *Social Indicators* (Bauer, 1966) began in the public sector as an assessment of the social impacts of the National Aeronautics and Space Administration (NASA) programs. The book itself had notable impacts: it popularized the term "social indicators," and presaged the production of widespread research by scholars in private agencies and universities. Among these were the *Annals of the American Academy of Political and Social Science* (Gross, 1967); *Indicators of Social Change—Concepts and Measurement* (Sheldon and Moore, 1968); and *Toward Social Reporting: Next Steps* (Duncan, 1969).

A list of the notable government work in this area must include *Toward a Social Report* (U. S. Department of HEW, 1969). The National Science Foundation has funded scholarly research about measuring social change and, with the help of the Social Science Research Council, has established a clearinghouse for social indicator research. More recently and significantly the Office of Management and Budget (OMB) in the Executive Office of the President has published *Social Indicators, 1973*. This compendium, without analysis of the data, contains selected statistics on social conditions and trends in the United States. It covers eight different fields: health, public safety, education, employment, income, housing, leisure and recreation, and population. As explained by the director of OMB:

> In each case the focus is on widely held basic objectives: good health, long life, and access to medical care; freedom from crime and the fear of crime; sufficient education to take part in society and make the most of one's abilities; the opportunity to work at a job that is satisfying and rewarding; income sufficient to cover the necessities of life with opportunities for improving income; housing that is comfortable within a congenial environment; and time and opportunity for discretionary activities.

In brief, it is the purpose of the compendium of statistics in relation to the goals stated to provide a basis for judging the quality of life in America. The OMB plans to publish a second edition in 1976 in time for the American bicentennial celebration.

Almost all of the efforts to conceptualize, define, and to obtain measurements of social indicators have addressed themselves to the problem of devising a single aggregative measure of the state of society. And, in every discussion of the problem, a similar conclusion was reached: that it is not possible, at least not in the present state of knowledge and development of social statistics. Some approximations of such a desired index were from time to time suggested, and these will be discussed after examining some of the major considerations involved in the effort to measure the state of society.

CONSTRUCTING SOCIAL INDICATORS

As the definition above indicated, the development of social indicators necessarily involves concern with norms—the standards or goals against which the social statistics can be compared. This comparison, based on values embodied in the standards or goals used, converts "social statistics" into "social indicators." The process involved in developing social indicators may be summarized by referring to three essential steps. The first step is the determination of the realms or social areas for which social statistics are desired. The second step is the achievement of valid measurements of selected realms; that is, the collection of information and their reduction into valid statistics. The third step is the setting of standards or goals—the social targets in respect to which the statistics indicate progress or retrogression. As we turn to a longer discussion of each of these steps, it is well to remember that all efforts to develop social indicators have dealt reasonably well with the first two steps. The third step, requiring as it does value judgments, has been much more difficult and will necessarily remain an area of conflicting judgments and controversy.

Selecting Areas of Concern

The first step in constructing social indicators is the selection of the important areas in which to collect data. This step has resulted in many varied lists of concerns. Each of the efforts considered above has its own set of areas. For example, in the volume by Sheldon and Moore (1968), chapters are devoted to each of the following topics:

Population
Measurement, Knowledge, and Technology
Politics
Family
Religion
Consumption
Leisure
Health
Education
Stratification and Mobility
Welfare

The hurried volume published in the lame-duck days of the Johnson administration (U. S. Department of HEW, 1969) also included public order and safety, income and poverty, and participation and alienation, as well as some variants on Sheldon and Moore's areas (e.g., "learning, science, and art" in place of "education"). The variations in areas treated reflect developments in measurement (e.g., illness), new areas of concern (e.g., environment and public safety), and advances in social science (e.g., measurement of social mobility). Such variable listings make international comparisons difficult, for not every country collects data in every area. It is for this reason that Phase I of the OECD Social Indicator project concentrated on listing common areas of social concern.

Eleanor Bernert Sheldon (1971) suggests that the areas in which social indicators are collected are set by three sorts of problems. The first is the problem of evaluating ongoing public programs. For example, an evaluation of Head Start would suggest the need for data in at least the three areas of education, family income, and perhaps social mobility. Dr. Sheldon suggests that not only acknowledged social goals such as industrial safety should be taken into account in establishing substantive areas of concern, but, also, emerging areas of concern should be included. For example, although safe machinery is an acknowledged area of industrial safety, the monotony of attending that machine is not an explicit area of concern. Job satisfaction may be an emerging goal.

The second sort of problem which determines the selection of areas of concern is description of the general state of society and of social change, even when no public policy is directly involved. For example, an indicator of how Americans budget their time could illustrate social change in leisure activities and family life.

Finally, the problems which social scientists study determine areas in which social indicators are needed. Social indicators may be explicit operationalizations of concepts in a causal model of the social system. For example, a hypothesis specifying the relationship of education to social mobility cannot be tested unless there are adequate measures of both education and mobility available.

The preceding discussion suggests that even when an official or quasi-official list of social indicators has been compiled, as in Great Britain, Denmark, and France, the substantive areas included are subject to change. When areas of concern have been selected, it is necessary to pick appropriate measurements in each area.

Measurements in Substantive Areas of Concern

Finding appropriate measurements within each area of concern can be difficult in highly abstract areas which are removed from government policy-making. For example, measuring the productivity of scientists is a difficult problem, involving subtle definitions and value judgments even in the selection of an appropriate statistic. Many social statistics are by-products of government administration, and there is a natural tendency for persons to deal with the data already available. The *Statistical Abstract of the United States* brings together a great deal of statistical matter which the government collects in the course of administration. Much of the data in the *Statistical Abstract* deals with areas of substantive social concern, but not all areas are included.

One frontier of measurement specification in social indicator research is the attempt to collect relatively "soft" or more subjective kinds of data. For example, people's confidence in the president usually is measured by a national sample survey of the population. Whenever people's attitudes or values are proper areas of measurement, more subjective kinds of data are needed. Subjective data may also be applied to areas of concern in which other social statistics, easier to quantify and therefore "harder," also are reported. For example, recidivism rates, judicial caseloads, and the distribution of sentences to convicted criminals are all relatively easy to quantify when the area of concern is public order and criminal justice. More subjective data may be equally enlightening. For example, victimization surveys have demonstrated that many crimes are never reported. This piece of "soft" data makes one wonder about the accuracy of crime rates. Attitudes toward the death penalty, feelings of personal security, and support of the police are more qualitative kinds of measurement which might be useful in describing the state of public order and criminal justice.

Just which statistics are the best ones to collect in an area of concern is another problem of measurement. Statistical correlation of statistics with one another, comparison with arbitrary profiles, or the results of previous evaluations provide clues about selecting particular measurements.

Goal Setting

Goals, or social targets, provide the standard against which the social indicator is measured. Sometimes these goals may be consensually arrived at; for example, nearly every citizen would measure social indicators of crime against a normative scale which implied that less crime is a better state of society. Standards or goals may be set by using the aspirations of the population. Norms may also be set by experts based on varying mixtures of judgment and basic requirements determined by research; in cross-national studies, an arbitrary intermediate level actually achieved by some nation or by a socioeconomic group within a nation may be taken as the goal. In some areas—for example, infant mortality—only the *best* record of any nation may be considered to be the goal.

Goal setting is not an unambiguous task. Not every goal can be reached simultaneously, and the priority ranking of goals is a normative procedure in itself. Further, most social phenomena have multiple outputs. To determine whether President Johnson's war on poverty was successful, you must include some unintended outcomes in the evaluation—for example, higher rates of inflation. A higher rate of unemployment may be taken as a measure of retrogression against the goal of full employment by some persons; other persons may consider a higher rate of unemployment to be a measure of advance toward controlling inflation, or a measure of advances in technology. Thus, a single social indicator may be taken as a measure for several competing goals.

The U. N. Expert Committee, to which reference is made above, was concerned with the measurement of levels or standards of living. Earlier undertakings agreed on the differentiation of "levels" of living and standards of living. The former is a measurement of what the situation actually is; the latter is a measure of what it ought to be. That is, the "standard of living" is a goal or a target embodying value judgments. Accepting this differentiation between "level" and "standard" is the first step in efforts to measure levels of living. The word "components" has been adopted widely to describe the elements of the level of living.

The discussion below documents the attempts to measure levels and standards of living as a case study in the construction of social indicators.

Case Study: Indicators of Levels of Living

The International Labor Organization (1938) set forth the following criteria for determining the components of the level of living:

1. Its importance in the well-being of the individual according to generally accepted norms
2. How widely its deficiency in relation to "felt" wants constitutes a problem
3. The extent to which its deficiency could be remedied by human action
4. Its susceptibility to statistical measurement

The components, in turn, determine the choice of social concerns to be investigated.

Because normative considerations were necessarily involved in the result of the exercise, it is not surprising that values were taken into account in the criteria for selecting components. Using these criteria, the ILO proposed the following list of major components of the level of living:

Health
Food and nutrition
Education
Housing

Conditions of work
Unemployment
General levels of consumption
Individual security and welfare

The list clearly shows that in considering levels of living the ILO was interested in the social as well as the economic aspects.

A more extensive listing of components of the levels of living is that of the Food and Agriculture Organization. Although focusing on "elements of rural welfare," the list obviously has broad general implications.

A. Health
    1. Demographic conditions
    2. State of physical health
    3. State of mental health
B. Levels of income and consumption
    1. Income
    2. Material standards of consumption
        a. Diet
        b. Housing
        c. Others
    3. Savings
C. Conditions of work
    1. Literacy and skills
    2. Social adjustment
    3. Individual security
        a. Security of person
        b. Security of income
        c. Security of property
        d. Emotional security

Beliefs, Customs, and Standards of Behavior

The list of beliefs, customs, etc., is definitely more responsive to the United Nations Educational, Scientific and Cultural Organization's concern with paying "full regard to differences of cultures and values as well as to material measurements." However, it obviously strains the ILO criterion of "susceptibility to statistical measurement."

The U. N. Expert Committee adopted essentially the same approach and, keeping international comparability in mind, developed the following list of components:

1. Health, including demographic conditions
2. Food and nutrition
3. Education, including literacy and skills
4. Conditions of work

5. Employment situation
6. Aggregate consumption and saving
7. Transportation
8. Housing, including household facilities
9. Clothing
10. Recreation and entertainment
11. Social security
12. Human freedoms

It was the judgment of the Expert Committee that although the proposed components did not include all the significant aspects of life which in their entirety properly constitute the level of living, they did include those aspects which were likely to be universally accepted as significant. The committee then explored a long list of "indicators" within each of the listed components—that is, it examined the extent to which reliable statistics were available to provide measurements of the respective components. This approach, pursued in 1953, is still the basic approach being followed in present efforts to develop social indicators.

After investigating a large number of indicators for each component, the committee considered the availability of data for international comparability and, setting priorities, proposed that the following indicators be given emphasis in developing and utilizing statistics for comparing levels of living:

1. Expectation of life at birth
2. Infant mortality rate
3. National average food supplies in terms of calorie requirements at the "retail level," compared with estimated calorie requirements
4. Proportion of children five to fourteen years of age enrolled in schools
5. Percentage of population literate, above some appropriate age, total and by sex
6. Proportion of economically active population unemployed
7. Percentage distribution of economically active population by principal industrial and occupational categories
8. Personal consumption as a proportion of national income and indices of changes therein

The committee also placed high priority on three "synthetic indicators":

9. Subitems included under "national income data"
10. Change in per capita national income (in constant prices)
11. Average expectation of life (at birth and at various ages)

The Expert Committee considered the problem of devising a single synthetic indicator—a measurement of the overall status of a society. In its report the following statement appears: "It would obviously be desirable if the numerous separate indicators of the different components or elements of the level of living could be synthesized in such a manner as to present a single picture of the whole. In the opinion of the Committee, however, there is no satisfactory means at present of statistically combining existing indicators of health, education, employment, etc., into a single comprehensive indicator." This is a judgment in which up to this point virtually all who have tackled the problem have concurred. At least one exception, however, will be noted below.

Also significant is the committee's response to the U. N. General Assembly's request for annual reports on differences and changes in levels of living of the world's various countries. Its report states: "The Committee felt it necessary to emphasize the impracticability of expecting at the present time or in the near future significant measurements of changes in levels of living on an annual basis." This statement made over two decades ago still holds, certainly in respect to changes in the levels of living of nations, especially the developing nations. It does not necessarily hold for social indicators in an economically advanced nation.

The Increasing Need for Social Indicators

In preceding chapters we observed that statistics in the United States evolved in response to emergent government needs. The history of the decennial census and the expansion and changing character of the census schedule reflected the transformation from an agrarian society to an urban one. The proliferation of current statistics—economic and social—was a response to the need for more information for policy and program development, administration, and the evaluation of problems in both the public and private sector.

The depression decade of the 1930s and the increased government functions of the New Deal generated the need for considerable expansion in the production of economic and social statistics by government. World War II and its cold war aftermath required an increased flow of information from all segments of society and its reduction into statistics. Social unrest, increasing alienation, and physical violence associated with minority group problems stimulated further statistical expansion.

Perhaps the most important stimulus to the expansion and improvement of government statistics was the passage of the Employment Act of 1946 and the creation of the Council of Economic Advisors. Although the major impact of this development was felt in the realm of the "economic," the "social" also was affected. The act required annual economic reports by the president to the nation about the state of the economy, and so the more important economic statistics became "economic indicators" that were used to assess the economic health of the country. They indicated whether the economy was progressing or retrogressing. Key economic indicators, such as GNP, rate of unemployment, the Consumer Price Index, the Federal Research Board Index of Production, the balance of foreign trade and the balance of payments, and the Department of Commerce's synthetic "leading" economic indicators have become familiar to the public, commonplace in political debate, especially in election years, and have been closely monitored by the Council of Economic Advisors and by economists at large. The strengthening and broadening of the base for these types of economic statistics have made them increasingly reliable as economic indicators and even have led economists to talk about "fine tuning" the economy—that is, controlling fluctuations through the cycle of prosperity and recession. The advent of the Council of Economic Advisors and the increased government and private-sector use of the economic indicators have certainly been factors in the dampening of business-cycle fluctuations and the avoidance of serious depression, even if they have not prevented recessions and have not yet resulted in "fine tuning."

Despite the utility of GNP and other economic measurements, many have felt that such economic measurements give a poor picture of the state of the society. Thus one impetus to the development of social indicators has been dissatisfaction with GNP; one proposed source of new, broader indicators is manipulation of the definition of GNP.

For purposes of analysis, let us divide all goods and services into those which carry a price and those which do not carry a price. Further, let us consider that goods and services may be prized—sought after and desired—or unprized. Then we have a fourfold classification. Goods may be priced and prized, as, for example, are most consumer goods which are desired and are purchased in the market. Goods in the most general sense may be prized but have no price tag. Were the best things in life really free, they would fall into this category. Sunshine, oxygen, and leisure time are examples of this category. Some economists, notably James Tobin and William Nordhaus of Yale (1972), believe that to reflect the quality of life, such measures as GNP should put a price tag on unpriced but valued aspects of life. Other economists, including Arthur Okun (1971), maintain that it is impossible to put a price tag on human happiness, and so the positive aspects of human welfare can never be quantified completely.

There are still two categories of the classification to consider. Unprized but priced goods are what Tobin and Nordhaus call "regrettable expenses." They would include military spending here; most persons could find better alternate uses for the money, but they conclude that some expenditures for defense are regrettably necessary. In the final category—unprized and unpriced goods—we put, among other things, the noxious side effects of economic growth, including pollution in the water and air. Some have argued that unprized expenses, rather than being added to GNP should be considered to be offsets to the quality life, and that the unpriced, unprized goods should have dollar values assigned to be subtracted from GNP. Tobin and Nordhaus have tentatively offered an index of consumption, rather than of output, which they call Measure of Economic Welfare (MEW). Paul Samuelson (1973) has called it Net Economic Welfare (NEW).

A further complication with GNP is its aggregate nature. GNP measures the production of goods and services, but not their distribution; consequently, even GNP per capita is a poor measure of individual economic welfare.

Besides such dissatisfaction with current economic measures, a second impetus to the development of social indicators was the sharper awareness of social problems. The social turmoil of the 1960s—manifest in the unrest of racial minorities; the disaffection and outbursts of radical student groups; the alienation and demonstrations of Vietnam war protesters; the growing discontent of environmentalists; and the ubiquitous and depressing menace of the "urban crisis"—prompted some leaders to feel the need for a Council of Social Advisors to parallel the Council of Economic Advisors. A Council of Social Advisors would monitor the state of society as the Council of Economic Advisors monitors the state of the economy, and it would require a Presidential Social Report to the nation to parallel the Economic Report.

On February 6, 1967, Senator Walter Mondale (D-Minn.), for himself and other senators, introduced a bill entitled the Full Opportunity and Social Accounting Act. This bill provided for the creation of a "Council of Social Advisors to the President," and a "Social Report of the President" to parallel the provisions for the Council of Economic Advisors. The bill spells out the goals in respect to which the social indicators would measure change—progress toward their attainment or retrogression. The statement, although in very general terms, explicitly provides a setting within which social statistics could be used to monitor change and to assay whether it was in the desired direction. The "Declaration of Policy" declares:

> Sec. 2. In order to promote the general welfare, the Congress declares that it is the continuing policy and responsibility of the Federal Government, consistent with the primary responsibilities of states and local governments and the private sector, to promote and encourage such conditions as will give every American the opportunity to live in decency and dignity, and to provide a clear and precise picture of whether such conditions are promoted and encouraged in such areas as health, education and training, rehabilitation, housing, vocational opportunities, the arts and humanities, and special assistance for the mentally ill and retarded, the deprived, the abandoned, and the criminal, and by measuring progress in meeting such needs.

The writer was among those who testified on behalf of the bill before the

Senate Subcommittee on Government Research of the Committee of Government Operations. The writer's belief in the role that a Council of Social Advisors and a Social Report could play as expressed at the Senate Hearings is relevant:

> ... I should like to express the judgment that over the years, had there been a Social Report to the Nation to parallel the Economic Report, among other things, we might not have had to face the consequences of accumulated social tensions as manifest in the guerrilla warfare sweeping this Nation on the home front . . . There is no question but that our most severe problems on the domestic front, including our racial problems, are directly traceable to this Nation's failure to face up to her social problems with the same candor and determination that have characterized her approach to economic problems over the past 20 years [U. S. Senate, 1967, p. 154].

In July 1972, the Senate passed a Full Opportunity and National Goals and Priorities Act (S. 5). The administration testified against the bill, primarily on the grounds that a Council of Social Advisors would represent duplication of effort and would raise jurisdictional problems with the Council of Economic Advisors and other agencies. Further, the administration argued that social measurement is not sufficiently advanced for a meaningful social report.

Synthetic Social Indicators

There is no framework in the realm of the social area comparable to GNP as a single indicator of the state of society. This fact has led some to conclude that, therefore, it is not really possible to monitor the health of society. This is an erroneous conclusion because there are social statistics which tell a great deal about the state of a society even if they cannot be integrated into a single index.

One such statistic is the expectation of life at birth or at other ages. For example, in 1969 expectation of life at birth for white males in the United States was 67.8 years, whereas that for Negro and other males was 60.5 years. For white females and Negro and other females, respectively, the figures were 75.1 years and 68.4 years. Thus, despite convergence in mortality rates over the years, Negro and other minority males, on the average, died 7.3 years before white males; and Negro and other minority females, on the average, died 6.7 years earlier than white females. Because expectation of life may be interpreted as the net effect of all factors—physical, social, economic, political, etc.—on the ability of a people to survive, it has broad special significance for assaying the health of society. Certainly the differentials in life expectation between the majority and minority peoples in the United States is not consistent with our profession of equality of opportunity for all.

Another statistic with broad social significance is the infant mortality rate—an important factor in the differentials in expectation of life at birth. In 1968, the Negro and other minority infant mortality rate, at a level of 34.8 (infant deaths per 1000 births) was almost twice as high as white infant mortality at 19.2. The ability of infants to survive their first year of life is also a measurement of the net effect of social, economic, and political factors, as well as biological factors. The decline of total infant mortality in the nation, from 47.0 in 1940 to 19.8 in 1970, can certainly be taken as a measurement of progress in the general level of health and welfare of the population.

Similarly, statistics on years of schooling for the various population groupings over time have special significance as an indicator of societal health in our urban order in which education, as a reflection of investment in human resources, plays a major role in the achievement potential of individuals and in the cultural, as well as economic, level of the nation.

Another example of an especially significant social statistic for use as a social indicator is afforded by the statistics on poverty in the United States. On the basis of available data it was estimated by the writer, as presented in testimony at the Senate hearings on the Full Opportunity and Social Accounting Act, that over 90 percent of youngsters in Negro families having five or more children were being reared in poverty. Such a statistic has great import in anticipating the problems likely to face the next generations of Americans. Moreover, the statistics on income distribution, revealing the extent to which, in this most affluent of all nations, large-scale poverty is still in evidence, point to the problems which affect the social order as well as to an aspect of the state of our economy.

It should be abundantly clear that the absence of a social accounting framework comparable to that which GNP provides for economics does not mean that social accounting in the sense discussed is not possible. Furthermore, although a single synthetic indicator is not at hand, research is underway which may produce better general social indicators. For example, at the United Nations Research Institute on Social Development a synthetic summary indicator has been developed as an index of economic development for international comparative purposes which appears to have many advantages over GNP per capita as a general economic indicator and which has important and separable social components that can also be synthesized.

CONCLUDING OBSERVATIONS

As concern over social problems increases it may be anticipated that social statistics will continue to proliferate and that social science research will find better ways to use statistics as social indicators. The social statistics which have been discussed in the preceding chapters and other social data not touched upon in this volume will continue to be used in the interest of society even if not in as systematic and effective a manner as are our economic statistics through the Council of Economic Advisors to the President and the President's Economic Report.

The previous chapters have pointed to some of the gaps in the data with which they are concerned. It may be anticipated that these gaps will be filled and that such statistics will continue to expand in base and content as new needs are felt and new demands are placed upon them.

Much progress has been achieved in the development of social statistics since Professor Richard Mayo-Smith (1910) said:

> We are surrounded by sociological or social problems which urgently demand solution. We cannot wait for the completed science; we must seek to understand the conditions affecting the particular problem before us. This may be called practical sociology. Everywhere in this domain we find statistics a useful instrument of investigation [p. 16].

But there is yet a long way to go in the development of social statistics and their use in the solution of social problems. This is attested to in a National Science Foundation Report (1969). In its recommendations the Special Commission on the Social Sciences of the National Science Board stated:

> The Federal Government, universities and private funding groups should provide the resources necessary for both government and private research organizations to develop new, more frequent, and better social statistics to record the important aspects of American life as yet relatively unstructured [p. xvi].

The record is clear that social statistics have evolved in response to the needs of the changing social order. As social change has generated new and unprecedented problems, both government and the private sector have, in efforts to cope, required more and more information as a foundation for policy formation and action programs. Economic statistics have been more rapidly developed than social statistics, especially since the passage of the Employment Act of 1946; and under the requirements of that act economic statistics have been used as a basis for monitoring the state of the economy and the development of policies and programs to stimulate economic change in desired directions.

There is as yet no legislation requiring parallel uses of data in the realm of the social, although consideration of such legislation has begun. The major barrier which still exists to the passage of such legislation is to be found in the fact that the nation has achieved reasonable consensus in respect of economic goals but has yet to do so in respect to social goals. Certainly, there is no widespread concerted national effort to achieve such goals as the elimination of the disadvantaged position of minority groups, or the initiation of effective programs to assure a more equitable distribution of income, health services, housing, and education. There is no concerted national effort to eliminate racism, poverty, slums, and ghettos. But there is increasing awareness of these types of social problems and determination on the part of many to come to grips with them. As the nation increasingly makes its social goals explicit, it may be expected that the need for and the utilization of statistics as social indicators will result in substantially the same course being followed in the social area that has already been traversed in the economic area.

REFERENCES

Bauer, Raymond. *Social Indicators*. Cambridge, Mass.: M.I.T. Press, 1966.
Duncan, Otis Dudley. *Toward Social Reporting: Next Steps*. New York: Russell Sage Foundation, 1967.
Economic Planning Agency of Japan (Keizai Kikakucho). *Report of National Life in 1972*.
Gross, Bertram (Ed.). *Social Goals and Indicators of American Society. Annals of the American Academy of Political and Social Science*. Vol. 1, May 1967; Vol. 2, September 1970.
Nissen, Muriel (Ed.). *Social Trends*. Central Statistical Office. London: Her Majesty's Stationery Office, annual.
Okun, Arthur. "Social Welfare Has No Price Tag." *Survey of Current Business*, July 1971.
President's Research Committee on Social Trends. *Recent Social Trends in the United States*. New York: McGraw-Hill, 1933.
Samuelson, Paul A. *Economics*. 9th ed. New York: McGraw-Hill, 1973.
Sheldon, Eleanor Bernert. "Social Reporting for the 1970s." *Federal Statistics, Report of the President's Commission*, Vol. II. Washington, D. C.: Government Printing Office, 1971, 403–436.
———, and Wilbert E. Moore. *Indicators of Social Change—Concepts and Measurements*. New York: Russell Sage Foundation, 1968.

Tobin, James, and William Nordhaus. *Papers on Economic Growth,* Vol. 5. New York: National Bureau of Economic Research, 1972.

U. S. Department of Commerce, Bureau of the Census. *Statistical Abstract of the United States.* Washington, D. C.: Government Printing Office, annual.

U. S. Department of Health, Education and Welfare. *Toward a Social Report.* Washington, D. C.: Government Printing Office, 1969.

U. S. Congress, Senate, Committee on Government Operations, Subcommittee on Government Research. *Hearings on the Full Opportunity and Social Accounting Act (S. 843).* 90th Congress, 1st sess. Washington, D. C.: Government Printing Office, 1967.

Index

Accidents, automobile, 57
Accountability, 79, 81, 89
Accounting, 5–6
Achievement, educational, 83, 92
Activist, 164
Adams, F. G., 201
Addicts, narcotics, 166, 167–168
Adult Basic Education Act, 25
Adult education, 88
Advertising
    and construction data, 226
    and consumer data, 202
    and crime, 177–179
    and population data, 35, 37, 38
    and recreation data, 252, 266
    See also Business.
Advisory Commission on Intergovernmental Relations, 28–29, 278, 283, 290
Advisory committees, and education data, 94–95
Age
    and crime data, 183–184
    data, 24, 27
    distribution, and education data, 80
Age Discrimination Employment Act, 132
Aged, the, 136
    and labor-force data, 132–133
    and public opinion *re* pensions for, 312–318
Aging, President's Council on, 132
Agriculture, employment in, 114
Agriculture, Quinquennial Census of, 15

Agriculture, U.S. Department of, 15, 64, 111, 194, 200, 202, 280
    Agricultural Experimental Stations, 25
    Agricultural Research Service, 201, 203, 206, 207
    Cooperative Agricultural Extension Service, 25
    Cooperative State Research Service, 25
    Economic Research Service, 15, 114, 228
    Family Economics Review, 201, 206
    Farmers Home Administration, 211
    Food Stamp Program, 136, 141
    Forest Service, 255–256, 264
Ahmed, P. I., 71
Aid, foreign, public opinion on, 330–333
Aid to the Blind (AB), 136, 141, 142, 144, 157
Aid to Families with Dependent Children (AFDC), 74, 96, 136, 141, 142, 143–144, 152, 153, 154, 157
Aid to the Permanently and Totally Disabled (APTD), 136, 141, 142, 144, 157
Alabama
    pupil expenditures in, 82
    recreation data in, 262
Alarm systems, as industry, 176–177
Alaska, voting data in, 301
Alexander, Frank D., 92, 104

Allstate Insurance Company, 177
Almond, Gabriel, 334, 335–336, 338
America at the Polls (Governmental Affairs Institute), 300, 310
America Votes (Governmental Affairs Institute), 300, 301, 306, 310
American Association of University Women, 131
American Automobile Association, 256
American Correctional Association, 185
American Council on Consumer Interests, 179
American Council on Education, 87, 99
American Federation of Labor and Congress of Industrial Organizations (AFL-CIO), 171–172, 188
American Federationist, The, 171, 172, 188
American Institute of Public Opinion (AIPO), 314, 317–338
American Journal of Sociology, 69
American Medical Association, 47, 318
American Opinion, 164
American Philosophical Society, 10
American Public Health Association, 47
American Rifleman, The, 183
American Sociological Review, 69
American Statistical Association, 11
American Trucking Association, 235, 249
American Trucking—Trends (American Trucking Ass'n), 235, 249
Amtrak, 236
Annals of the American Academy of Political and Social Science (Gross), 342, 355
Annual Report on Transport Statistics in the United States, Part 7, Motor Carriers (ICC), 235, 250
Appalachian Redevelopment Act, 25
Area Trends in Employment and Unemployment (Dept. of Labor), 115, 134
Argentina, use of U.S. recreation data by, 264
Arizona, marriage records in, 61
Arkansas, voting data in, 301
Assault, aggravated, interactions in, 170
Assessing Officers, National Association of, 292
Assistance programs, 135–157
Athletic Institute, 256
Atlanta, employment survey in, 113
Atom bombings, opinions on, 329–330
Atomic Energy Commission, 87
Attainment, educational, 81, 86, 92, 102
"Attitudes Toward Desegregation" (Hyman & Sheatsley), 325, 338
Audits and Surveys, 15
Australia, and use of U.S. travel data, 265
Automobile
  accidents, 57
  data, 235
  industry, 192
  registration data, 194
"Average Statistician (641.07 Words About a Pain in the Neck), The" (Miksch), 2, 21

Bahr, Stephen J., 164–165, 180–182, 188
Baltimore (MD)
  Eastern Health District, 60
  welfare data in, 143
Bankhead Jones Act, 96
Bankruptcy, as crime, 176
Banks
  incorporating, 29
  locating branches of, 35, 37, 38
Bauer, Raymond, 342, 355
Beall, George, 265
Bean, Alan L., 168
Bean, Louis H., 309

Index

Bennett, Edward H., 243, 249
Bernstein, Barton J., 317, 331, 338
Bexar County (TX), voting data in, 503
Bills of credit, statistics on, 9
Birch, John, Society, 164
Birth rates, 40, 46, 49
Births, statistics on, 20, 43–58
Black Panther, 164, 181
Black World, 164
Blacks
    comparative life expectations of, 352
    and crime data, 180–182
    and divorce, 70
    and fear levels, 163
    infant mortality rate of, 353
    and labor-force data, 130
    and the labor market, 122
    opinions concerning, 320, 323–327
    and poverty, 353
    and unemployment rates, 117
    and use of election data, 305
Bolivia, use of U.S. recreation data by, 264
Bond issues, school, 82, 92
Bonds, selling of, and population data, 32
Boston (MA), 127
Brimmer, Andrew F., 201
Brody, D. S., 201
Budget planning, and construction data, 220
Budgets, standard, 200
Budgets, state, 281–284. *See also* Funding; Funds.
Building permits, and housing data, 221
Burchinal, Lee G., 70
Burgess, Ernest W., 68, 75
Burglar alarms, as booming industry, 176–177
Burglary, cost of
    to business, 173
    to homeowners, 176
Burma, John H., 69

Burnham, Daniel H., 243, 249
Burnham, Walter Dean, 299, 310
Bus Facts (National Ass'n of Motor Bus Owners), 236, 250
Bus transport data, 236
Business
    and consumer data, 194–198
    and crime data, 172–177
    and family data, 71–72
    and labor-force data, 126–127
    and recreation data, 252, 265–267
    and use of data on governments, 286–287
    and use of housing data, 225–227, 229
    and use of population data, 34–38
Business Conditions Digest (Dept. of Commerce), 118, 134
Business Economics, U.S. Office of, 83, 193, 277
Business Week, 172
Busing, 324
Buy American Act, 120
Buying plans data, 204

Cade, June G., 300, 310
California
    Bureau of Criminal Statistics, 180
    Corona Unified School District, 96
    Department of Education, 95–96, 104
    Los Angeles, 69, 113, 177
    New Haven Unified School District, 96
    San Francisco Bay region, 124, 143
    Serrano case in, 102
    Vallejo Unified School District in, 96
    voting data in, 301, 302–303
    welfare data in, 145
California Achievement Test, 83
California Votes (Lee), 301, 311
Campaigns, political
    and population data, 38
    and public opinion polls, 313

360 Index

Canada
  use of U.S. recreation data by, 265
  and youth employment, 125
Career Guide for Demand Occupations, 128
Carey, Hugh, 165
Carnegie Commission on the Future of Higher Education, 87
Carter, Hugh, 59n, 68, 70, 75
Cash, Norman E., 172, 174, 188
Catalog (Census Bureau), 276
Census, U.S. Bureau of the, 300
  and CPS (*see* Current Population Survey)
  and confidentiality, 42
  and consumer data, 194
  and crime data, 162, 186
  and data on governments, 273–297 *passim*
  and education surveys, 79, 80, 86, 94, 99, 102
  Governments Division, 294
  Historical Statistics on Governmental Finances and Employment, 275, 297
  Historical Statistics of the United States, 16, 21
  history of, 47
  and housing and construction data, 210–211, 212, 213, 231
  and income questions, 3–4
  and marriage surveys, 62
  Pocket Book Data, 16, 21
  and poverty surveys, 67, 76, 113
  and recreation data, 253, 264, 271
  and special tabulations, 33–34
  Statistical Abstract of the United States, 16, 21, 236, 345, 356
Census Committee (House of Representatives), 7
Census of the Construction Industries, 209, 213, 220, 232
Census data, 28
  and the labor force, 112
  and the schools, 102–103
Census of Distribution, 15

Census Employment Survey, 112
Census of Governments, 280, 288, 290, 291, 294, 295, 296, 297
Census of Governments Act, 274
Census of Housing, 13–14, 15, 60, 209, 210, 221
Census of Manufacturers, 15
Census of Population, 108
  Decennial, 3, 23
Census of Religious Bodies, 15
Census of Transportation, 15, 253
Census of Unemployment (1937), 108
Censuses, 24
  decennial, 3, 23, 102, 103, 112
  development of, in U.S., 9–13
  of military manpower, 6
  opposition to, 3–5
  quinquennial, 15, 103
  and data on families, 59–60
Central Statistical Office (London), 341
Changing Patterns of Consumer Spending in the 1970s (NICB), 203, 206
Changing Times, "Spending Yardstick," 203
Checks, bad, cost of, 173
Chicago (IL)
  Area Transportation Study (CATS), 241, 244–246
  Community Inventory, 243
  employment survey in, 113
  Department of Development and Planning, 243, 245
  Land Use Survey, 239–240, 243
  metropolitan planning in, 242–246
  Plan Commission (CPC), 239, 243, 249
  Regional Planning Association, 243, 244
  Standard Metropolitan Statistical Area, 244
  transit traffic study in, 238
  welfare data in, 145
Child-care centers, and labor-force data, 122

Index

Children's Bureau, 162, 183
Chilton Research Service, 256, 260
China
    Communist, 332–333
    early census in, 6
    opinions on, 332–334
Chorness, Maury H., 89, 104
Christaller, Walter, 248, 249
Christensen, Harold T., 69
Churches, and population data, 39
Cities, classifying, 30. *See also* Governments, state and local.
Citizen's Advisory Council on the Status of Women, Task Force on Labor Standards, 131
Civil Aeronautics Board, 236
Civil Disorders, President's Commission on, 327
Civil liberties and civil rights, public opinions on, 319–327, 337
Civil Rights, U.S. Office of, 80, 104–105
Civil Rights Act, 25, 122, 132
Civil Rights Commission, 95
Clark, Joseph S., 121
Clawson, Marion, 267, 272
Cohen, Albert K., 181–183, 188
Cohort fertility analysis, 49
Colleges, 85–88
Colliers, 2
Columbia University, Center for Research and Education in American Liberties, 180
Commerce, U.S. Department of, 3, 38, 120, 194, 195, 198, 219, 350, 356
    Bureau of the Census (*see* Census Bureau)
    Bureau of Economic Analysis, 207, 217
    Bureau of Domestic Commerce, 231
    Business Conditions Digest, 118, 134
    National Income and Product Accounts, 200
    Office of Business Economics, 85, 193, 277
    State Technical Services, 25
Committee for Economic Development, 228, 286
Committee on Educational Data Systems (CEDS), 94, 99, 101
Committee on Evaluation and Information Systems (CEIS), 91, 94, 102
Committee on Government Statistics, 15
Common Core of Data for the 1970s, The, 102
Common Core of State Educational Information (USOE), 99
Communication data, 233–234
Communist party, 321, 322–323
Communists, 332–333
Communities, classifying, 30
Community Chest, and population data, 39
Comprehensive Health Planning Program, 45
Comprehensive Plan of Chicago (Dept. of Development & Planning), 245, 246
Computers, use of, 52, 57, 122, 291, 292
"Concentrated Employment Program," 119
Conference Board Record, The, 172, 174n, 175n, 176n, 188, 189, 202, 206
Confidentiality, 5, 13–14, 42, 140, 276
Congressional districts, 23–24
Congressional Quarterly, 301
Connecticut, voting data in, 302
Conrad, Charles, Jr., 168
Conservative Journal, The, 164
Construction
    data on, 20, 194, 209–232
    nonresidential, 212, 231
    President's Cabinet Committee on, 218

Construction Act Amendments, 96
Construction contracts data, 231–232
Construction Industries, Census of the, 209, 213, 220, 232
Construction industry, unemployment in, 121–122
Construction Industry Stabilization Committee, 218
Construction materials, requirements for, 213
Construction prices, measures of, 212
Construction trade, and use of construction data, 227
Consumer attitudes, data on, 204–205
Consumer Expenditure Surveys, 194, 199–203
Consumer Frauds and Protection, U.S. Bureau of, 179
Consumer Markets (NICB), 202, 206
Consumer Price Index (CPI), 193–194, 199–200, 203, 209, 350
Consumer Product Safety Commission, 51
Consumer Protection Hearings, 178
Consumer Sentiment, Index of, 195, 204
Consumer statistics, 20, 191–207
  economic and social, 193
  goals of, 192–193
  uses of, 198–205
Consumers
  and crime data, 177–179
  and use of consumer data, 203
Consumption and consumers, 20, 191–207
Contemporary Social Problems (Merton & Nisbet), 182n, 188
Contrasts in Spending by Urban Families: Trends Since 1950 and Variations in 1960–61 (BLS), 200, 207
Cooperative Agricultural Extension Service, 25
Cooperative State Research Service, 25
"Corporate Vulnerability to Crime" (Wilson), 175–176, 189

Corps of Engineers, U.S. Army, 247, 256
Cosman, Bernard, 308, 310
Cost-benefit analysis, 50
Cost of living index. *See* Consumer Price Index.
Council of Chief State School Officers, 94, 99, 101
Council of Economic Advisors, 16, 20, 117–118, 124, 134, 198, 217, 340, 341, 349, 350, 351, 354
Council of Oriental Organizations, 131
Council of Social Advisors, 17, 340, 341, 351, 352
Council of State Governments, 283
Counselor Education and Supervision, 180
"Counting the Poor: Before and After Federal Income-Support Programs" (Orshansky), 154, 156
Court statistics, 161–162
Credit, bills of, 9
Crime, organized, 75
  income of, 173–174
Crime, white collar, 161, 173–176, 187
Crime Commission, 160, 169–170, 173, 178, 186
Crime control, politics of, 166–168
"Crime and the Corporation" (Cash), 173–174, 188
Crime and Delinquency, National Council on (NCCD), 184
Crime and delinquency statistics, 20, 159–187
  deficiencies in, 159–162
  uses and users of, 162–187
Crossley S–D Surveys, Inc., 271
Current Population Survey (CPS), 60, 80, 81, 94, 102, 109, 110, 111, 112, 115, 118, 120, 126, 130, 133, 154, 254, 270

Daily Evergreen, 180
Daley, Richard, 309
Dan Ryan rapid transit, 245

Index

Dark Side of the Marketplace, The (Magnuson), 178
Davis-Bacon Act, 218
Death rates, 44–45, 46
Deaths, statistics on, 20, 43–58
Debt, consumer, 194
Decennial Census Review Committee, 4, 14
Defense, national, and population data, 27
Defense, U.S. Department of, 64, 87, 247, 280
 U.S. Army Corps of Engineers, 247, 256
Defense Education Act, National, 96, 128
Defense Manpower Policy No. 4, 119–120
Delaware River basin, 124
Delinquency data, 20, 159–189
Democracy, and public opinion, 334–338
Demographic Yearbook (United Nations), 73, 75
Demonstration Cities and Metropolitan Development Act, 25
Denmark, 69, 71
 and social data, 341, 344
Dennis, Samuel J., 209n
Desegregation, school, 95. *See also* Integration.
Detroit (MI)
 employment survey in, 113
 transportation study in, 241
 welfare data in, 145
Developers, land, and use of construction data, 226–227
Dewey, Thomas E., 315
Dickinson, John, 335
Diets, statistics on, 9
Digest of Educational Statistics (USOE), 79, 84–85
Directory of Public Elementary and Secondary Schools . . . (Civil Rights Office), 80, 104
Disability, data on, 47–48

Disadvantaged, the, 120. *See also* Minorities.
Diseases
 degenerative, 45
 infectious, 44
 notifiable, 47
Distribution, Census of, 15
District of Columbia
 crime in, 176
 pupil expenditures in, 82, 102
 welfare data in, 145
Divorce, interfaith and interracial marriages and, 69–70
Divorce statistics, 20, 43, 59–75
Divorce Reform League, National, 61
Divorce registration area (DRA), 63
Dodge, F. W., Division, McGraw-Hill, 15, 194, 231–232
Dodge Construction Contracts, 232
Domestic Commerce, U.S. Bureau of, 231
Douglas, Paul H., 278, 316–317, 338
Dun & Bradstreet, 15
Duncan, Otis Dudley, 342, 355

Ebony, 164, 181
Economic Advisors Council, 16, 20, 117–118, 124, 134, 198, 217, 340, 341, 349, 350, 351, 354
Economic Analysis, U.S. Bureau of, 207, 217
Economic Cooperation and Development, Organization for (OECD), 341, 344
Economic Development Committee, 228, 286
Economic Development Act, 124
Economic impact studies, 267–269
Economic Indicators (Council of Economic Advisors), 118, 134
Economic Opportunity, Office of (OEO), 25, 56–57, 101, 111, 148
Economic Opportunity, Survey of, 112, 126
Economic Opportunity Act, 124, 128, 129

Economic Opportunity Amendments, 26
Economic Planning Agency of Japan, 342, 355
Economic policy, housing and, 216–217
Economic Research Service, 15, 114, 228
Economic vs. social indicators, 339–341, 349–355
"Economic Trends in the Negro Market" (Brimmer), 201
Economics of the Property Tax (Netzer), 288, 297
Economy, domestic, 191–206
Education
 adult, 88
 higher, 84–85
 National Institute of, 92
 statistics on, 20, 77–105
Education, U.S. Office of (USOE), 79–105, 129, 201, 294
 Advisory Committees of, 94
 Bureau of Elementary and Secondary Education (BESE), 97
 Bureau of the Handicapped, 97
 Common Core of State Educational Information, 99
 Council of Chief State School Officers, 94, 99, 101
 Digest of Educational Statistics, 79, 84–85
 Education Directory, 86
 Office of the Deputy Commissioner for Development, 100
 Opening Fall Enrollment in Higher Education, 85
 Socioeconomic Research Abstract Series, 201
 Standard Terminology for Curriculum and Instruction . . ., 99
Education Directory (USOE), 86
Education programs, evaluation of, 100–102

Educational Communication, National Center for (NCEC), 80, 84
Educational Data Systems Committee (CEDS), 94, 99, 101
Educational Resources Information Center (ERIC), 80, 84
Educational Statistics, National Center for (NCES), 79–104
Educators
 and election data, 306–307
 and labor-force data, 129–130
 and use of data on governments, 288–289
 and use of housing data, 228
 See also Education; Students.
Elections, prediction of, 309
Elections data, 20, 299–310
 uses of, 304–310
Elementary and Secondary Education Act (ESEA), 25, 84, 90, 95, 96–97, 101
Emergency Planning, Office of, 27
Emerging Republican Majority, The (Phillips), 308, 311
Employment
 data on, 107–134
 governmental, 274–275, 277
 guaranteed, 318
 youth, 125
Employment Act, 16, 20, 117, 121, 349, 354
Employment Security, U.S. Bureau of, 113–114, 124
Employment Security Amendments, 120
Employment and Training Service, 113–114, 124, 128
England, Domesday inquiry in, 6
Ennis, Philip H., 186, 188
Eno Foundation for Transportation, 237, 249
Enrollment data, 80–81, 85–86, 88, 96–97, 102
 college, 129
"Equal Justice and the Problem of

Index **365**

White Collar Crime" (Morgenthau), 174–175, 188
Equal Opportunity Commission, 131
"Establishment data," 108
Europe, Western, and youth employment, 125
Evaluation of Family Service Program of Clinton County, N.Y. (Alexander), 91–92, 104
"Evaluation of the Guidance Program in the Los Angeles City Adult Schools" (Stewart), 91, 104
Evaluation and Information Systems Committee (CEIS), 91, 94, 102
Evaluation studies, 100–101
Executive Office of the President
    Council of Economic Advisors, 16, 20, 117–118, 124, 134, 198, 217, 349, 350, 351, 354
    Office of Economic Opportunity, 25, 56–57, 101, 111, 148
    Office of Management and Budget, 15, 17, 21, 100, 342
    War Production Board, 8
Executive Order of Sept. 10, 1963, 68
Expenditure Patterns of Low-Consumption Families (BLS), 200, 207
Expenditures, education, 77, 81–82
Exports and imports, statistics on, 9

Fair Labor Standards Act, 25
Fairfax County (VA), school system in, 97–98
Family, the, statistics on, 20, 59–75
Family Assistance Plan (FAP), 123, 145, 150
Family Economics Review (USDA), 201, 206
"Family Money Profile" (Pittsburgh National Bank), 203
Farmers Home Administration, 211
Fear levels, 163
Federal Aid Highways, 26
Federal Bureau of Investigation (FBI), 160, 165, 170

Federal Communications Commission, 161
Federal Highway Administration, 235
Federal Home Loan Bank Board, 62, 211
Federal Housing Administration (FHA), 211, 217, 224
Federal Power Commission, 256
Federal Reports Act, 15, 100
Federal Research Board, Index of Production, 350
Federal Reserve System, 281
    Board of Governors, 194, 198, 217
Federal Trade Commission, 161, 169, 178
    Bureau of Consumer Frauds and Protection, 179
Ferriss, Abbott L., 251, 266
Fertility analysis, 49
Fertility data, 69
Fesler, James W., 287, 296
50 States and Their Local Governments, The (Fesler), 287, 296
Figlio, Robert M., 189
Finances
    city and state, 274–289, 295–296
    educational, 81–82, 86
    See also Funding; Funds.
Fish and Wildlife Service, U.S., 254, 255, 271
Fishing and Hunting Survey, 253–254, 263, 265, 267, 271
Five States for Goldwater (Cosman), 308, 310
Florida
    Jacksonville, 143, 288
    recreation information in, 260, 261–262
    travel data in, 263
Florida Votes (Hartsfield), 300, 310
Foley, Warendorf and Company, 203
Food and Agricultural Organization (Rome), 265
Food and Agriculture Organization of the U.N. (FAO), 341, 347

Food Expenditures of Urban Families (BLS), 200, 207
Food Stamp Program, 136, 141
Foreign aid, opinions on, 330–333
Foreign policy, opinions on, 327–338
Forest Service, U.S., 255–256, 264
Fortune, 172, 317
Framingham (MA), 52
France
    constituent assembly, 6
    Planning Commissariat, 341
    and social data, 341, 344
    use of U.S. recreation data by, 264, 265
Franchises, and population data, 35
Francis, Wayne L., 300, 310
Fraud statistics, 178–179
Freedom of expression, public opinions on, 321–323
Friedheim, Jerry, 308, 310
Fuchsberg, R. R., 71
Full Opportunity and National Goals and Priorities Act, 352
Full Opportunity and Social Accounting Act, 351, 353
Funding, educational, 77, 78–79, 80, 81–82, 96–97, 102
Funds
    allocation of, 25, 31
    federal, to states, 29
    recreational, 259
    See also Finances; Revenue sharing.
Future of American Politics, The (Lubell), 311
"Future of Home Economics Research, The" (Leverton), 201, 206

Gallup, George, 310, 314, 338
Gallup Monthly Report, 314, 316, 338
Gallup Political Almanac, 301, 310
Gallup survey organization, 15
    Poll by, 163
    See also American Institute of Public Opinion.
Garelik, Sanford, 167, 168

Gary (IN), income maintenance experiment in, 151
General Assistance (GA), 136, 141, 142, 148, 157
General Household Survey, 341
Georgia, recreation survey in, 256
German American Bund, 321
Glaser, Ezra, 77n
Glick, Paul C., 68, 69, 75
Goode, William J., 68, 75
Goodman, Samuel M., 92, 104
Gone, Samuel Kimball, 300, 310
Government
    and consumer data, 201
    and crime data, 169–171
    and labor-force data, 117–125
    and use of the CPI, 199
Government, federal
    and education data, 95, 97, 102
    and educational programs, 84, 87–88
    and use of data on governments, 277–281
    and use of housing data, 215–221, 229, 230
    and use of population data, 24–27
    and use of recreation data, 264
    and use of family statistics, 66–68
Government, state and local
    and data on governments, 281–286, 292
    and education data, 95, 97
    and use of housing data, 221–224, 229
    and use of population data, 27–33
    and use of recreation data, 263
    and use of family statistics, 68
Government Statistics Committee, 15
Governmental Affairs Institute, 300, 310
Governments, Census of, 280, 288, 290, 291, 294, 295, 296, 297
Governments, foreign, and use of U.S. recreation data, 264–265
Governments data, 20, 273–296
    outlook for, 290–294

Index

types of, 295–296
uses of, 276–290
Grabhill, Wilson H., 69
Grants, educational, 152
Grants-in-aid, 25, 29
and data on governments, 278–279, 280, 284
Great Britain
and social indicator research, 341, 344
and use of U.S. travel data, 265
Gross, Bertram, 342, 355
Gross National Product (GNP), 124, 191, 193, 220, 225, 339–340, 350–351, 353
and education expenditures, 82
Guide to Family Living Costs (United Community Services of Metropolitan Boston), 201, 206
Guidelines to the Measurement of Ability to Pay for Health and Social Services (New Jersey Welfare Council), 201, 206
Gun control, 172, 263
Guttman scale, 325n

Haight-Ashbury (CA), 168
Hajnal, John, 69
Hammarskjöld, Dag, 341
Hansen, Harry L., 72
Hare, E. H., 70
Harris, Louis, Associates (HAR), 15, 163, 314, 322, 326
Harris, Seymour E., 88, 104
Hartsfield, Annie Mary, 300, 310
Hasten, William A., 165
Hatch Act, 25
Hawaii
LEA in, 81
and use of travel survey, 263
voting data in, 301
Health
and family size, 70–71
National Institute of Mental, 57, 177, 179
National Institutes of, 87

Health, Education and Welfare, U.S. Department of (HEW), 15, 25, 95, 99, 141
Children's Bureau, 162, 183
Health Services and Mental Health Administration, 43n, 57
Indian Health Service, 130
National Center for Educational Statistics, 79–104
National Center for Health Services Research and Development, 57
National Center for Health Statistics, 43n, 53, 54–56, 63–64, 66, 75
National Institute of Mental Health, 57, 177, 179
National Institutes of Health, 87
Office of Civil Rights, 80, 104–105
Public Health Service, 116, 294
Social Security Administration (*see* Social Security)
Toward a Social Report, 17, 21, 342, 356
Welfare Administration, 96
Health care programs, 56–57
Health Careers Guidance, 128
Health Examination Survey, 47, 48
Health industry, and vital statistics, 43–58
Health insurance programs, public opinion and, 317–318
Health Interview Survey, 47–48
Health Planning Program, Comprehensive, 45
Health resources, data on, 48
Health services
and census data, 41
and labor-force data, 122
and population data, 33
Health Services and Mental Health Administration, 43n, 57
Health Services Research and Development, National Center for, 57

Health statistics, 20, 43–58
  history of, 44–49
  users and uses of, 49–56
Health Statistics, National Center for (NCHS), 43n, 53, 54–56, 63–64, 66, 75
Health Survey Act, National, 47
Heart Disease, Cancer and Stroke, National Commission on, 51
Heath, Edward, 315
Helping Families Manage Their Finances (Agricultural Research Service), 203, 207
Hendrix, Paul, 263
Hidden Crisis in American Politics, The (Lubell), 311
High School Graduating Class of 1972, A Survey of the, 94, 101
Higher Education Act, 96
Higher Education Facilities Act, 25
Highway Research Board, 237
Highway transport data, 235–237
Highways
  data on, 236–237
  federal aid to, 26
Historical Statistics on Governmental Finances and Employment (Census Bureau), 275, 297
Historical Statistics of the United States: . . . (Census Bureau), 16, 21
Home Loan Bank, 62, 211
Home owners and renters, and use of data on governments, 290
Home ownership data, 202
"Home Ownership: 1980" (Linden), 202, 206
Homicide studies, interactions in, 170–171
Hoover, Herbert, 340
Hospital Discharge Study, 48, 54
Hospital services, and population data, 32
Household survey and data, 108, 109–110, 114
Households, income and expenditures of, 191–206

Housing, 20, 209–232
  Census of, 13–14, 15, 60, 209, 210, 221
  construction and repair of, 211–213, 230–231
  Inventory of, 210–211
  and population data, 33
Housing Act, 25, 26, 215, 216, 245
Housing contracts data, 194
Housing data, 13–14, 28
  uses of, 213–229
Housing programs, government, 211, 229, 230
Housing and Urban Development, U.S. Department of (HUD), 28, 211, 216, 241–242
  Federal Housing Administration, 211, 217, 224
  "Model Cities" program, 119
  Operation Breakthrough, 219
Housing and Urban Development Act, 25, 26
Houston (TX), employment survey in, 113
How to Lie With Statistics (Huff), 2
How Wisconsin Voted (University of Wisconsin), 300, 311
Howard, John, Association, 185
Hoyt, Homer, 238
Huff, Darrell, 2
"Human interest," crime as, 168–169
Hunting and Fishing Survey, 253–254, 263, 265–267, 271
Hurd, Richard M., 238
Hyman, Herbert, 325, 338

Idaho, voting data in, 301
Illinois
  metropolitan planning in, 244–246
  voting data in, 301
  See also Chicago.
Illinois Votes (Gone), 300, 310
Immigration Act, 25
Immunization, 44
Improving Ethnic Balance and Inter-

Index

group Relations (Calif. State Dept. of Education), 95–96, 104
Income data, 26, 60. *See also* Consumer data.
Income questions, 3–4
Income maintenance experiment, 145–151
Income tax
 "negative," 147–151
 public opinion on, 319, 320
Indian Affairs, U.S. Bureau of, 130
Indian Awareness, National Conference on, 131
Indian Health Service, 130
Indian Opportunity, National Council on, 130
Indian reservations, as concentrated unemployment areas, 119
Indiana
 and divorce records, 61, 69
 income maintenance experiment in, 151
 O-D survey technique in, 244
Indiana Votes (Pitchell; Francis), 300, 311
Indians
 and crime data, 181
 and enrollment data, 80
 and labor-force data, 130–131
Indicators, 118
 economic vs. social, 339–341, 349–355
 social, 17, 20, 205, 339–356
 synthetic, 348–349, 352–353
Indicators of Social Change—Concepts and Measurements (Sheldon & Moore), 342, 343, 355
Industry
 and population data, 35–38
 and vital statistics, 50
 See also Business.
Infant mortality, 45, 353
Inflation, and use of construction data, 218, 219
Information systems, 255–256
 and education data, 90–91

See also Computers.
Institutional Population Survey, 48
Institutions
 educational, 86
 nonprofit, 228–229
 See also Educators; Schools; Research.
Insurance company records, 9
Instructor, The, 180
Integration
 public opinion on, 324, 325
 school, 95
Interactions, criminal, 170–171
Intergovernmental Relations, Advisory Commission on, 28–29, 278, 283, 290
Intergovernmental Revenue Act, 279
Interior, U.S. Department of the, 25
 Bureau of Indian Affairs, 130
 Bureau of Land Management, 254–255
 Bureau of Outdoor Recreation, 253, 256–257, 259, 260, 271
 Bureau of Reclamation, 255, 256
 Bureau of Sport Fisheries and Wildlife, 254
 National Park Service, 255, 264
 U.S. Fish and Wildlife Service, 254, 255, 271
Internal Revenue Service (IRS), 175, 201
International City Management Association, 284, 297
International Labor Organization (ILO), 340–341, 346–347
International Statistical Institute, 16
International Union for the Conservation of Nature and Natural Resources, 265
Interstate Commerce Commission, 235, 250
Investment Bankers Association of America, 82
Iowa, 70
 income maintenance experiment in, 151

Iowa Test of Basic Skills, 83
Israel, war support in, 329
Italy
    use of U.S. recreation data by, 265
    welfare data in, 145
Jacksonville (FL), 143
    use of census data on governments in, 288
Jacobson, Paul H., 68, 75
Japan
    criminals in, 182–183
    social indicators in, 342
    use of U.S. recreation data by, 264
    and youth employment, 125
Japanese-American Citizens' League, 131
Japanese-Americans, and labor-force data, 131
Japanese Community Youth Council, 131
Jefferson, Thomas, 10
Jersey City (NJ), income tax experiment in, 149–150
Jewelers, and marriage data, 62
Jeweler's Circular-Bulletin, The, 62
Jewell, Malcolm E., 301, 311
Jews
    and crime data, 181
    polling attitudes toward, 316
Job banks, 122
Job Corps, 123
Job Guide for Young Workers, 128
John Birch Society, 164
Johnson, Lyndon B., 173
Joint Committee on the Economic Report, 118, 121, 125, 278, 297
Joint Federal/State Task Force on Evaluation, 91, 94
Journal of General Education, 180
Journal of Marriage and the Family, 69
Journal of Research in Crime and Delinquency, 184, 188
Journalists, and election data, 306, 307–309. *See also* News; Newspapers.
Jury Selection and Service Act, 26

Justice, U.S. Department of, 64, 179, 186, 188, 291
    Bureau of Prisons, 162
    FBI, 160, 165, 170
    National Criminal Justice Information and Statistics Center, 186
    "National Prisoner Statistics," 162
    surveys for, 280
"Juvenile Court Statistics" (NCSS), 183
Juvenile delinquency
    and population data, 32
    statistics on, 159–187

Kansas Votes (Cade), 300, 310
Katona, George, 191n
Kelley, Clarence M., 160, 188
Kenkel, William F., 68, 75
Kennedy, John F., 131
Kennedy Expressway rapid transit, 245
Kentucky, city classifications in, 30–31
Kentucky Votes (Jewell), 300, 311
Kephart, William M., 68, 75
Kershaw, David N., 150, 157
Key, V. O., 334, 335, 338
Kirkpatrick, Clifford, 68, 75
Knetsch, Jack L., 267, 271
Korean conflict, opinions on, 328, 330
Ku Klux Klan, 164

Labor, organized
    and crime data, 171–172
    and use of data on governments, 286
    and use of labor-force data, 125–126
Labor, U.S. Department of, 15, 64, 90, 92, 97, 112, 132, 219, 281
    Area Trends in Employment and Unemployment, 115, 134
    "Concentrated Employment Program," 119
    Employment Security Bureau, 113–114, 124
    Employment and Training Service, 113–114, 124, 128

Index   **371**

Job Corps, 123
Labor Statistics Bureau (*see* Labor Statistics. . . .)
Manpower Development and Training Administration, 123, 128, 132
Monthly Report on the Labor Force, 13, 254, 272
Women's Bureau, 131
Work Incentive Program, 123, 144
Youth Development and Delinquency Prevention Administration, 179
Labor force
 measuring, 13
 women in, 150
Labor-force statistics, 20, 90, 107–134
 definition and scope of, 107–109
 uses and users of, 116–134
Labor Standards, Task Force on, 131
Labor Statisticians, Seventh International Conference of, 340
Labor Statistics, U.S. Bureau of (BLS), 107–134 *passim*, 193–194, 199, 200, 202, 207, 213, 277
 Consumer Expenditure Study, 203
 Occupational Outlook Handbook and *Quarterly,* 124, 128, 134
Labor unions, and use of housing data, 224–225
Lake-Porter County Transportation and Planning Commission, 244
Lamale, Helen H., 191n
Land Management, U.S. Bureau of, 254–255
Land use, 20, 233–249
Land-use planning, and housing data, 221–222
Land and Water Conservation Fund Act, 259
Landon, Alfred, 315
Lanham Act, 98
Latin American Committee on National Parks, 265
Law Enforcement, President's Commission on, 160, 169–170
Law and order, public opinion on, 163–168
Laws, census data and, 25–26, 42. *See also* Legislation.
Lawsuits, vital statistics and, 53
League of Nations, 331
League of Women Voters, 214, 277
Lee, Eugene C., 301, 311
Lee, Ivan M., 267, 272
Lefkowitz, Louis J., 179
Legal provisions, and population data, 31
Legislation
 census data and, 25–26, 42
 and data on governments, 277–279
 and education data, 95–96, 97
 and public opinion polls, 316–317
 and use of family data, 66–67
 and welfare statistics, 152
Legislative Reference Service, 169, 278
Legislative Research Checklist (Council of State Governments), 283
Leisure-time data, 251–271
Lending institutions, and use of construction data, 226
Leverton, Ruth M., 201, 206
Lewiston (ID) *Tribune,* 164
Liberties, civil, public opinion data on, 319–323
Library of Congress, 64
 Legislative Reference Service, 169, 278
Library General Information System (LIBGIS), 94
Library Services, 96
Licenses, 29
 hunting and fishing, 254, 263
Life expectation data, 352–353
Life Insurance Agency Management Association, Division of Marketing Research, 201
Life, 164, 195, 202
Linden, Fabian, 202, 206
Lindsay, John V., 152, 165, 166–167

Literary Digest, 314, 315
Local educational agency (LEA), 81, 88–98
Locke, Harvey W., 68, 75
Longitudinal Retirement History Survey, 116
Longitudinal studies, 101
Look, 164
Los Angeles (CA), 69
 crime in, 177
 employment survey in, 113
Los Angeles County (CA), voting data in, 302–303
Lubell, Samuel, 308, 311
Lumio, J. S., 71
Lyle, Jack, 165, 188

McCarthy, Eugene J., 121
McCarthy, Joseph, 322, 332
McGraw-Hill, 15
 F. W. Dodge Division, 194, 231–232
McNally, Gertrude Bancroft, 107n
Macro and micro data, 195–196
Magazines, and criminal data, 164–165
Magnuson, Warren G., 178
Maine, recreation survey in, 256
Making of the President, The (White), 311
Malpractice suits, 53
Management and Budget, U.S. Office of (OMB), 17, 21, 100, 342
 Office of Statistical Standards, 15
Manpower Development and Training Act, 25, 120, 121, 123, 124, 128–129, 133
Manpower Development and Training Administration (MDTA), 123, 128, 132
Manpower Report of the President, 119, 134
Manufacturers, Census of, 15
Manvel, Allen D., 273n
Mao Tse-tung, 332
Marijuana, estimated use of, 177
Maritime Administration, 247

Maritime Transportation Research Board, Ports and Cargo Systems Committee, 247
Market analyses, 60, 217
 and family data, 71–72, 73
 and recreation data, 265–266
 vital statistics and, 50
 See also Consumer data.
"Market Profiles of Consumer Products" (NICB), 203
Market research, and public opinion, 316
Marketing
 and construction data, 226
 and consumer data, 201–203
Marriage and divorce statistics, 20, 43, 59–75
 users and uses of, 63–72
Marriage registration area (MRA), 63
Marriages, interracial and interfaith, 69–70
Marshall Plan, opinions on, 331, 337
Maryland
 Baltimore, 60, 143
 Dept. of Game and Inland Fish, 263
 Hagerstown, 54
 travel data in, 263
Master Plan of Residential Land Use of Chicago (CPC), 243, 249
Matuson, Allen J., 317, 331, 338
Mayer, Harold M., 233n
Mayo-Smith, Richard, 354
Meany, George, 172
Measure of Economic Welfare (MEW), 351
Medicaid, 45–46, 48, 136, 141
Medicare, 45, 48, 51, 67, 137
 public opinion and, 317–318
Mental Health, National Institute of, 57, 177, 179
Merton, Robert K., 182n, 188
Metropolitan Achievement Test of Reading, 83
Metropolitan Life Insurance Company, 62, 75

Index **373**

Mexicans, and crime data, 181
Michigan
   Tecumseh, 52
   and use of travel survey, 263
   voting data in, 302
   welfare data in, 145
   See also University of Michigan.
Michigan Votes (White), 301, 311
Miksch, W. F., 2, 21
Military manpower censuses, 9
Minnesota
   and divorce records, 61
   and recreation data, 262, 268
   University of, 268
Minorities, 3
   and crime data, 180–182
   and labor-force data, 130–131
   See also Blacks; Women; Aged.
Mississippi
   pupil expenditures in, 81
   school integration in, 95
Missouri
   St. Louis, 95, 143
   voting data in, 302
Mitchell, Robert A., 241, 250
Mondale, Walter, 17, 351
Montana Politics Since 1864
   (Waldron), 300, 311
Monthly Report on the Labor Force
   (Labor Dept.), 13, 254, 271
Monthly Vital Statistics Report, 64
Moore, Arthur L., 272
Moore, Geoffrey, 199
Moore, Wilbert E., 342, 343, 355
Morbidity statistics, 43 ff.
Morgenthau, Robert M., 174–175, 188
Moriyama, I. M., 43n
Morrill Act, 87
Mortality statistics, 43
   infant, 353
Mortgage insurance, and housing data, 217
Mosteller, Frederick, 19, 21
Motivation research, 205
Motor Bus Owners, National Association of, 236, 250

Mount Vernon (NY), crime in, 168
Moynihan, Patrick, 318
Multiple sclerosis, 52
Mulvihill, Donald J., 162, 186, 187, 188
Municipal Finance Officers Association, 292
Municipal Yearbook (International City Management Association), 31, 42, 284, 297
Muskie, Edmund, 279

Narcotics, alleged use of, 166, 167–168
Nashville (TN), use of census statistics on governments in, 288
Nassau County (NY) Vocational Center for Women, 90, 104
National Academy of Sciences, National Research Council Highway Research Board, 237
National Advisory Council on Vocational Education, 130
National Aeronautics and Space Administration (NASA), 342
National Analysts, 15
National Assessment of Educational Progress (NAEP), 83
National Association of Assessing Officers, 292
National Association of Counties, 284
National Association of Motor Bus Owners, 236, 250
National Association of Railroads, 286
National Association of Tax Administrators, 282
National Association of Travel Organizations, 253
National Catholic Welfare Conference, 79
National Center for Educational Communication (NCEC), 80, 84
National Center for Educational Statistics (NCES), 79–104
National Center for Health Services Research and Development, 57

National Center for Health Statistics (NCHS), 43n, 53, 54–56, 66, 75
  Marriage and Divorce Statistics Branch, 63–64
National Center for Social Statistics (NCSS), 142, 145, 183
National Commission on the Causes and Prevention of Violence, 169–170
  Task Force on Acts of Violence, 162, 186–187
National Commission on Heart Disease, Cancer and Stroke, 51
National Commission on Urban Problems, 278, 280, 290
National Committee on Vital and Health Statistics, 63, 66, 75
National Conference on Indian Awareness, 131
National Consumer Protection Hearings, 178
National Council on Crime and Delinquency (NCCD), 184, 188
National Council on Indian Opportunity, 130
National Criminal Justice Information and Statistics Center, 186
National Defense Education Act, 96, 128
National Divorce Reform League, 61
National Education Association (NEA), 83, 93, 99, 284
National Health Survey, 116, 294
National Health Survey Act, 47
National Income and Products Accounts, 200
National Industrial Conference Board, 15, 172, 203
  Department of Consumer Economics, 202
National Institute of Education, 92
National Institute of Mental Health, 57, 177
  Center for Studies of Crime and Delinquency, 180
National Institute of Social Research (Denmark), 341
National Institutes of Health, 87
National League of Cities, 284, 285
National Municipal League, 277
National Observer, The, 164
National Opinion Research Center (NORC), 15, 314, 324, 331
National Park Service, 255, 264
National Planning Association, 124, 228
"National Prisoner Statistics" (Justice Dept.), 162
National Recreation and Park Association, 256
National Recreation Survey, 252, 253, 254, 260, 268, 270
National Safety Council, 177
National Science Foundation, 87, 281, 342, 354
National Register, 115–116
National Student Vocational Loan Insurance Act, 96
National Survey of Hunting and Fishing, 253–254, 263, 265–267, 271
National System of Interstate and Defense Highways, 236–237
National Tax Journal, The, 289, 297
National Travel Survey, 253, 262–264, 269, 270
Nazi, American, Party, 164
Nebraska, LEAs in, 81
Negroes. *See* Blacks.
Neighborhood Youth Corps, 123
Net Economic Welfare (NEW), 351
Netherlands, the, use of U.S. recreation data by, 264–265
Netzer, Dick, 288, 290, 297
Nevada, voting data in, 301
New Beneficiaries, Survey of, 116
New England
  travel industry in, 263
  use of family data in, 72
  voting data in, 302
New England Divorce Reform League, 61

Index **375**

"New Federalism," 26, 133
New Hampshire, voting data in, 301
New Haven (CA) Unified School District, 96
New Jersey
    crime data in, 166
    income tax experiment in, 149–150
    welfare recipients in, 152
New Jersey Graduated Work Incentive Experiment, 148–151
"New Jersey Graduated Work Incentive Experiment" (Kershaw & Skidmore), 150–151, 157
New Jersey Welfare Council, 201
New Mexico, 61
    voting data in, 301
New York City (NY), 71, 143
    consumer expenditures in, 202
    crime in, 165–168
    employment survey in, 113
    heroin deaths in, 180
    voting data in, 302
    welfare data in, 145
    welfare recipients in, 152
New York City (NY) *Record*, 302
"New York's 19¼ Billion Dollars—Who Spends It and How" (*New York Times*), 202
New York State
    Educational Information System (NYSEIS), 90-91, 104
    Joint Legislative Committee, 166
    Mount Vernon, 168
    pupil expenditures in, 81, 82
    regional planning in, 242
    Scarsdale, 177
    school administration in, 285
    travel data in, 263
    voting data in, 302
    welfare data in, 145
New York Stock Exchange, 72, 194
New York Times, 164–169, 172, 176–177
    Research Dept., 202
Newark (NJ), welfare recipients in, 152

News, crime as, 164–168
Newspapers
    and criminal data, 164–165
    and population data, 37
Newsweek, 164, 177
Nisbet, Robert, 182n, 188
Nissen, Muriel, 341, 355
Nixon, Richard M., 66, 145, 150, 173, 218, 333
Nordhaus, William, 350, 351, 356
North Carolina
    income maintenance experiment in, 151
    University of, 300, 311
North Carolina Votes (Univ. of N.C.), 300, 311
North Dakota, voting data in, 301
Northeastern Illinois Planning Commission (NIPC), 244-246
Northwest Territories Ordinance, 242
Nuclear power, public opinion on, 329–330
Nuclear Test Ban Treaty, 330
Nutrition deficiencies, 49, 51

Occupational Outlook Handbook (BLS), 124, 128, 134
Occupational Outlook Quarterly (BLS), 128, 134
Office of Economic Opportunity (OEO), 25, 56–57, 101, 111, 148
Office of Management and Budget, 17, 21, 100, 342
    Office of Statistical Standards, 15
Office of Public Opinion Research (OPOR), 321
Officials, municipal, salaries of, 30–31
Ogburn, William F., 340
Ohio
    voting data in, 302
    welfare applications in, 144–145
Oklahoma, 61
    University of, 301, 311
    voting data in, 301
Oklahoma Votes (Univ. of Okla.), 301, 311

Okun, Arthur, 350, 355
Old Age Assistance (OAA), 136, 141, 142, 144, 154, 157
Old Age Income Insurance, 154, 157
Olmsted, Frederick, 242
Omnibus Crime Control and Safe Streets Act, 280
Opening Fall Enrollment in Higher Education (USOE), 85
Operation Breakthrough, 219
"Operation Shakedown," 174
Opinion, public, 313–338
  and election data, 306, 309
Oregon, recreation survey in, 256
Organization for Economic Cooperation and Development (OECD), 341, 344
Oriental Organizations Council, 131
Orientals, and crime data, 181
Origin-Destination survey (O-D), 240–241, 244–247
Orshansky, Mollie, 154, 157
Osborne Association, 185
Outdoor Life, 266
Outdoor Recreation, U.S. Bureau of (BOR), 253, 256–257, 259, 260, 272
Outdoor recreation data, 20
  background of, 251–252
  types of, 252–256
  uses of, 256–269
Outdoor Recreation Activities, Survey of, 270
Outdoor Recreation Resources Review Commission (ORRRC), 253, 256, 260, 267, 268, 272

PTA Magazine, 180
Palmer, James M., 95, 104
Parade, 180
Parnes, Herbert, 112
Paterson (NJ), crime data in, 166
Paterson-Passaic (NJ), income tax experiment in, 149–150
"Payroll statistics," 108
Penn-Jersey Study, 241

Pennsylvania
  income tax experiment in, 149–150
  voting data in, 302
Pennsylvania State Manual, 302
Pensions, old age, and public opinion, 316–318
"Performance contracting," 101, 102
Permits and licenses, 29, 221, 254, 263
Petersen, Svend, 299, 311
Phillips, Kevin, 308, 311
Pitchell, Robert J., 300, 311
Pittsburgh Area Transportation Study, 241
Pittsburgh National Bank, 203
Plan of Chicago (Burnham & Bennett), 243, 249
Planning, city and metropolitan, and use of transportation data, 241–246
Planning, recreation, 259–262
Planning Commissariat (France), 341
Plateris, Dr. Alex, 64
Plumbing questions, 4, 13–14
Pocket Book Data, 16, 21
Point Four Program, opinions on, 331
Police data, 159–162 ff., 186
Policemen's Benevolent Association, 167
Politicians
  and crime data, 165–168
  and use of statistics, 2
  and welfare statistics, 152
Politics, American
  data on, 299–310
  and public opinion polls, 313–314, 334 ff.
Politz, Alfred, Research, Inc., 195, 206
Polk, R. L., and Company, 194
Polling, public opinion, 313–338
  and election data, 306, 309
"Polling Day in America" (ABC-TV), 163
Polling groups, 60
Polls, 162–168
  data on, 313–338

Index

Pollution, 46
    and family statistics, 67–68
Pools, public, and population data, 32
Poor, the, 136, 146, 147, 152, 196
    health services and, 45–46
    types of data on, 27
Population
    Census of, 108
    Decennial Census of, 3, 23
Population Association of America, 63
Population data, 9, 19–20, 23–42, 102
Population growth, 46
    forecasting, 40–42
Population Research Center, 243
Port cities, and transportation data, 247–248
Poverty, assessing, 67
Poverty data, 353. *See also* Poor, the.
Precinct voting data, 302–303, 306, 307, 310
Presidential Ballots (Burnham), 299, 310
Presidential Vote, The (Robinson), 299, 311
President's Cabinet Committee on Construction, Subcommittee on Construction Statistics, 218
President's Cabinet Committee on Opportunity for Spanish-Americans, 130
President's Commission on Civil Disorders, 327
President's Commission on Law Enforcement and Administration of Justice, 160, 169–170, 173, 178, 186
President's Commission on the Status of Women, 131
President's Council on Aging, 132
President's Economic Report, 118
President's Research Committee on Social Trends, 355
President's Social Report, 351, 352
Press, Charles, 301, 311
Pretrial statistics, 186–187

Price indexes, 9. *See also* Consumer Price Index.
Primaries, data on, 301, 304
Prisons, U.S. Bureau of, 162
Prison statistics, 162
Private sector, and use of population data, 33–39
Privacy, right to, 3, 4, 13–14. *See also* Confidentiality.
Procaccino, Mario, 165
Projections
    and education data, 93
    and labor-force data, 123–124
    revenue, 282–283
Projections of Educational Statistics (NCES), 93
Public, general
    and labor-force data, 116–117
    and use of data on governments, 276–277
    and use of housing data, 213–215
Public assistance, 135–157
Public Health Service
    National Health Survey, 116, 294
    National Institutes of Health, 87
    National Institute of Mental Health, 57, 177, 179
Public Health Service Act, 56
Public Land Statistics, 254–255
Public opinion data, 20, 313–338
    accuracy of, 314–316
    and election data, 306, 309
    on law and order, 163–168
    review of, 316–334
    sources on, 314–316
    topics used, 316 ff.
    uses of, 334–338
Public Opinion Quarterly, 314, 316, 338
Public Opinion Research, Office of (OPOR), 321
Public Roads, U.S. Bureau of, 235, 236, 240, 250, 294
Public Roads (Public Roads Bureau), 236, 250

Public Works and Economic Development Act, 25, 120
Puerto Ricans, and crime data, 181
Puerto Rico
  as concentrated unemployment area, 119
  crime in, 168

Quality Measurement Project (Goodman), 92, 104
Questions, census, types of, 9–13
Quinquennial Census of Agriculture, 15

Radicals, public opinion concerning, 321–323
Race relations, and population data, 33
Railroads, National Association of, 286
Rape cases, interactions in, 170
Rapkin, Chester, 241, 250
Real Majority, The (Scammon & Wattenberg), 308, 311
Real Property Inventory, 210
Recent Social Trends (Ogburn), 340
Records
  marriage and divorce, 61
  medical, 53–54
  See also Vital statistics.
Recreation data, 251–271
  information requested from, 257–259
  uses and users of, 256–269
Recreation Information Management (RIM), 255–256
Regional Medical Program, 45
Reischauer, Robert D., 135n
Reiss, Albert J., Jr., 186, 188
Religious Bodies, Census of, 15
Report of the Decennial Census Review Committee to the Secretary of Commerce, 42
Report of National Life in 1972 (Economic Planning Agency of Japan), 342, 355
"Reporting to Management on Business Affairs" (NICB), 172–174

Research
  educational, 84, 87
  and health statistics, 52
  manpower, 128–129
  and use of construction data, 228
  and use of family statistics, 68–71
  and use of recreation data, 267–269
Research Facilities Act, 25
Residential Finance, Survey of, 210
Resources for the Future, 228
Retirement systems data, 275
Revenue projections, 282–283
Revenue sharing, 26, 31, 152, 279, 280, 294
Revenue Sharing and Its Alternatives: What Future for Fiscal Federalism? (Joint Committee on the Economic Report), 278, 297
Rice, David, 178
Ridley, Jean Clare, 69
Rights, civil, public opinion on, 320, 323–327
Rittenhouse, Carl H., 89, 104
River basin planning, 268
Rivlin, Alice M., 135n
Robbery
  cost of, to business, 173
  interactions in, 170
Robinson, Edgar Eugene, 299–300, 311
Roosevelt, Franklin D., 309, 315
Roosevelt, Theodore, 62
Roper Research Associates (ROP), 15, 321
  Public Opinion Research Center, 314

St. Louis (MO), 143
  Board of Education, 95
Salaries, official, 30–31
Salerno, Ralph, 173
Samuelson, Paul A., 351, 355
San Francisco (CA), 143
  Bay region, 124
Savings data, 194

Index **379**

Scammon, Richard M., 299n, 308, 311
Scarsdale (NY), alarm systems in, 177
Scheur, James, 166
School districts, census data for, 103. *See also* LEA.
School funds, and population data, 33
Schools, 281, 285
    church-related, 80
    elementary and secondary, 79–84
    and population data, 33
Scranton (PA), income tax experiment in, 149–150
Seattle (WA), income maintenance experiment in, 151
Securities and Exchange Commission, 161, 194
Segregation, residential, and population data, 32
Selective Service System, 27, 64
    and marriage data, 68
Sellin, Thorsten, 186, 188, 189
Serrano v. *Priest,* 102
Seventh International Conference of Labor Statisticians, 340
Sewer lines, and population data, 32
Sex data, 24
Sex ratios, crime, 182–183
Shapiro, Leo J., and Associates, Inc., 203, 206
Sharkansky, Ira, 289, 297
Shaw, G. G., 70
Sheatsley, Paul, 325, 338
Sheldon, Eleanor Bernert, 342, 343, 344, 355
Shoplifting, cost of, 173
Short, James F., 159n
Short, James F., Jr., 181–183, 188
Sielaff, Richard O., 268, 271
Simon, Rita J., 313n
Skidmore, Felicity, 150, 157
Slave trade, statistics on, 9
Slaves, 24
    census of, 11
Smith Lever Act, 25
Social Advisors Council, 17, 340, 341, 351, 352

"Social and Economic Characteristics of the School Districts" (NCES), 103
Social indicators, 17, 20, 205, 339–356
    areas of need for, 161
    constructing, 343–353
    vs. economic indicators, 339–341, 349–355
    synthetic, 348–349, 352–353
Social Indicators (Bauer), 342, 355
Social Indicators, 1973 (OMB), 17, 21, 342
Social Report of the President, 351, 352
Social Science Research Council, 342
Social Security, 20, 67, 135–157, 317
Social Security Act, 25, 128, 129, 141
    public opinion and, 316–318
Social Security Administration, 48, 115, 116, 133, 140, 294
    Medicare and Medicaid, 45
    and uses of statistics, 137–140
Social Security Bulletin (Soc. Sec. Adm.), 138, 142, 143, 157
Social Security in the United States (Douglas), 316–317, 338
Social Statistics, National Center for (NCSS), 142, 145, 183
Social Trends, President's Research Committee on, 356
Social Trends (Nissen), 341, 355
Socioeconomic Research Abstract Series (USOE), 201
South Carolina
    recreation information in, 262
    welfare data in, 144–145
Southall, Mart T., 166
Spanish-Americans, President's Cabinet Committee on Opportunity for, 130
Special Mobility Census Reports, 72
Speech, freedom of, public opinion on, 321–323
Spencer, L. M., 62
Spending in the American States (Sharkansky), 289, 297

"Spending Yardstick" (*Changing Times*), 203
Spokane (WA) *Chronicle,* 164
Sport Fisheries and Wildlife, U.S. Bureau of, 254
Standard Industrial Classification, 126, 127, 249
Standard Metropolitan Statistical Areas (SMSAs), 110, 114, 160, 199, 244–245
Standard and Poor, 15
Standard Terminology for Curriculum and Instruction in Local and State School Systems (USOE), 99
Standards of living, measuring, 339–355
Stanford Reading Tests, 83
Stanford Research Institute, 89
State, U.S. Department of, 332
State educational agencies (SEA), 88–98, 101
State Educational Records and Reports Series (USOE), 99
State Farm Mutual Automobile Insurance Company, 177
State government. *See* Government, state and local.
State Governments Council, 283
State Manuals, Blue Books, and Election Results (Press & Williams), 301, 311
State Technical Services, 25
Statistical Abstract of the United States (Census Bureau), 16, 21, 236, 345, 356
Statistical Bulletin (Metropolitan Life Insurance Co.), 62
Statistical History of the American Presidential Elections (Petersen), 299, 311
Statistical Portrait of Higher Education, A (Harris), 88, 104
Statistical Society of London, 7
Statistical Standards, U.S. Office of, 15
Statistician, role of, 1

Statistics: A Guide to the Unknown (Tanur, Mosteller *et al.*), 19, 21
"Status of Integration in the St. Louis Public Schools in the 1966–1967 School Year, The" (St. Louis Bd. of Education), 95
Statutes, census data in, 25. *See also* Legislation.
Stempel, Guido H., III, 165
Stewart, Robert M., 91, 104
Stocks data, 194
Stouffer, Samuel, 62, 335, 338
Students
 and crime data, 179–180
 and labor-force data, 127–129
 and use of data on governments, 287–288
 and use of election data, 306–307
 See also Education; Educators.
Sullivan, Teresa A., 339n
Supermarkets, and population data, 35, 37, 38
Survey of Consumer Finances, 195, 206
Survey of Current Business (Dept. of Commerce), 193, 207, 355
"Survey of the Decision Processes and Related Informational Requirements for Educational Planning and Innovation, A" (Rittenhouse & Chorness), 89
Survey Research Center (Univ. of Mich.), 204–205, 206, 300, 306
Surveys, 125, 126, 194–195
 Census Employment, 112
 Chicago Land Use, 239–240, 243
 Consumer Expenditure, 194, 199–203
 consumer information, 196–198 ff.
 Economic Opportunity, 112, 126
 General Household, 341
 of governments, 280–281
 Health Interview, 47–48
 High School Graduating Class of 1972, 94, 101

Index

household, 109–110, 114
housing and construction, 210
Institutional Population, 48
land-use, 239–241
Longitudinal Retirement History, 116
marriage and divorce, 61–62
National Health, 116
New Beneficiaries, 116
offense and arrest reports, 170–171
Origin-Destination, 240–241, 244–247
Outdoor Recreation Activities, 270
recreation, 268–271
Residential Finance, 210
Travel, 253, 262–264, 269, 270
Urban Employment, 113
victim and victimization, 186, 345
welfare recipients, 144–145, 155
See also Public opinion polls.
Swimming pools, and population data, 32
Switzerland, use of U.S. recreation data by, 265

Taeuber, Conrad D., 23n
Tanur, Judith M., 19, 21
Tarrance, Lance, Jr., 303, 311
Tax Administrators, National Association of, 282
Tax collection indexes, 9
Tax money sharing, 31. *See also* Revenue sharing.
Tax revenue data, 274–275
Tax-structure studies, 283
Taxes
    income, 147–151, 319, 320
    property, 279, 281, 284, 286, 290, 295–296
Teachers, data on, 82–83, 87. *See also* Education; Educators.
Teen-agers, unemployment rate of, 121, 124–125
Telephone companies, and use of construction data, 226
Television Bureau of Advertising, Inc., 172
Tennessee
    Nashville, 288
    recreation survey in, 256
    voting data in, 302
Tennessee Valley Authority (T.V.A.), 256
Terminology, educational, 99–100
Tests, achievement, 83
Texas, employment survey in, 113
Texas Precinct Votes (Tarrance), 303, 311
Textbooks, and data on governments, 287–288
Theft, employee, cost of, 173. *See also* Burglary; Robbery; Crime.
They Voted for Roosevelt (Robinson), 299, 311
Time, 164, 165, 172, 177
Tobin, James, 350, 351, 356
Tourism, 251–271 *passim*
Toward a Social Report (HEW), 17, 21, 342, 344, 356
Toward Social Reporting: Next Steps (Duncan), 342, 355
Traffic data. *See* Transportation.
Traffic planning, and transportation data, 246–247
Traffic Quarterly (Eno Foundation), 237, 249
Training and Employment Service, 113–114, 124, 128
Transportation, 20, 233–249
    Census of, 15, 253
    and population data, 32
    studies of, 237–241
    uses of data on, 241–249
Transportation, U.S. Department of (DOT), 235, 241–242, 264
    Federal Aid Highways Program, 26
    Federal Highway Administration, 235
    National System of Interstate and

Transportation, U.S. Department of *(cont.)*
  Defense Highways, 236–237
  U.S. Coast Guard, 247, 256
"Travel Expectancy Tables," 262
Travel Organizations, National Association of, 253
Travel Survey, 253, 262–264, 269, 270
Treasury, U.S. Department of, 198, 217, 277
  Internal Revenue Service, 175, 201
Treasury notes, statistics on, 9
Trenton (NJ), income tax experiment in, 149–150
Tri-State Regional Planning Commission, 242
Tri-State Transportation Commission, 242
Truck data, 235–236
Truman, Harry, 309, 315, 317, 318, 328, 331
Tumin, Melvin M., 162, 186, 187, 188
Twentieth Century Fund, 228

Udry, J. Richard, 68, 75
Unemployment
  Census of, 108
  data on, 108–134
  insured, 115, 120
  measuring, 13
  polled attitudes toward, 317
Unemployment compensation, 145
Unemployment Problems, Special Senate Committee on, 120–121
Uniform Crime Reports (UCR), 160–161, 164–165, 166, 168, 176, 179, 188
United Community Services of Metropolitan Boston, 201
United Kingdom, and youth employment, 125
United Nations, 16, 76, 185, 225, 331, 337
  admission of Red China to, 332–334
  Educational, Scientific and Cultural Organization (UNESCO), 341, 347
  Expert Committee, 341, 346, 347–349
  Food and Agriculture Organization, 341, 347
  General Assembly, 340, 349
  and marriage data, 73
  public opinion on, 330
  public support for, 336, 338
  Research Institute for Social Development (UNRISD), 341, 353
United States (government) agencies: *see pages and items under* Agriculture Dept.; Atomic Energy Commission; Citizen's Advisory Council . . . ; Civil Aeronautics Board; Civil Rights Commission; Commerce Dept.; Consumer Product Safety Commission; Crime Commission; Defense Dept.; Equal Opportunity Commission; Executive Office; *items under* Federal; Governmental Affairs Institute; Health, Education and Welfare; Housing and Urban Development; Interior Dept.; Interstate Commerce Commission; Justice Dept.; Labor Dept.; *items under* National; Outdoor Recreation Resources Review Commission; *items under* President's; Securities and Exchange Commission; Selective Service System; Tennessee Valley Authority; Transportation Dept.; Treasury Dept.; U.S. Civil Service Commission; U.S. Congress; U.S. Information Agency; U.S. Postal Service; U.S. Supreme Court; Veterans Administration; Violence Commission.
United States of America v. *William F. Rickenbacker,* 42

Index

United States Catholic Conference, 79, 99
U.S. Chamber of Commerce, 286–287
U.S. Civil Service Commission, 122
U.S. Coast Guard, 247, 256
U.S. Conference of Mayors, 284
U.S. Congress, 42, 47, 49, 66, 108, 118, 124, 253, 274, 291, 317–318, 337
   black caucus in, 305
   and development of censuses, 10–13
   House of Representatives, 7, 23–24, 64, 300
   Joint Committee on the Economic Report, 118, 121, 125, 278, 297
   Library of Congress, 64, 169, 278
   Senate, 64, 120–121, 352, 356
   U.S. Government Printing Office, 99
U.S. Constitution, 6
   First Amendment, 321
   Fourteenth Amendment, 12
U.S. Fish and Wildlife Service, 254, 255, 271
U.S. Government Printing Office, 99
U.S. House of Representatives, 23–24, 64
   Census Committee, 7
   Clerk of, 300
U.S. Information Agency, 64
U.S. News and World Report, 164, 176
U.S. Postal Service, 53
U.S. Senate, 64
   Special Committee on Unemployment Problems, 120–121
   Subcommittee on Employment and Manpower, Committee on Labor and Public Welfare, 121
   Subcommittee on Government Research, Committee on Government Operations, 352, 356
U.S. Supreme Court, 337
Universities, 85–88

University of Chicago, 62
   National Opinion Research Center, 15, 314, 324, 331
   Population Research Center, 243
   Sociology Dept., 243
   Survey Research Center, 15, 195
University of Michigan, 268
   Survey Research Center, 204–205, 206, 300, 306
University of Minnesota—Duluth Campus, 268
University of North Carolina, 300, 311
University of Oklahoma, 301, 311
University of Wisconsin, 300, 311
Upper Midwest Recreation Resources Institute, 268
Urban Coalition, 172
Urban crises, 17
   and welfare data, 152
Urban Employment Survey, 113
Urban League, 130, 228
Urban Mass Transportation Act, 25
Urban Problems, National Commission on, 278, 280, 290
Urban programs, and population data, 28
Urban Traffic: A Function of Land Use (Mitchell & Rapkin), 241, 250
Urban transportation, 237–241
"Use and Abuse of Criminal Statistics in Minority and 'Hate' Literature, The" (Bahr), 164, 180–182, 188
Utah, 69, 301
Utilities, public,
   and population data, 35
   and use of construction data, 226

Vallejo Unified School District, 96
Vandalism, cost of, to business, 173
Vermont, pupil expenditures in, 82
Vertical or short take-off and landing (V-STOL) plane, 264
Veterans Administration, 64, 211
Victims and victimization, 163, 178–179
   surveys of, 186, 345

Vietnam war, public opinion on, 320, 321–322, 328, 336
Violence Commission, 169–170
  Task Force on Acts of Violence, 162, 186–187
Virginia
  schools in, 97–98
  travel data in, 263
  voting data in, 301
Vital and Health Statistics, National Committee on, 63, 66, 75
Vital statistics, 43–58
  history of, 44–49
  uses and users of, 49–56
Vital Statistics Data, 72
Vital Statistics of the U.S., 63
Vocational Agriculture, 31
Vocational education, and labor-force data, 129
Vocational Education
  National Advisory Council on, 130
  State Boards of, 124
Vocational Education Act, 25, 96, 123, 124, 129
Vocational system, redesign of, 122
Voter registration, and population data, 32
Voters and voting
  data on, 299–310
  and public opinion polls, 313–316
  and use of data on goverments, 287
Voting Rights Act, 25

Wage standards, public opinion on, 318
Wages, statistics on, 9. *See also* Income items.
Wagner, Robert F., 165
Waldron, Ellis Comp, 300, 311
Walker, General Francis A., 11
Wall Street Journal, 126, 172, 176–177
War, public opinion on, 320, 321–322, 327–331
War Production Board, 8

Washington [DC]—Boston travel corridor, assessing, 264
Washington State
  income maintenance experiment in, 151
  recreation survey in, 256
  travel data in, 263
Washington State University, 180
Wattenberg, Ben J., 308, 311
Welfare, 20, 135–157, 285
Welfare Administration, 96
Welfare in Review, 142, 157
Welfare recipients
  characteristics of, 152
  surveys of, 144–145, 155
  and welfare data, 152–153, 154
Welfare reform, and family data, 66–67
Welfare Rights Organization, 153
Welfare statistics
  limitations of, 153–155
  outlook for, 155–156
  summary of, 157
  users and uses of, 151–153
Welfare system
  criticisms of, 144
  reform of, 66–67, 155
Westinghouse, 176
Weston, Allen F., 180
Where Are the Voters? (Friedheim), 308, 310
White, John Patrick, 301, 311
White, Theodore, 308, 311
White, William M., 266
Williams, Oliver, 301, 311
Wilson, Harold, 315
Wilson, Will, 175–176, 189
Winch, Robert F., 68, 76
Wisconsin Regional Planning Commission, 244
Wolfgang, Marvin E., 186, 188, 189
Women
  Citizen's Advisory Council on, 131
  and crime, 182–183, 184
  and fear levels, 163

in the labor force, 117, 127, 128, 150
and labor-force data, 131–132
President's Commission on the Status of, 131
Women's Bureau, 131
Woolsey, Theodore D., 43n
Work incentive, 146–153, 155
Work Incentive Program (WIN), 123, 144
Work Projects Administration, 109
Workers, discouraged, 110. *See also* Labor force.
World War I, opinions on, 328
World War II, 8, 27
opinions on, 328

World's Columbia Exposition, 242
Wright, Carroll D., 10, 21, 61

Youth
and crime data, 183–184
employment of, 125
Youth Development and Delinquency Prevention Administration, 179
Youth training programs, 121
Youth Unemployment and Minimum Wages (BLS), 125

Zoning, 239
and population data, 32, 37